AN INTRODUCTION
TO THE
THEORY OF INTEREST

A PUBLICATION OF THE BUREAU OF BUSINESS AND ECONOMIC RESEARCH OF THE UNIVERSITY OF CALIFORNIA

AN INTRODUCTION TO THE THEORY OF INTEREST

By JOSEPH W. CONARD

UNIVERSITY OF CALIFORNIA PRESS

Berkeley and Los Angeles 1959

UNIVERSITY OF CALIFORNIA PRESS
BERKELEY AND LOS ANGELES
CALIFORNIA

CAMBRIDGE UNIVERSITY PRESS
LONDON, ENGLAND

LIBRARY OF CONGRESS CATALOG CARD NUMBER: 59:10463

PRINTED IN THE UNITED STATES OF AMERICA

To MY MOTHER
    and FLORENCE, *my wife*
and JOHN, *my son*

FOREWORD

From the very earliest beginnings of the intellectual history of Western civilization, the phenomenon of interest has piqued the curiosity and challenged the analytical powers of the philosophers. As students of political science and economic thought know, Aristotle had a word to say about interest; and his word, supported by similar reflections on the part of the Church Fathers, persisted through the time of Thomas Aquinas and beyond. For a whole millennium, from the eighth century through the French Revolution, the receipt of usury was at least formally banned by canon law, and frequently also by civil law.

In the history of economic thought, after it began to be differentiated from social ethics and politics by the Mercantilists, Physiocrats, and Adam Smith, the theory of interest has held a very central position and interest has usually engendered more speculation than other kinds of income, such as profits, rents, or wages. Thus it is that some—perhaps most—of the really outstanding economists of the past two centuries have tried to make some significant contribution to the theory of capital and interest. The generalization certainly holds for Ricardo, Marx, Schumpeter, Fisher, and—most recently—J. M. Keynes.

Professor Conard enters one of the contentious and difficult areas of economic thought. But if the terrain is particularly treacherous and difficult, the rewards of conscientious and patient research are correspondingly great. Many issues, some of them quite basic, have yielded to his sustained effort, which has extended well over a decade. Not only has he explored the purely theoretical aspects of the interest problem, but he has subjected his analysis to the test of empiric facts. The findings of the present study rest upon intensive studies at the University of California and other universities and upon first-hand experience in the New York money market.

Students of the history of economic thought will find in this volume an authoritative and exhaustive review of modern doctrines of interest. General students of economics will be brought up to date on the most recent issues, and will be supplied with a vade mecum to guide them through some of its most tortuous phases. Those concerned with fiscal and monetary policy will find valuable insights into the practical operations of interest rates. Whatever the viewpoint, Professor Conard will command respect for his profound scholarship and the vigor and penetration of his analysis.

HOWARD S. ELLIS

PREFACE

The purpose which motivated the choice of subject matter in this study is too ambitious for a single book, and the present work must be viewed as the first step in a larger endeavor. My basic objectives are, first, to provide an understanding of the nature of interest and of the forces determining rates of interest, and second, to consider the implications of these for social policy, especially montary policy.

In his *Prosperity and Depression* Haberler states that "the theory of interest has for a long time been a weak spot in the science of economics, and the explanation and determination of the interest rate gives rise to more disagreement among economists than any other branch of economic theory." [1] Vera and Friedrich Lutz begin their 1951 "Remarks on the Theory of Interest" with the sentence, "The theory of interest is, at present, in a state of great confusion." [2]

As I have examined my own difficulties with the theory of interest, it has seemed that the quest for clarification might require at least five steps. First, to gain an understanding of the meaning and the degree of validity of the so-called nonmonetary theories of interest, such as those of Boehm-Bawerk and Irving Fisher. Second, to examine contemporary monetary theories, such as the loanable-funds and the liquidity-preference theories, studying their relation to one another and to nonmonetary theories. Third, to recognize the existence not only of one "rate of interest," but of an entire structure of rates, depending upon term to maturity even when there is no risk of nonpayment. Fourth, to take into account the implications of market imperfections, uncertainty, and dynamic elements in relation to the general levels of rates as well as to the term structure. And finally to utilize the results of empirical studies

---

[1] Gottfried von Haberler, *Prosperity and Depression.* New rev. and enl. ed. (Geneva: League of Nations, 1939), p. 195.

[2] Vera and Friedrich Lutz, *The Theory of Investment of the Firm* (Princeton: Princeton University Press, 1951), p. 237.

in order to suggest the probable shapes and shifts of functions used in the theory of interest.

This book is titled *An Introduction to the Theory of Interest* because it leads only part of the way down the path described above. Its stopping point at the end of the third step is determined by the limitations of available time rather than by logic, but readers of the manuscript have kindly suggested that it would be useful to publish this introduction even though it does not achieve the full purpose of the study. I claim no major originality, though the interpretation and evaluation of various ideas is, of course, my own. What I do hope to do is to make available in one book the most helpful elements in many writings that deal with the knotty problems of interest theory. I hope I have clarified conflicting views on controversial issues and indicated a possible resolution of arguments when such a resolution seemed possible. If the study is successful it will have cleared away some rubble and laid a foundation for a more dynamic and realistic superstructure.

In Part I, I have attempted to describe and evaluate the nonmonetary theories of interest, primarily by summarizing and relating to one another the theories of Boehm-Bawerk, Fisher, and Knight. Other references to the history of ideas are included, and nonmonetary aspects of Schumpeter's theory, among others, are discussed, but the approach is intended to provide an understanding of issues relating to the theory of interest rather than a history of doctrine. In Part II an examination of the loanable-funds and the liquidity-preference theories leads inevitably to an analysis of macroeconomic general equilibrium, and here a comparison of the Keynesian with the "classical" system according to the familiar models of Klein and McKenna is related both to my own method of approach and to that of Patinkin. The resulting model is used to examine a number of issues such as unemployment in underdeveloped areas, "cost-push" versus "excessive-demand" inflation, and escalator clauses.

In Part III a study of the term structure of interest rates is used to develop some theoretical notions about the probable shapes and shifts of yield curves under varying circumstances. In the first section of this part the static assumptions of "the theory of interest" described in Parts I and II are retained, and the resulting theory of the structure of rates is related directly to that theory. It soon becomes evident, however, that any realistic study of rate structure must recognize uncertainty and segmentation of markets by type of security. These considerations are therefore admitted to the analysis, and theoretical implications are derived. Finally, an attempt is made to test these theoretical expectations against empirical evidence, and it is argued that the facts appear to be consistent with the theory advanced.

An important limitation of Part III is that it was completed in the summer of 1955, so that there are no data from the excitingly revealing period since that time. Despite its limitation, this section is included for two reasons. First, an early revision is not feasible. Second, the orientation of the study is toward theory rather than history, and a recent study of experience since 1954 suggests that none of the major theoretical conclusions would have to be revised on the basis of that experience. Indeed, the conclusions are confirmed by the later study, which was made by Edward Stevens, a senior at Haverford College, during the spring of 1957, and is based on data that come up to the beginning of that year.

Eight of the figures in this book should be used while reading the corresponding parts of the text. In order to facilitate such use, they are printed in a separate booklet which will be found in a pocket on the inside of the back cover. All figures in that booklet have been given Roman numerals, and are thus distinguished in the text. Should the booklet be lost, a duplicate may be secured from the author at Swarthmore College for 50¢.

This study has, of course, been greatly aided by the work of others. The footnotes give the sources used directly. Special mention should be made, however, of the debt which Part III owes to a study prepared by Braddock Hickman for the National Bureau of Economic Research in 1942 under the title, "The Term Structure of Interest Rates: An Exploratory Analysis." I mention this source especially because the study has not been published, and hence the extent of my indebtedness to Hickman's work is not readily apparent.

Direct help has come from many persons. The study was originally prepared as a doctoral dissertation for the University of California, where every member of my committee gave helpful criticism and suggestion. Professors Howard S. Ellis and Robert A. Gordon, who served successively as chairman, were, of course, of especially great assistance, but the other members of the committee also gave generous and important help. These include Professors Earl R. Rolph, Sidney S. Hoos, David A. Alhadeff, and Andreas G. Papendreou. I owe very special thanks to Dr. Edward S. Herman of the University of Pennsylvania for carefully reading the entire text and making innumerable helpful suggestions for improvement. Particular appreciation is due Mr. Henry T. Gayley of Swarthmore, who patiently and painstakingly experimented with me in an effort to make the figures most clearly reveal complex ideas, often in three dimensions. Professors Frank Pierson and William Brown of Swarthmore College have also read the manuscript and given important suggestions for improvement. Others who have read parts of the study to check special points include Professors Karl Brunner of the University of California, Los Angeles; Hobart Carr of New York University;

Alvin Marty of Northwestern University; and James Tobin of Yale University. In Part III I was greatly helped by Leroy S. Wherley of Yale University, and by friends at the Federal Reserve Bank of New York, including especially Lawrence Ritter, Tilford Gaines, Frank Schiff, and Albert Wojnilower. Finally, I should like to express my gratitude to Mr. John Gildersleeve of the University of California Press for an editing job which surely goes far beyond the normal call of duty. His detailed care and his insight have made this book clearer and more readable in innumerable ways.

Authors of books have become accustomed to two other kinds of assistance upon which publication commonly depends. One is the tireless and patient slave labor supplied by a wife. Mine has contributed far more than her share of this. The second is the provision of the money needed to meet the many costs incidental to publication. I am deeply indebted to the Bureau of Business and Economic Research of the University of California for their generous aid, without which this book could not have been published.

To all of these I give my hearty thanks, but on behalf of all I must emphasize that I alone am responsible for any errors, especially since very few have seen the book in its present form. This caveat should be reëmphasized in relation to my friends at the Federal Reserve Bank, for policy implications reflect my own judgments exclusively.

CONTENTS

Figures I to VIII are in a booklet in back-cover pocket

I

INTRODUCTION: THE RELEVANCE AND NATURE OF INTEREST AND INTEREST THEORY

THE RELEVANCE OF THE THEORY OF INTEREST

Ever since the mid-1930's large numbers of economists have taken the position that interest rates have relatively little influence upon economic life. Although Keynes went less far in this direction than many of his followers, his *General Theory*[1] provided much of the theoretical basis for this view. As a complement to this theoretical development, a series of studies made at Oxford in 1938 and 1939[2] gave strong empirical support to those who were skeptical about the economic significance of interest rates. Finally, the inability of monetary policy to relieve the great depression strengthened this idea.[3]

Keynes himself stated that the volume of saving is not greatly influenced by interest rates. Many of his followers believe that investment also is quite insensitive to these rates. Large numbers of persons who would not call themselves Keynesians would agree that interest has little effect on saving and investment, so that substantial changes in spending could not be expected to follow feasible changes in interest rates. Although fluctuations in rates during the past three years have been large in relation to the experience of the previous two decades, even these changes may be small compared with those required for substantial effects on aggregate spending. Furthermore, these years have given shocks to the bond market and have imposed increases in the cost of Treasury refunding that suggest the problems to be faced, both economic and political, if still greater rate fluctuations were to be permitted or encouraged. Even those persons who still place great faith in monetary policy — and there are many more of them now than in the 30's and early 40's — even these faithful often support their convictions by doctrines which ascribe

---

[1] J. M. Keynes, *The General Theory of Employment, Interest and Money* (New York: Harcourt, Brace, 1936).

[2] For reprints of six articles describing these studies see *Oxford Studies in the Price Mechanism*, edited by T. Wilson and P. W. S. Andrews (Oxford: Clarendon Press, 1951), chapter 1, pp. 1–74.

[3] For a good review and critique of ideas discussed here, see W. H. White, "Interest Inelasticity of Investment Demand," *American Economic Review*, 46 (1956): 565–587.

the influence of monetary policy to aspects of the availability of funds other than "costs" as represented by interest charges. Finally, if one turns from economic activity to the distribution of income, he again finds evidence that interest rates are less important than might be supposed. For example, Department of Commerce data reveal that interest accounts for only about five per cent of personal income.

The obvious question posed by considerations like those just cited is, "why study the theory of interest?" My reply is neither original nor profound, but it seems helpful despite that fact to state it at the outset. In the first place, an economic theorist cannot rest comfortably so long as there remains an unfilled gap in his general theoretical structure. Whether or not interest rates are "important" variables, they are prices whose derivation and influence must be understood if economic theory is to be complete.

This "pure-theory" argument alone would justify the study of interest rates; but the case for such an inquiry does not rest here. Even the view that interest rates do not influence economic activity significantly cannot be accepted without a theory of interest which leads to that conclusion. Even the atheist has his creed. And the economic agnostic will quickly discover that there are powerful arguments on both sides of the question of the influence of interest rates on economic activity. Although a marked elasticity of saving and investment curves is no longer assumed by most writers, assumption of near-zero elasticity is now equally unpopular. In the context of a fiscal policy which maintains relatively full employment, even a slight elasticity may be significant for the maintenance of stability without inflation. Furthermore, to discard the theory of interest on the grounds that availability of credit now moves in another dimension would be to oversimplify the implications of the availability doctrine. Changing interest rates play a significant role even according to this view.

Thus we may conclude that in order to understand the effects of monetary policy on employment and prices it is necessary to have some theory of interest, even if it leads to the conviction that such a policy is impotent. Furthermore the assumption of impotence is far less general today than it has been in the recent past.

The usefulness of a theory of interest is not confined to its value in predicting the consequences of monetary policy. Debt management cannot be conducted wisely except upon the basis of some theory of interest and interest rates. Here again the concern will be in part with the influence of interest rates on employment and prices, but emphasis will also rest on the problems of borrowing-costs to the Treasury and of stability in the government securities market. The implications of the theory of interest, with special emphasis upon the structure of rates in this case, are too obvious to require elaboration. It may be worth noting in passing, however, that inelasticity of the investment and saving curves would increase the importance of interest theory in this connection, for shifts of inelastic curves would cause more violent changes in interest rates and security prices than would shifts of elastic curves.

Although the influence of interest rates upon the personal distribution of income is not nearly so great as some political controversy would suggest, it is appreciably greater than is implied by the share shown as "interest" in the Department of Commerce data on personal income. Chiefly this is because we must allow for the effects of interest rates upon all return from property, including dividends, rental income of persons, and proprietors' net income. It is beyond the scope of this study to estimate the quantitative influence of interest rates upon the distribution of income, but it may be noted that in 1956 about 12 per cent of personal income was net interest (including government interest payments), dividends, and rental income of persons: if undistributed profits were included the total would be about 15 per cent. It would, of course, be a gross error to presume that there is any simple direct correlation between changing interest rates and the changing size of property income: outstanding contracts are typically long-term, and changing capital values must sometimes be set against changes in going interest rates. But it is true that interest rates may be presumed to have a substantial direct effect upon these components of personal income.

If one grants that some elements of investment and consumption spending are affected by the rates of interest, then another important function of interest theory would be its contribution to the investigation of the allocative effects of interest charges. One of the common arguments for traditional monetary controls, as against rationing and other direct controls, is that such devices as discount rates and open-market operations impinge on the market impersonally and generally, so that the monetary authority is not compelled to determine just "how much" of "what" may be sold. This argument is valid as far as it goes, but those who administer our traditional "general" controls can hardly be oblivious to the allocative effects of their policies just because the goods rationed are not named in the orders issued. After all, if monetary policy is effective it squeezes or relieves somebody, and who that somebody is may matter. The view that monetary policy has substantially different effects on different segments of the economy provided part of the reason for the 1934 legislation granting the Federal Reserve Board power to regulate margin requirements, and this view is even more clearly expressed in arguments today for laws granting the Federal Reserve similar control over consumer credit.[4] The

---

[4] In December, 1955, Allan Sproul, then President of the Federal Reserve Bank of New York, upheld this view in an address to the American Economic Association, "Reflections of a Central Banker." It should be stated that the Federal Reserve System

major concern of Federal Reserve officials is, of course with the ways whereby certain segments may, through lack of response to tight money, thwart the attempts of monetary authorities to provide economic stability. But their argument rests on the assumption that some persons are pinched much more than others by monetary tightness. Furthermore, there are many today who believe that monetary restriction is discriminatory even within segments, bearing down much more sharply on the small than on the large borrower.[5]

Interest theory has thus far been viewed from the standpoint of social policy. The businessman must also make many decisions that require an understanding of the behavior of interest rates. Such understanding is especially important to the investment officer of any financial institution that shifts funds between securities of different term, or between bonds and equities, or between securities and real property. Likewise, the firm which must borrow will frequently find it profitable to be familiar with the forces shaping rates of interest in different markets and at different times. To the extent that changing rates and monetary policy exert an influence on the general level of economic activity, the wise businessman will also keep an eye on them in planning his own activities.

Finally, beyond the practical problems of the present there always stand the broad ethical and philosophical questions which have occupied the minds of many earlier writers. Are interest payments a form of exploitation? Are such payments socially desirable or necessary? Would interest exist in a socialistic economy? Would interest rates be zero in a stationary state? Although some of these questions can be answered only after explicit value judgments have been made, and others prove to be largely semantic, nonetheless the issues they raise can be greatly clarified by a well-developed theory of interest. In the United States these questions have lain quiescent throughout almost two decades of prosperity. But the revolutions which are now shaking the world beyond our shores — and very possibly domestic problems that now appear to be held in check — will not permit them to rest forever. They may one day prove to be as "practical" as any raised in this book.

THE NATURE OF INTEREST

Interest and the Functional Distribution of Income

Throughout most of the period in which we have had a reasonably comprehensive corpus of formalized economic theory — that is, since the

---

as a whole has not supported Sproul's position, but the differences do not rest on a repudiation of the argument that monetary policy causes substantially different impacts on different segments of the economy.

[5] See, for example, J. K. Galbraith, "Market Structure and Stabilization Policy," *Review of Economics and Statistics*, 39 (1957): 124–133.

Physiocrats and Adam Smith — interest theory has been studied as a part of the theory of distribution. The traditional view is that our economy comprises four productive groups, each of which receives a different type of income. Thus workers receive wages, landholders receive rent, the owners of capital receive interest, and entrepreneurs receive profits. If this general pattern is qualified, it is usually because of some hesitation concerning profits; the other three classifications are commonly accepted.

In sharpest contrast to this view we have that of Irving Fisher, who wrote in 1930, "Distribution has been erroneously defined as the division of the income of society into 'interest, rent, wages, and profits.' " [6] For Fisher, interest is not a distributive share at all, but a way of looking at income of every kind (except capital gains). Every productive agent provides a stream of income. Given the appropriate interest rates for the present and future, it is possible to capitalize these income streams. This capitalized *value* is precisely the meaning of the word "capital" for Fisher. When the individual looks at his prospective income in its relation to the capitalized value of that stream he sees it as interest. "Viewed as above outlined, *interest is not a part, but the whole of income.*" [7]

F. H. Knight is perhaps less specific than Fisher, but much of his writing appears to reflect the same concept.[8] He is quite explicit in denying the validity of a distinction between interest and rent. "Only historical accident or 'psychology' can explain the fact that 'interest' and 'rent' have been viewed as coming from different sources, specifically natural agents and capital goods. The difference is clearly one of contractual form, or even of arbitrary 'point of view.' " [9] Although he does not specify that incomes other than rent can be comprehended within the concept of interest, he surely implies it in passages like these: ". . . the general and fundamental meaning of real capital includes all sources or objects which have productive capacity." [10] "All sources are properly productive agents, and are also 'capital goods' in the most inclusive meaning." [11] He is quite explicit in stating that labor is to be included with other sources in these generalizations, and finally, having thus reduced all sources to "capital goods," he proceeds, like Fisher, to state that "capital," as opposed to "capital goods" must be regarded as "productive capacity, viewed in ab-

---

[6] Irving Fisher, *The Theory of Interest* (New York: Macmillan, 1930), p. 331.

[7] *Ibid.*, p. 332 (Fisher's italics).

[8] The following quotations are taken from his 1946 article in the Encyclopaedia Britannica, "Capital and Interest," reprinted in American Economic Association, *Readings in the Theory of Income Distribution* (Philadelphia: Blakiston, 1946), pp. 384–417. See also F. H. Knight, "On the Theory of Capital," *Econometrica*, 6 (1938): 74 and elsewhere.

[9] "Capital and Interest," p. 392 in reprint.

[10] *Ibid.*, p. 389.

[11] *Ibid.*, p. 388.

stract quantitative terms," [12] the evaluation being secured "by 'capitaliz-ing' their expected income yield." [13]

Here, then, are two contrasting concepts of interest. In the first, the traditional, interest is considered to be one specific type of income, namely, the functional share earned by "capital goods," these being defined as man-made goods used for further production. According to the second, that of Fisher and Knight, interest is a way of looking at all income: specifically, that of seeing it as a percentage of the capitalized value of all income sources. Between these two concepts lies Schumpeter's, as pre-sented in his *Theory of Economic Development*. Schumpeter seems to vacillate between two possible intermediate positions. In places he is very close to Fisher and Knight, though he regards wages as a form of income which should not be included as interest, in part because the capitaliza-tion of labor seems inappropriate in a society where workers are not bought and sold.[14] Thus he speaks of the "fact that interest finally be-comes a form of expression for all returns with the exception of wages." [15] Throughout most of his analysis, however, he seems closer to those who regard interest as a specific part of the total income, though he would object to calling it a functional share: rather, it is a deduction from prof-its. "Development . . . sweeps a part of profit to the capitalist [as op-posed to the entrepreneur, who would otherwise receive it all]. Interest acts as a tax upon profit." [16]

In this part of my study I make no attempt to explain the *theory* of in-terest as presented by any of these writers. My only purpose is to give here some of the different ideas of the *meaning* of interest. Definitions, of course, cannot be judged "right" or "wrong" except to the degree that they may or may not be self-contradictory. But they may legitimately be appraised in terms of usefulness and convenience.

Fisher's concept is logically tenable. With given expectations and inter-est rates one can capitalize all his income and then think of it as "interest" on this capitalized value. This approach has the virtue of showing that there is a logical similarity between capital values acquired through the investment of funds and capital values derivable from other types of claim to future income. But it may mislead by tending to hide the crucial implications of the freedom of labor, and it also robs us of a name for a particular type of income that needs a name if it is to be discussed sepa-rately. It seems useful, therefore, to retain the term "interest" for refer-ence to a particular part of the total flow of income (I shall define it more

---

[12] *Ibid.*, p. 389.

[13] *Ibid.*, p. 396.

[14] Joseph A. Schumpeter, *The Theory of Economic Development* (Cambridge: Har-vard University Press, 1934), pp. 202–203.

[15] *Ibid.*, p. 202.

[16] *Ibid.*, p. 175.

precisely), and at the same time to recognize with Fisher that the point of view which relates this flow to its capitalized value can be applied equally to that of other types of income.

These remarks suggest a return to the familiar division of income into functional shares. But the traditional fourfold classification presents some marked inconveniences and confusions. In the first place, the factor of production called "capital" must mean "capital goods," since it is these which actually participate in the productive process. Yet analysis shows that capital goods earn quasi-rents, not interest. This is not a mere semantic quibble. The forces determining the return on capital goods are those described in the theory of rents and quasi-rents, not those described in the theory of interest.

In his *Pricing, Distribution and Employment,* Bain points the way to a marked clarification of these issues, but in my view he could helpfully go farther down the road on which he has started. He states that "interest paid for invested money is thus a third distributive share, in addition to wages and rents. It is paid for the services of invested money [may I say capital?] *and it is earned* (as a part of quasi-rents) *by the capital goods in which the funds are invested.*" [17] The crucial contribution of this passage is its distinction between the agent which "earns" the income share and the investor who receives it. The question which remains unresolved, however, is that of the relation between interest and the concept of distributive shares. Interest is here called a "third distributive share." Does this mean a share in *functional* distribution? If so, are loanable funds factors after all, in some sort of second-hand way? Obviously they cannot be full-fledged factors, because the income received for their services cannot be added to that earned by the capital goods in which they are invested without double counting. Yet it is clearly stated that they do provide services for which payment is received. When the concept of profits is examined within the familiar framework of functional distribution difficulties similar to those arising in relation to interest are encountered: this time quasi-rents raise the problem of double counting. This dilemma forces Stigler to argue that profits are really zero if one imputes quasi-rents, as should be done for many purposes.[18]

As indicated above, the way out of these difficulties lies in pursuing Bain's distinction between income-earning agents and income-receiving claimants. I suggest that this distinction should be applied systematically to the entire analysis of income distribution. Enterprise may be thought of as an abstract entity — much like the corporation — which owns some income-producing sources and hires others. These sources together "earn"

---

[17] Joe S. Bain, *Pricing, Distribution, and Employment,* Rev. ed. (New York: Henry Holt, 1953), p. 462.
[18] George Stigler, *The Theory of Price* (New York: Macmillan, 1947), p. 247.

(but do not "receive") all income in return for the services they provide. This income is then "redistributed" to ultimate claimants according to the nature of their claims. The earnings of the agents of production are determined by the familiar theory of marginal productivity; the payments made to claimants of income are determined by contractual and other institutional considerations. The terms of these contracts, when established, are of course largely determined by expected earnings of the productive agents made available directly or indirectly by the claimant, and thus a clear relation is established between "factor" earnings and income receipts; but this relation is not entirely direct. Mistaken expectations, ineptness in bargaining, and many other elements may cause sharp divergence between today's earnings of John Doe's land and his receipts from the farmer to whom he hired it out.

If this general structure is accepted, then the next question is whether we can usefully classify groups of productive agents on the one hand, and receivers of income on the other. First, productive agents: is it possible to distinguish broad categories of these within which there is enough homogeneity to justify the term "factor of production"? Since "homogeneity" is always a relative term unless it implies complete identity, the answer to this question must depend upon the purpose for which the classification is being made, but it is frequently legitimate and convenient to adopt a classification that would distinguish between (*a*) labor, (*b*) the nonaugmentable element in nature (i.e., basic natural resources), and (*c*) augmentable productive goods (roughly, "capital goods"). For many purposes it would be useful to note a distinction within *b* between indestructible "land," such as land space, and destructible "land," as represented by all the resources that can be and are exploited, including even the fertility of the soil.

Knight has shown the dangers and difficulties of any such classification, by emphasizing, among other things, the inseparable contribution of man's efforts in creating and maintaining the economic capacity of both "land" and "labor." [19] When one considers the drainage of swamps and the education of children the difficulty of distinguishing sharply between man-made and natural factors becomes obvious. At one point Knight declares that "the entire notion of 'factor of production' is an incubus on economic analysis, and should be eliminated from economic discussion as summarily as possible." [20]

By his statements Knight has demonstrated the difficulty (or impossibility) of drawing distinctions between the three "factors" which make it possible categorically and without qualification to classify any given agent of production into one or another group. This provides a useful

---

[19] "On the Theory of Capital," esp. pp. 75–82.
[20] *Ibid.*, p. 81.

warning against reading too much into our definitional distinctions. We are reminded of Triffin's similar objections to the concepts "product" and "industry." Yet, for better or for worse, despite Knight and Triffin, economists continue to find it convenient to use such imperfect systems of classification, since they do relate to substantial, if not absolute, differences among members of economic categories. Free labor does not, either in its working activity or in its long-run supply behavior, function as would the "ideal" slave component which is implied by treating labor as inert capital goods. And much of the "gift of nature" represents a given datum in a way that capital goods do not. Finally, lest we push Knight farther than he would really want to go, it may be said that he too recognizes differences in degree if not altogether in kind. He concedes that for some purposes labor may be usefully distinguished from other productive agents, and with some hesitation he even admits a kind of vague difference between "land" and "capital goods," if properly defined: "I should not even say," he remarks, "that it is never possible to recognize differences in the 'proportions' of 'natural resources' to labor capacity, or to 'artificial' capital," though he continues by adding that it would be "rash in the extreme" to assign any numerical values to these ratios.[21]

If, then, we make the provisional classification of factors described above, we can accept the conventional statement that labor earns wages, land earns rent, and capital goods earn quasi-rents. The earnings of all these agents of production are determined according to the familiar analysis relating marginal productivity to supply. The significance of the classification rests upon differences in supply functions and, for labor, upon social implications relating to the ultimate purposes of production and the "costs" of factor use. At the same time, this classification is inherently crude and it is desirable for many purposes to use a different framework. Since any taxonomic system in this context is subject to important limitations, it should be emphasized that our basic approach to the problem of distribution, namely the separation of "agent earnings" from receipts of ultimate claimants, does not depend upon this or any other classification of agents of production into "factors."

I turn now from productive agents to the ultimate claimants of income, of which the following groups may be conveniently distinguished: (1) workers, who receive wages; (2) those who hire out nonlabor factors to enterprise, and who receive a hire price for the services of these factors; (3) those who lend money to enterprise, and who receive interest; and (4) ultimate owners, who receive profits or a claim to profits.[22] This simple model may be expanded as much as wished. It seems useful to adopt the

---

[21] *Ibid.*, p. 82.

[22] It may be noted that we are now abstracting from government and the issues raised by its existence.

familiar procedure of breaking down interest into pure interest — the payments made for borrowed funds when there is no risk of nonpayment — and gross interest including a risk premium. It is also appropriate, and for some purposes essential, to say that because the owner has invested funds in an enterprise, part of his returns should be regarded as imputed interest rather than as part of pure profits. There is nothing in this model to prevent those who wish to do so from going on to say, with Schumpeter, that persons who receive a hire price for the use of their earning assets are also receiving imputed interest for the funds invested in those assets; or to continue with Fisher and capitalize labor services as well.

It will be noted at once that I have given no explanation of why the lenders of money receive a payment in the form of interest. To answer that question is the function of this book. All I have done so far is to describe a structure of concepts for the analysis of income distribution, and to indicate that this structure is consistent with the concept of interest which I adopt, namely, the return on borrowed funds.

The Meaning of Interest Rates

Given this concept of interest, how shall interest rates be defined? I suggest that they be regarded as the effective yield on claims to loaned funds, where yield is calculated on the basis of present market price, or an appropriate equivalent if the security that represents the claim is not readily marketable. If markets are perfect these interest rates will be equal to the contractual rates on new loans, but they will at most times presumably differ from rates established in earlier contracts. This divergence necessitates our distinguishing between three basic concepts of yield on securities. One is the contract rate itself, or, for many securities, the coupon rate. A second is the "current yield," which represents the annual income divided by the market value of the security. The third, yield to maturity, is more complex but also more significant: it is the rate at which it would be necessary to discount all subsequent payments, including interest and the repayment of principal, in order to make the present value of these payments equal to the present price of the security. What this definition does is to delineate the effective yield for the person who holds the security to maturity, making due allowance for the capital gain or loss which results whenever the current market price is not equal to the maturity value.

This long discussion of conflicting, or at least alternative, concepts of interest has led to the very simple and common view that interest is the income received by those who lend their funds, and that interest rates are the effective yields on such invested funds; but the discussion was necessary to suggest the relation of this simple view to the more complex ideas of those who have tried to think deeply about the ultimate nature and source of interest. An understanding of the relation of interest to the functional distribution of income may remove some confusions and clear the way to the subsequent analysis of the theory of interest. In saying that interest is the return to those who lend their funds, I also say that it is not the return to a factor of production. These payments may best be viewed as a transfer, to the ultimate claimant, of a portion of enterprise earnings. Precisely how this transfer relates to the earnings of the factor "capital goods," remains to be discussed in the development of the theory of interest.

The Classical Identification of Interest and Profits

The foregoing comments really complete my examination of the *meaning* of interest. But I have deliberately omitted one important method of dealing with this problem, namely, that of the classical economists, because I could not discuss that method without becoming involved in controversy over the theory as well as the meaning of interest, and it seemed useful to avoid confusing these two issues before I had stated my own conclusions concerning the meaning of interest.

The theories of interest presented by the classical writers are almost exclusively described by those writers as theories of "profits." Nassau Senior, for example, whose abstinence theory is one of the most important pillars in the classical theory of interest, describes that concept exclusively as an explanation of "profits," and the term "interest" appears nowhere in the index of his *Political Economy*.[23] The obvious question is, did the classical writers completely identify the concepts of interest and profits, using the term profits to describe the single concept? They are commonly accused of so doing, this charge being leveled particularly against Ricardo and his successors. Thus Schumpeter writes that for "Ricardo and his epigoni . . . the two [are] plainly synonymous." [24] Much can be said to support Schumpeter's interpretation, and many aspects of the classical analysis can best be understood if the reader assumes the model to be one in which the capitalist and the entrepreneur are one and the same person, whose income share is an inseparable combination of what we would call "profits" and "interest." He invests his funds in the enterprise which he directs, and his income is to be studied as profits. John Stuart Mill, to be sure, had a concept of gross profits, which, he said, consist of interest, insurance, and wages of superintendence. But when he explains the level of profits he generally omits reference to the last two elements and writes simply, ". . . the profits of the capitalist are . . . the remuneration of abstinence." [25] One reason, then, for the common classical failure to dis-

[23] Nassau Senior, *An Outline of the Science of Political Economy* (New York: Farrar and Rinehart, 1939).

[24] Schumpeter, *op. cit.*, p. 180.

[25] J. S. Mill, *Principles of Political Economy*, Ashley ed. (London, New York, Toronto: Longmans, Green, 1940), p. 405.

tinguish between profits and interest was the identification of entrepreneur and capitalist.

It is interesting to note that this tendency to identify profits with interest was in no sense characteristic of preclassical economists. As Schumpeter points out, Cantillon, who was himself a banker, makes an especially clear distinction, as did Hume, Petty, Locke and Steuart.[26] Adam Smith neatly distinguishes interest from profits by stating that the share of income "derived from stock by the person who manages or employs it is called profit. That derived from it by the person who does not employ it himself, but lends it to another, is called the interest, or the use of money." Smith then continues by pointing out that the reason a lender can secure interest is because the borrower can make a profit, so that "the interest of money is always a derivative revenue." [27] In this last statement we see a second reason for the frequent post-Smith classical treatment of interest as identical with profits. When the classical writer did make a distinction between capitalist and entrepreneur, then the former could demand a return for his funds essentially equal to the profits that the capitalist was able to acquire from their use, with the result that the rate of interest would be roughly equal to the rate of profit, and determined by it. Ricardo himself, in a statement which in a measure belies Schumpeter's accusation against him, spells out this point precisely. "The rate of interest," he writes, "though ultimately and permanently governed by the rate of profit, is, however, subject to temporary variations from other causes." [28]

The common identification of interest and profits by classical economists may thus be understood in the light of at least two elements in their thinking. One was the identification of capitalist and entrepreneur, the other was the view that interest was after all derived from profits, and its rate was roughly determined by and equal to that of profits. The question now arises: How serious is this classical oversimplification? Schumpeter argues that the error is fundamental. Although interest is for him, as for Smith, derived from profits and therefore necessarily limited by them, the central problem of interest theory is that of discovering why such a derivation exists, and how great it will be. "If traditional theory links up contractual interest with entrepreneur's profits, it only traces the problem to what it believes to be its fundamental cause, and has, after having done so, still to perform the main part of the task . . . *how* does interest arise from entrepreneurial profit?" [29] (One is reminded of the

---

[26] Schumpeter, *The Theory of Economic Development*, p. 179.

[27] Adam Smith, *The Wealth of Nations*, ed. by Edwin Cannan (New York: Modern Library, 1937), p. 52.

[28] David Ricardo, *Principles of Political Economy and Taxation*, Everyman's Library (New York: E. P. Dutton, 1948), p. 198.

[29] Schumpeter, *The Theory of Economic Development*, pp. 182–183.

statement by A. T. Hadley that interest results from a contract between two capitalists, one who wishes fixed and sure returns, the other who wants to accept control together with the speculative possibilities and the risks that adhere thereto.)[30] Unquestionably Schumpeter is right: an adequate analysis must differentiate between interest and profits, and the classical economists often failed to do this. But I am inclined to believe that the burden of this failure falls upon their theory of profit rather than on that of interest, for the concepts which they developed are directly applicable to what we would call the theory of interest, whereas they scarcely develop any theory of what we might call "profits." Their views will be evaluated below, but I suggest that the classical theory may be related to our study legitimately by simply substituting the word "interest" for "profit" in most parts of their analysis. Given the concept of interest which I have proposed, as the payment for the use of borrowed funds, then the analysis of interest rates involves the description and analysis of the supply and demand for these funds. The classical economists discussed the demand for these funds largely in terms of the profit possibilities available to the borrower, and they described the supply in terms of the supply price of abstinence. It seems entirely appropriate to regard this as an attempt to analyze what I have called the rate of interest.

THE NATURE OF THE THEORY OF INTEREST

The Problem Posed for the Theory of Interest

Arthur Hadley, toward the close of the last century, stated that "the causes which have produced the *system* of interest are radically different from those which determine the *rate* of interest." [31] Much of the literature on interest theory makes it seem easy indeed to reach this conclusion. Some discussions, like those of Schumpeter and Knight, are broad, philosophic essays on why interest exists, and seem only remotely concerned with the actual determination of the rate of interest in the market. Other discussions, such as those which focus on the money market, and the liquidity preference theory itself, direct attention to the many and volatile forces which move daily rates about with little apparent relation to the fundamental elements described by the classical essays. Harrod seems to accept this apparent dichotomy as a real one, expressing views which Robertson summarizes (and rejects) to the effect that "we must have a

---

[30] A. T. Hadley, "Interest and Profits," *Annals of the American Academy of Political and Social Science,* 4 (1893–94): 342. Hadley's statement differs in that he calls entrepreneur and lender both capitalists, but his thought is clearly the same as Schumpeter's.

[31] *Ibid.,* p. 338.

classical theory to tell us why there is a rate of interest at all, and a liquidity theory to tell us why it is what it is." [32]

If there is such a dichotomy, then the theory of interest is concerned with both questions: "Why interest?" and "How high interest?" In my view the dichotomy is a false one, if for no other reason than that given simply and directly by Fisher, who says: "Some writers have chosen, for purposes of exposition, to postulate two questions involved in the theory of the rate of interest, viz., (1) why any rate of interest exists and (2) how the rate of interest is determined. This second question, however, embraces also the first, since to explain how the rate of interest is determined involves the question of whether the rate can or cannot be zero, i.e., whether a positive rate of interest must necessarily exist." [33] Until this simple logic is proved false I shall continue to accept Fisher's conclusion.

The theory of interest, then, must rest upon an analysis of all the elements which determine rates of interest. If the classical theory gives alleged reasons for the existence of interest which do not actually enter into the determination of interest rates, then I should simply conclude that these were not reasons at all, and that the classical theory was wrong. If contemporary theory describes any element in the determination of market rates which does in fact operate, then this element is also a "reason for the existence of interest."

A Classification of Theories of Interest

The many attempts that have been made to develop a theory of interest almost defy any comprehensive classification, but a broad general statement may perhaps clarify without doing too much violence to the truth. Many theorists, including most of the well-known classical economists, have been concerned primarily with what might be called "nonmonetary" theories of interest. Recent writers of this school would include F. H. Knight and Irving Fisher. These theories are characterized by the fact that their central models include no explicit variable for the quantity or velocity of money. I assume in this statement that "hoards" or "idle balances" are alternative expressions for velocity.

Both before and after the classical writers, "monetary" theories of interest have been prominent. These make central to their major models the influences of changes in the quantity of money supplied and changes in the demand for idle balances. Recent monetary theories may be usefully divided between (1) two major types of partial-equilibrium theory and (2) various ways of presenting interest theory as a part of a general-equi-

---

[32] D. H. Robertson, "Some Notes on the Theory of Interest," in *Money, Trade, and Economic Growth* (New York: Macmillan, 1951), p. 200. Harrod's statement is in R. F. Harrod, *Towards a Dynamic Economics* (London: Macmillan, 1948), p. 67.

[33] Fisher, *The Theory of Interest*, pp. 13–14.

librium system. The two partial-equilibrium models are the loanable-funds theory and the liquidity-preference theory. Whether these are merely different ways of stating the same thing or significantly different theories will be discussed at length in Part Two.

Notes on Preclassical Doctrine

Although this study makes no attempt to provide a history of doctrine, it may be useful to comment briefly on the broad sweep of changing ideas in relation to various types of interest theory, in order to gain some insight into the reasons for the kinds of oversimplification which are characteristic of many approaches.

The earliest writers of the 18th Century were active participants in the development of the quantity theory of money, and they had a general tendency to think of the value of money quite indiscriminately as the amount one can get for it when lending (the interest rate) or when buying goods (the price level). Just as increases in the quantity of money tended to reduce its value for purchase of commodities, so these increases were assumed also to reduce the return for lending. In the context of the quantity theory of money this confusion of two basically different concepts of the "value of money" made the theory of interest of the period almost exclusively a monetary theory; the theory of interest, indeed, was simply part of a crude quantity theory of money. Schumpeter takes to task Law, Locke, and Montesquieu, who, he says, like "others were undoubtedly quite wrong in making the rate of interest simply depend on the quantity of money." [34] This charge is not wholly justified in relation to Locke, who faces the question why borrowers are willing to pay interest for the use of money, and answers by pointing out that the borrower can use the funds to produce more than the cost of borrowing.[35] Here we see the elements of clearly nonmonetary determinants of the rate of interest. But Schumpeter's charge appears legitimate as a criticism of most writers in the early part of the 18th Century.

By the latter part of the century, however, the theory of interest had become surprisingly sophisticated. Charles Rist states that by this time it "was particularly penetrating and provided the foundation for all subsequent studies of the rate of interest." [36] Cantillon had clearly made the necessary distinction between the purchasing power of money and the

[34] Schumpeter, *The Theory of Economic Development*, p. 186.

[35] John Locke, "Some Considerations of the Consequences of Lowering the Interest and Raising the Value of Money," in *Locke's Works*, IV (London: Longman's, 1794), p. 36. Edward S. Herman has pointed out to me that Schumpeter himself later gives Locke credit for expressing precisely the ideas we have attributed to him here. See Joseph Schumpeter, *History of Economic Analysis* (Oxford: Oxford University Press, 1954), p. 329.

[36] Charles Rist, *History of Monetary and Credit Theory*, translated by Jane Degras (New York: Macmillan, 1940), p. 123.

rate for lending it.[37] He went on to describe the way in which an increase in the quantity of money might either raise or lower the rate of interest, depending upon the way in which it is injected into the economy. "If the abundance of money in the state comes from the hands of money lenders it will doubtless bring down the current rate of interest by increasing the number of money lenders: but if it comes from the intervention of spenders it will have just the opposite effect and will raise the rate of interest by increasing the number of Undertakers who will have employment from this increased expense, and will need to borrow to equip their business in all classes of interest." [38] Today, we might refer to Cantillon's first example as one of increase only in the quantity of money, and to his second as an increase in the quantity of money supplied in response to an increase in the demand for investment or for consumption. In any event the distinction he described here would clarify many an argument over the effects of changes in the quantity of money. In his characteristic way, Cantillon supported his theoretical generalization with empirical evidence drawn from the experience in 1720, when large increases in both the quantity and velocity of money in London were associated with sharply *rising* money rates.[39] Underlying his conclusions was a theory of the determination of interest rates which is highly suggestive of the loanable funds doctrine. Cantillon states that "the Interest of Money in a State is settled by the proportionate number of Lenders and Borrowers." [40] In words that could as well have come from Schumpeter two centuries later, Cantillon then describes the reasons for the demand of the borrowers: "If there were in a State no Undertakers who could make a profit on the money or goods which they borrow, the use of interest would probably be less frequent than it is. Only the extravagant and prodigal people would contract loans." [41] Turgot likewise emphasized the role of entrepreneurial borrowers, but he also added that we must not forget the borrowing of both individuals and states for purposes of consumption. On the supply side of the market for loanable funds all of these writers had in mind both saving and newly created money, the latter being very much on their minds because of the great influx of gold and silver from the New World.

---

[37] Cantillon is really an exception to the midcentury dividing line suggested by Rist, since he died in 1734, but it is obvious that a sharp demarcation is not intended.

[38] Richard Cantillon, *Essai sur la Nature du Commerce,* Higgs edition (London: Macmillan, 1931), p. 215. Quoted by Charles Rist, *History of Monetary and Credit Theory,* p. 127.

[39] Cantillon, *ibid.,* p. 212.

[40] *Ibid.,* p. 198.

[41] *Ibid.,* p. 210.

Notes on Classical Doctrine

One wonders how it can be that the classical writers following Smith could have disregarded so much that was valid in earlier thought, and developed in contrast to these theories a much narrower and less inclusive doctrine. Specifically, why did they omit monetary elements and develop a nonmonetary theory of interest? The answer to this query lies primarily in the fact that the classical economists were asking different questions from those raised by their predecessors, and secondarily in the classical tendency to regard as unimportant all those events of "temporary" nature that characterized disequilibrium situations.[42]

Preclassical writers were men of affairs, concerned with and immersed in the daily events of the market and of politics. They saw interest rates fluctuating sharply under the impact of short-run forces. Monetary effects were ever-present and obvious. The classical writers, on the other hand, were mostly philosophers of political economy whose interest was less in daily changes than in long-run movements and basic forces that determined the levels about which daily rates might be expected to fluctuate. This objective is well stated by Irving Fisher, one of the most recent nonmonetary theorists, who made the following comment concerning his own book on the theory of interest:

This volume makes no claim to being the monumental work necessary to analyze every possible influence that acts upon such a rate. The purpose of the book is rather to isolate the fundamental or basic forces which are operative in the interest problem. . . . The aim in view has therefore dictated the suppression of the innumerable secondary factors in order to focus the analysis upon the primary factors involved. . . . Laws, gold movements, . . . banking customs and policies, governmental finance . . . and many other factors work their influences on the so-called money market where interest rates are determined. Practically these matters are of equal importance with fundamental theory. While theory, in other words, assumes a waveless sea, actual, practical life represents a choppy one.[43]

It may be gravely doubted that most of the classical economists — or possibly even Fisher — fully recognized how very important the waves are. The surface may often be disturbed by tides or by storms too enduring or too powerful to be represented by a sea that is only "choppy." And disequilibrium is far more characteristic of our world than is equilibrium. But right or wrong, that was essentially the classical view, and their error was not so much to forget money as to deny its relevance to the long-run problems with which they were concerned. Thus, Ricardo wrote in his

[42] A discussion of the legitimacy of this treatment is summarized in chapter xiii, pp. 280–282.

[43] Fisher, *The Theory of Interest*, pp. 487–488 and 491.

Principles, "If, by the discovery of a new mine, by the abuses of banking, or by any other cause the quantity of money be greatly increased, its ultimate effect is to raise the level of prices of commodities in proportion to the increased quantity of money; but there is probably always an interval during which some effect is produced on the rate of interest." [44] Even if the increase of money in the hands of lenders should at first reduce the rate of interest, the increased demand for goods will soon raise their prices so that the money needed to purchase them removes the superfluity of funds and forces interest rates to rise once more to their original level.[45] In a copiously documented section of his work, *The Theory of Prices,* Marget argues that the economists "from Thornton and Ricardo . . . down to Marshall" showed a sophisticated understanding of the way in which changes in the quantity of money operate on prices via the link provided by the rate of interest.[46] It is an illusion, in this view, to suppose that interest rates can be held for long by monetary policy above or below the level they would find without such a policy. As Ricardo put it, the interest rate "is not regulated by the rate at which the Bank will lend, whether it be 5, 4, or 3 per cent, but by the rate of profits which can be made by the employment of capital, and which is totally independent of the quantity or of the value of money. Whether a Bank lent one million, ten million, or a hundred million, they would not *permanently* alter the market rate of interest; they would alter only the value of the money which they thus issued." [47] Given this analysis of economic behavior it becomes clear why classical writers relegated the operation of monetary phenomena to secondary consideration. I am not here concerned with the validity of these views, a question to which I shall return when the analysis has been more fully developed:[48] my purpose is only to show the reason why economists for over one hundred years laid to one side the consideration of monetary effects upon the rate of interest, and developed a nonmonetary theory of interest instead.

Whatever conclusion one may reach regarding the adequacy of the nonmonetary theories, it cannot be denied that they provide important elements for any acceptable theory. A "complete" theory of interest cannot eliminate but can only supplement the factors described in these theories. In fact, Vera and Friedrich Lutz go so far as to say:

One cannot help feeling that this modern discussion of the theory of interest, which centered around the 'loanable funds approach' versus the

---

[44] Ricardo, *Principles of Political Economy and Taxation,* p. 198.

[45] A clear review of Ricardo's position on this issue is given by Knut Wicksell, in his *Lectures on Political Economy,* II (London: Routledge and Sons, 1946), p. 179.

[46] A. W. Marget, *The Theory of Prices,* I (New York: Prentice-Hall, 1938), pp. 173 ff.

[47] Ricardo, *Principles of Political Economy and Taxation,* p. 246. Italics mine.

[48] See chapter xiii, pp. 280–282.

'liquidity preference approach' moved on a much lower plane than the discussion among the older generation of economists. . . . The main problem for them was to analyze what lies behind the demand for (and supply of) loanable funds. . . . The results of this investigation . . . have to be incorporated into any theory of interest.[49]

The "older generation" referred to here includes, to be sure, early monetary theorists like Wicksell, but prominent place is given to the classical economists and, even more important, to Boehm-Bawerk and Irving Fisher.

THE DILEMMA POSED BY THE EXISTENCE OF INTEREST

Schumpeter, drawing upon the work of Boehm-Bawerk and others, gives an excellent statement of the basic reason why interest has presented a conundrum for many economists. After describing this dilemma he indicates the only logical ways he can see by which theorists can escape it. A review of Schumpeter's analysis will provide a frame of reference to which we shall frequently recur in the interpretation and evaluation of proposed theories of interest.

According to the theory of long-run competitive equilibrium all the value received from the sale of a product should accrue to the factors used in its production. It would thus appear that if land, labor and capital goods participate in producing a final consumer good, then the value of their services must exactly equal the value of the final good. But capital goods are also produced goods, and their value must, therefore, exactly equal the value of the factors entering their production. We may carry this process of analysis back until we reach the point at which only the "original" factors, land and labor, enter the product. The logic of such a procedure drives us to the conclusion that the value of final consumer goods must be equal to the value of the ultimate factors of production, land and labor, used in producing them (including both their direct application, and their indirect application through capital goods). There is no room for a net return to capital goods. In Schumpeter's own words,

The existence of interest constitutes a problem because we know that in the normal circular flow the whole value product must be imputed to the original factors, that is to the services of labor and land; hence . . . there can be no permanent net income other than wages and rent.[50] . . . a machine has a value corresponding to its product, but has only received it from the services of labor and land which existed before it was created, to which the value has already been imputed as a whole. It is true that a

---

[49] Vera and Friedrich Lutz, *The Theory of Investment of the Firm* (Princeton: Princeton University Press, 1951), p. 237.

[50] Joseph A. Schumpeter, *The Theory of Economic Development*, p. 160.

stream of goods flows to the machine, but it also flows through it. . . .
The machine itself is a product, and therefore just like a consumption
good its value is conducted on to a reservoir, from which no interest can
flow any more.[51]

In the real world, of course, we observe an exception to these conclusions in relation to profits as well as to interest. But profits present no
dilemma for the theory of perfect competition, because they emerge only
temporarily or as a result of monopoly. Interest, on the other hand, is a
permanent flow, and it would exist with or without monopoly. It "is a
permanent net income," says Schumpeter,[52] taking the same position as
Boehm-Bawerk before him, who wrote, ". . . it flows in to the capitalist
without ever exhausting the capital from which it comes, and therefore
without any necessary limit to its continuance." [53] Likewise, interest cannot be explained by monopoly, since ". . . monopoly positions do not
occur regularly and numerously enough for this explanation to be accepted, and moreover interest exists without them." [54]

For Schumpeter, then, the dilemma posed by the existence of interest
is this: How can a permanent flow of income accrue to the capitalist if
there are only two original factors of production, land and labor, and if
conventional theory is correct in holding that in long-run competitive
equilibrium the total value of goods produced must be absorbed by the
factors producing them? Only three ways out of this dilemma suggest
themselves to Schumpeter. The first is that there may be not two but
three ultimate factors of production. The second is that there is a flaw
in the theory which states that in competitive equilibrium all value of
products sold must accrue to the factors of production. The third is to
suggest that interest would not exist in equilibrium of the type visualized
in conventional competitive theory, but exists as a permanent flow in the
real world only because this is a noncompetitive world, and/or one of
development rather than of static equilibrium.

Since I believe that Schumpeter has, indeed, put his finger on what has
been for many a central problem in understanding interest, it seems
necessary to deal with an argument which might imply that the problem
posed is essentially specious. Knight argues eloquently and with much
validity that the very concept of "original factors" is entirely erroneous:
". . . no general classification as between 'primary' and 'derived' factors
is realistic or useful. . . . If we go back to any supposable beginning we
shall undoubtedly find that the first things on which man came to set a

---

[51] *Ibid.*, pp. 162–163. See also p. 190 ff.

[52] *Ibid.*, p. 159.

[53] Eugen von Boehm-Bawerk, *Capital and Interest,* translated by William Smart
(London and New York: Macmillan, 1922), p. 1.

[54] Schumpeter, *The Theory of Economic Development*, p. 169.

value, in something like our present understanding of the concept, were either artifacts or slaves, — 'capital' in either event. This certainly occurred long before any such thing as free labor had economic value, or there was 'property' in natural resources." [55] If these statements are valid what becomes of the dilemma arising out of the supposed ultimate reversion of all values to these phantom "original" or "primary" factors?

I suggest that the hypothetical history which would give literal meaning to "original" factors is not really relevant to the essential point that Schumpeter is making. We could as well start today, with some existing land, capital goods, and free labor available, and produce future consumer goods by any of many alternative methods. The application of a given amount of today's factors over the next two years may, by one method, produce a fairly steady output, whereas another method may require the production of more intermediate goods, yielding very little of the desired consumer goods in the first year, but more by the end of two years than the first method. If we desire to maximize the two-year flow we must, then, make many intermediate goods. He who advances the funds to tide us over until consumer goods begin to flow will receive a return for doing so. We might well imagine him buying the intermediate goods as we produce them, and in turn using them for production of the final goods. The fact that the lender can receive interest is equivalent to saying that he who buys the newly produced capital goods can secure them for less than he will ultimately obtain for sale of the finished product. Schumpeter's dilemma of interest, then, may be expressed in this way: since all factors receive remuneration equal to the value of their contribution to final products, why is not the full final value of these products swept back to today's factors? Why is it that the intermediate factor produced with their aid can also demand and obtain a payment over and above what is necessary to pay the factors for producing it? Is not the admitted fact of such payments a contradiction to competitive theory?

These questions do not in any sense dispense with the issue Knight has raised, and I shall show later[56] the way in which I believe a more adequate answer to his criticism contributes to a resolution of the dilemma created by the existence of interest. For the present, however, I wish only to indicate my reason for believing that Schumpeter has, indeed, posed a real, even if solvable, problem despite the criticisms that may be leveled at the concept of "original factors."

---

[55] "Note on Dr. Lange's Interest Theory," *Review of Economic Studies*, 4 (1937): 226.
[56] See pp. 111–113.

PART ONE

NONMONETARY THEORIES OF INTEREST

BOEHM-BAWERK'S REVIEW
AND CRITICISM OF EARLIER DOCTRINES

New ideas are seldom born full blown, and the views which fill the pages written by the "father" of a doctrine may usually be found scattered among the writings of his predecessors. This is as true of Keynes as it was of Smith, and it is equally true of Boehm-Bawerk, as he would have been the first to admit. His contribution to the theory of interest, like that of Smith to the broader field of economic analysis, was to a large extent that of winnower and binder.[1] Although we start with him we recognize that a case might be made for going back to the Mercantilists, or even to the Old Testament. But the purpose of this book is analytical, not historical, and Boehm-Bawerk provides an excellent point at which to begin the construction of modern interest theory. One reason for this is that he himself prepared an excellent review of earlier ideas, some of which contributed to his own construction, and some of which he rejected for reasons that help clarify the theory of interest.

It should be understood that Boehm-Bawerk's history of doctrine, comprehensive and well documented though it is, has not gone without criticism. Francis A. Walker especially rebuked him for citing, as attempts to explain interest, statements in earlier writings, which, in Walker's view, were intended rather as social justifications for interest.[2] Boehm-Bawerk effectively defended himself against this charge in "The Positive Theory of Capital and Its Critics." [3] Walker made a second criticism, however, which was also voiced by Alfred Marshall [4] — and which seems to me more

---

[1] Special mention should be made of John Rae, who anticipated much of Boehm-Bawerk's analysis by half a century in his 1834 publication of *A Statement of Some New Principles on the Subject of Political Economy*. . . . (Boston: Hilliard, Gray and Co., 1834). In his second edition (1900) Boehm-Bawerk recognizes Rae's achievements, of which he was not even aware at the time of his first edition (1890).

[2] Francis A. Walker, "Dr. Boehm-Bawerk's Theory of Interest," *Quarterly Journal of Economics*, 6 (1892): 399–416.

[3] *Quarterly Journal of Economics*, 9 (1895): especially pp. 235–239.

[4] Alfred Marshall, *Principles of Economics*, 8th ed. (London: Macmillan, 1930), p. 583 n. and p. 790 n. For further discussion, see also "Translator's Preface," by William A. Scott, in Boehm-Bawerk, *Recent Literature on Interest* (London and New York: Macmillan, 1903), p. ix ff.

telling. According to this criticism Boehm-Bawerk's attempt to classify theories into categories such as "abstinence theories," "productivity theories," "use theories" and so forth, suggests that the doctrines involved were narrow and single-cause theories of interest. In my own view, the earlier writers themselves often encourage this misunderstanding by discussing different aspects of the interest problem at entirely different parts of their books, with the result that one will read a section carefully and suppose he has grasped the author's full view, only to discover a hundred pages later that he has seen but a part of it.

Nassau Senior illustrates this problem well. He is famous for having introduced the "abstinence theory" of interest, and he is criticized both for its one-sidedness and for using it to imply that the "pain" of the capitalist is in some sense proportional to the "reward" he "earns" by abstaining. On page 89 of *Political Economy,* Senior describes abstinence as the cause of interest in terms which would readily explain this general interpretation, and in his public-policy pronouncements he further supports it. Yet on page 192 he points out precisely what many have criticized him for "not realizing," namely, that the capitalist soon finds accumulation a goal in itself: "The capitalist soon regards the increase of his capital as the great business of his life." [5] In this section he makes it abundantly clear that the "pain" of the abstainer may be close to zero or even negative (i.e., pleasure). Senior here describes interest (profit) in terms which could legitimately be characterized as those of a productivity theory, making the productivity of capital depend upon the relationship between the quantity of capital supplied and the quantity of labor and land.

Senior is by no means the only classical economist whose writing could be adduced to support Marshall's conclusion that "some writers have laid more stress on the supply side and others on the demand side, but the difference between them has often been little more than a difference in emphasis. . . . In short there is no reason to believe that the accounts which Professor Boehm-Bawerk has given of the 'naive productivity theories,' the 'use theories,' etc. of capital and interest would have been accepted by the older writers themselves as well balanced and complete presentations of their several positions." [6]

Since my purpose, like that of Boehm-Bawerk himself, is essentially analytical, these limitations of his presentation will not reduce its usefulness. Indeed, they serve in some measure to highlight types of analysis. I shall, therefore, largely follow Boehm-Bawerk's summaries of earlier theories without thereby passing judgment on the degree to which they actually represent the whole view of those whose theories he reviews. The

[5] Nassau Senior, *An Outline of the Science of Political Economy* (New York: Farrar and Rinehart, 1939), p. 192.
[6] Alfred Marshall, *Principles of Economics,* p. 790 n.

function of these descriptions from *Capital and Interest* will be to present ideas which deserve appraisal, to show Boehm-Bawerk's criticisms of these ideas, and to note the way in which he uses these "theories" as a spring-board for the exposition of his own analysis.

DEFINITIONS

Before summarizing and appraising the work of others, Boehm-Bawerk presents a number of definitions, several of which should be reviewed at this point. He defines capital as "a complex of goods that originate in a previous process of production, and are destined, not for immediate consumption, but to serve as a means of acquiring further goods. Objects of immediate consumption, then, and land (as not produced) stand outside our conception of capital." [7] In short, the term capital as here defined refers to what we conventionally call "capital goods."

"The income that flows from capital . . . we shall simply call Interest." [8] Gross Interest must be distinguished from Net Interest. The former includes "besides the true interest, such things as part of replacement of the substance of capital expended, compensation for all sorts of current costs, outlays on repairs, premiums for risk, and so on. . . . Net Interest, on the other hand, is just this true income of capital which appears after these heterogeneous elements are deducted from Gross Interest. It is the explanation of Net Interest with which the theory of interest naturally has to do." [9]

Next, Boehm-Bawerk faces the problem of the relation of interest to profits. He follows John Stuart Mill in assuming that the entrepreneur is the supplier of both funds and managerial effort, which leads him to the view that interest is one element in profits. "It may with reason appear questionable if the entire profit realized by an undertaker from a process of production should be put to the account of his capital. . . . On this point opinions are divided. Most economists draw some . . . distinction. From the total profit obtained by the productive undertaking they regard one part as profit of capital, another as undertaker's profit." In order to determine the proper imputation between these two shares, "we find what in other circumstances a capital of definite amount generally yields. That is shown most simply by the usual rate of interest obtainable for a perfectly safe loan of capital." [10] Boehm-Bawerk then admits that such

---

[7] Eugen von Boehm-Bawerk, *Capital and Interest,* translated by William Smart (London and New York: Macmillan, 1922), p. 6.

[8] *Ibid.,* p. 7. For further refinement see Boehm-Bawerk, *The Positive Theory of Capital,* translated by William Smart (New York: G. E. Stechert, 1923), Book I, chapter iv.

[9] Boehm-Bawerk, *Capital and Interest,* p. 7.

[10] *Ibid.,* pp. 8–9.

a process of imputation is not universally accepted as admissible, but points out that "the difficulties . . . which surround . . . the problem of interest are so considerable that I do not feel it my duty to add to them by taking up another. I purposely refrain then from entering on any investigation . . . of undertaker's profit." [11]

Following these introductory definitions, Boehm-Bawerk presents an outline of the history of the theory of interest from classical and medieval times through Turgot, Smith, and a number of writers whose theories he classifies as "colorless," including in this category, along with many less known writers, the theories of Ricardo, Torrens and McCulloch. I shall not dwell on this section, since the essential points that have not already been suggested are expounded in the subsequent parts of Boehm-Bawerk's review. The remainder of his volume comprises an outline and criticism of theories classified into the following groups: Productivity Theories, Abstinence Theory, Labor Theories, Exploitation Theory, and Minor Systems.

PRODUCTIVITY THEORIES

The theories called "productivity theories" include those of Say, Roscher, Riedel, Lauderdale, Malthus, Carey, and von Thünen. Although the concept of productivity envisaged by these writers is not always clear, and is not entirely the same for each, the fundamental notion of all is that capital goods are in some sense productive, and hence must receive a functional share in distribution of income. Three very common illustrations of this idea may be mentioned. (1) With the aid of a net we can catch more fish than without it. A stronger statement would be that with the aid of a net we can catch more fish than could be caught without it, even allowing for the time required to construct the net. (2) A grain of wheat or a tree planted today will yield considerably more wheat or lumber tomorrow. Here the material which constitutes capital goods reproduces more of itself over time. (3) Wine which we abstain from consuming today will become more satisfying and more valuable by next year.

Superficially, these considerations might appear to provide direct and obvious reasons for the existence of interest. Since capital goods are in these various ways productive, it is reasonable that he who provides them or the wherewithal to secure them, should receive a net return for making them available. Unlike the Marxists, Boehm-Bawerk makes no attempt to deny that capital goods should be recognized as "productive." Capital, he says, "actually possesses the physical productivity ascribed to it — that

---

[11] *Ibid.*, p. 9.

is to say by its assistance more goods can be produced than without it." [12] Indeed, this characteristic of capital goods is given a crucial role in his own theory under the title of the technical superiority of present goods over future goods. But he argues that the productivity theories have failed to show that this provides an adequate reason for the existence of interest, because of their failure to face two basic questions. In the first place they do not adequately consider the problem of value. To explain interest by reference to productivity, he argues, it would be necessary to show not only that more goods are produced with the aid of capital, but also that the value of such goods is greater than the value of the former, smaller output. By creating goods one does not necessarily produce value. "What production can do is never anything more than to create goods, in the hope that, according to the anticipated relations of demand and supply, they will obtain value." [13] The very fact that tomorrow's output can be larger than today's might, indeed, cause the value of that output to be less than today's.

Although Boehm-Bawerk considers this oversight in the attempted proofs by the productivity theorists to be important, he does not make it central to his major criticism. Indeed, he is willing to grant the probability that this unproved assumption may generally be valid. The crucial fact is that "there is not one single feature in the whole circumstances to indicate that this greater amount of goods must be worth more than the capital consumed in its production, — and it is this phenomenon of *surplus* value we have to explain." [14] If capital produced nothing, it would presumably be of no value. If it produces goods of much value, it will presumably be of much value itself. The dilemma of interest is the fact that the value of the capital is not equal to the value of its (ultimate) product. Somehow a surplus emerges. "Why should a concrete capital that yields a great return not be highly valued on that account — so highly that its capital value would be equal to the value of the abundant return that flows from it? Why, e.g., should a boat and net which, during the time that they last, help to procure an extra return of 2,700 fish, not be considered exactly equal in value to these 2,700 fish?" [15] If this occurred, there would be no surplus value despite physical productivity; and the value of the boat and net would be swept back to the original factors, land and labor, so that there would be no interest. Essentially the same question is raised by Menger and ably paraphrased by Boehm-Bawerk: "If it

---

[12] *Ibid.*, p. 138. This and many of the following quotations from Boehm-Bawerk were cited in William A. Scott's excellent chapter xxii of *The Development of Economics* (New York and London: Century, 1932). These references have been checked in the original source for context and interpretation.

[13] Boehm-Bawerk, *Capital and Interest*, p. 135.

[14] *Ibid.*, p. 138. (Italics mine.)

[15] *Ibid.*, p. 139.

is true that the anticipated value of the product is the source and the measure of the value of its means of production, how is it that real capital is not valued as highly as its product?" [16] This is the problem of interest, and this problem is in no sense solved by the physical productivity of capital.

USE THEORIES

A second type of attempt to explain the existence of interest is that described by Boehm-Bawerk as "use theories." Of the many writers whose theories fall into this category special attention is given to the ideas of Hermann and Menger. These theories seem very closely related to the productivity theories, and I should even incline to regard them as particular developments of that approach: yet their statement of the problem is characteristically different, and I shall follow Boehm-Bawerk's review. These theories imply that "besides the substance of capital, the use of capital is an object of independent nature and of independent value." [17] He who buys the product of capital must pay both for the substance of the capital and for the use of it. This latter payment provides the surplus, which is interest. Thus, for instance, a house or land provides a service to the user even if it is not consumed. Menger describes this "use" in terms of "disposal over capital" during a period of time, in return for which a payment must be made in the form of interest.

Boehm-Bawerk criticized these theories by arguing that all value of all goods always arises from their use, and that therefore it is meaningless to try to separate use value from the value of the substance: ". . . we value and desire goods only on account of the material services we expect from them." [18] These services form the "substance" with which we have to do, the goods themselves forming only the bodily shell: ". . . the value and price of a good is nothing else than the value and price of all its material services thrown together into a lump sum . . ." [19] Thus the value of a capital good must already include any use value anticipated from it. Furthermore, if Menger were correct in believing that interest is a necessary payment for "disposal over goods" during a period of time, then why should not the value of ownership of land be infinite, since it gives the power of disposal over infinite time?

Returning now to Schumpeter's basic dilemma, presented by the existence of interest in view of competitive price theory, it is not clear how the productivity and use theories avoid the logical impasse described there. They have sought to find a productivity in capital, but they have made

[16] *Ibid.*, p. 211.
[17] *Ibid.*, p. 186.
[18] *Ibid.*, p. 226.
[19] *Ibid.*, p. 227.

no attempt either to trace that productivity back to any original factor other than labor and land, *or* to show why that "tracing back" is not incumbent upon us.

ABSTINENCE THEORIES

Senior came much more directly to grips with the basic problem of interest as posed in Schumpeter's dilemma. He recognized explicitly that the discovery of a third original factor would solve the problem of interest. Capital goods were not original factors, and so they would not fill the bill. But behind the existence of capital goods he thought he saw a contributing service besides labor and land. This was abstinence. Its role was in a sense similar to that of labor; it also came from sacrifice for which a reward had to be provided. If the concept of such an independent factor of production could be justified, then the problem of interest would be solved.

In a certain sense Senior's introduction of the concept of abstinence rounded out the classical theory of cost. "The real price of everything," Smith had said, "is the toil and trouble of acquiring it." Ricardo appears to lay little if any stress on "sacrifice," but even more than Smith he found the source of exchange value in embodied labor. Senior, who explicitly emphasized sacrifice *as the essential nature* of cost, was enabled by his concept of abstinence to relate interest as well as wages to "real cost." Only rent remained as a payment of dubious justification from the standpoint of a real cost ethics.

Boehm-Bawerk rejected this theory, partly in consonance with his general rejection of the entire pain-cost theory of value, which he and the other Austrians were replacing by the idea that all value arises from the utility of goods.[20] Specifically, he pointed out that in many cases the existence and rate of interest failed utterly to correspond in any way with the "sacrifice from abstinence" by the capitalist. Indeed, he argued that interest is often paid when there is no "pain" whatever felt by the capitalist.[21] Taken at its face value, this criticism, which is common among those with socioethical objections to the payment of interest,[22] is partly confused and partly wrong. Modern value theory never implies that the total pain of labor, or any other sacrifice, need equal the total pleasure obtained from the resulting product. Such an equation of utilities would require measurements that are impossible to make, and which, even if possible, would not be relevant to the determination of outputs. If the principle of abstinence were applied in a modern value theory it would only suggest that

[20] *Ibid.*, pp. 285–286.

[21] *Ibid.*, p. 277.

[22] This reference does not imply that Boehm-Bawerk had such objections: he did not.

when equilibrium has been achieved the "pain" of further abstinence would exceed the satisfaction from the use of the additional product that it provided. Put in this way, the abstinence principle may be wholly consistent with Fisher's and other contemporary views. As Boehm-Bawerk himself implies, considerations of the sort referred to here do not invalidate the theory of abstinence if that theory is properly stated.[23] They do, of course, invalidate the naive argument that interest payments are socially desirable because they compensate the capitalist for the "pain" of his abstinence.

The ultimate and irrefutable objection to Senior's theory, in Boehm-Bawerk's view, is that abstinence simply cannot be regarded as an independent factor of production. It is "a logical blunder to represent the renunciation or postponement of gratification, or abstinence, as a second independent sacrifice in addition to the labor sacrificed in production." [24] To support this conclusion we need only consider the nature of a factor of production; it is an entity — e.g., a good or a person — which is capable of providing productive services. Any use of these services in production implies abstinence from some other use: if I labor, I abstain from swimming or playing tennis. As Boehm-Bawerk pointed out, payment for labor already includes payment for abstention from other activities. Abstinence simply is not an independent factor, but is the act by which factors are permitted to perform their services in production.

This view does not deny that abstinence from present consumption in order to enjoy a later benefit may not involve a sacrifice and hence require a reward in an economy permitting freedom of choice to those who own control over factors. Indeed, we shall see that the existence of this supply price is an essential element in any adequate theory of interest, and in this sense Senior's contribution was a crucial one. But the very nature of a factor of production denies to abstinence the role of an independent "factor," and this denial closes to us the simple road out of Schumpeter's and Boehm-Bawerk's dilemma which Senior's theory might have provided. If an independent factor has not been found, then we must either continue to seek one, or else we must choose one of the two other roads which Schumpeter offers: we must say either that there is a flaw in long-run competitive-price theory, or we must deny that interest would exist under the conditions which that theory posits.

LABOR THEORIES

Labor theories of interest also attempt to explain the existence of interest by the discovery of a third original and independent factor of production. Many of these theories allege that interest is a payment legitimately earned

---

[23] *Capital and Interest*, p. 278.
[24] *Ibid.*

by the capitalist through some sort of labor he has performed, or over which he has obtained rights. The latter form of the theory is presented by James Mill, who regarded interest as payment for "stored-up labor" embodied in capital goods. Here again, as in the productivity theories, Boehm-Bawerk points out that such an analysis cannot explain the emergence of a surplus. Why should stored-up labor receive a higher reward than direct labor? Interest is a surplus over and above the cost of the capital — that is over and above the value of the labor that is stored up.[25]

A French version of the labor theory (represented in Boehm-Bawerk's review chiefly by Courcelle-Seneuil) gives credit directly to the capitalist for the additional labor embodied in capital goods.[26] When one examines the nature of such labor it turns out to be essentially that of enduring the trials of saving, and Boehm-Bawerk dismisses this approach as merely a variant of the abstinence theory. A German labor theory (Schäffle) held that the capitalist performed the services which, in the ideal state, public officials would perform, directing economic activity in consonance with the national need. This approach has the virtue of at least describing what purports to be an actual, additional productive service. Unfortunately for this theory, however, it fails entirely to show any relation between the alleged labor and the interest received. If interest "can be so explained, then there must be shown some normal relation between the alleged result, the interest of capital, and the asserted cause, the expenditure of labour on the part of the capitalist." [27] Not only do we fail to find any such relation in the real world, but indeed we may even find the opposite. "The borrower who guards another man's capital and employs it, notwithstanding this expenditure of labour, receives no interest; the owner receives it although his labour be nil. . . . Just as surely as interest bears no proportion to the labour put forth by the capitalist, does it stand in exact proportion to the fact of possession and to the amount of possession. Interest on capital, to repeat my former words, is not an income from labour, but an income from ownership." [28]

EXPLOITATION THEORIES

Although Boehm-Bawerk supported many parts of the Marxian theory, and criticized many of the specific objections raised by those who tried to refute Marx, his own theory was in no small measure developed to disprove the essential conclusions of the exploitation theory of interest.

Boehm-Bawerk's views were similar to those of the Marxists in the fol-

[25] *Ibid.*, p. 299.
[26] *Ibid.*, p. 300 ff.
[27] *Ibid.*, p. 311.
[28] *Ibid.*

lowing respects. (1) He accepted the Marxian frame of reference — which was also that of the classical English economists — namely, that society is composed of economic classes, including propertied capitalists and propertyless laborers. (2) He rejected the idea that capital, or abstinence, represented an independent entity in production, a factor in some sense parallel to the two original factors, land and labor. (3) He denied that interest is a necessary reward either for abstinence or for some mysterious hidden labor of the capitalist. "It owes its existence to no personal activity of the capitalist, and flows to him even where he has not moved a finger in its making." [29] (4) Interest is thus seen as a surplus value, a payment representing the difference between the value of capital goods and the value of the goods they produce.

Despite these important similarities between Boehm-Bawerk's views and those of the Marxists, his ultimate conclusions diverge sharply from theirs. The general tenor of Marxian analysis is summarized by Boehm-Bawerk to be, ". . . that the value of goods is measured by quantity of labour; that labour alone creates all value; that in the loan contract the worker receives less value than he creates, and that necessity compels him to acquiesce in this; that the capitalist appropriates the surplus to himself; and that consequently profit so obtained has the character of plunder from the produce of the labour of others." [30] This seems to be a legitimate interpretation of the Marxian analysis, and I should think Marxists would themselves accept it except for possible debate over the term "plunder." It is common for Marxists to argue that the labor theory of value is scientific and does not directly imply value judgments, but I have been quite unable to separate the word "exploitation" as they use it from value judgments that are essentially similar to the overtones of the word "plunder."

Boehm-Bawerk's first attack on this theory is directed against the labor theory of value upon which it rests. Again he presents a summary which seems as accurate as any brief statement could be, and which he supports by pages of direct quotation from *Capital*. Here is his summary of the Marxian argument:

First step. Since in exchange two goods are made equal to one another, there must be a common element of similar quantity in the two, and in this common element must reside the principle of Exchange value.

Second step. This common element cannot be the Use value, for in the exchange of goods the Use value is disregarded.

Third step. If the Use value of commodities be disregarded, there remains in them only one common property—that of being products of labour. Consequently, so runs the conclusion, Labour is the principle of

---
[29] *Ibid.*, p. 1.
[30] *Ibid.*, p. 374.

value; or, as Marx says, the Use value or 'good' only has a value because human labour is made objective in it, is materialized in it.[31]

Boehm-Bawerk introduces his attack on this analysis with the statement, "I have seldom read anything to equal this for bad reasoning and carelessness in drawing conclusion." [32] He says he will let the first step pass, but the second and third he rejects with all the vigor of a proponent of the Austrian school whose central approach to value theory is precisely through the "use values" whose role Marx is here denying. The place of utility in the determination of exchange values is so well understood today that there is no need of retracing Boehm-Bawerk's comments on this issue, except to say that he supports his own views by showing both that use value does have bearing on exchange value, and that labor quantities are not proportional to exchange values. Labor does enter into the determination of value, he says, but only through its influence on scarcity.

Boehm-Bawerk's next major criticism of the Marxian doctrine is more directly bound up with the specific problem of interest, and we shall find that discussion of this issue leads us directly to his own positive theory. Having demonstrated that labor does not create all value, he raises the question whether labor ought to receive all the product of the economy. In answer, he concedes that labor should receive all of *its* product, but he also argues that since labor does not create all value there is no reason to suppose that it should receive all the fruits of production. "The perfectly just proposition that the laborer should receive the entire value of his product may be understood to mean, either that the laborer should *now* receive the entire *present* value of his product, or should receive the entire *future* value of his product *in the future*." [33] The fact that there is a difference between the present value and the future value of a given good is what Boehm-Bawerk sets out to explain. Given this fact, it becomes obvious that if labor is paid now for a product that will emerge only in the future, then his present payment must be different from the value of the product when sold. So long as we assume that the right of labor is to the value of its own product, there is no exploitation involved in payment to others of whatever value accretion emerges between the time of the worker's effort and the final sale of the good. The task of interest theory is to demonstrate why this difference in value emerges.

[31] *Ibid.*, p. 381.
[32] *Ibid.*
[33] *Ibid.*, p. 342.

THE THEORY OF BOEHM-BAWERK

"Present goods are, as a rule, worth more than future goods of like kind and number. This proposition is the kernel and center of the interest theory which I have to present." [1] So wrote Boehm-Bawerk. Once this fact is established, he continued, then the willingness of persons to pay interest for the loan of funds becomes obvious. Earlier attempts to explain the difference in value between present goods and a claim to identical future goods have been reviewed and found unsatisfactory: this difference does not arise simply because of the physical productivity of some types of present goods; "abstinence" cannot qualify as some third "original factor" to explain it; it does not arise because of some obscure form of labor or other productive quality inhering in capital goods or existing in relation to their owner. Yet there *is* a difference between present and future values, so that interest payments cannot simply be attributed to exploitation of one class by another. Wherein, then, lies the explanation of this value differential? [2]

Boehm-Bawerk replies that there are three basic Reasons[3] for the fact that people generally value present goods more highly than future goods. These may be outlined as follows:

1. There is a difference between present and future needs relative to the scarcity of means to meet those needs, chiefly for the following reasons:

   a. Some people recognize that their earning capacity will be greater in the future than at present (e.g., young doctors).

   b. Some people are in more urgent need now because of illness, loss, etc.

   c. Although either of these elements might sometimes work in reverse, he who possesses a durable asset is always at liberty to use it either now

---

[1] Boehm-Bawerk, *Positive Theory of Capital,* translated by William Smart (New York: Stechert, 1923), p. 237.

[2] For the discussion reviewed here, see *ibid.,* Book V.

[3] To simplify identification we shall capitalize the R in Boehm-Bawerk's three "Reasons."

or in the future. Present possession of the durable asset therefore gives all the advantage of both present and future goods, whereas future possession gives only the advantage of the latter. Since money is especially durable and costs little to store, persons preferring future over present goods would be virtually indifferent between money now and money to be delivered later, but even they may prefer present money, because possible needs of which they do not already know may arise. And those who prefer present over future goods will clearly prefer present money. Therefore an "agio" will normally be established for present over future goods if they can be converted into durable form (e.g., sold for money).

2. Most people tend to underestimate the future relative to the present, because:

    a. They lack imagination.

    b. They lack will power.

    c. They are uncertain about their length of life.

3. Present goods have technical superiority over future goods.

This last consideration is the one that reflects the physical productivity of capital goods, but just how it reflects this productivity is not wholly clear. Indeed, Irving Fisher and Boehm-Bawerk had a long debate over whether technical superiority provides an independent reason for the existence of an interest rate, as alleged by Boehm-Bawerk, or whether interest can exist only if technical superiority is combined with one or both of the other two Reasons. Apparently most economists agree with Fisher's conclusions, but Guy Arvidsson, in a study that examines the problem in some detail, gives his support to the conclusions of Boehm-Bawerk.[4] My view is that each was correct in what he was trying to say, that each misinterpreted the other and therefore made a legitimate attack on what he thought was the other's view. Boehm-Bawerk's statement surely includes passages which justify Fisher's interpretation of his position. I shall review only that part of the controversy which casts light on two important issues where misinterpretation is common: the meaning of "technical superiority," and the relation between time preference and the productivity of capital. As a prelude to this discussion, however, it is necessary to clarify the meaning of another concept which is utilized throughout the

---

[4] For this debate, see Boehm-Bawerk, *The Positive Theory of Capital,* esp. pp. 260–275; Irving Fisher, *The Theory of Interest* (New York: Macmillan, 1930), pp. 476–485; Guy Arvidsson, "On the Reasons for a Rate of Interest," translated by Alan Williams, in *International Economic Papers,* no. 6 (New York and London: Macmillan, 1956), pp. 23–33, from *Ekonomisk Tidskrift,* March, 1953; and sources cited in the latter article, including especially the third edition of Boehm-Bawerk's *Positive Theorie des Kapitals* (Innsbruck: 1912), Exkurse iv and xii.

controversy. This is the "period of production," a concept which is one of the bases of Austrian capital theory.[5]

Partly in order to emphasize the view that capital goods are not original and independent factors of production, but are simply intermediate products of the ultimate factors, land and labor, Boehm-Bawerk identifies a "more capitalistic" process of production with one requiring a longer period of production. In this view the investment of input must be measured in two dimensions. In one dimension we measure the number of man-hours of labor expended and the number of acre-hours of land utilized; in the other dimension we measure the average period of waiting from the time the input is employed to the time the output materializes. If labor and land are used today to produce two bottles of wine, but one is marketed today and the other ten years hence, then the investment in the two is not equal even though equal amounts of the original factors were employed. The period of production of the second was much greater than that of the first. In this view the production of goods by the aid of capital goods requires a longer period of production because there is no final output during the time the capital goods are being constructed. In the familiar model of fishing, a "one-year" method might represent the use of a simple wooden spear, a "two-year" method would represent the manufacture and use of a net, and a "three-year" method would represent the use of both boat and net. To summarize, the "period of production" refers to the period of time during which the average unit of the services

---

[5] A long and involved controversy between F. H. Knight and Nicholas Kaldor will be illuminating for those wishing to appraise the Austrian capital theory, with special emphasis on the concept of a "period of production." One hesitates to interpret "findings," but I believe it would be reasonable to conclude that (1) under simplified enough assumptions the concept of a "period of production" — defined much more rigorously than I have done here — could be regarded as a meaningful measure of the capital intensitivity of an economy; (2) realistic conditions do not permit such an application of the concept, important reasons being (a) "original" agents of production are heterogeneous and their proportions are altered by changes in the quantity of capital goods, so that there is no unambiguous measure of "ultimate" input, (b) products are heterogeneous, and changes in capital goods may alter their prices, so that there is no unambiguous measure of output, and (c) capital goods are constantly maintained and are used in the production of other capital goods, so that no calculation can be made until the whole life of the economy is known from birth to death. For the Knight-Kaldor discussion, plus related discussions, see the following: Oskar Lange, "The Place of Interest in the Theory of Production," *Review of Economic Studies,* 3 (1936): 159–192; Frank H. Knight, "Note on Dr. Lange's Interest Theory," *Review of Economic Studies,* 4 (1937): 223–230; Oskar Lange, "Professor Knight's Note on Interest Theory," *Review of Economic Studies,* 4 (1937): 231–235; Nicholas Kaldor, "Annual Survey of Economic Theory: The Recent Controversy on the Theory of Capital," *Econometrica,* 5 (1937): 201–233; Frank H. Knight, "On the Theory of Capital: In Reply to Mr. Kaldor," *Econometrica,* 6 (1938): 63–84; Nicholas Kaldor, "On the Theory of Capital: A Rejoinder to Professor Knight," *Econometrica,* 6 (1938): 163–176; and other sources listed in footnotes 1–3, pp. 201–202, in the first Kaldor article cited above.

of labor and land lie invested in the productive process to obtain a unit
of the desired product: this time does not refer to the hours of labor spent,
but to the interval from the date of input to that of the output; and this
interval represents an average that includes the "waiting time" of both
the land and labor used in production of capital goods and that used in
production of the final goods with their aid.

It goes without saying that this method of measuring capital intensity
would be wholly inoperable under the complexities of real-world situations. The computation would be difficult enough in highly simplified
cases when the capital goods have all worn out and one can look back on
a history that is complete with all input and output dates recorded, and
with all input and all output homogeneous. Consider then the difficulties
introduced when a large plant is maintained indefinitely, and when all
capital goods used are the product of processes using previously produced
capital goods in a long chain that reaches back indefinitely. How would
one calculate the period of production in the manufacture of Ford cars?

Despite the inoperability of the period of production as a device for
measurement of capital, one can readily see how the concept had meaning
to the Austrians, and Boehm-Bawerk uses it directly in his exposition of
the technical superiority of roundabout methods of production. This exposition utilizes a hypothetical example, the essential parts of which are
given in columns 1 to 7 of table 1. Column 2 shows that *one month's
labor* applied this year in a one-year method (let us say production with
virtually no use of capital) would yield 100 units of product by the end of
the year; if a two-year method of production were used (i.e., first employ-
ing labor to produce capital goods) then the product *attributable to one
month's labor* (i.e., the same amount of labor as before) would be 200
units. Similarly the product attributable to a month's labor in a three-year
method (one involving still more capital goods) would be 280 units. The
construction of column 3 is similar to that of column 2, the only difference being that it is assumed that the first application of labor is made
one year later, with the result that the product attributable to a month's
labor maturing at any given time is equal to that shown a year earlier in
column 2.

In the application of these hypothetical data to the problem of interest
the next task is to examine *present values* of a month's labor when applied
according to various methods of production. In order to show values,
Boehm-Bawerk calls upon his two other Reasons for the existence of an
agio for present over future goods. The effect of these considerations is
shown in columns 4 to 7. Column 4 presents his admittedly arbitrary
assumption that because of greater present need relative to supply the
marginal utility of a unit this year is greater than that of the same good
next year. The declining marginal utility continues throughout the

TABLE 1

Hypothetical Values of One Month's Labor, Present and Future

	Boehm-Bawerk's Tables						Fisher's Refutation of Boehm-Bawerk		
(1)	(2)	(3)	(4)	(5)	(6)	(7)	(8)	(9)	(10)
Years from present to product maturity	Units of product		Present true marginal utility	M. U. reduced by present bias	Present value of product		Constant marginal utility	Present value of product	
	Labor applied now	Labor applied next yr.			Begun now	Begun next yr.		Begun now	Begun next yr.
1	100	0	5.0	5.0	500	0	5	500	0
2	200	100	4.0	3.8	760	380	5	1000	500
3	280	200	3.3	3.0	**840**	600	5	1400	1000
4	350	280	2.5	2.2	770	616	5	1750	1400
5	400	350	2.2	2.0	800	700	5	2000	1750
6	440	400	2.1	1.8	792	720	5	2200	2000
7	470	440	2.0	1.5	705	660	5	2350	2200
8	500	470	1.5	1.0	500	470	5	**2500**	2350
9	490	500	...	...	...	...	5	2450	**2500**
10	475	490	...	...	...	...	5	2375	2450

Note: It should be carefully noted that the goods will be forthcoming only after the number of years shown in column 1, but that the values are always present values of claims to goods forthcoming at the time shown.

period of years shown in the table. Column 5 modifies column 4 to allow for underestimation of future, relative to present, utilities. Columns 6 and 7 show the present values of outputs described by columns 2 and 3 respectively. These figures are obtained by multiplying the appropriate marginal utilities by the appropriate outputs. Thus, for example, one's present estimate of the value of a month's labor employed now in a three-year method of production would be 840 — i.e. the 280 units of product which would be forthcoming at the end of three years multiplied by the marginal utility of 3.0.

Column 6 of this table shows that one can secure the maximum value (as now envisaged) from this year's "month of labor" if he employs it in a three-year method of production. The resulting value will be 840 units. On the other hand, if one had only a claim to next year's labor, the maximum present value he could achieve would be that shown by column 7 to be 720 units, made available by use of a five-year method of production.

There is at least one aspect of technical superiority on which there is no confusion. The technical superiority of present goods is in part due to the fact that the present investment of resources has a greater present value than next year's investment of those same resources, and this is true even if both procedures involve roundabout methods of production and thereby exploit the technical productivity of capital goods. To be sure, the productivity of capital goods is centrally involved, for without it values could not have risen, either to 840 by the one method or to 720 by the other. But the technical superiority of present goods is not seen by the comparison of the value obtained by the one-year method (value 500) with that of the three-year method (840). Rather, it is seen by comparing the most productive use of this year's labor (a three-year method yielding 840) with the most productive use of next year's labor (which happens to be a five-year method, yielding 720).

A second aspect of the meaning of technical superiority is less clear, and it is about this that the debate with Fisher developed. Boehm-Bawerk seems to say (and I believe he does say) that the 840 of column 6 is higher than the 720 of column 7 *whether or not* we assume declining marginal utility as illustrated here in columns 4 and 5. These are his words:

I must, further, lay particular weight on the fact, that this result does not make its appearance simply because, in our hypothesis, we have introduced, as already active, those other two circumstances which are fitted to account for a surplus value of present as against future goods — namely, a difference in the circumstances of provision at the various periods of time, and a diminution of the future utility by way of perspective. The superiority in value of present means of production, which is based on

their technical superiority, is not one borrowed from these circumstances . . .[6]

Irving Fisher has interpreted these statements to mean what I have
indicated they mean to me also. He proves that if they do mean this they
are wrong. His proof will be given because it has significance for the relation between the productivity of capital goods and time preference. At
the close of this chapter I shall show that later passages in Boehm-Bawerk
indicate that he may not mean to say what I believe the above passages
say, and that in reality his view may be entirely consistent with that of
Fisher. From our standpoint, of course, the important issue is not the
proof or disproof of an alleged error in writing, but the validity of basic
ideas, and the following review is intended to focus on that issue.

Fisher's analysis is based on the use of Boehm-Bawerk's own hypothetical table. His object is to demonstrate that if Boehm-Bawerk really abstracted from Reasons one and two, that is from "time preference proper,"
then the present values of the two production procedures would be identical. In order to illustrate this argument, column 5 is replaced by column
8, in which it is presumed that there is no diminishing marginal utility as
a function of time. Columns 9 and 10 replace columns 6 and 7 to show
present values of the ultimate income resulting from this year's and next
year's labor respectively, each according to various production methods.
As is obvious from the construction of the table, and should have been
obvious to Boehm-Bawerk, the result is that all values in column 10 are
identical with those for the preceding year in column 9. It is impossible
to find a "maximum value" in either column without making the assumption that a time comes when the use of more roundabout methods of production no longer increase the physical product of land and labor. The
nine-year method which we have added for illustrative purposes presumes
that such a diminution would set in during that year. Two conclusions
of importance are revealed by the table as thus developed. If we assume
the total absence of time preference, then either of two results follows:
(1) If total product increases indefinitely as the period of production increases, then the present value of labor is infinite, whether that labor be
applied this year or next: there is no reason to prefer this year's labor over
next year's labor even though capital is "productive." (2) If there is an
optimum degree of roundaboutness beyond which total product actually
declines, then a maximum value will be achieved by producing with the
amount of capital that such roundaboutness creates. But present labor is
still no better than next year's labor, for the only difference between the
two is that the product of this optimum production method will be avail-

---

[6] Boehm-Bawerk, *Positive Theory of Capital*, p. 268.

able one year eariler if present labor is used. Since there is no time preference, this is a matter of indifference, and present values of both this
year's and next year's labor are identical (in this illustration the value of
each is 2500).

The conclusion reached by this analysis is exactly the opposite of that
which Boehm-Bawerk's argument seems to state. The admitted greater
physical productivity of roundabout methods of production does not, by
itself, cause a difference in value between present and subsequent application of labor. In modern terms, the physical productivity of capital goods
does not by itself establish a case for preferring present over future goods,
and hence does not establish a case for a rate of interest.

Many people find it difficult to accept this conclusion, and it may be
useful to present the basic idea on which it rests in a more straightforward
way. Suppose we ask ourselves this question: Granting that total product
per man-hour will probably increase if we use more capital goods per man,
at least up to a point not yet reached, then why do we not devote all our
energies to producing that capital before we begin to consume at all? If
we were interested only in securing the maximum ultimate product —
if we were in no sense concerned about when that product emerged — then
we should do exactly this. Furthermore, the productivity of capital would
not cause us to prefer capital today over capital tomorrow, for the only
consequence of the difference would be that the final product would
emerge earlier in the one case than in the other, and this should not
matter if the size of the product, regardless of time, were all that concerned us. If interest represents the payment we are willing to make in
order to have goods today instead of tomorrow, then it is related to time
preference by definition and cannot be explained by the productivity of
capital in the absence of time preference.

This argument does not imply that with time preference given, productivity is of no consequence to the rate of interest. In Fisher's own
analysis, the physical productivity of capital goods substantially influences
the relative scarcity of goods today and tomorrow, with the result that
the accumulation of capital today lowers the marginal utility of tomorrow's goods relative to those of today by providing greater abundance
then. This also causes shifts of income between today and tomorrow
(through investment and disinvestment), thereby directly affecting relative marginal utilities of today and tomorrow. Thus, time preference and
productivity interact to determine the degree of preference for today's
income over that of the future, and hence the rate of interest.

These comments suggest the need to distinguish between three terms
that are often confused: Fisher's time preference, myopia, and Boehm-
Bawerk's agio for present over future goods. A more complete discussion

of time preference and its relation to interest-rate determination will be possible after presentation of Fisher's theory, but a brief distinction between these three terms is possible now. The most serious but widespread error is to identify myopia with time preference and suggest that Fisher's insistence on the importance of time preference implies that his theory makes the existence of interest depend upon shortsightedness. In fact, as the preceding paragraph indicates, the tendency for equilibrium to be established in a situation where people prefer present goods over an equal claim to future goods requires no myopia whatever. Rather it is based chiefly on the assumption of diminishing marginal utility of income in conjunction with the physical productivity of capital goods.

An example may clarify this argument. Suppose that an individual initially enjoys equal claims to present and future income, faces equal prospective needs in the two periods, and exhibits no myopia at all. He will then presumably be indifferent to a marginal shift of income between present and future. Suppose now that the productivity of capital goods is such that by sacrificing one unit of today's consumption goods through investment, the individual can receive two tomorrow. He will, of course, make this investment. As similar undertakings are adopted today's income for consumption becomes more scarce, and tomorrow's becomes more plentiful. If the principle of diminishing marginal utility of income applies, then a time will come when the rising marginal utility of today's sacrificed consumption just equals the falling utility of the resulting additions to tomorrow's consumption. At this point investment will stop. And at this point the marginal utility of a single unit of today's goods is clearly greater than the marginal utility of an equal unit available tomorrow. Thus the productivity of capital calls forth such a shift of consumption between today and tomorrow that marginal time preference becomes positive even if no such relation existed initially.

Harrod, in his book on dynamic economics, draws the same emphatic distinction that I have drawn between myopia and diminishing marginal utility of income as explanations of time preference "in its broader sense." [7] When he denies the significance of "pure" time preference, as he repeatedly does, he is in fact only denying the adequacy of myopia as an explanation of interest. He thus supports my view, though in words that may appear to contradict it.[8]

One further comment: Boehm-Bawerk's "agio" does not refer to my-

---

[7] R. F. Harrod, *Towards a Dynamic Economics* (London: Macmillan, 1948), p. 35 ff.

[8] Further discussion of conflicting concepts of time preference will be found on pp. 56–58 below.

opia, though myopia was believed by him to be one cause for an agio for present over future goods. An agio is nothing more than a premium which people are willing to pay for present income over a claim to future income. It is caused by all the elements resulting in a rate of interest.

Fisher's criticism leads directly to the consideration of his own theory, but two other points concerning Boehm-Bawerk require brief mention first. One is his analysis of market equilibrium, the other is a closing comment on his controversy with Fisher over the independence of technical superiority. Boehm-Bawerk's analysis of market equilibrium is quite incomplete: the needy and the prodigal will prefer present over future goods because of first and second Reasons; the thrifty will prefer present over future income because of its technical superiority (the third Reason); and thus there will be a general tendency to prefer present over future income. Boehm-Bawerk also notes that the first two Reasons may be cumulative, each adding to the desire for present income to be used for consumption. The third is alternative, providing a basis for seeking income for investment instead. Yet these Reasons interact, both among persons and within a single person. Each person will consume and invest up to the point where the marginal utility of the last dollar used each way is equal. And the price of present income in relation to future income (the rate of interest) will adjust until supply equals demand (or, in Boehm-Bawerk's conception, ". . . the market price will be settled between the subjective valuations . . . of the two marginal pairs").[9]

This discussion of the interaction among Boehm-Bawerk's three Reasons gives good cause to believe that his statements recited earlier regarding the independence of technical superiority as a potential cause of interest do not in fact represent his whole thought, and a careful reading of his controversy with Fisher suggests the possibility of an interpretation different from the one described above and assumed by Fisher. Boehm-Bawerk states quite clearly that the increased future product made possible by the third Reason will be a partial determinant of the difference between want and provision that make up his first Reason. Furthermore, he states that if the first Reason did not exist, then the third would bring it into being by creating a difference in provision between present and future. In order to make Boehm-Bawerk's whole position internally consistent it seems legitimate to presume that what he meant to say about the independence of the third Reason is this: whatever relation between provision and need we may assume to exist without respect to technical superiority, is unimportant; given *any* assumed relation, technical superiority can still create the emergence of a rate of interest, for the tech-

---

[9] Boehm-Bawerk, *Positive Theory of Capital,* pp. 278–279.

nical productivity of capital goods would withdraw current income until consumer goods were so scarce that an agio would be created. If we may interpret Boehm-Bawerk in this way, then his argument becomes quite similar to Fisher's.[10]

---

[10] See Arvidsson, "On the Reasons for a Rate of Interest," p. 27, for a still different interpretation of the independence of the third Reason, and for further discussion of the controversy.

IV

IRVING FISHER'S THEORY OF INTEREST

Despite the controversy between Boehm-Bawerk and Fisher, their theories of interest are constructed with similar building blocks, and Fisher dedicates his book, *The Theory of Interest,* to John Rae and Boehm-Bawerk, "Who laid the foundation on which I have endeavored to build." The two major elements in Boehm-Bawerk's theory, time preference and the productivity of capital, provide Fisher's first two "approximations": the third is risk.

Fisher presents his theory in three successive ways. First he gives it in words, next he presents it graphically, and finally he states it in systems of equations. I shall proceed directly to the graphic method, translating into words as I go, and following this by comments on the wider comprehensiveness which can be attained by use of equations instead of two-dimensional graphs.

GEOMETRIC PRESENTATION

As in general price theory, so also in the theory of interest it is useful to consider two aspects of the process by which equilibrium is approached. In the first place, individuals in competition take prices as given, and adjust quantities until their satisfactions are maximized. Secondly, the aggregate effect of these simultaneous individual acts may be described by an analysis of market equilibrium, where prices are not given, but adjust until total market supply and demand are equated. Fisher's analysis proceeds in a similar way, the goods in trade being present and future income, the price being the rate of interest. Figure I [1] illustrates both the adjustment of the individual, with price (interest rates) given, and the adjustment of the market, wherein the equilibrium rate of interest is determined.

In this figure, present income is represented on the x-axis, and "next

---

[1] Figures I through VIII will be found in a booklet inserted in the back of this book in order that they may be studied as the text is read without constant turning of pages.

year's income" is represented on the y-axis. The presumption is that the individuals X and Y start with claims to both present and future income in amounts indicated by the points O_x and O_y respectively. Thus X begins with 35 units of present income and a claim to 10 units next year, whereas Y starts with 58 units of current income and a claim to 20 next year.

Opportunity Curves

A brief illustration may help to clarify the economic meaning of both the "claims to income" just discussed and the "opportunities for investment" which will be examined in this section. If we own a mine that will soon be exhausted, we hold a claim to much present income and little future income. If we own a seedling forest, we hold a claim to no present income, but substantial future income. Likewise, if we hold a bond we hold a claim to future income.

There are various ways by which we may change the relation between our claims to present and to future income. (1) We may lend or borrow. Also we may buy or sell debt instruments, which is equivalent to lending or borrowing and will be so regarded throughout this analysis. (2) We may plant forests and manufacture capital goods, or we may cut the former and let the latter deteriorate. These activities whereby we increase or reduce the existing amounts of real earning assets may be regarded as investment and disinvestment. (3) Finally we may exchange ownership title to real earning assets, including share ownership in corporate enterprise. Fisher does not seem to be wholly clear about the treatment of this last type of transaction, and it will be best to make our first approach to his analysis by abstracting entirely from the exchange of claims to real assets. We then have two distinct types of transaction to examine. One is the act of borrowing and lending — or its equivalent, the sale and purchase of debt instruments — the geometric representation of which will be discussed in the following section. The other is the act of "real" investment or disinvestment, the presentation of which will be described here.

The investment opportunities, in this "real" sense, presented to X and Y are indicated by the "opportunity" curves passing through O_x and O_y respectively. By investing in capital goods, X could secure 18 additional units of income next year at a cost of only 7 units this year (moving from O_x to S_x); alternatively, he could sacrifice 15 units of current income and secure in exchange 28 additional units of income next year, assuming he places the 15 units in capital goods. Obviously X could invest the 15 units less wisely, securing in return some amount less than 28 units of next year's income; thus the OP curve is really an envelope indicating the most profitable of all possible investments. It surrounds an infinite number of points that lie between it and the axes, each of which represents a less attractive investment opportunity. The OP curve is concave to the origin, reflecting the assumption of diminishing returns to investment.[2] This assumption is illustrated in the example cited above by the fact that an investment of 7 will be rewarded with a return payment of 18, providing a gain of 11 against the investment of 7, or a "rate of return over cost" of 11/7, whereas an investment of 15 yields a rate of return over cost of "only" 13/15, i.e., (28 − 15)/15.

It may be noted that the average rate of return over cost for any investment is shown by deducting 1 from the slope of the line connecting the initial point (e.g., O_x) with the point where the investment stops (e.g., P_x). In this statement, and in all similar references to figure I throughout this book, we greatly simplify our expression by disregarding the negative sign of the slope of OP (and, correspondingly in other references, the slopes of AB and W curves). Illustrating our previous statement, then, the slope of a line connecting O_x with P_x is 28/15; the indicated rate of return for this investment has been shown to be (28 − 15)/15 which equals (28/15) − 1. The fact that rates of return are indicated by slopes of the relevant lines *minus one* may be made intuitively plausible by noting that a slope of unity implies a gain of future income precisely equal to current sacrifice, and hence represents a zero rate of return over cost.

The figures just described are of course *average* rates of return. The *marginal* rate of return at any point is shown by the slope of the opportunity curve at that point, and is equal to that slope (again disregarding sign) minus one.

Interest Lines

A straight line may be drawn through any point on the graph to indicate any assumed rate of interest. Thus the AB lines[3] show that from any point on them a person can *lend* on the market 10 units of present income in return for a claim to 11 units next year (moving to the left and upward on the A_1B_1 line, as from E to A_1), or he can borrow by sacrificing 11 units of next year's income in return for 10 units of current income (moving down to the right on the A_1B_1 line, as from A_1 to E). The rate of interest in this case is 10 per cent (11 − 10)/10, which is read from the graph as the slope of the AB line minus one. Thus a 45 degree line represents zero rate of interest (repayment = original loan), and higher interest rates are shown by the increasing slope of the AB line above 45 degrees. A given interest rate may be represented by a family of an infinite number of AB lines of given slope.

---

[2] The legitimacy of this assumption is discussed on pp. 53–55.

[3] We shall hereafter refer to the lines whose "slope minus 1 = the interest rate" as the AB lines, without subscript. There are, of course, an infinite number of these for each rate of interest, all parallel to one another. A_1B_1 and A_2B_2 in figure I are two of them.

Willingness Curve

The third type of curve shown here is the "willingness" curve, the W curves shown convex to the origin being illustrative. These are essentially indifference curves. Every individual will have a whole family of such curves, each indicating combinations of present and future income that yield him equal satisfaction. I have drawn W_x and $W_{x'}$ to represent two of X's willingness curves, and I have similarly drawn W_y and $W_{y'}$ for Y.

Individual Equilibrium

As stated above, figure I may be used to illustrate either the equilibrium of the individual or that of the market. We shall begin with the former. Consider, for example, the adjustments made by citizen X, whose income claims at the start provide him with $35 this year and assurance of $10 next year. He can alter this income by either of two types of procedure: (1) he can borrow or lend at interest, or (2) he can engage in real investment or disinvestment. It is obvious that his optimum investment position will be shown by the point of tangency of the opportunity line with the interest line (A_1B_1). This follows because he can then attain any position on the tangent AB line by merely borrowing and lending; and any location he might attain on some other AB line (by stopping at a different point on the opportunity line) would be inferior to *some* position on the tangent AB line. Thus an AB line through S_x, parallel to A_1B_1 as I have drawn it, would lie closer to the origin throughout its length. From any point on the line through S_x an investor could, by moving to A_1B_1, either increase this year's income without loss of next years', or increase next year's income without loss of this year's, or increase each simultaneously. A simple way of stating this conclusion is to say that the market value of the individual's income stream will be maximized if he moves along the opportunity curve until he reaches the point of tangency with the interest line.[4]

Let us suppose that the interest rate is shown by the AB line. X will find it most profitable to invest in real capital goods until he reaches the

---

[4] The fact that X would maximize the market value of his income by investing to the point P assuming the market rate of interest $= 10\%$ and OP is as drawn may be illustrated by comparing the value of this stream with that of alternative points on each side of P along OP. Using the familiar discount formula we may write:

$$V \text{ at P} = Y_0 + \text{Discounted Value of } Y_1 = Y_0 + \frac{Y_1}{1 + 10\%} = 20 + \frac{38}{1.1} = 54.54$$

$$V \text{ slightly left of P} = Y_0 + \frac{Y_1}{1.1} = 18 + \frac{40}{1.1} = 54.36$$

$$V \text{ slightly right of P} = Y_0 + \frac{Y_1}{1.1} = 25 + \frac{32}{1.1} = 54.09$$

position P_x, and Y will find it most profitable to invest along his opportunity line to the point P_y. But neither X nor Y is now satisfied with his distribution of income between present and future. X finds himself with a claim to only 20 units of income this year, when all his children are in college and he needs every cent he can muster; whereas he has a claim to 38 units "next year" when they will have graduated and his needs are small. He will therefore borrow until he reaches the highest possible indifference curve, which will, for familiar reasons, be the one tangent to the A_1B_1 line. He ends at R_x. As a result of investing and borrowing, X has increased his current income from 35 to 40, and he has simultaneously raised his future income from 10 to 16. No other plan for investment or for borrowing and lending could reach so high an indifference curve.

While the analytical problem must proceed by investing first, then borrowing and lending, there is obviously no implication regarding the chronology of the action taken. All that is suggested is that X borrows a total of 20 units (horizontal distance from P_x to R_x), invests 15 (horizontal distance from O_x to P_x), and dissaves 5 (spends 5 in excess of his current income; horizontal distance from O_x to R_x).

Similar interpretation shows that Y lends 20 (P_y to R_y), invests 18 (O_y to P_y), and saves 38 (O_y to R_y). Equilibrium is established for each individual, for he maximizes his satisfaction under the given conditions and tastes; it is established for the market because, at the given interest rates, lending by Y (20) precisely equals borrowing by X.

Market Equilibrium

We have now examined the adjustment of individuals in a market where an equilibrium rate of interest had already been established. We next observe the way in which the rate might adjust toward such an equilibrium if it were at first in disequilibrium. Suppose the situation is identical to that just described except that the initial rate is shown by the CD lines instead of by the AB lines. X will now wish to invest 7 (O_x to S_x), borrow 8 (S_x to T_x), and dissave 1 (O_x to T_x). Y, in the meantime, will want to invest 11 (O_y to S_y), lend 27 (S_y to T_y), and save 38 (O_y to T_y). The crucial point is that Y wishes to lend 27 and X wishes to borrow only 8. Assuming, in order to avoid problems of bilateral monopoly, that the market consists of many such individuals, it is clear that the rate of interest will be pushed down because of Y's desire to lend more than he can at going rates, and because X's desire to borrow far less than is available at going rates. The fall of the interest rate under these "forces" is recorded by the shift of the CD lines toward more nearly horizontal slope. When they reach the position of the AB lines, they move no further, for at this point the quantity which lenders wish to make available exactly equals the quantity that borrowers wish to secure.

It will be noted that in Fisher's model as thus far presented (his first two approximations)[5] equilibrium requires that the marginal rate of return over cost equal the rate of interest, which in turn must also equal the marginal rate of time preference (the slope of the willingness curve minus one). The first of these conditions is parallel to the familiar proposition that in equilibrium investment will be carried to the point where the marginal efficiency of capital (Keynes' vocabulary) will be just equal to the rate of interest.[6] The second condition is essentially a definition of the psychology which lies behind the construction of a supply curve that shows saving as a function of the rate of interest.

By a slight transformation we can show that this equilibrium is also characterized by the equality of planned saving and investment, which Keynes regards as the "classical" theory of interest. This equivalence may be derived as follows. In Fisher's equilibrium, desired lending equals desired borrowing. But Y's desired lending equals his desired saving (horizontal O_y to $R_y = 38$) minus his desired investment (O_y to $P_y = 18$). X's desired borrowing, on the other hand, equals his desired investment (horizontal O_x to $P_x = 15$) plus his desired dissaving, which may be conveniently stated as "minus his desired (negative) saving" (horizontal O_x to $R_x = 5$). With these substitutions we may restate the condition of equilibrium as follows:

$$\text{Desired lending} \quad = \quad \text{Desired borrowing}$$
$$S_y\,(=38) - I_y\,(=18) = I_x\,(=15) - S_x\,(=-5)$$

By transposing we have:

$$S_y\,(=38) + S_x\,(=-5) = I_x\,(=15) + I_y\,(=18)$$

or

$$S\,(=33) = I\,(=33).$$

In short, Fisher's theory states that the rate of interest equates saving and investment, assuming these to be "desired" or "ex ante" magnitudes.

We may note also that this model takes income as given (presumably on the full-employment assumption), except to the extent that it is altered by the output flowing from real investment. The decision of persons to increase saving reduces interest rates, with the result that (1) the amount of desired saving is, typically, somewhat less than if rates had not fallen, and (2) the quantity invested increases. The same result can be shown by moving a saving curve to the right in a simplified loanable funds

---

[5] Discussion of the third approximation is presented on pp. 65–67.

[6] Keynes recognizes the identity explicitly, though it should be qualified by the important fact that Keynes' term is an "expected value." See J. M. Keynes, *The General Theory of Employment, Interest and Money* (New York: Harcourt, Brace, 1936), p. 140. For discussion of a context in which essential differences emerge between MEC and marginal rate of return over cost, see pp. 76–77 below.

model in which demand is represented by investment and supply by saving.

It may be noted in passing that this transformation from equality of lending and borrowing to equality of saving and investing slightly modifies Fisher's supply and demand curves by netting out dissaving and disinvestment. (Fisher's supply curve would include both saving and disinvestment, his demand curve would include both investment and dissaving.) The resulting interest rate is, of course, unchanged by this transformation.

NOTES ON ALGEBRAIC PRESENTATION

In most graphical presentations of economic problems, the confinement to two (or at most three) dimensions makes for difficulties in exposition which can be overcome by conversion to algebra. The behavioral assumptions and the market equalities that characterize the equilibrium described above provide the bases for a set of equations wherein Fisher derives a determinate equilibrium assuming n individuals instead of 2, and m time periods instead of only "this year" and "next year."[7] His resulting solutions provide him with not one but many interest rates, each being the rate that will rule during some future year. With the aid of Friedrich Lutz' analysis (see chapter xv below) one can then determine the rates on securities of different term, retaining Fisher's assumption of perfect foresight. This reduction of the system to algebra not only permits the solution of multidimensional problems, but it also removes the awkwardness which arises because the curves in the system will in fact shift as one moves toward equilibrium. Thus, for instance, changing interest rates will change a person's income if he borrows or lends extensively, and this will cause his indifference pattern to shift. Geometrically the problem is most awkward, algebraically it need not present any difficulty.

SOME PROBLEMS OF INTERPRETATION

Shape of OP Curve

A few problems which sometimes arise in the interpretation of this theory deserve comment. First, why is not the investment opportunity curve a straight line for the ordinary individual? Fisher explains the concavity toward the origin by the law of diminishing returns: "Every investment *in his farm* will have a variable decreasing return . . ."[8] But the question raised at once is, why not buy more land? In a perfectly competitive society such as that which underlies Fisher's model, will the *individual* face decreasing returns to scale as expansion takes place? The answer consistent with conventional theory would appear to be that managerial limi-

---

[7] The system of equations described here is presented in the appendix to this chapter.
[8] Irving Fisher, *The Theory of Interest* (New York: Macmillan, 1930), pp. 278–279.

tations will cause any firm's returns to decrease when it reaches a certain size. But why should we presume that point to be within the upper right-hand quadrant of the graph — that is, why should we presume that diminishing returns will set in while the size of operations is still that which could be financed by use of the individual's initial income? Here it is probable that one should recognize the possibility of P lying well over in the left-hand upper quadrant. In the real world this situation occurs whenever the entrepreneur borrows more than his claim to current income.[9]

In the perspective of a very-long-run competitive theory, this might suffice to explain mild concavity of the OP curve. A number of other considerations, however, justify the use of a much more concave curve, though some would involve redefinition of the curve employed. The first is uncertainty, which will often cause any single-valued expression for the "expected rate of return over cost" to decline when money is invested in activities that go beyond the scope of past experience.

A second consideration does not actually make the OP curve as defined above more concave but suggests the use of a differently defined opportunity curve that would be more concave than OP: I shall call this new Opportunity curve OP'. Its concavity reflects the fact that as the rate of investment expands the cost of capital goods relative to other goods rises, so that for this reason there is a fall in rate of return from current income sacrificed, in terms of future income acquired. The difficulty in using this curve arises from the fact that in competition the expansion of any individual firm can have no effect on the prices of factors bought. Hence the individual's OP curve cannot reflect the rising prices of capital goods. What happens is that as all firms expand, each individual's OP curve becomes more nearly horizontal. Thus if all do indeed expand together, the locus of the new P's to which any one individual can move is not shown by a movement up his original OP curve, but rather by points that trace a new curve that rises less and less steeply — in other words, a curve that is more concave than the original one. It is this locus which I have defined as the OP' curve.[10]

---

[9] In this procedure the movement to P, analytically intervening en route from O to T, can hardly be said to be economically meaningful, but we have pointed out above that in economic reality the borrowing may well be expected to precede the investment, in which case no problem is presented by this mechanical device to analyze events. Other devices that are a bit more complex could be used if preferred in order to avoid use of the second quadrant.

[10] Precedent for a curve somewhat though not wholly analogous to this one is given in Edward Chamberlin's *Theory of Monopolistic Competition*, 3d ed. (Cambridge: Harvard University Press, 1939), p. 90. In Chamberlin's illustration the problem is that of showing the effects on the quantity demanded of a firm's output if (a) he and he only changes price, and if (b) he and others change prices simultaneously. The firm's demand curve under assumption a is drawn and labeled "dd," whereas the demand curve under assumption b is labeled "DD." Our concept is admittedly more vague than Chamberlin's, since the rate at which others are expanding their investment is not defined. The

There are obviously some questions which this procedure slurs over. It does not reveal, for instance, the fact that X's actual level of investment in a finite period would depend partly upon how fast others had moved during the same period. In other words, although it goes farther than Fisher did by recognizing interdependence of the various OP curves, it does not wholly reflect that interdependence because it assumes some given relation between the expansion of the various firms. Without such an assumption OP′ could not be drawn. Those who prefer to reject this device may operate in terms of shifting OP curves instead of a stable OP′ curve. That procedure is more clumsy geometrically and equally vague, but its vagueness is not hidden under an apparently well defined and clear-cut curve. I believe, however, that with these warnings about its limitations, the use of the OP′ curve is justified, and I shall use it in the future.

Still another consideration might influence the shape of the opportunity curve: the introduction of monopoly might alter its concavity in either direction. The first reason given above for concavity, namely, diminishing returns to scale for an individual firm, which is a necessary corollary of the assumption of pure competition, need not apply within the relevant range for monopoly: From this standpoint the OP curve *might* be more nearly straight. On the other hand monopsony would permit the expansion of individual firms to raise the prices of factors bought, thus causing the OP curve to acquire the concavity of the OP′ curve.

Since Fisher's analysis did not introduce uncertainty at this point, and since it abstracts from the interdependence of opportunity curves, his explanation of concavity of an individual's opportunity curve is incomplete in his first two approximations. On the other hand he does introduce the implications of uncertainty in his third approximation, as reviewed in the last section of this chapter. And the interdependence of opportunity curves may well be included in his algebraic presentation,[11] even though the geometric application is complex.

Production of Goods versus Production of Value

A second problem in interpreting Fisher's theory is that raised by Boehm-Bawerk concerning the difference between the production of goods and the production of values. As he put it, how can we be sure that tomorrow's larger output will have greater value than today's smaller one? Actually this question is quite ambiguous, but fortunately, we shall find that it

---

general nature of the path toward equilibrium, and the conditions of equilibrium itself, however, are of the kind suggested by the use of our OP′ curve, and this method of exposition seems legitimate, therefore, where the purpose is only schematic as is ours.

[11] One need only admit all values of i from 1 to n in the function shown in paragraph 6 of the appendix to this chapter.

need not concern us anyway. The question is essentially irrelevant to both the theory of pure competition and the theory of social optimum.

The difficulty in giving meaning to a comparison of future with present values is that there is no measuring rod that does not stretch or contract with time. If one maximizes the exchange values of goods possessed at a moment of time by any standard, then he maximizes them by all standards at going prices. But it is a very different proposition to compare the present value of a collection of some good with the future value of some other collection. In money terms the present value may be higher, in wheat terms the future value may be higher. Conceptually it may seem attractive to measure values in terms of utility, but this presents all the problems of both interpersonal and intertemporal comparisons of utility. All one can really do is to compare the present values of claims to present goods or income with the present value of claims to future goods or income. This is what Boehm-Bawerk actually did in his tables; and it is all one needs to do in order to determine the rate of interest. The individual is faced only with present choices, and it is his present appraisals of present options that determine his behavior.

In Fisher's theory the individual is given objective choices among claims to different combinations of present and future income. With any given rate of interest he can determine the combination with the maximum present value. Having chosen the alternative that maximizes this market value, he can then exchange present for future income, or vice versa in such a way as to maximize his total ultimate satisfactions according to his present assessment of these satisfactions.

Unique OP Curve for Each Individual

A question sometimes raised by students is: Why could not X, after moving up to P and back to R, again move to the left and upward along some "parallel" opportunity line to some new and higher P', then back to an R', and so on indefinitely? The answer is that in this theory each individual has one and only one opportunity line: OP is not a member of a family of curves, as W is. In the real world, however, this curve will be an "expected" curve, as described in the third approximation below, and its shape will be influenced as much by imagination, courage, and resources as by technical possibilities.

Conflicting Concepts of Time Preference

I have already indicated that it is common to regard myopia as synonymous with time preference, but that I believe this interpretation confuses the essential views of both Boehm-Bawerk and Fisher. Indeed, Fisher's analysis, which emphasizes time preference in his own sense, may be used to prove that positive rates of interest could exist without the presence of myopia. In this demonstration and those that follow, I shall simplify the exposition without altering any essentials by assuming that all persons have identical opportunity curves and identical willingness maps. There will be no cause for borrowing and lending, but the implicit rate of interest will be indicated by the slope of the OP curve (and the equal slope of a W curve) at the point of their tangency. Investment or disinvestment will be employed to shift each person from O (initial income position, not origin) to this point of tangency to P. The interest rate will be zero if the slope of the curves at this point is forty-five degrees. The question before us is to see whether the absence of myopia would require such a solution. The answer is No, as can easily be seen. The absence of myopia gives no indication of where the W curves have a forty-five degree slope, because this will depend also upon the time-shape of expected needs. Thus any point on a given OP curve would be a possible point of tangency even if there is no myopia.

A second, and perhaps the most appropriate concept of time preference, would be one that describes the desired time-shape of income under the assumption of zero interest rates. Thus a person who preferred more present than future income when the interest rate was zero would be said to have positive time preference; one preferring more future income would be said to have negative time preference; and one who wished equal present and future income would be said to have zero time preference. All the willingness curves of such a person would have a negative slope of forty-five degrees at their intersection with the ray from the origin that had a positive slope of forty-five degrees. This configuration would imply that whenever a person had equal claims to present and future income, one was a perfect substitute for the other.

Such a situation is entirely consistent with a positive rate of interest. Indeed, whenever the OP curve is steeper than forty-five degrees where the forty-five degree ray from the origin intersects it, a willingness curve of the kind described above cannot be tangent to it at that ray, but must be tangent to it at a higher point in the figure. But the W curve of the person with neutral time preference in this sense must be steeper than forty-five degrees at any point above the ray, since it is convex toward the origin. This means that the point of tangency must imply a positive rate of interest, despite zero time preference, whenever the opportunity curve offers a positive marginal rate of return over cost at the point that indicates equal present and future income.

In Fisher's broad concept of time preference, persons are said to exhibit time preference of one sort or another if, under any condition, they have some clear preference as to the shape of their income stream. The willingness curves of persons with no capacity for time preference would be straight, and each would slope at forty-five degrees throughout its length, indicating that present and future income are perfect substitutes for one another with reference to all time-shapes of income. If persons have no time preference in *this* sense, then interest rates cannot be positive except in the impossible situation in which no present consumption takes place. This conclusion follows because no point of tangency with a straight forty-five degree line can imply any interest rate other than zero. The exception would occur only at the axes, where a kind of equilibrium would result if the OP curve were at all points steeper than forty-five degrees (giving equilibrium at the y-axis) or at all points less steep than forty-five degrees (giving equilibrium at the x-axis). At these points the rate of interest would be indeterminate within the limiting positions set by the slopes of the W and the OP curves at the axis involved. When a person has time preference in this broad sense, then we may say that his time preference is positive if, in a given context of claims to present and future income, he would accept an offer to exchange a marginal unit of future consumption for an equal amount of present consumption.

In summary: (1) Neither Boehm-Bawerk nor Fisher used the term time preference to refer to myopia, though shortsightedness was an important part of Boehm-Bawerk's explanation for time preference. There seems to be no useful reason to give time preference the connotation of myopia. (2) For some purposes it is convenient to have a term for describing a person whose attitude toward consumption is such that if he were given equal present and future claims he would be indifferent to a marginal shift between them. We shall later refer to this as the "second concept" of time preference. Positive time preference in this sense would result from Boehm-Bawerk's first two Reasons, not only from myopia. (3) If Fisher said a man exhibited positive time preference he would not be referring to the general structure of tastes concerning time of consumption, but rather to the specific attitude in a particular context. If, with his *given* time shape of income claims, he would prefer to exchange one unit of future consumption for one present, then, in this circumstance, he exhibits positive time preference. (4) Finally, if persons are capable of having positive time preference in the sense just cited, then the phenomenon of time preference exists. In this broadest sense of all we may say with Fisher that time preference is essential for the occurrence of a positive rate of interest. And no theory of interest can be complete unless it includes consideration of time preference as well as of the productivity of capital.

Fisher's Theory and Inelastic Saving Curves

In light of the widespread acceptance of the view that aggregate saving may be quite interest inelastic it seems important to inquire whether this assumption could be fitted into Fisher's model.[12] Fellner shows that it can be, and he suggests the following procedure: "The indifference map underlying the time-preference theory . . . may easily be drawn so that the line connecting the points of tangency . . . for different rates of interest will reflect the identical amount of present consumption for all conceivable rates of interest — just as the Allen-Hicks indifference map for two consumers' goods may be drawn so that the price-consumption line will reflect the identical amount of consumption for one of the two goods irrespective of the price ratios. The validity of the time-preference theory is not affected by the shape of the savings function." [13] With Fellner's conclusion I fully agree, but his analysis illustrates only one of

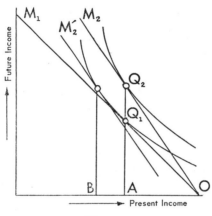

Figure 1

two commonly asserted reasons for inelasticity of the saving curve, and a somewhat different method may be used to illustrate another commonly emphasized reason for Keynes' assumption concerning the inelasticity of saving to the rate of interest. We shall describe in turn these two methods of reconciling Fisher's analysis with inelastic saving curves.

When the Allen-Hicks indifference map is drawn as indicated by Fellner, what it really does is to suggest that the income effect of a price change exactly cancels the substitution effect. By analogy, a rise in rates would cause those engaged in positive saving to increase their saving still more (substitution effect) except for the fact that the higher income from

[12] Robertson, for example, implies that any behavior such as that of the man who saves *more* when rates are low because of a goal of fixed retirement income is "in defiance of the Fisherine calculus." "Some Notes on the Theory of Interest," in *Money, Trade and Economic Growth: In Honor of John Henry Williams* (New York: Macmillan, 1951), p. 196, n. 11.

[13] William Fellner, *Monetary Policies and Full Employment* (Berkeley and Los Angeles: University of California Press, 1946), p. 144.

their interest receipts encourages current consumption enough to cancel this tendency. An extreme case is the person whose total claim is to present income (shown at O in figure 1). When rates rise from M_1 to M_2 the substitution effect would tend to cause saving to rise from OA to OB, but

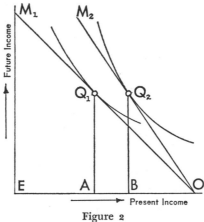

Figure 2

because of the income effect consumption is unchanged and the equilibrium position shifts directly upward from Q_1 to Q_2.

A special and well-known example of this kind of income effect is that of the person who wishes a given income following retirement and who

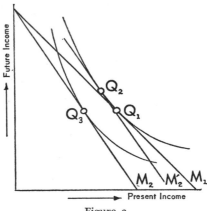

Figure 3

therefore finds he can afford to consume more and save less when rates rise. The behavior of such a person is illustrated in figure 2: rising rates result in unchanged future income but permit current consumption to increase from EA to EB — that is, saving *drops* (by AB) when interest rates rise. A reason often given for believing that the aggregate saving function for society is probably vertical is that those who, as in this last case, respond more to the income effect than to the substitution effect approximately cancel those who are more influenced by the substitution effect. Figure 3 illustrates the opposite impact of income effect on *dis-savers*. Higher rates here increase the cost of dissaving and tend to supplement the substitution effect, both working to increase saving (i.e., reduce dissaving) as shown by the relations of Q_1, Q_2, and Q_3. Because the substitution effect of higher rates on dissavers must necessarily be to increase aggregate saving (reduce dissaving), the only assumption that would be consistent with a zero-elastic saving curve for them would be the assumption that they increase current consumption when their income is reduced. Since it is difficult to conceive of such a behavior pattern, we should have to presume that the saving curve of dissavers has the traditional slope, i.e., the slope exemplifying positive elasticity.

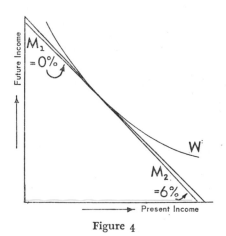

Figure 4

Fellner's reason — the one just given — for the low elasticity of the saving curve probably has more validity than it seems to have at first glance. The typical individual may not neatly balance substitution effects against income effects when he makes his saving decision. But increasing numbers of people follow insurance schedules and general saving programs that are carefully calculated to provide a desired retirement income. Furthermore, even though most savers may not calculate their saving with reference to interest rates, the wealthy few who do make such calculations are responsible for a large part of total personal saving.

Despite these comments it is useful to consider also the way that Fisher's model can illustrate the behavior of those other savers whom Keynesians have had in mind: persons who pay little or no attention to interest rates when they make their saving decisions. Their behavior is illustrated in figures 4 and 5.

In order to show effects of changing rates in figures 1 to 3, I have greatly exaggerated rate changes. In figure 4 I have attempted to be more realistic, but even here I show a change of rates from 0 to 6 per cent (still enormous by current standards). The point of tangency is moved negligibly even on a fairly "open" willingness curve (W). But just how open are most willingness curves? If it is true that we decide how much to spend almost entirely on the basis of our income (in the context of a given environment, of course), then up to a certain point we would sacrifice current income even on fairly unsatisfactory terms in exchange for future income, but beyond that point we would not continue the exchange even on much more favorable terms. This is to say that our willingness

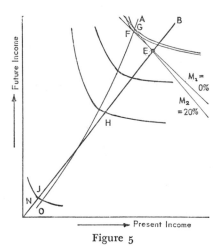

Figure 5

curves are rather sharply bent at a point determined by our psychological propensity to consume. A number of such curves might produce the map shown in figure 5, in which the locus of their "points" (curve OA) is essentially a portrayal of the consumption function. It assumes small (but not zero) changes in consumption in response to changes of interest rates. Points along NB indicate possible incomes for various individuals, each of whom expects slowly rising income (i.e., the ratio of future to present income is slightly greater than unity). A line from any point on this curve at a slope indicating feasible rates would touch a willingness curve in the neighborhood of OA. This procedure suggests the derivation of what is, in effect, the Keynesian consumption function for an individual, modified by Lange's model in which a small effect of changing interest rates is felt. To illustrate this configuration, consider first the person whose present and future incomes are shown by the point E. M_1 and M_2 represent a change of 20 per cent in the rate of interest, yet the lending of Mr. E took him to F in one case and to G in the other — two points which are exceedingly close together. The interest rate has little effect on the amount saved — i.e., the horizontal distance between E and the final position. Mr. H, whose income is considerably less than that of Mr. E, will save far less, and Mr. J will actually dissave, each amount being little affected by feasible changes in the rate of interest. It may be noted that OA is so drawn that saving increases both absolutely and relatively to income as income increases. It may be of interest also to note that if Mr. E had the same present income but considerably more future income (raise the point vertically on the graph), he might not only save less, but even dissave. This seems intuitively reasonable. All in all this construction presents relations similar to those of the conventional Keynesian consumption function, but it also permits illustration of the effects upon consumption not only of current income, but also of interest rates and of expected future income. Furthermore, it permits us to draw the willingness curves in such a way as to indicate as little interest impact as we believe to characterize actual behavior patterns.

This model, with its "pointed" willingness curves, expresses the ideas that account for one major element in the view that the saving curve is interest inelastic; Fellner's exposition expresses the assumptions that provide another major element in that view — assumptions especially relevant for those having large incomes.

Equities

As indicated in the earlier discussion of opportunity curves, Fisher is not clear about the treatment of exchanges of title to ownership of real assets. In some contexts he seems to include these transactions among "investment" operations. Thus, for instance, he writes, "Will a new harvesting machine at market prices make enough difference in the harvest to be worth while? Will a merger of two companies make a return in future profits sufficient to make the temporary costs involved in the merging process worth while? It will be seen, then, that the concept here used of investment opportunity is not contrary to ordinary ideas." [14] In other contexts Fisher appears to exclude all mere exchanges from his investment category. Consider, for example, this statement: "To invest in the original telephone enterprise . . . seems somehow different from today buying telephone or railway securities. In the latter transactions we feel we are dealing with men — trading; in the former we feel we are dealing with Nature or our technical environment — exploiting. In fact, I came near selecting the term exploitation for a suitable catch word rather than investment opportunity to express the objective factor of a return over cost." [15]

[14] Fisher, *The Theory of Interest,* pp. 157–158.
[15] *Ibid.,* pp. 179–180.

It is my view that the most appropriate procedure is to treat the acquisition or relinquishment of title to real assets as wholly equivalent, for the individual, to "real investment." I see little difference, for the individual, between planting one's own land to forest and exchanging one's unplanted land for an existing seedling forest. For society as a whole the difference is, of course, crucial. But this difference for society will be cared for in the process of aggregation, where all exchanges will cancel out, but "real investment" will not be canceled.

Persons Without Investment Opportunities

Large numbers of people are unable, for financial or institutional and psychological reasons, to engage in any real investment. Their situation can be readily pictured in figure I, and indeed a world of such people was the one described by Fisher as his "first approximation." If Mr. X were such a person he would have no opportunity curve, but could move only along the AB line that passes through O_x. He would be in equilibrium at the point where this AB line is tangent to a willingness curve. In the configuration shown in figure I the result would be to reduce borrowing to less than it would be if investment were a possible option, and the rate of interest would be forced below the level shown by A_1B_1 as the figure is now drawn.

Fisher's Theory and Schumpeter's "Dilemma of Interest"

Although Fisher does not explicitly deal with the question posed by Schumpeter concerning the apparent conflict between that part of the theory of pure competition that holds that the total value of goods is absorbed by the factors of production and the fact that the existence of interest implies a greater value of final consumer goods than that paid to the factors producing them, his theory does provide an answer. One way to put that answer would be to say that the conventional theory of perfect competition does not explain the price differentials associated with the existence of a rate of interest because the conventional competitive theory is simply not constructed to deal with problems in which time plays the crucial role that it does whenever the issue of interest arises. Conventional competitive theory envisages a circular flow in which goods are not dated and people do not choose between present and future. Current flows of supply simply equal current flows demanded. Once goods are given dates, and the desires for them are related to these dates, new elements enter.

As Boehm-Bawerk rightly emphasized, an interest rate will exist when, for whatever reason, persons prefer present goods over a claim to equal future goods. Whenever such a preference exists, it will follow that today's payment to a factor must be less than the value of the goods matur-

ing a year hence as a result of its present service. Indeed, given a preference for present goods, the laborer would be paid more than the value of
his marginal product if he were paid today the full amount that will come
forth later, since a claim to this ultimate product is worth less than a
claim for its spot delivery. So long as people have any consciousness of
time preference in the broadest sense — that is, so long as their willingness curves are not straight lines sloping at forty-five degrees throughout
their length — interest rates can emerge. The difference between the value
of consumer goods and the value of today's factors, whether these be labor, land, or capital goods, becomes nothing more than an instance of this
ubiquitous time differential.

Boehm-Bawerk's basic explanation of interest also provides this same
road out of Schumpeter's dilemma. The difficulty, it turns out, does not
lie in any contradiction between the theory of pure competition and the
fact of interest, but rather in a careless reading of competitive theory. To
be sure, that theory indicates that the factor should receive a payment
equal to the value of its marginal product. But nothing in the theory
indicates that the product of today's service by a factor should be identified
with the ultimate consumer's good toward which it contributes. The introduction of time into the analysis, by permitting a difference between the
value of claims to present and to future goods, raises problems that are
not inconsistent with competitive theory but that go beyond it.[16]

RECAPITULATION AND MODIFICATION
FOR UNCERTAINTY

In the analysis thus far I have assumed perfect foresight. Fisher himself
developed his theory by a series of three successive "approximations," the
first two of which, i.e. time preference and the productivity of capital, I
have telescoped in a single presentation. His third approximation introduced uncertainty. The clearest way to present the implications of this
amendment will be to review each of the equilibrium conditions thus
far described or implied, and in each case show how this condition is
modified by the existence of uncertainty.

1. There are two principles of investment opportunity.
   a. *Empirical.* — The individual at O finds before him a large number of investment opportunities, represented not only by all the points
on OP, but also by all the inferior opportunities which may be imag-
ined as dotting the area between that curve and the x–y axes. These

---

[16] For a presentation of this view, see Earl Rolph, "The Discounted Marginal Productivity Doctrine," *Journal of Political Economy*, 47 (1939): 542–546, reprinted in
American Economic Association, *Readings in the Theory of Income Distribution* (Philadelphia: Blakiston, 1946), pp. 278–293.

opportunities differ in size, time shape, composition, and — we may now add — in degree of risk.

b. *Maximizing principle.* — The choice of option. The individual selects that investment opportunity which maximizes the present value of his income stream by equating marginal rate of return over cost with the interest rate. Now that risk is explicitly included in the analysis, we must say he equates marginal rate of *anticipated* return over cost to the interest rate.[17] Consequences are:

i. *Realized* rate of return may *not* equal the interest rate.

ii. The choice of options will take account of the varying degrees of risk involved.

iii. Inability to borrow (lack of security) may bar even highly profitable options.

2. There are two principles of impatience.

a. *Empirical.* — Each person may be thought of as having an indifference map which relates his marginal rate of time preference to the size and time-shape of his income stream. One must now add that the marginal rate of time preference will also be affected by the degree of uncertainty about various aspects of that anticipated income.

b. *Maximizing principle.* — Each person maximizes his satisfaction by borrowing or lending until his marginal rate of time preference equals the interest rate. Two important qualifications must now be added:

i. He may not actually maximize satisfaction because he may judge wrongly about what will bring satisfaction.

ii. The market may not permit him to maximize even his anticipated satisfaction, because the risk of lending to him may exclude him from the loan market. Therefore marginal rate of time preference may *not* be equal to the interest rate.

3. There are two principles of equilibrium in the market.

a. *Clearing the market.* — The market is cleared. Fisher says this means that "the additions, through loans, to some persons' real income must equal the subtraction from others'." [18] He admits this is an identity as stated. I would amend the statement to read, "In equilibrium the interest rate will have so adjusted that the amount people *want* to

---

[17] This statement is Fisher's and it is now the conventional statement. As the availability doctrine shows, however, the fact of uncertainty must influence not only the income, but also the cost side. In other words, we need not only to replace "return over cost" by "anticipated return over cost," but also to recognize the influence of expectations concerning future interest-rate movements on amounts borrowed. This uncertainty affects action both because of refunding problems, and also because borrowing may be postponed if lower rates are expected to rule shortly.

[18] Fisher, *The Theory of Interest*, facing p. 226.

borrow equals the amount that other people *want* to lend." When risk is admitted, this principle (by either Fisher's version or mine) is of course unchanged, but Fisher adds parenthetically that with risk there is the possibility of default, so that anticipated payments may not equal realized payments.

  b. *Repayment principle.* — For any individual the present value of all loans must equal the present value of anticipated repayment. When risk is admitted, this remains true at the moment the loan is made, but the equality may not persist; subsequent expectations may be very different from those at the time of the contract.

Fisher concludes that under conditions of uncertainty those equalities which are assumed to exist under the first two approximations (interest rate, marginal rate of return over cost, and marginal rate of time preference) become only idealized tendencies toward equality.

APPENDIX: ALGEBRAIC PRESENTATION OF FISHER'S THEORY OF INTEREST

(A brief summary outline of Fisher's algebraic statement of his theory of interest (omitting the third approximation) as presented in pages 288 to 315 of *The Theory of Interest*.[19])

  1. Income streams are defined as follows.
  a) Elements in Mr. 1's income stream are

$$(y_1' + x_1'), (y_1'' + x_1''), \ldots (y_1^m + x_1^m).$$

  b) Symbols:
  y represents income stream after "investment" or "disinvestment" but before receipts or payments arising from loans and interest. To put this another way, y values represent the various income dimensions of the point P on the opportunity surface, i.e. of the point which will have been chosen by the process of maximizing the present value of the income stream.
  x represents receipts (or payments if negative) from borrowing (or lending) and from repayments received from former loans, including interest.
  Subscript indicates the person whose income is involved.
  The number of primes in the superscript indicates the year of income.
  m represents the last year under consideration.
  Thus Mr. 2's total receipts in year 3 would be

$$(y_2''' + x_2''').$$

---

[19] (New York: Macmillan, 1930). I have changed some symbols and reorganized the presentation, but the basic structure is Fisher's.

2. Impatience principle A describes time preference (marginal rate of substitution between income of one year and that of another) as a function of the prospective income streams during the current and all future years.

a) Form of equation:

$$f_i^j = F_i^j[(y_i^j + x_i^j), (y_i^{j+1} + x_i^{j+1}), \ldots (y_i^m + x_i^m)].$$

b) Symbols:

f_i^j represents Mr. i's marginal rate of substitution between income of year j and year $j + 1$.

F is simply a functional notation.

n represents the number of individuals in the economy.

c) Number of equations:

An equation for each individual for each pair of successive years from the one beginning now to the one ending with the last year under consideration: $n(m - 1)$ equations.

3. Impatience principle B states the equilibrium equality between the marginal rates of time preference and the corresponding rate of interest.

a) Form of equation:

$$f_i^j = r^j.$$

b) Symbols:

r^j represents the "short" rate of interest between year j and year $j + 1$.

c) Number of equations:

An equation for each individual for each pair of successive years from the one beginning now to the one ending with the last year: $n(m - 1)$ equations.

4. Market principle A states that the total receipts resulting from borrowing and lending (including interest) in any year must equal the total payments the same year.

a) Form of equation:

$$x_1^j + x_2^j + x_3^j \ldots + x_n^j = 0.$$

b) Number of equations:

One for each year: m equations.

5. Market principle B states that the *present value* of each individual's income stream is not altered by borrowing and lending; i.e. the sum of all changes in present value of an individual's income resulting from all future borrowing and lending and repayments must equal zero.

a) Form of equation:

$$x_1' + \frac{x_1''}{1 + r'} + \frac{x_1'''}{(1 + r')(1 + r'')} + \cdots \frac{x_1^m}{(1 + r')(1 + r'') \ldots (1 + r^{m-1})} = 0.$$

b) Number of equations:

One for each individual: n equations.

6. Opportunity principle A defines the possible combinations of different year's income streams available to each individual. This is simply the equation of his opportunity "surface."

a) Form of equation:

$$\phi_i(y_i', y_i'', y_i''' \ldots y_i^m) = 0.$$

b) Number of equations:

One for each individual: n equations.

7. Opportunity principle B states that each individual invests and disinvests to the point which maximizes the present value of his income stream, with the result that the marginal rate of return over cost (s) between any year and the succeeding year is equal to the rate of interest between those same two years.

a) Form of equation:

$$s_i^j = r^j.$$

b) Symbols:

s_i^j represents Mr. i's marginal rate of return over cost for investment activity of year j extending to year $j + 1$.

c) Number of equations:

An equation for each individual for each pair of years from the one beginning now to the one ending with the last year: $n\,(m - 1)$ equations.

8. Equations may be derived to relate each s to the opportunity curve on which it depends. We have shown in the two dimensional case that s, the marginal rate of return over cost, is the slope of the opportunity curve minus one. In terms of our present problem and notation this means that each s may be derived from the relations of the y's defined by the equation for the opportunity "surface." [20] We assume here that "years" are infinitesimal.

a) Form of equation:

$$s_i^j = -\frac{\partial y_i^{j+1}}{\partial y_i^j} - 1.$$

b) Number of equations:

An equation for each individual's s as between each pair of successive years: $n(m - 1)$ equations.

9. Independence of equations: it may now be noted that if one considers paragraphs 4 and 5 together, one equation of that combined system

---

[20] Fisher used the relations described here to "reduce the number of unknowns," (see *ibid.*, p. 309), but the outline of my summary seems simpler: to use these considerations as providing an additional set of equations.

is not independent, but may be derived from the others. We shall show, for example, how the first equation of the set described in paragraph 4 may be derived from the other equations of paragraphs 4 and 5.

a) We may add together the n equations of paragraph 5, yielding:

$$x_1' + x_2' + \ldots x_n' + \frac{x_1'' + x_2'' + \ldots x_n''}{1 + r'}$$

$$+ \frac{x_1''' + x_2''' + \ldots x_n'''}{(1 + r')(1 + r'')} + \ldots \frac{x_1^m + x_2^m + \ldots x_n^m}{(1 + r')(1 + r'') \ldots (1 + r^{m-1})} = 0.$$

But the second equation of the set shown in paragraph 4 shows that the numerator of the first fraction above equals zero. Similarly the third and succeeding equations of that set show the other numerators to equal zero. Thus we may reduce the equation above to:

$$x_1' + x_2' + \ldots x_n' = 0.$$

But this is precisely the first equation of the set shown in paragraph 4, which proves that one equation of the set is redundant.

b) This reduces the number of equations that may be regarded as independent by 1, i.e.: subtract 1 equation

10. The number of unknowns are:

a) The "present income" of each individual for each year, after investment and disinvestment, but before borrowing, lending, repayments, and interest; i.e. y_i^j for $i = 1$ to $i = n$ and $j = 1$ to $j = m$: mn unknowns.

b) The additional receipts (positive or negative) of each individual each year resulting from borrowing, lending, repayment, and interest; i.e. x_i^j for $i = 1$ to $i = n$, and for $j = 1$ to $j = m$: mn unknowns.

c) The marginal rate of substitution between each pair of years for each individual; i.e. f_i^j for each individual (i) from 1 to n for each year (j) from 1 to $m - 1$: $n(m - 1)$ unknowns.

d) The interest rate as between each pair of successive years; i.e. r^j for $j = 1$ to $j = m - 1$: $m - 1$ unknowns.

e) The marginal rate of return over cost in investment for each individual for each pair of years; i.e. s_i^j for $i = 1$ to $i = n$ and for $j = 1$ to $j = m - 1$: $n(m - 1)$ unknowns.

11. Counting equations and unknowns:

a) The number of equations shown in paragraphs 2 to 9 inclusive is:

$$4n(m - 1) + 2n + m - 1 = 4mn + m - 2n - 1.$$

b) The number of unknowns shown in paragraph 10, (a) to (e), is:

$$2n(m - 1) + 2mn + m - 1 = 4mn + m - 2n - 1.$$

c) Since the number of independent equations equals the number of unknowns a major test for the determinateness of the system is satisfied. We shall not examine the conditions under which no solution or many solutions would result in this system.

V

OTHER NONMONETARY THEORIES OF INTEREST

The exposition of Fisher's theory has already indicated its usefulness both as a technique for showing the relations between nonmonetary elements in the determination of interest rates (time preference and productivity of capital), and as a framework for evaluating theories such as that of Boehm-Bawerk. It remains now to use Fisher's analysis as an instrument for clarifying other and more recent nonmonetary theories, and for helping to provide answers to a number of age-old questions about the nature of interest.

The major part of this chapter will be devoted to study of two important recent theories of interest. One, that of Knight, may be legitimately classified as a nonmonetary theory. The other, that of Schumpeter, is a monetary theory, but places such emphasis on nonmonetary issues as to make discussion here useful. These studies will be preceded by brief comment on some post-Marxian views regarding interest as a monopoly return, and by an examination of the curve that describes the demand for investment. This apparent digression into a study of ideas developed chiefly by Lerner will facilitate the subsequent analysis and, together with Fisher's theory of interest, will provide methods to assist in the appraisal of Knight's and Schumpeter's theories.

LERNER'S ANALYSIS OF
INVESTMENT-DEMAND CURVES

Three concepts that have been used to describe the demand for capital as a function of the rate of interest will be discussed in this section. These three concepts are the "marginal productivity of capital," the "marginal efficiency of investment," and the "marginal efficiency of capital." Lerner has made major contributions to an understanding of these relations, and the following discussion is based largely on his work. In 1953[1] he rejected part of his earlier analysis[2] but his first study has much merit, and

---

[1] A. P. Lerner, "On the Marginal Productivity of Capital and Marginal Efficiency of Investment," *Journal of Political Economy*, 61 (1953), pp. 1–14.

[2] Lerner, *The Economics of Control* (New York: Macmillan, 1944), pp. 330–338. An excellent summary of this earlier analysis is given by D. H. Robertson in "Some Notes on the Theory of Interest" in *Money, Trade and Economic Growth: In Honor of John Henry Williams* (New York: Macmillan, 1951), pp. 198–199.

I shall draw upon both sources. First I shall summarize his 1953 discussion of the Marginal Productivity of Capital and the Marginal Efficiency of Investment.

1. Literature on the theory of investment has presented us with two very different curves for investment demand without adequately distinguishing one from the other. These curves may be described as follows.

a. The Marginal Productivity of Capital (MPC) curve purports to show the rate of change of income with respect to capital. This curve is a logical impossibility, and the concept should be discarded. Furthermore, even if one could give meaning to the curve, it would not be the measure to compare with the rate of interest in order to determine the level of investment demand. An explanation of this point follows shortly.

b. The Marginal Efficiency of Investment (MEI) curve shows the rate of change of income with respect to the sacrifice of income represented by investment. This curve can be given clear meaning and should be used for investment analysis in place of the alleged MPC curve.

2. An interest rate is a ratio in which numerator and denominator are defined in identical units, and is therefore a pure number.

3. The investment-demand curve, be it MPC or MEI, must be expressed in terms of a pure number if it is to be compared with the rate of interest.

4. Even if it were found to be logically tenable, the concept of MPC would not be appropriate as an investment-demand curve because numerator and denominator are not measured in homogeneous units, so that MPC is not a pure number.

a. The numerator is the rate of change of income, the denominator is the rate of change in capital.

b. Even in the primitive illustration of a growing forest the numerator is measured in terms of board feet and the denominator is measured in trees of different ages.

c. This problem cannot be solved by reducing both income and capital to money terms. Indeed, the measure of capital by its money value would lead to serious confusion, because every change in either the rate of interest or the yield of capital goods would drastically change the value of existing capital goods. By employment of a money measure of capital, therefore, the "change in capital" found in the denominator of MPC would provide no measure at all of changes in "real capital" stock. Indeed, the two might move in opposite directions.

5. MEI is a pure number because both numerator and denominator are measures of income. Therefore MEI *can* be equated to the rate of interest, and this gives us the concept with which we wish to operate in our analysis of investment. This conclusion is, Lerner continues, a reasonable one, since investment decisions are, after all, decisions concerning current outlays of funds over given time periods in return for future receipt of funds.

With the aid of Lerner's discussion of the general nature of the investment-demand curve, it is now possible to review his ideas regarding its shape and shifts.

1. The rate of return from investment activity is influenced by both the amount of capital in existence and the rate at which investment is taking place.

a. With given technology it seems reasonable to presume that the most profitable investment activity will take place first. Therefore, as the quantity of capital increases, the rate of return expected from the next unit of investment activity will decline. This explains the fact that the rate of return on investment will be a function of the capital stock.

b. With given technology and given capital stock, the relative cost of investment goods will be positively correlated with the rate of investment. In short-run analysis with full employment this increase in costs as a function of the rate of investment will be great because of factor immobilities. But even in long-run analysis *some* cost differential may be normally expected because one may presume that except in the rarest coincidence labor and land will not be used in the same proportions in capital goods as in consumer goods.[3]

2. The preceding paragraphs suggest that at a moment of time one may draw a curve showing MEI on the y-axis and the rate of investment on the x-axis. The curve will *slope* negatively because of the increasing cost of capital goods as a function of the *rate* of investment, but it will also *shift* downward over time as a function of the *amount of capital stock*. This discussion of the shift of the curve is, of course, based on a *ceteris paribus* clause concerning technology, population, expectation changes, and other possible influences.

In this analysis Lerner has helpfully emphasized the danger of widespread and plausible confusions. I am not sure that he has demonstrated

---

[3] A fuller explanation may be readily adapted from Jacob Viner's discussion of increasing costs, supplement to his article on "Cost Curves and Supply Curves," in *Readings in Economic Analysis*, ed. by Richard V. Clemence, II (Cambridge, Mass.: Addison-Wesley Press, 1950), pp. 31 ff.

the logical impossibility of the MPC concept,[4] but his really central points seem valid. In the first place he shows the need to solve a difficult index-number problem in relation to the measurement of real capital in order to give the concept of MPC unambiguous meaning. In the second place, and more important, he has shown that even if we do give meaning to the concept of MPC, we cannot use it as a figure to be related to the interest rate, since it is not a pure number. Finally, if either of these two curves is to be used in context with the rate of interest to serve as the demand curve for investment funds, it must be the MEI curve.

Lerner next argues that Keynes' investment demand curve, called by him Marginal Efficiency of Capital (MEC), is really analogous to MEI, not to MPC, and is, therefore, appropriately used by Keynes even if not felicitously named. With one qualification I agree with this assertion, for Keynes' MEC is clearly defined as a pure number (like the rate of interest) and is found by relating the future returns from an investment to the current income that would have to be sacrificed in making that investment. Despite this similarity, however, an important and difficult problem is raised by the comparison of Keynes' MEC with Lerner's MEI. In *The General Theory* Keynes gives two reasons for the negative slope of his MEC curve: first, the fact that rapid investment activity uses up the most attractive opportunities quickly and leaves only less profitable ones for subsequent investment, and second, the rising cost of capital goods associated with a more rapid rate of investment.[5] Thus Keynes permits the negative slope of his MEC curve to reflect not only the consideration that gives Lerner's MEI its negative slope, but also that which causes Lerner's curve to shift with time. The problem posed is this: Should the investment-demand curve have the characteristics of Keynes' MEC or of Lerner's MEI?

If one abstracts from expectations concerning the future rate of investment, Lerner is surely right. Today's capital stock together with the production function and with input and output prices determines the current rate of return on today's investment. It is obvious, however, that the ultimate rate of return on this investment will be profoundly influenced not only by today's capital stock, but also by that throughout the life

---

[4] His argument is presented in the article cited in footnote 1. I omit discussion of this complex issue because its conclusion is irrelevant to the following analysis.

[5] Keynes clearly described these two determinants of the rate of return on investment. "If there is an increased investment in any given type of capital during any period of time, the marginal efficiency of that type of capital will diminish as the investment in it is increased, partly because the prospective yield will fall . . . and partly because, as a rule, pressure on the facilities for producing that type of capital will cause its supply price to increase; the second of these factors being usually the more important in producing equilibrium in the short run, but the longer the period in view the more does the first factor take its place." *The General Theory of Employment, Interest and Money* (New York: Harcourt, Brace, 1936), p. 136.

of these investment goods. If it is reasonable to presume that the present rate of investment provides the basis for investors' judgments about the changing levels of capital stock throughout the life of capital goods produced today, then Keynes' position seems well taken. Furthermore, if one thinks of today's investment decisions as being lumpy, then the expected rate of return on the last dollar of that lump will be influenced by the size of the lump, and again Keynes' approach would be vindicated. In the final analysis the choice between Keynes and Lerner would appear to be dependent upon behavioral assumptions regarding investors, and I shall offer no judgment on these. But I shall use the term MEI as introduced by Lerner, since that seems to be a better description of the investment demand curve whether one chooses to attribute to it the properties indicated by Keynes or those of Lerner.

KEYNES' MEC AND FISHER'S RATE
OF RETURN OVER COST

The analysis of Fisher's opportunity curve shows that this curve clearly provides the data required for an investment demand curve. Any given rate of interest implies a unique point P on a convex opportunity curve, and thus the horizontal distance between O (initial claims to income) and P shows the quantity of investment to be undertaken by any individual with given rates of interest. The question immediately posed is whether an investment demand curve derived in this way would be identical with the curve defined by Keynes as the marginal efficiency of capital curve.

Keynes states explicitly that his concept is the same as that of Fisher. "Professor Fisher uses his 'rate of return over cost' in the same sense and for precisely the same purpose as I employ the 'marginal efficiency of capital.' " (see note 6, p. 52 above). The view appears to be generally held that this identification is valid, and that the investment demand curves implied by Keynes' MEC and the use of Fisher's opportunity curve are the same. A. A. Alchian has challenged this assumption, and states that "unfortunately Keynes was wrong; they are not the same and they were not used for the same purpose." [6]

Alchian's analysis is interesting and important. I do not agree with the sweeping conceptual dichotomy he presents, but believe, on the contrary, that under the simplifying assumptions which both Keynes and Fisher were making these concepts are identical and were similarly used. However, I believe Alchian has demonstrated that a crucial difference does emerge between MEC and marginal rate of return over cost wher-

---

[6] A. A. Alchian, "The Rate of Interest, Fisher's Rate of Return over Costs and Keynes' Internal Rate of Return," *American Economic Review*, 45 (1955): 938–942.

ever mutually exclusive investment opportunities are presented. It would obviously not make sense to rank such options along a Keynesian MEC curve, which implies that the entrepreneur moves successively from one project to the next, fulfilling each until he reaches one whose MEC is lower than the rate of interest. The central question posed by this consideration is how to decide which of two mutually exclusive options to elect. The answer to that question cannot be found by simply taking the one with the higher MEC. Basically this is because, if each yields more than the going rate of interest, a much larger investment at a slightly lower yield might well provide greater total profits.

Although an unmodified application of the Keynesian concept of MEC would not give a solution to the problem posed by mutually exclusive options, the Fisherian procedure would provide the correct answer directly. Using this method implies selection of the option for which the return has the greatest present value when discounted at going rates of interest. To put this statement another way, one should calculate the marginal rate of return over cost for replacing option 1 with that of option 2: if this rate is greater than the rate of interest, option 2 should be taken; otherwise number 1 should be preferred.

The importance of Alchian's point is realized if one considers how many investment options are, indeed, mutually exclusive. Any decision between building plant to manufacture by one process or by another, or of one size or another, or at one location or another, would be illustrative. Similarly, budget restrictions may force a decision between two procedures, each of which would be desirable in itself.

Aside from the difference between MEC and marginal rate of return over cost described here, it is important also to remember, of course, that Keynes' MEC describes *expected* rates of return in a context where uncertainty is given central importance, whereas Fisher's marginal rate of return as developed in his second approximation abstracts from the problem of uncertainty.

INTEREST AS A MONOPOLY RETURN

Boehm-Bawerk disposed of the Marxian "exploitation theories" of interest by discrediting the labor theory of value upon which they rested. (See pp. 34–35.) For better or for worse that procedure is inadequate. Although the foundation on which Marx built his theoretical framework was the labor theory of value, it is now clear that many of his conclusions do not fall if that theory is destroyed.[7] Many non-Marxists regard interest

---

[7] See Joan Robinson, *An Essay on Marxian Economics* (London: Macmillan, 1947), and Leo Rogin, *The Meaning and Validity of Economic Theory* (New York: Harper, 1956).

as a monopoly return. According to the economic historian Arthur Birnie, for example, ". . . interest is a scarcity or monopoly charge; the owner of a relatively scarce article, the capitalist, takes advantage of the purchaser's need to charge a non-competitive price." [8] Since one need not subscribe to a labor theory of value in order to believe in the possibility of "monopolistic exploitation," constructions like Birnie's are not destroyed by Boehm-Bawerk's arguments.

This widely prevalent attribution of interest to monopoly power serves to confuse the issue in at least two ways. In the first place, the valid assertion that a disproportionately large part of total wealth is owned by a relatively few people does not imply monopoly, as that word is used in economic analysis, unless there is collusion among the holders of wealth. If all who could lend agreed to demand of all borrowers a higher rate of interest than the market would provide when they bid against one another, then a monopoly return would exist. There is no evidence that the existence of interest depends upon such a process, nor do the Marxists or those agreeing with Professor Birnie's views attempt to show that it does. Secondly, this theory implies that there would be no interest if wealth were evenly divided. Fisher's analysis enables us to see that such a conclusion is not valid, and it also helps us to see what Birnie may be trying to say. If figure I is redrawn with both X and Y having identical original claims, identical production-possibility curves, and identical indifference maps, then, of course, a solution is found in which no borrowing or lending occurs. Investment will take place, however, and the solution will lie somewhere between O_x and P_x at a point of tangency between the opportunity curve and some willingness curve. This absence of lending, and of receiving interest as a payment from one to another, is doubtless what Birnie means in asserting that there would be no interest. Properly stated, the observation is not without significance, but the imputed interest rate proves in this case to be even greater than in the society of unequal distribution illustrated in the original figure I. The slope of the OP and the W curves at their point of tangency would be greater than that at P_x. Furthermore, if even the slightest difference in tastes existed, so that a small amount of borrowing took place, this high interest rate would be revealed on the market. Put very simply, if it is true that the rich have a larger marginal propensity to save than the poor, then a more equal distribution of income would in all probability tend to raise interest rates rather than to lower them. Thus Fisher helps us see the analytical error in a popular explanation of interest rates. Going beyond Fisher's model, in which everybody is in some sense an entrepreneur, and visualizing a society of large-scale corporate production, even the allegation of

---

[8] Arthur Birnie, *The History and Ethics of Interest* (Glasgow, London, and Edinburgh: Hodge, 1952), p. 34.

smaller interest payments becomes questionable. All that Professor Birnie has shown is that if wealth were more equally divided, income would also be more equally divided.

Although I believe the analysis I have given here is valid for a discussion of interest rates under the assumptions of my model, in which I assume only one rate to exist and in which I abstract from risk, it should be added that the problem of monopoly can be an important one in real markets for certain kinds of loans, just as for other goods. Loan sharks represent a clear case, and there may well be important monopoly elements even in legitimate loan markets. I should be only too glad to endorse Professor Birnie's strictures against any such elements. But it seems to me that one identifies the wrong enemy if he presumes that interest *per se* arises because of the existence of monopoly.

KNIGHT'S THEORY OF INTEREST

A widely respected contemporary theory of interest has been developed by F. H. Knight in a long series of studies which he himself summarized in an article in the *Encyclopaedia Britannica*.[9] Knight, like Boehm-Bawerk and Fisher, presents an explicitly nonmonetary theory: ". . . even in an entrepreneurial economy using money, the relation between capital and its yield, or between rent and interest, has no essential connection with the borrowing and lending of money." [10] Furthermore, "If the role of capital in a situation without exchange or lending is understood, the explanation of the market value of sources, and of the yield as an annual rate per cent of their value, will present no difficulty." [11]

Knight states that in order to understand the nature of interest one must discard the economically useless distinction between capital goods, in the sense of produced goods used for further production, and other sources of productive power such as land and labor. Each person who has control over productive capacity must constantly decide whether to use that capacity to produce goods for immediate consumption or to produce intermediate goods. He will employ any or all sources (land, labor, capital goods) in such a way as to maximize the return for their use.

In order to facilitate comparison of different shapes of income flows Knight reminds us that through investment or disinvestment the individual can always exchange any claim to future income, however dis-

---

[9] "Capital and Interest," *Encyclopaedia Britannica*, 1946, reprinted in American Economic Association, *Readings in the Theory of Income Distribution* (Philadelphia: Blakiston, 1946), p. 384–417. For a considerably less difficult article which seems to me to clarify the views expressed in this one, see Frank H. Knight, *The Ethics of Competition and Other Essays* (London: Allen and Unwin, 1951), pp. 251–276.

[10] Knight, "Capital and Interest," p. 393 in reprint.

[11] *Ibid.*, p. 394.

tributed through time, for a perpetual annual flow. Whatever any source actually produces, minus maintenance cost, is its imputed yield for the period considered. The annual *rate* of yield is the ratio between the uniform, annual return provided by the perpetuity and the amount invested in the source (factor).

Under perfectly competitive equilibrium the maximizing principle described above will cause all sources to be so used that the return from each use, whether it be for production of investment goods or of consumption goods, will exchange for perpetuities of equal annual yield. That is, the marginal rates of return from all uses will be equal when measured by the common denominator of an equivalent uniform perpetuity. Under "real world" conditions the rates of return (in relation to initial investment) on various specific old capital goods may of course be very different from one another because expectations are never entirely fulfilled; but this equality will tend to hold, at least for expected rates of return, on currently produced investment goods. If the expected yield from the use of one good is higher than that from the use of another, more of that good and less of the other will be produced until the equality is reëstablished between their marginal rates of return.

Thus, in the real world, an equality between marginal rates of return will tend to be established at the margin of growth. It is because the amount of investment in *existing* capital goods is already set, whereas yields from those goods may change with time, that equality in rates of return calculated in relation to original investment will not hold for existing assets. But the price, or value, of these assets will rise or fall in the market until their yield divided by their current price will equal the yield divided by the cost of newly produced capital goods. This proposition may be stated in either of two ways. (1) Existing sources will be valued by capitalizing their expected income (or that of the equivalent perpetuity) at the rate fixed at the margin of growth; or (2) the value of existing sources will be the market estimation of the minimum cost of producing any source that will yield an income equal to that yielded by the source being priced.

Thus far what Knight has presented is wholly consistent with the conclusions of Fisher: in equilibrium, equality is established between the marginal rate of return over cost of production and the interest rate. But when he turns to causation, he differs significantly from all of the more eclectic schools, for he ends with what seems to be best classified as a pure productivity theory of interest.[12]

---

[12] This characterization is subject to argument. In the *Ethics of Competition* Knight classifies what seems to me to be his own view among the eclectic theories. Rolph prefers to call it a cost theory on the basis that the cost of producing new resources determines their price and hence the rate of return. Actually if one reduces either Rolph's or

In reference to the similarity with Fisher, it will be noted that the foregoing implies the equation:

$$\text{interest rate at time of investment} = \frac{\text{(expected) annual yield}}{\text{cost of investment}}.$$

Abstracting from problems arising in relation to expectations, Knight's equation gives the same ratio as that established at Fisher's P, where the AB line touches the OP curve. This identity may be readily shown as follows:

By Knight's equation, $r = $ annual yield $\div$ cost. But, in Fisher's figure, $r = $ slope of AB $-$ 1, and, annual yield $\div$ cost $= (\Delta y - \Delta x) \div \Delta x$, referred to positions on OP. Knight's equation thus becomes in Fisher's symbols,

$$\text{slope of AB} - 1 = (\Delta y - \Delta x)/\Delta x$$
$$= \Delta y/\Delta x - 1,$$

the limit of which, as $\Delta x \to 0$,

$$= \text{slope of OP} - 1.$$

Adding 1 to both sides of this equation we obtain one of the conditions required by equilibrium in Fisher's analysis, namely the condition that the slope of OP be equal to that of AB. In words, again, the marginal rate of return over cost is equal to the rate of interest. In Fisher's system, however, this is a necessary but not a sufficient condition for determination of the equilibrium rate of interest. Indeed, this point was found by Fisher only by assuming the rate of interest already known. So far as this equation alone goes one could draw AB of any slope found along OP, and nothing yet stated about Knight's theory would make one solution more appropriate than another. Fisher secured an equilibrium rate of interest by admitting to the analysis time preference and corresponding levels of desired lending and borrowing. But none of these appear in Knight's statement. How, then, can he secure a solution? The same question may be posed in direct relation to his own equation: if both the annual yield and the cost of investment are in part dependent upon the rate of investment, how can r be determined without further equations?

---

my own description of Knight's theory to mathematics it becomes clear that the rate of interest is dependent upon both cost and productivity. I prefer the "productivity" characterization because by Knight's theory it is the slope of the OP' line that determines the interest rate (see below) and this may be called a "productivity" theory because the slope of OP' depends upon the relation between current income sacrificed and subsequent income made available through production by that sacrifice. Costs of capital goods and values of future output are both involved, but are in a sense comprehended by the over-all relation between present and future income. Knight himself gives support to this interpretation by writing that the view of his theory which says it would "make the marginal productivity of capital the causal determinant of the interest rate . . ." is essentially correct. *Ibid.*, p. 397.

To pose this question is to suggest Knight's answer: the rate of return on capital is determined by the world's stock of capital and by the production function; the rate of investment cannot significantly influence this rate of return in any short period. In terms of Fisher's diagram, the OP′ curve (see p. 54 for definition) is a straight line and the rate of interest is therefore determined by its slope regardless of time preference. The point where equilibrium is reached along OP′ is, to be sure, determined in part by the willingness curves. Where they are tangent, as in Fisher's analysis, equilibrium will be found. Thus the quantity of investment is determined by the amount that people wish to save at the already predetermined rate of interest. In Knight's words, people will "save enough of their income to make their marginal time preference equal to this rate." But "this rate will not be appreciably affected by ordinary changes in the amount saved per unit of time." [13]

Thus, it is entirely possible to transpose Knight's theory into Fisher's language and geometry. But Knight's case is clearly a special case of Fisher's, since it presumes that OP′ must be straight. And how can that be argued in view of the reasons already presented for its being concave to the origin?

In the first place, Knight apparently abstracts from uncertainty in this part of his analysis, and thus removes a major reason for curvature in OP′. Two other major reasons remain to be dealt with. One is the Keynesian argument that the prices of capital goods will increase as the rate of investment increases. Knight answers this view by saying that in the long run all factors are fluid, so that shifts from consumer goods to capital goods need not have any ultimate effect on the cost of capital goods in relation to that of consumer goods. ". . . there is little or no permanent specialization of productive agents between the consumption and the investment use, so that the alternative-cost curve for capital goods in terms of sacrificed consumption is practically horizontal." [14]

The second major argument (see p. 75) for the view that the OP′ curve is concave toward the origin is that persons will always tend to choose the most attractive investment opportunity first, and thus each succeeding choice will yield less than the previous one. Knight's answer to this argument is that the total amount of capital in existence at any one time is so great that the change in this amount that can occur in any short period can never be large enough to have an appreciable effect on its yield. In his own words, the capital stock ". . . in any society at any moment . . . is the total accumulation made through all past time." Furthermore ". . . this is so large that the net production in a short period of time will not make an appreciable difference in the demand price." He

---

[13] *Ibid.*, p. 401.
[14] *Ibid.*, p. 399.

grants that ". . . total investment is doubtless subject to 'diminishing returns.' . . . But the decline in the rate [of return] would be slow, in historical terms." [15]

In summary, then, Knight's basic theory of interest may be regarded as a special case of Fisher's, and he gives reasons for his view that this "special case" is, because of the nature of the elements involved, one of general validity. However, Knight fully recognizes the modifications imposed in any realistic, short-run determination of interest rates. He indicates willingness to "admit [that] 'liquidity preference' is the main cause of the extremely high short run interest rate at the moment of a crisis and the abnormally low rates of deep depression." Furthermore, he agrees that government policy, bank policy, or public activities may "bring about a substantial deviation, for a considerable period, in the apparent market loan rate and in general prices or in the prices of securities." [16] Furthermore, "analysis of capital in terms of economically rational behavior and theoretical equilibrium seems unrealistic, and its explanatory and predictive value are rather limited." [17] He recognizes the force of ignorance, prejudice, and psychological and institutional elements. He also emphasizes that the productivity of investment, and hence the interest rate, may be altered sharply by new technology.

I shall give a critical appraisal of Knight's theory of interest after a brief outline of a similar analysis by F. P. Ramsey.

RAMSEY'S MODEL

Knight does not stand alone in espousing a theory according to which the rate of interest at any given time may be determined directly from consideration of the quantity of capital in society and the marginal productivity of investment which this quantity determines. D. H. Robertson commends Ramsey[18] for applying a pure theory of saving to the laws of growth in a community, and presenting an analysis that implies the same determination of interest rates as that of Knight.[19]

Figure 6, a is copied directly from Ramsey. In it a demand curve relates the quantity of capital to the rate of return it will yield (the partial derivative of income with respect to capital). A vertical line (C_0) then shows the existing amount of capital, and its intersection with the demand curve determines the rate of interest. A horizontal line (ρ) is drawn at a level showing the rate at which all persons, now and in the future,

[15] Ibid., pp. 400–401.
[16] Ibid., p. 406.
[17] Ibid., p. 403.
[18] "Some Notes on the Theory of Interest," p. 195.
[19] F. P. Ramsey, "A Mathematical Theory of Saving," Economic Journal, 38 (1928): 543–559.

discount future utilities. Since the rate of interest (r) is greater than e in this example, abstinence takes place. That is, net saving is greater than zero. The rate of saving (or investment) is not determined in this analysis, but Ramsey states that this will depend roughly on the ratio PM/QN, that is, the ratio of ρ to r. The similarity of Ramsey's theory to that of Knight is at once apparent. In each construction the existing stock of capital determines the rate of interest without reference to time preference or the rate of investment, though the latter would of course determine the rate at which the gradual descent along the demand curve takes place over time (assuming no innovation meanwhile).

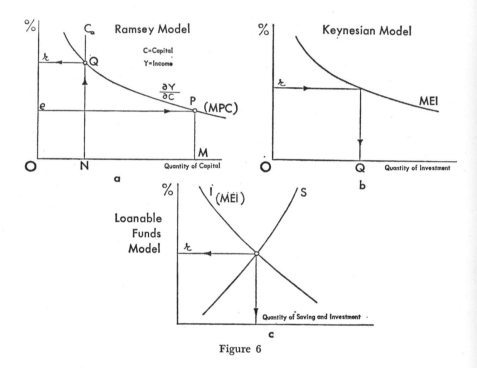

Figure 6

APPRAISAL OF THE KNIGHT-RAMSEY THEORIES OF INTEREST

The central proposition of the Knight-Ramsey theories is that the interest rate at any time is determined, given the production function, by the existing stock of capital without reference to time preference or to the rate of investment. Their justification for abstraction from time preference is their assumption that the rate of investment, which, they agree, will be substantially influenced by time preference, is not relevant to the determination of the rate of interest. I have shown that this is equivalent to saying that OP', in my modification of Fisher's geometry, is a straight line.

Since I have argued for the validity of the general framework used by Fisher, my evaluation of Knight's theory must depend to an important degree upon my appraisal of the arguments which are used to justify the straight OP' curve — i.e., the essential irrelevance of the rate of investment in society to the marginal rate of return on capital goods. An examination of these arguments leads increasingly to the conviction that the central issue is not the logic of the analysis but rather the usefulness of the frame of reference.

When one examines the central structure of Knight's theory, he feels as if he is breathing the clean, pure, but thin air of the stratosphere. The logic is clear, but the model is extremely abstract. In some senses it is a very-long-run theory. Not only does it, like other nonmonetary theories, explicitly abstract from such "temporary" phenomena as changes in the desire to "hoard" and changes in the quantity of money, but it presumes also that real investment is permitted to expand only in the directions consistent with ultimate equilibrium, so that the rate of return by expanding enterprise is not distorted by either uncertainty or lags in other parts of the developing economy. It abstracts from any short-run changes in the relationship of the costs of capital goods to the values of final products that might result from changing the rate of investment; indeed, in order to justify this constant cost assumption it assumes the complete adaptability of all productive agents. Thus the long-run nature of the theory yields a virtually horizontal MEI curve, and its abstraction from problems related to "expectations" permits this MEI curve to serve as the demand curve for capital. Yet this last consideration suggests a way in which Knight's perspective is also so short-run as to be instantaneous: the relevant rate of return over cost is the rate applying to the present moment only, uninfluenced by the rate at which capital is growing and forcing the MEI curve to shift.

I see nothing logically untenable about this juxtaposition of very-long-run and instantaneous perspectives. Indeed, the entire analysis seems essentially valid in the frame of reference Knight has chosen. The only analytical criticism which I see arises from the fact that even long-run costs of capital goods may be affected by changing rates of investment, but I suspect that Knight may be justified in regarding this element as having little weight.

The next question for evaluation, then, concerns the function of a theory set in this frame of reference. The major contribution of such a theory, it seems to me, is to force us to careful thought about the kind of assumptions we make when we seek to derive a theory for life below the stratosphere. To be sure, Knight also describes real-world qualifications of his analysis — I believe it would be difficult to find considerations which have not entered his thought — but I confess some feeling that he may not adequately emphasize the sharpness of the changes which his descent toward earth imposes on the implications of his abstract theory. The demand curve for capital may often, in fact, have very little interest elasticity at all, in contrast to the horizontal curve of Knight's theory, and for practical purposes the difference is, of course, extremely important. It means that the central characteristic of the theory is entirely reversed when realism is admitted, and that, among other things, the rate of saving, and hence time preference, must be recognized as an important determinant of the rate of interest. Although this does not destroy the usefulness of Knight's model as an analytical device, it points up the necessity of fully emphasizing the fact that the theory gives us only the remotest kind of approximation to a real-world theory of interest.

Because I believe it essential to make this sharp distinction between Knight's abstract model and a real-world model I question his defense of his MEI curve by an appeal to a realistic frame of reference, as in his treatment of diminishing returns to capital. His argument is that diminishing returns do not measurably influence the demand for capital because short-period changes in capital stock are small, relative to the total accumulated stock. "The virtually unlimited possibility of using more capital in production means that future incomes can be provided in correspondingly large volume at a slowly increasing cost." [20] But the emphasis here is on the "slowness" of the increase in cost, so that ". . . it is correct to consider the supply of future income at a given time as practically unlimited, indefinitely elastic." [21]

If Knight remained on the level of complete abstraction, the logic of his theory might have remained free of criticism. But the kind of argument just cited is clearly an appeal to a real-world frame of reference. Once he starts down this road he must decide just what time period he *is* using, and what behavioral assumptions are appropriate for that period. In my view the most appropriate time period would be that period which is taken into consideration by enterprise when it plans expansion. Firms do not borrow infinitesimal amounts in a succession of infinitesimal time periods, but they project a finite expansion program and borrow substantial blocks of funds in order to finance that program. The amount they wish to borrow at any one time is the amount directly relevant to the demand curve that enters the determination of the rate of interest. This amount will depend in part upon the certainty with which they feel they can forecast the results of investments of different size, and it will depend in part upon the rate at which other firms in the industry

[20] *Ethics of Competition*, p. 262, n. 9.
[21] *Loc. cit.*

are expanding plant and equipment. Thus a marked slope is given to the demand curve for capital by the element of realism that enters once abstraction and its pure MEI curve is left behind.

Particularly in the context of the kinds of uncertainties implied above, I doubt that the change in capital stock of even a single year could be regarded as negligible. In 1953, for instance, gross private domestic investment in the United States was equal to about five and a quarter per cent of the total estimated stock of reproducible national wealth existing at the start of the year, and about four and a half per cent of all wealth including land.[22] The time perspective implied by my analysis would surely be more than a single year.

With reference to the increasing costs of capital goods in the short run, Knight argues that sudden changes in saving "might" alter these costs, as implied by a sloping MEI curve, but that important changes of this kind are related to the business cycle and should be considered separately. Although I wholly agree that an adequate analysis of short-period changes in the rate of interest must introduce many dynamic elements not considered here, it still seems appropriate to show a slope in any short-period MEI curve if one believes that the functional relationship implied by that slope is valid. In this connection one may note an interesting anomaly: Keynes and Lerner emphasize the effects of the rate of investment on the cost of capital goods, whereas under the assumptions of underemployment that characterize their typical model this effect might be small; but Knight abstracts from these cost effects, though they might be expected to be most noticeable in the full-employment world of his model.

This examination of Knight's theory of interest has led to certain conclusions which may be summarized here. Although he has recognized at one point or another almost every element that can be thought of as influencing interest rates — including monetary as well as nonmonetary factors, and dynamic as well as static considerations — his basic theory of interest is one that attempts to abstract from passing phenomena and from considerations of minor importance. When this theory is recognized as a highly abstract model it seems to be open to little if any important criticism. Some of his presentation, however, implies recognition of such real-world phenomena as finite time periods and expectations, and at these points Knight has not adequately emphasized the importance of

---

[22] Estimates from Department of Commerce, *Survey of Current Business* (July, 1957), and *Statistical Abstract of the United States* (1955), p. 308, based on R. W. Goldsmith, *A Study of Saving in the United States*, III (Princeton: Princeton University Press, 1953). Reproducible wealth was estimated at 968.4 billion dollars at the end of 1952; gross private domestic investment was estimated at 50.3 billion in 1953. The most recent land estimate was 160 billion dollars in 1949. Omitting consumers' capital of 141.5 billion dollars, the proportion of gross private domestic investment to reproducible wealth would have been about 6 per cent.

the changes imposed on the implications of his basic theory. Explicitly and primarily, any relaxation of the assumptions inherent in his abstract model should recognize a marked inelasticity in the investment-demand curve. Many consequences of social importance would follow this recognition. And on the level of theory, it implies a convex OP' curve, and hence prevents the determination of interest rates without recognition of time preference. Put another way, once the investment-demand curve is given slope, the location of the saving curve influences the equilibrium rate of interest.

The abstract model of Knight's theory is of great value in clarifying the logic that must underlie any theory of interest, but as a working model to give one a feeling for real-world relations Keynes' MEC curve gives a much more appropriate concept of the nature of the demand curve for capital. And as a general model useful for over-all analysis Fisher's construction is the most convenient (so far as nonmonetary considerations are concerned) because it may be used to illustrate the implications of Knight's theory, or of Keynes', or of Lerner's: it is thus of general applicability, and serves also to clarify the relations between different theoretical structures.

It should be mentioned, however, that Knight has made an important and valid criticism of the term "time preference" (or perhaps even more the term "impatience") that Fisher employs to describe the psychology behind the willingness curves. "In reality the net accumulation of capital depends on the fact that savers maintain their capital and leave it behind when they die. . . . It does not seem very realistic to call the decision to save and invest, looking beyond one's own life, a choice of future rather than present satisfaction." [23] Since I have found it convenient to use Fisher's terminology, Knight's point leads me to emphasize that the motivation underlying the shape of the willingness curves may be best regarded as relating the desire for present income to the desire for future claims to income without specification of the many reasons for wishing to accumulate these latter claims.

Before leaving the Knight-Ramsey exposition it may be of interest to contrast briefly three familiar models in which the rate of interest, an MPC or MEI curve, and the quantity of investment appear. Figure 6 provides an illustration of these three approaches. Each model implies that in equilibrium the rate of interest will be equal to the marginal rate of return on investment. The differences are important, however. (1) In the Knight-Ramsey model (figure 6, *a*) the MPC curve relates the rate of return on investment to the *amount of capital* in existence (x-axis), without any dependence upon the rate at which investment takes place. Thus the rate of interest is wholly determined by the existing amount of capital

---

[23] *Ethics of Competition*, p. 263.

goods in conjunction with the MPC curve. I have already shown that the same fact may be illustrated in the Fisher model by the use of a straight OP' line, which then determines r without reference to the rate of investment (and saving). (2) In the familiar Keynesian picture (figure 6, b) the MEI curve (called MEC by Keynes) relates the rate of return on investment directly to the *rate at which investment is taking place* (the x-axis), and the influence of the quantity of capital in existence is hidden behind this curve, determining its location. In this model the rate of interest is determined elsewhere, and this figure merely shows how individuals in aggregate adjust to that rate by so varying their investment activity as to equate its marginal rate of return with the given interest rate. This process is shown in the Fisher model by the way in which persons move along a nonlinear OP' curve from O to P. (3) The simplified loanable-funds model referred to by Keynes as the "classical" theory (figure 6, c) may be pictured as including an MEI curve just like the preceding one. But instead of locating the equilibrium point thereon by assuming a given rate of interest, this theory describes the saving behavior of the society by a saving curve, and permits the simultaneous determination of both the rate of interest and the rate of investment (and of saving) by the intersection of these two curves. This, as we have shown above, is the full Fisher model, with the rate of interest determined at the unique rate which equates the marginal rate of return on investment and the marginal rate of time preference. A much more comprehensive comparison of the Keynesian and the "classical" theories of interest will be given in Part Two.

SCHUMPETER'S THEORY OF INTEREST

Joseph Schumpeter states emphatically that his is a monetary theory of interest. In the study of interest, he says, ". . . it is impossible to pierce the money veil. . . . If one penetrates through it one penetrates into a void." [24] Again, ". . . this money form is not shell but kernel." [25] In its fullest form Schumpeter's theory may well be described as a modern loanable funds theory of the kind we shall examine in Part Two. Briefly, he sees the rate of interest as determined by the forces of supply and demand in the market for money loans. The demand is determined chiefly by the investment demand of entrepreneurs, the supply consisting not only of saving, but also of newly created bank credit and funds released from hoards.[26]

One may wonder why I discuss Schumpeter in the part of this book

---

[24] Joseph Schumpeter, *The Theory of Economic Development* (Cambridge: Harvard University Press, 1951), p. 184; see also pp. 183, 195, 200.

[25] *Ibid.*, p. 184.

[26] *Ibid.*, pp. 193–195; 198–201.

dealing with nonmonetary theories while supporting his contention that his is a monetary theory. The reason is that, however much he admitted monetary elements to his analysis, he placed great emphasis on non-monetary considerations, and raised many interesting issues in relation to nonmonetary theories. I shall not now enter into the issues raised by the monetary phenomena to which he refers. My procedure will be first to review sketchily the main outline of his theory of interest, and then to examine central questions raised by his treatment of the relation between interest, development, and time preference.

Schumpeter discusses two types of cause for the emergence of interest, largely as if they operated independently of one another. One he deals with very briefly: the kind of cause that might generate a rate of interest even in a static (circular flow) economy. This general class includes a variety of specific causes, but these ". . . constitute no problem. Interest on consumptive loans is a case in point. That any one in unexpected distress . . . or in expectation of a future increase in income . . . values a hundred present more highly than a hundred future marks requires no explanation, and it is self evident that interest may exist in such cases. All categories of government credit requirements belong here. There have always been such cases of interest, and obviously they could also exist in the circular flow in which there is no development." [27] But the existence of interest arising from causes like these "does not constitute the great social phenomenon that needs explaining. This consists of interest on productive loans." [28]

Having said this, Schumpeter gives over virtually all the rest of his discussion to a second type of cause, treating it as an essentially independent phenomenon and often writing as if the first kind had been wholly forgotten. According to his theory, *the socially significant kind of interest is the payment made by the entrepreneur to the capitalist for the use of purchasing power.* This simple statement suggests not only a definition, but also three basic questions raised for Schumpeter by the existence of interest. These questions are: (1) Why can, and why does, the entrepreneur pay for the use of purchasing power? (2) Why is interest a permanent, not merely a temporary flow of income to the capitalist? (3) Whence come the funds the capitalist lends to the entrepreneur?

In answer to the first question Schumpeter says that the entrepreneur is willing and able to pay interest because the loan of purchasing power enables him to acquire capital goods with which he can make profits. These profits arise from the employment of specific physical agents of production, and therein lies an important fact: wherever competition exists, it will quickly drive to zero the profit on any particular product or productive method. Thus, profits will be only temporary except where

---

[27] *Ibid.*, p. 157.
[28] *Ibid.*

monopoly exists, and even few monopolies can long withstand the winds of creative destruction which are born of the competitive struggle. New sources of profits continue to emerge ubiquitously from the innovation and development of new goods and processes.

These comments lead directly to the second question. Since interest is derived from profits — being paid by the entrepreneur in order to acquire them — how can it be a permanent flow when profits themselves are always temporary? Schumpeter answers this by saying that though profits are earned on specific goods and are therefore temporary, interest is earned on liquid purchasing power, which can flow from one source of profit to another in a constantly developing society. Indeed, much of the reason that money is "not shell but kernel" of the theory of interest appears to lie in a sharp distinction between profits, which arise from specific goods, and interest, which arises from the use of purchasing power. Schumpeter repudiates completely the post-Ricardian classical identification of profits with interest. For him, interest, far from being synonymous with profits, is a tax on profits, a payment out of profits by the entrepreneur to another party, the capitalist. Its source is profits, and without them it could not exist, but it is a withdrawal from them. He arrives, then, at these three conclusions: "that interest as a great social phenomenon is a product of development, that it flows from profit, and that it does not adhere to concrete goods . . ." These three propositions, Schumpeter continues, "are the basis of our theory of interest." [29]

In answer to the third of his questions — What provides the supply of loanable funds? — he makes a number of extremely interesting observations, but the part of his answer that concerns nonmonetary aspects seems to contain a gap which allows a number of unclear, incomplete, or even erroneous elements to enter his theory. The insights that I should accept in whole or in large part include both his emphasis on monetary elements, and a very interesting discussion of the important degree to which loan funds arise directly or indirectly from the reinvestment of profits. This reminder is useful today for those who explain saving with too exclusive dependence upon the personal consumption function.[30] The elements of error or omission can be best discussed as part of a general

---

[29] *Ibid.*, p. 175.

[30] Schumpeter argues that most saving that actually takes place would not occur in the circular flow. Much "saving" is financed directly by the reinvestment of profits; most of the rest "does not come from thrift in the strict sense, that is, from abstaining from the consumption of part of one's regular income, but it consists of funds which are themselves the result of successful innovation and in which we shall later recognize entrepreneurial profit." (*Ibid.*, p. 72.) With reference to a category that is somewhat similar to the first source of these "savings" it is interesting to note the findings of Irwin Friend and I. B. Kravis regarding the proportion of American saving attributable to reinvestment of corporate and entrepreneurial income. Estimates of this portion vary widely for unexplainable reasons, running from about 40 per cent to 80 per cent. See their "Entrepreneurial Income, Saving, and Investment," *American Economic Review*, 47 (1957): 269–301.

appraisal of his theory, and I therefore turn now to this over-all evaluation.

Any evaluation of Schumpeter's analysis must contain an expression of enthusiasm for the broad scope and the stimulating insights he has given. For one who has read *The Theory of Economic Development* my criticism will appear extremely pedestrian after the grand sweep of Schumpeter's outlook. Despite this, however, it seems useful to examine closely the adequacy of his theoretical structure. My major criticism would be that he has separated time preference and innovation, as though they provide two different and independent explanations for the emergence of interest, instead of recognizing that they must always enter simultaneously into any determination of interest rates. Perhaps Schumpeter has too closely followed Boehm-Bawerk, whose emphasis on the independence of technical superiority of present goods over future goods as a reason for the existence of interest led to the debate with Fisher.[31] Partly because of this incomplete analysis Schumpeter does not seem to have answered adequately his own question concerning the dilemma of interest. And partly also because of this incompleteness he errs or at least misleads in a second way: that of seeming to make development not only an empirically important, but also a logically essential element in causing the existence of interest on production loans.

Early in his discussion Schumpeter describes and attempts to deal with the "dilemma of interest," [32] wherein the theory of perfect competition appears to deny the possibility of interest because it seems to imply that the full value of finished consumers' goods must be swept back to the original factors of production, land and labor. The answer to this contradiction, he says, lies in the fact that the theory of perfect competition is a theory of static equilibrium, and that the real world is one in which development is a permanent characteristic. "The number of possible innovations is practically unlimited. . . . Improvements can always be made . . . Every step forward opens new prospects. . . . Consequently the demand for productive loan funds with interest at zero would always be greater than the supply, which is always limited." [33] Thus interest rates will always be forced above zero by the excess demand, which in turn owes its existence to innovation and development.

The question that this analysis immediately suggests is: if demand for development is so great, why does this not result in bidding up factor prices by entrepreneurs until they do, after all, receive payments equal to the full final value of the final product? Schumpeter anticipated this question: the prices of the factors, he says, will have been determined by

---

[31] See pp. 41–46 above.
[32] See chapter i, pp. 19–21.
[33] Schumpeter, *The Theory of Economic Development*, p. 197.

the previous uses to which they were put, not by the more profitable uses to which innovation now makes it possible to apply them. Thus it is innovation and that alone which makes productive interest possible, for only with innovation can we produce capital goods whose return will be greater than the payment made to land and labor for producing them.[34] Now the only difficulty with this answer is that Schumpeter gives no reason for believing it to be valid. He simply asserts that the factors will be paid according to their previous uses rather than their present uses. To be sure, by assuming that innovation creates a disequilibrium, Schumpeter makes possible an escape from his dilemma, since the characteristics of competitive equilibrium are no longer binding. But it is still quite unclear why the entrepreneurs, if they have many profitable and unexploited innovations before them, may not bid against one another for factors until those factor prices exhaust the value of the total product under the new and more profitable opportunity. In short, Schumpeter has opened a door that could well lead to one possible resolution of his dilemma, but his analysis beyond that point is neither compelling nor complete. It is not compelling because it gives no clear reason why the derived demand from innovation should not be swept in full to the factors of production. It is incomplete because it leaves almost no room for interest without continuous innovation.

An analysis of this last point should further clarify my view. The major source of interest, according to Schumpeter, is the continuous disequilibrium in which our system operates because of development. This development creates the profits for the entrepreneur (a disequilibrium phenomenon in a competitive model) from which the capitalist can "tax" a share called interest. The question raised is whether the existence of interest, outside of that arising from myopia and similar phenomena, does indeed depend upon development. And in order to answer this question we must first discover just what Schumpeter means by the term "development." Would the extension of the existing stock of capital goods with present technological methods represent "development"? (In today's parlance this might be called the "development of under-developed areas or segments.") Would Schumpeter also accept this interpretation of his term, or would he insist upon the necessity of innovation?

In *The Theory of Economic Development* there are some passages which seem to support the first interpretation,[35] but the clearest and sharpest statements all support the opposite: mere growth is not enough to establish development; innovation is an essential ingredient. For example: "Continuous changes, which may in time . . . make a great

---

[34] *Ibid.*, p. 190.

[35] E.g., *ibid.*, p. 71; ". . . the running of the latter circular flow presupposes given quantities of means of production."

department store out of a small retail business, come under the 'static' analysis.[36] . . . Nor will the mere growth of the economy, as shown by the growth of population and wealth, be designated here as a process of development. For it calls forth no qualitatively new phenomena . . .[37] Development in our sense is a distinct phenomenon, entirely foreign to what may be observed in the circular flow or the tendency toward equilibrium." [38]

Given this concept of development, then, we may return to the initial question, "Can interest arise without these types of revolutionary, innovational changes? If so, then under what circumstances?" Fisher's analysis would seem to provide a convenient tool for seeking an answer to this question.[39] I see no reason to presume that the OP′ curve may not, even after the long absence of innovation, have a greater slope than unity in the area of the initial income points (i.e., O_x and O_y in figure I). In fact this condition should hold until no further efficiency in production could be achieved by extension of existing types of capital goods. And that might be a long time indeed. If OP′ is so sloped, then it could be tangent to any of a wide variety of willingness curves at points indicating both positive investment and positive rates of interest. Indeed, even if all persons had zero time preference in the second sense described above (p. 58), OP′ curves of this nature would necessarily imply positive interest rates whenever the time shape of initial claims involves future income equal to or greater than present income; and positive rates could readily occur even if present income claims initially exceed future claims.

It would probably be possible to bring together enough of Schumpeter's statements to argue the consistency of his position with the solution just derived from Fisher, but Schumpeter's implication clearly seems to be that positive rates of interest would not emerge in even a growing society unless either innovation took place or people on the average exhibited positive time preference. As an empirical postulate this view may be valid, but as a theoretical, logical necessity it is not.

In conclusion, then, there is certainly a great deal of validity in Schumpeter's view that in the real world interest emerges primarily because of innovation and development, and Schumpeter's statement of his theory has a breadth and simplicity which lend it great usefulness. But anyone who wishes to analyze more fully the complex relationships between development and time preference will do well to make use of Fisher's construction. This model permits analysis on the basis of Schumpeter's special assumptions, but it does not tie the analysis to these assumptions.

---

[36] *Ibid.*, p. 62.

[37] *Ibid.*, p. 63.

[38] *Ibid.*, p. 64.

[39] In the following analysis I shall again simplify procedures by the same device used in chapter iv, p. 57.

VI

THE DESIRABILITY OF INTEREST

It would be inappropriate to enter here any thorough analysis of the many issues involved in appraising the social desirability of the existence of interest payments. Furthermore, it must be recognized that in touching these questions we are entering upon a fundamentally different type of discussion from that which has preceded and that which will follow. These issues directly involve value judgments as well as analysis. Yet these questions are continually and properly raised in relation to the discussion of interest, and it seems useful in this final section of Part One to observe the ways in which the nonmonetary theory of interest can clarify the discussion of the social implications of these payments.

For the purpose of this analysis it is useful to break down the question of "desirability" into at least four parts: (1) Is it desirable that those who must pay interest under free enterprise be required to do so? (2) Is it desirable that interest be secured and retained by those who receive it in a free-enterprise economy? (3) Should interest rates be permitted to seek their levels as determined in free markets? (4) Is there a role for interest under socialism? I shall comment on these questions in the order listed.

1. Is it desirable that those who must pay interest be required to do so?

In 1893 Arthur Hadley wrote, concerning the function of interest in our economy, "The system of interest is justified by its effect on the natural selection of employers and methods rather than by any contribution made by the individual receiver of interest to the good of society." [1] In this statement Hadley neatly separates the first two questions we have proposed for discussion, implying an affirmative answer to the first and possibly a negative reply to the second.

The service allegedly performed by interest payments (as opposed to receipts) includes rationing in at least three dimensions: they ration factors between types of goods to be produced, between entrepreneurs,

---

[1] A. T. Hadley, "Interest and Profits," *Annals of the American Academy of Political and Social Sciences*, 4 (1893–94): 339.

and between methods of production. Fisher's analysis indicates that the time when a good is forthcoming has definite social importance. The differences between supply-need relations today and tomorrow, as described by Boehm-Bawerk and maintained by Fisher, almost inevitably cause goods to have different utility today from that they would have tomorrow, even if we completely exclude myopia. This means that there is always a social cost (positive or negative) in shifting output from one time to another. Any price system which fails to allow for this social cost will fail to maximize real income. If a consumer is indifferent to the use of two different goods which require precisely the same amount of land, labor, and existing capital goods, it does not follow that society is indifferent to his choice. If the resources expended upon one of these goods can produce it directly and at once, whereas the other can be produced by use of the same resources only after many years, then the latter has a different and presumably greater social cost. The only way by which a price system can encourage the consumer to choose goods in such a way as to maximize real income is to impose a charge that appropriately evaluates the social cost resulting from time preference.

On the basis of this consideration it would seem that the first part of Hadley's statement is justified, and social welfare will be greater if interest is appropriately charged against producers than if it is not. But what of consumptive borrowing? In strict logic the same considerations justify a similar conclusion. There is no reason that the prodigal should not be charged for the social cost involved in his prodigality. This conclusion does not imply that subsidy should not be given generously to the needy, but it implies that the true cost of that subsidy will be recognized only if an appropriate interest charge is included in the accounting.

The preceding analysis is based upon the assumption that producers calculate interest costs when they make their decisions, and it presumes that interest rates reflect the public's time preference in some meaningful way. Although there is much debate over how far businessmen consider interest differentials when deciding whether to engage in major investment undertakings, I doubt that there could be any serious question that businessmen do calculate interest costs very carefully when considering methods of production or type of product. The second question, whether interest rates reflect the public's time preference in any meaningful way, is a much more knotty problem. There is of course the ubiquitous welfare problem of comparing utilities among people. But beyond that are all the problems which arise because interest rates in the real world are greatly influenced by monetary elements not yet introduced into our analysis, by uncertainty and expectations, and by governmental decisions oriented toward stability. These considerations would surely qualify the effectiveness of actual interest rates as a device for rationing investment according to consumer sovereignty, but they do not imply the social desirability of replacing an imperfect charge with none at all.

2. Is it desirable that interest be retained by those who receive it in a free-enterprise economy?

An affirmative answer to the question concerning the desirability of charging interest as a cost to producers does not make the present query pointless. It is conceptually possible to permit the payment of interest by borrowers but to tax away interest income from those who receive it — or at least to impose taxes which take part of it. The problem is quite analogous to that of the taxation of rents. A discussion of this issue may also shed some light on the desirability of tax provisions like some of today which have exactly the opposite effect, favoring particular kinds of property income as compared with that from labor.

It is, of course, well known that the taking of interest was condemned by dominant western thought for many centuries. Old Testament objections were apparently directed to the taking of interest from fellow Jews, although the poor are included without clear national distinction in some contexts. Aristotle condemned interest as the unnatural fruit of a barren parent, money. The Christian church condemned usury at the Council of Nicea in 325. The Scholastics persisted in their opposition, but following the thirteenth century increasing evidence of the profitable use of borrowed funds undermined the logic of the interdict and also made enforcement increasingly difficult.

Most of the earlier opposition was based on the fact that interest was regarded as the means by which the wealthy received an unearned return from the unfortunate. Modern interest payments are primarily made for productive loans, and cases of need can generally be dealt with better by direct subsidy than by the provision of interest-free loans. But the ethical objection to "unearned income" is not weakened by the fact that the loan is a productive one, and so this part of the historic objection to interest is not removed.

There are a number of criteria which bear on the social desirability of interest, and these criteria to some degree conflict with one another, so that a compromise among competing values has to be reached. I shall list and examine briefly five widely held value judgments relating to the distribution of income, and discuss the appropriateness of each together with its relevance to the receipt and retention of interest payments by those with funds to invest. First are three criteria related directly to ethical value judgments. (*a*) Many persons believe that for one or more reasons extreme inequality in the distribution of income should be avoided, though almost all would also oppose complete equality. (*b*) Many persons believe that need should be one element that might modify

a desirable distribution pattern from whatever form it might take before
consideration of need. (*c*) Many believe that he who works hard should
normally receive more compensation than he who refuses to work, and
that this judgment stands on grounds of ethics ("fairness"), not just on
the ground of providing a necessary work incentive.

In addition to these three direct ethical considerations, many people
hold strong convictions about the indirect effects of income distribution
on social well-being. These views include the belief that (*d*) the distribution of income may affect economic productivity and progress, and that
(*e*) it may be critically related to acceptable, as opposed to unacceptable,
social systems, thus affecting not only economic but also social and cul-
tural values.

a) *Equality.* — Two major reasons for advocating equalitarian objectives are commonly found among economists. One is a direct and frank
value judgment that people ought to have equal opportunity to enjoy a
good life. The second is that equality is the best way to maximize total
social welfare. Little need be said, or can be said, about the first, since it
is a direct value judgment. It is significant to note, however, that Robert
Lampman finds the general acceptance of this position in western societies increasing. "The recent history of Western nations reveals an increasingly widespread adoption of the idea that substantial equality of
social and economic conditions among individuals is a good thing." [2]
Lampman goes on to cite David Thomson's finding that egalitarianism
has spread gradually across many social fronts, "from concern with re-
ligious equality, to political equality, and most recently to economic
equality." [3]

Although acceptance of equality as an end in itself has grown, the argument that it is desirable because it maximizes social welfare has lost
ground steadily since its heyday, when it was given a central place in
Pigou's *Economics of Welfare*.[4] The argument was essentially simple and
straightforward. Assuming that all persons have diminishing marginal
utility of income, and assuming all persons roughly equivalent to one
another, it follows logically that a dollar taken from the rich and given
to the poor will increase the total welfare by increasing the satisfactions
of the latter more than it reduces those of the former. Increasing dis-
satisfaction with this view among economists is associated chiefly with
two developments of thought. First, there is growing distrust of the as-

---

[2] Robert J. Lampman, "Recent Thought on Egalitarianism," *Quarterly Journal of
Economics,* 71 (1957): 234. Anyone interested in the question of egalitarianism will find
this article useful.

[3] David Thomson, *Equality* (Cambridge: Cambridge University Press, 1949), chapter
ii, quoted by Lampman, *ibid.,* p. 235.

[4] A. C. Pigou, *The Economics of Welfare,* 2d ed. (London: Macmillan, 1924), Part I,
chapter vii.

sumption that the law of diminishing marginal utility applies to income as a whole, even though this principle would seem generally acceptable as applied to individual products. Secondly, there is virtually unanimous distrust of any attempt to make interpersonal utility comparisons. It should be said for Pigou that his discussion is quite sophisticated, and does not rest on the view that all individuals are homogeneous, but rather that there is no basis for the presumption that differences among them are such that the rich should always be those who by their nature gain more satisfaction from income than those who are poor. I must confess to being old fashioned enough to think there is much merit in Pigou's views, but I am doubtless in the minority, and I fully agree with Lampman that this approach has been under increasingly widespread attack.

In addition to these two egalitarian arguments, in which economic equality is appraised in terms of its direct economic consequences on well-being, a third concerns the implications of economic equality for political and other forms of power. It would be impossible in this space to assess the changing attitudes on this complex question, but I feel sure that there would be strong support in democratic societies for the view that concentration of wealth can have undesirable effects through its bearing on the distribution of power.

Given these value judgments, what is the effect of interest receipts on the "desirability" of the income distribution? The general nature of the influence of interest is in just the direction one would expect, but the quantitative significance of the influence may be considerably less than is commonly supposed. The actual calculation of this effect would raise problems that lead far beyond the scope of this book, but some of the issues involved should be mentioned. The distribution of explicit monetary interest is more nearly equal than that of the other major source of property income, dividends; on the other hand, interest income is distributed less equally than aggregate income, and, of course, much less equally than employee compensation. Table 2 presents relevant data for 1948.

The *direction* of the influence of interest payments on the distribution of income is suggested by these data, but the *amount* of the influence may appear greater here than it really is. In 1948, monetary interest payments amounted to only 2.6 per cent of total personal income receipts.[5] Furthermore, the trend in both the inequality of interest distribution and the importance of interest in total income had been quite steadily downward since the early thirties or before. At least the latter trend has been sharply reversed since 1948.[6]

---

[5] Lawrence H. Seltzer, *Interest as a Source of Personal Income and Tax Revenue,* Occasional Paper 51 (New York: National Bureau of Economic Research, 1955), p. 1253.

[6] The following ratios of personal interest income to total personal income may be derived from Department of Commerce data. 1948: 4.3 per cent; 1952: 4.5 per cent;

TABLE 2

PERCENTAGE SHARE OF VARIOUS TYPES OF INCOME RECEIVED
BY SELECTED UPPER INCOME GROUPS, 1948

Type of income	Proportion received by			
	Top 1%	Top 5%	Top 10%	Top 20%
Employee compensation	3.8	10.9	18.8	31.9
Entrepreneurial income	15.2	30.7	36.1	41.6
Dividends	53.6	69.9	74.0	77.5
Interest	15.8	26.5	30.8	35.3
Rent	12.8	22.6	26.4	30.1
Total property income	31.1	43.9	48.1	51.9
Total income	8.4	17.6	24.7	35.6

SOURCE: Simon Kuznets, *Shares of Upper Income Groups in Income and Savings* (New York: National Bureau of Economic Research, 1953). All rows but last taken from Table 123, pp. 646 ff.; last row calculated from Table 108, p. 455. Parts of the former table were cited in Lawrence H. Seltzer, *Interest as a Source of Personal Income and Tax Revenue*, Occasional Paper 51 (New York: National Bureau of Economic Research, 1955), p. 1253.

All this indicates a fairly moderate effect of interest payments on the inequality of income distribution. Its importance would appear considerably greater, however, if one assumes that imputed interest as a part of other types of property income should also be included. My analysis would suggest that such an inclusion would be legitimate, but there are many knotty problems involved in determining the influence of interest rates on property income generally. A major difficulty is that of measuring the effects of interest rates on profits in a dynamic economy. Also a problem arises because the effect on capital values of existing assets is in the opposite direction from that on returns from subsequent investment.

In conclusion, then, widely held value judgments about the desirability of equality in the distribution of income would indicate that from this standpoint the effect of interest receipts by lenders is undesirable, but the importance of this effect is difficult to assess. At present the proportion of interest to total income is increasing, following a twenty-year downtrend that began in the early thirties.

b) Need. — On the basis of personal, random observations, including repeated questioning of both graduate and undergradute students, I believe it safe to conclude that most persons in our culture accept the

---

1954: 5.2 per cent; 1956: 5.4 per cent. (U. S. Department of Commerce, *Survey of Current Business,* July, 1957, Table 3.) These data are not entirely comparable with Seltzer's, but the trend is suggestive.

view that a "just" distribution of income would take "need" into account. The laws of the United States acknowledge this by permitting family exemptions for purposes of income tax calculations. This point, however, seems to have little independent bearing on the issue of interest payments. To be sure, many people believe that these are desirable because of the large part which is presumed to flow toward widows, orphans, and colleges — in short, to the needy. There is no doubt that a substantial amount of interest does go to these groups — but it should not be forgotten that some of our richest people are widows. Except for nonprofit institutions, however, this would appear to have been covered by the discussion of equality, where the indications are that the wealthy benefit appreciably more from interest income than do the "needy."

c) *Hard Work and the Distribution of Income.* — If I may again judge by student response to questions, it would appear that there is a widespread feeling that hard work should be rewarded, and that there is a general though not altogether consistent objection to people (except for ourselves and the winners of quiz programs) getting something for nothing. Confusion and inconsistencies often underlie the judgments: there may be resentment at the unemployed receiving payments when they are unwilling to accept proffered work, but no objection to permitting the man who finds oil on his property to retain it.

Two types of argument are commonly used to support the general contention that men should work for what they get. One is that a person has a right to whatever product results from his own activity. The second is that persons should receive a reward as compensation for the "pain" and sacrifice involved in their labors. These arguments are not usually distinguished from each other or applied systematically, but both of them are apparently generally held to be valid.

The right to the full value of what our labor produces but not to the contribution of our property is forcefully challenged by Knight: ". . . the sharp distinction, common to popular and reformist thinking, between ethical claims of property and personal services involves . . . fallacy. The possession of productive capacity in external things and in internal abilities stands in much the same position, particularly with respect to inheritance *versus* effort, foresight and initiative." [7] We might ask if a man is more worthy of a great reward for his inherited business acumen than for his inherited bonds? And further, to what degree is the value of the product of one's labor a matter of chance or social circumstance? How many persons have labored long hours to produce goods of relatively little

[7] F. H. Knight, "Capital and Interest," *Encyclopaedia Britannica*, 1946, reprinted in American Economic Association, *Readings in the Theory of Income Distribution* (Philadelphia: Blakiston, 1946), p. 408.

value, receiving a correspondingly small reward, although possessing undeveloped talents that could have given them the life and income of a
movie actor?

The second view, that property income can find no justification corresponding to the pain and sacrifice of labor, is given support in the work
of Boehm-Bawerk himself, the great defender of interest income. Even
he concedes that interest provides a reward out of all proportion to any
pain or abstinence, and that it accrues to the capitalist "even where he
has not moved a finger in its making." [8] This statement is in no way con-
troverted by the view that saving takes place until the marginal sacrifice
of further abstinence is equal to the satisfaction of the marginal interest
income, for the latter thesis rests on the idea of *marginal* changes. The
saver might wish to save $99,900 even if interest rates were zero, yet
find further abstinence unpleasant, and therefore save only $100,000 if
interest rates were 5 per cent. His total sacrifice for his total saving may
well be negative — he may very much prefer to save the whole $100,000
than not to save at all. Wherein lies the pain that ethical considerations
require us to reward?

So far as it goes this argument may appear acceptable, but it stops too
soon. Is it not likely that the laborer also finds life much pleasanter than
does the loafer? In the abstraction of our theories, the worker's limits of
sacrifice are at marginal equalities with satisfaction from pay for that
sacrifice, just as are those of the saver, and the ethical case for a reward in
return for the worker's sacrifice stands on no firmer footing than that of
the capitalist unless more can be said than has been reviewed thus far.

My own position on these arguments is a somewhat mixed one, but for
a combination of reasons I come down quite firmly on the side of those
who believe that, so far as direct ethical implications for distribution are
concerned, it would be generally desirable to minimize property income.
The indirect effects of such a procedure, of course, remain to be discussed.
But before turning to them, a few comments are in order concerning the
reasons for my stand on the issue of direct ethical implications. In the
first place I do not accept the productivity argument. On this issue I believe Knight has effectively shown that there is little ethical basis for
presuming a man's just deserts are at all closely correlated with the value
that emerges from his product. This applies even in pure competition;
and much more in the real world where values can be inflated by con-
trived scarcity.

My stand might be explained as follows. First, it is an unfortunate fact
that nature has not endowed us with talents of equivalent value. The
differing rewards that result from these differential capacities should

---

[8] Eugen von Boehm-Bawerk, *Capital and Interest,* translated by William Smart (London: Macmillan, 1890), p. 1.

be reduced where feasible by taxation, although the amount of correction it is desirable to make in this way is clearly limited. Surely, however, any additional inequalities should be avoided. To the extent that property income falls in this classification it is undesirable. In fact, property income is most unevenly divided, and one effective way to move toward equality would be to reduce the amount of income from this source. Second, whatever "reward for abstaining" may seem to be merited by the saver may be more than overbalanced by the privileged position that permits him to face that option. How gladly would I accept the pain of being in a position to abstain from spending a million dollars of income! Third — and perhaps the weakest of my arguments — I believe that those who labor sacrifice many more attractive alternatives than those who save, and thus merit greater compensation.

But all strictures against property income lose their force, in part or in full, if the indirect social consequences of eliminating it bring more damage in their wake than can be overcome by the gains of the "reform." I can not discuss here the consequences of removing the major type of property income, profits, but I shall try to sketch some of the issues involved in any attempt to reduce or remove interest payments. In this discussion I shall deal simultaneously with propositions (*d*) and (*e*) as given on page 98.

d and *e*) *The Indirect Social Consequences of Removing or Reducing the Payment of Interest.* — Those who believe that the values of free enterprise are superior to those of other systems will immediately ask themselves whether such an economy could operate without interest receipts — that is, if these were taxed away by the state. If the risk premiums that make up a substantial part of gross interest were to be included in the tax, it would create difficulties of a serious nature which will not be discussed in this study. Short of this, an endeavor might be made to tax all property income by an amount equal to the estimate of "pure interest": a category that should exclude all payments for sacrifice of liquidity as well as those for risk of nonpayment. The component of property income taxed would, therefore, have to be based on the approximate rate that Treasury bills would yield if they existed in such an economy. The consequences of such a program would be so pervasive that it is hazardous without a thorough study to attempt to judge whether a free-enterprise economy would be seriously undermined. In terms of practical politics I have little doubt that outright socialism would be a more likely development, for it would face opposition from few more groups, but would have a much greater appeal to those who did favor radical change. The complete confiscation of "pure interest" would revolutionize our present system of Treasury finance, eliminating the net yield on government bonds except for liquidity premiums related to the maturity and call dates of the securities, and making Treasury bills meaningless. Monetary policy would be correspondingly changed, with Federal Reserve operations shifting to long term or even private securities.

It seems useless to explore further this limiting case — i.e., total expropriation of interest payments under capitalism. But it is not pointless to consider the nature of changes that would result from a less drastic move. The major consequences that would result from moderate taxation of interest receipts (explicit and imputed) would appear to be these: (1) The distribution of income would be affected, presumably in the direction indicated to be desirable by the value judgments described above. (2) The quantity of desired saving at full employment might be reduced. If this occurred it would increase stability when deflation threatened, but would exacerbate inflationary problems. However, the effect on sav-

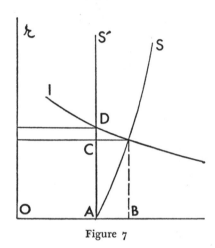

Figure 7

ing would be small if there is validity in the widely held view that the saving curve has very low interest elasticity and if this inelasticity extends to very low interest rates. (3) Corporations bidding for funds would have to offer higher rates. If the investment curve is fairly elastic, the rate might not be greatly increased, but if this curve too is quite inelastic the rate might rise appreciably. Figure 7 depicts the consequences if the tax is assumed to be completely confiscatory, and if it is assumed also that the saving curve is inelastic, and the investment curve elastic. The reduction in saving is AB, regardless of the slope of the investment curve. The smallness of the rise in interest rates (this increase being only CD) results from the high elasticity of the investment curve. (4) There would probably be a tendency for rates to rise more than the preceding analysis implies: the analysis abstracts from differences in risk on various securities, and it is probable that a substantial tax of the kind described here would cause a shift of funds from bonds, with their low after-tax yields, to equities. Since it is widely held that tax policy should encourage venture capital, this change might be desirable. Indeed, this procedure, if feasible, might achieve some of the purposes now sought by giving tax-status privileges to capital gains. (5) The reduced income of the provident aged might justify further increases in social security. No new difficulties would face charitable and educational institutions so long as their tax exemption was continued.

It is clear that any tax of the kind described here represents a distortion in the operation of a price system to the extent that the saving curve exhibits elasticity; perfect inelasticity would make the payment of interest a rent and hence would indicate no distortive consequences from such a tax except those (desirable ones) on the distribution of income. So long as taxation of "pure interest" is not virtually confiscatory, and so long as one believes that saving curves are highly inelastic, one need not presume that proposals of this kind must weaken the values commonly attributed to free enterprise. This analysis suggests, however, that the case against taxes that favor interest income may be much stronger than the argument for taxes that discriminate against interest income: the value judgments described earlier would tend to favor taxation of such income, and the price-system arguments tend to favor no discrimination in either direction.

3. Should interest rates be determined on free markets?

The theory of interest as we have developed it thus far seems to suggest that consumer sovereignty will be most fully effected if interest rates are set by market forces, for then saving is determined by time preference and costs for "waiting" are charged against goods on the basis determined by time preference. Two qualifications need to be examined, however. The less important one arises from the fact that time preference is partly determined by myopia. If we believe that this fact results in substantial undersaving in relation to the ideal, we may choose to follow the calculated time preference of society operating through the government, as we do in much of the legislation for conservation of natural resources. If we wish to extend this principle, we might either subsidize saving or provide for socialized saving to supplement private saving by way of extensive public works. The pros and cons of the second proposal are too familiar and extensive to enter into here, but they are of course centered upon the question of the appropriate scope of government investment activity. The disadvantage of the subsidized saving is that it goes directly in the opposite direction from that suggested by the ethical considerations discussed above.

A more important objection to market determination of interest rates is raised by a problem from which Fisher's theory of interest abstracts.

Fisher assumed by implication stable full employment without inflation, but there is, in fact, abundant theoretical and empirical evidence that *laissez faire* free enterprise results in substantial economic instability. This fact bears on the question at hand in at least two ways. In the first place, it means that the decision of persons to save is not necessarily associated with realized saving, but may result instead in underemployment and lower income. To this extent it is not true that "consumer sovereignty" is made effective by permitting people to "try to save" whatever they wish. Second, the methods now followed by our monetary authorities in an attempt to prevent unemployment or inflation seek their effectiveness through means which inevitably result in rates other than those that would be established in free markets.

4. Is there a role for interest under socialism?

Schumpeter has asserted that ". . . *in a communistic or nonexchange society in general there would be no interest as an independent value phenomenon. . . .* The agent for which interest is paid simply would not exist in a communist economy. Hence it could not be the object of a valuation. And consequently there could not be a net return corresponding to the interest form of income." [9] This is true, he says, in a very fundamental way. Wages and rent, like interest, would not be *paid*. But wages and rent would still be an economic category to be valued and reckoned in the economic plan. "Nothing of this holds good for interest." [10]

Schumpeter reaches this conclusion because of his fundamental definition of interest as the payment made by entrepreneurs to capitalists. I have already referred to his statement that the "main part of the task" of explaining interest is not to explain the profits from which interest is a deduction, but rather to explain why this deduction is made. The answer is that "it is only because other people have command of the necessary producers' goods that entrepreneurs must call in the capitalist. . . . Here, then, the function of capital comes in, and it becomes evident that nothing corresponding to it can exist . . . in a communist . . . society." [11]

I believe this analysis is seriously wrong. Its error is not in what it says, but in what it fails to say. So long as Schumpeter means by interest simply that share of entrepreneurial profits which is paid over to the capitalist, interest is of course defined away in a socialist economy. But unlike Schumpeter, I should argue that the *category* of interest as an *accounting* item is essential in the plans of a socialist economy: it needs

---

[9] Joseph A. Schumpeter, *The Theory of Economic Development* (Cambridge: Harvard University Press, 1951), p. 176.

[10] *Ibid.*

[11] *Ibid.*, 177.

very much to be included. The difference between us arises because of Schumpeter's almost total neglect of time preference in his analysis. In the United States such neglect may seem trivial. It is doubtless true that the "cost" of abstinence to the rich may be negative, and to the United States as a whole it may be negligible in either direction (positive or negative). But this is true only because we are wealthy, and because our social choices have resulted in saving small enough to allow consumption for most of us to reach a very tolerable level. However, there are underdeveloped areas in the world where poverty cannot afford abstinence except at enormous social cost — literally starvation, if there is too much. In other words, time preference means that social costs are involved in capital expansion, and no theory which neglects it is complete, whether it be for a capitalist or a socialist economy. Again the more general analysis of Fisher helps us toward insights which less complete theories cannot provide.

VII

NONMONETARY THEORIES OF INTEREST: SUMMARY AND CONCLUSIONS

A useful definition of "nonmonetary" theories of interest is that they are theories according to which the rate of interest is determined without reference to possible changes in the supply of money or in its velocity. The exclusion of reference to velocity from such theories is, of course, equivalent to the exclusion of reference to "hoarding" or to changes in the desired sizes of cash balances. In short, these theories leave the interest rate entirely outside the equation of exchange.[1] Since nonmonetary theorists have generally operated under the assumption of full employment, this threw exclusive effect of MV upon P, though it would have been assumed that economic growth was reflected in a rising T hence requiring a larger M in order to prevent price declines.

Nonmonetary theories of the rate of interest were developed by the classical economists for two major reasons. In part, these theories represented a reaction to previous theories which went to the opposite extreme and implied that interest rates were determined exclusively by changes in the quantity or rate of circulation of money. In part, they represented the classical preoccupation with "long-run" problems, together with the view that changes in the quantity of money would have only a temporary effect on the rate of interest — that after a lag, the full effect would be on prices, and interest rates would return to their former levels. However useful the classical reaction may have been in counteracting the one-sidedness of some earlier theories, it surely resulted in an equal if opposite distortion. The inadequacy of this approach lies partly in the fact that for many questions an understanding of short-run phenomena may be quite as important as an understanding of long-run relations, and partly in the fact that a modern theory of general equilibrium will suggest lasting as well as temporary effects of changes in the quantity

---

[1] I refer here to the familiar equation $MV = PT$, where M represents the quantity of money, V its velocity, P the level of prices, and T the volume of transactions. It would be equally appropriate to let V stand for income velocity, and T for real income.

of money or the desire to hoard. As a consequence nonmonetary theories provide no means for the clear analysis of some of our most pressing economic problems.

Despite the inadequacy of nonmonetary theories, an examination of them is important analytically as well as historically. In the first place, there is no complete theory of interest which does not include the variables studied in nonmonetary theory; the difference is only that other variables are added. In the second place, there are ways in which a true equilibrium must satisfy the conditions of nonmonetary equilibrium as well as the conditions more readily apparent in contemporary monetary theory. Finally, nonmonetary theories are not merely archaic notions of classical economists, but are in large measure the basic theory of several contemporary economists, including F. H. Knight and the late Irving Fisher. Especially through analyzing the recent nonmonetary theories do we gain insight into some of the most important aspects of the meaning, nature, and "necessity" of interest.

Schumpeter has well posed the dilemma which the existence of interest seemed to present to many economic theorists. The theory of perfect competition, by making the price of goods in equilibrium equal to the imputed value of the contribution of the factors producing them, would suggest that the value of final goods should precisely equal the total payments to the original factors of production. Since capital goods are intermediate products, this theory would appear to suggest that the value of the product attributable to these capital goods should exactly equal the payments made to the factors producing them. But these factors ultimately reduce to labor and land only. How, then, is there room for any flow of income to the owner of the capital goods over and above that necessary to compensate him for the invested labor and land? Yet interest exists in the real world, and its basic characteristic is precisely that it is a surplus over this original investment. How, then, can interest be explained?

Schumpeter suggests three possible escapes from this dilemma. The first would be to find a third original factor of production inherently related to capital goods, thereby explaining the return their owners receive. Early classical theorists generally tried to follow this road. Senior presented his abstinence theory explicitly as a demonstration of a third productive factor whose reward was interest (profit). Those theories labeled by Boehm-Bawerk as the "labor theories of interest" found a third factor in the labor of the capitalist himself or else in labor over which he had obtained title through the ownership of their intermediate product, capital goods. The use theories argued that use or disposal over capital somehow embodied an additional productive quality that could flow forth without diminishing the capital good from which it flowed, so that the final product acquired a value over and above that represented by the value of the capital goods themselves. All of these attempts to escape Schumpeter's dilemma by discovery of a third original factor seem to break down.

A second possible escape would be to deny the logical validity of the theory of competition. It may be that Marxian theory should be classified as one attempting to escape along this road. At least it introduces no additional factor. Only labor creates value. But labor does not receive the full value of its product, even under pure competition, because of the nature of the wage contract. The worker is exploited, part of his income going to the capitalist because the capitalist owns the land and capital goods with which labor must work in order to produce. Boehm-Bawerk has effectively demonstrated the weakness of the labor theory of value on which this theory was grounded.

A third way out of the dilemma would be to admit the logical validity but not the practical relevance of the competitive theory. Schumpeter himself chooses this course. There would be no interest, he says, in the circular flow of perfectly competitive equilibrium. At least, he argues, there would be no productive interest, and that is the crucial kind of interest in our society, not the interest on consumption loans. Competitive theory is correct enough, he says, but it simply does not describe the real world, which is inevitably and permanently one of development, not of circular flow. Productive interest exists only because of development, which provides the continuous possibility of profits on the ever-changing physical embodiments of capital. And thus a constant income is paid by the entrepreneur to the capitalist, the only one who is able to supply the wherewithal for the creation of capital goods and the exploitation of profit possibilities through innovation.

Schumpeter argues that interest exists because, given the fact of development, productive agents will receive a payment equal to the value of their product before the use of an innovation, and that the increased productivity caused by the innovation will result in a profit to the entrepreneur. But he fails to show why the innovation should not cause factor prices to be bid up until this profit disappears. Thus his theory, no less than older "productivity theories," fails to provide an adequate solution to the problem he has so well defined. In one fundamental sense, however, Schumpeter does point the correct general road out of the dilemma presented by the existence of interest: the theory of perfectly competitive equilibrium simply cannot solve the problem of interest, for it is descriptive of a circular-flow world in which time, though existing, plays no crucial role. Interest is, by its very nature, a phenomenon rooted in time. It is centrally related to the comparison of wants, not between two goods now, but between goods today and tomorrow. Competitive equilibrium theory is not constructed to solve such problems without admitting assumptions that go beyond those implied by the statement in which Schumpeter finds his dilemma. If the quantity of goods that can be produced by a given quantity of factor services depends upon the time span during which these given hours of factor service are applied, then a problem is raised with which the theory of competitive circular flow simply cannot cope.

The entire statement of Schumpeter's dilemma may seem mistaken to those who share Knight's belief in the essential difficulty of distinguishing "factors of production," together with his rejection of the concept of "original factors of production." I have indicated that in my view the difficulty of defining "original" factors does not really destroy the usefulness of posing the problem as Schumpeter has done. However, it may be interesting to note that a conclusion similar to the one I have proposed above may be reached by a route that may be much more acceptable to those who wish to emphasize the sense in which all factors are coördinate rather than that in which some are primary and others secondary.

It seems to me that the question Knight raises may be stated thus: Why should the so-called "capital goods" be remunerated in any other way than other factors, since the marginal-productivity theory can be applied uniformly to all factors, and the size of reward that each will earn is thus determined by that principle? My view would be that the marginal-productivity theory does indeed operate on all agents similarly, but that it explains only the demand for agents, whereas supply is also involved in pricing. At this point distinctions do arise among different varieties of factors.

1. Labor does not multiply to the point where the value of its return equals its cost of production (i.e., subsistence), because it makes its own decisions on the basis of maximizing elements other than the profits from its use. In this sense free labor cannot be identified with slave labor as though the two were essentially interchangeable, and in this sense free labor is not the equivalent of capital goods.

2. The distinction between "land" and capital goods is much more knotty. Yet I agree with Kaldor's argument that meaningful differences can be drawn by reference to the concept of the augmentability of the factor. Indeed, he points out that Knight's own assumption of diminishing returns to capital goods necessarily "presupposes the existence of some 'fixed factor' as their cause." [2] In rejoinder to Knight's objection that *all* resources are augmentable to a certain degree,[3] he presents his views more concisely than I could summarize them:

---

[2] Nicholas Kaldor, "Annual Survey of Economic Theory: The Recent Controversy on the Theory of Capital," *Econometrica*, 5 (1937): 218.

[3] Frank H. Knight, "On the Theory of Capital: In Reply to Mr. Kaldor," *Econometrica*, 6 (1938): 74–80.

There can be no doubt that most resources, *as defined and differenti-ated by the market,* are augmentable to a certain degree. Land can be im-proved by fertilization . . . coal available for consumption in large cities can be increased at will by sinking more shafts. . . . But all this is beside the point. Coal in the drawing room is not the same resource as coal in the earth, any more than the house is the same resource as the bricks out of which it is made. In all these cases augmentation is only possible at *increasing* cost, and it is only possible up to a point; for in all these cases production embodies an *invariable element,* which cannot be augmented at all. Analytically, at any rate, we must distinguish between hydro-elec-tric plants and mere waterfalls; and it is pertinent to inquire whether more electric power means more plants and more waterfalls or whether it merely means more plants combined with a given number of waterfalls. In the one case the stream of services can be expanded at constant cost; in the other case, at increasing cost.[4]

My own opinion is that there are some agents of production, or elements within them, which are given by nature and which cannot be produced, and that it would be entirely meaningless to state that their supply will increase until their cost of production equals the value of their yield.

3. Capital goods, finally, *can* be augmented, including the results of training workers and of fertilizing the soil. In relation to these, and to these only, it is pertinent to raise the question: Should not production take place until the cost of the agent equals the value of its service? It is in this sense that the pricing of capital goods raises a problem not raised in relation to other factors. And the answer is, as Rolph and others have emphasized, capital goods will indeed be produced up to the point where payments to agents producing them equal the *immediate* value of their output.[5] But the value of their service in this analysis is derived by dis-counting the value of a final consumers good, and thus any difference between the cost of producing a capital good and the ultimate value of consumer goods attributable to it already assumes the existence of a rate of interest. This analysis, correct though it is, does not provide the answer to Schumpeter's question. His question is — Why does not the cost of the machine exactly equal the *ultimate* value of the consumer goods attrib-utable to it? — and he refuses to accept a reply which itself already takes the rate of interest as given.[6]

I suggest that there is one reason that capital goods are not produced exclusively and indefinitely, until no more final goods can be produced

---

[4] Nicholas Kaldor, "On the Theory of Capital: A Rejoinder to Professor Knight," *Econometrica,* 6 (1938): 172–173.

[5] Earl Rolph, "The Discounted Marginal Productivity Doctrine," *Journal of Political Economy,* 47 (1939), pp. 542–556, reprinted in American Economic Association, *Read-ings in the Theory of Income Distribution* (Philadelphia: Blakiston, 1946), pp. 278–293.

[6] Joseph A. Schumpeter, *The Theory of Economic Development* (Cambridge: Harvard University Press, 1951), p. 164.

with the aid of new capital goods than can be produced without them. (It is at this point that the ultimate value of the product added by the use of capital goods would exactly equal the payments to the factors making the capital goods.) The reason is that people want final goods now. We are led directly to Fisher's analysis, with its suggestion that expansion of investment ceases when the marginal rate of return over cost in producing investment goods no longer exceeds the marginal rate of time preference. The purpose of these paragraphs has been to demonstrate that Schumpeter's dilemma may be stated without dependence on original factors — upon hypothetical ancient history — and to show that the dilemma does not rest upon an asymmetrical attitude toward the principles by which various factor prices are determined. At the same time it attempts to show that the problem, when posed in these terms, quite as much as in my previous exposition, leads toward a solution in which time preference plays a crucial role — a solution of the kind described in Fisher's theory.

Boehm-Bawerk had ably developed a similar concept before Fisher, but he had not properly (or at least not fully and clearly) applied it to the productive capacity of capital goods. Partly because of this his theory gives a crucial role to the assumption of positive time preference in the second sense of our earlier discussion (p. 58). This makes it easy for critics, interpreting him still more narrowly, mistakenly to presume that his theory depends upon myopia.

A much more serious error occurs when Fisher's emphasis on time preference leads to the view that his theory, too, depends centrally upon belief in the prevalence of shortsightedness. This identification of myopia with Fisher's time preference still haunts the literature and causes many to deny the relevance of time preference, when what they mean to deny is only the assumption that time preference would necessarily be positive under conditions of equal present and future income. It should be obvious that since interest is essentially a link between the present and the future, it cannot be understood without an analysis of the forces affecting people's relative desires for present versus future goods.

Once time preference is freed from its unholy alliance with myopia, we can understand its true determinants. Chiefly these are the character of a man's income, "as to its size, time-shape, and probability." [7] But this "character of a man's income" will itself be shaped by the decisions he makes in light of his structure of tastes, his investment opportunities, and the terms on which he can borrow or lend. Myopia, if it exists, is only one element in taste patterns. So long as capital goods are physically productive the shift of income from present to future through investment

---

[7] Irving Fisher, *The Theory of Interest* (New York: Macmillan, 1930), p. 80.

will, in the context of diminishing marginal utility of income, tend to establish a "character of income" that evokes positive time preference at the margin in Fisher's sense.

These comments on the role of time preference and productivity in Fisher's theory may be clarified by a review of the process by which equilibrium is achieved. With any given rate of interest each person can invest up to the point where the market value of his total income (present and future) is maximized regardless of whether or not he wishes to consume his income during the time periods when it would become available to him from such an investment program. Having maximized the market value of his income through investment or disinvestment, he next borrows or lends until the distribution of his present and future income provides the maximum possible satisfaction. When all individuals so act, the amount some seek to borrow may not equal that which others would lend. Fisher's analysis shows how the market rate of interest will be altered by the forces of supply and demand for these loanable funds until an equilibrium will presumably be achieved. At this point the rate of interest will be equal to both the marginal rate of return over cost in investment and the marginal rate of time preference.

Some of the implications of this theory are: (1) By equating desired lending with desired borrowing, the interest rate also equates desired saving with desired investment, and thus Fisher's theory becomes equivalent to what Keynes attacked as the "classical" theory of interest. (2) Even if the marginal efficiency of investment equals zero at zero net investment, it is technically possible to have an interest rate greater or less than zero. If it is greater than zero, however, disinvestment must be taking place, the proceeds being used to finance "impatience" (i.e., to supply consumer loans). (3) The social importance of time preference is indicated especially clearly in an undeveloped economy, where great social cost is involved in any sacrifice of current consumption. This illustrates the fact that interest is representative of a true social cost, and that an appropriate accounting charge should be made even in a socialist economy. (4) The most general economic case for interest has to do with the imposition of interest charges on those borrowing rather than with the receipt of interest by those supplying funds. The fundamental economic importance of the receipt of interest may be small if the supply curve of saving is quite inelastic (abstracting from problems of hoarding, which are introduced in Part Two below). Significant changes would be required in our present socioeconomic structure before it would be possible to tax away all pure interest receipts, and even greater changes would be involved in taxing all gross interest. Ethical arguments based on widely held value judgments can be advanced for such taxation, but a final answer would require weighing of values on which the economist qua economist cannot offer advice.

Knight's theory of interest may be clarified by translation into Fisher's terms. This theory makes the explicit assumption that the investment opportunity curve is straight and unshifting because (1) the quantity of capital at any time is so great that the current rate of investment activity cannot significantly alter its yield, and (2) the relation between the cost of investment goods and the value of their product is not affected by the rate of investment. Thus Knight's rate of interest is determined directly and fully by the slope of this opportunity curve, and time preference determines only the amount of investment that will take place.

Lerner argues that the yield of capital will depend not only upon the quantity of capital in existence, but also upon the rate at which new investment is taking place. He cannot, therefore, accept Knight's straight opportunity curve. His investment-demand curve is one showing the "marginal efficiency of investment," that is, the ratio of the annual increase of perpetual income to the sacrifice of current income through investment whereby this growth of income is generated. He suggests that this curve slopes negatively, and shifts downward over time unless prevented from doing so by innovation.

The graphical exposition of Fisher's theory has inevitable clumsiness because of its two-dimensional limitations, but it aids in visualization of relations which are more fully spelled out in Fisher's algebraic presentation. As developed there, Fisher's theory seems to be the most logically satisfactory and the most complete of the nonmonetary theories I have discussed. Theories like those of Knight and Schumpeter have the disadvantage of omitting the effects of time preference on the rate of interest, but their authors believe that for this very reason they serve better to highlight crucial variables.

The major limitation of Fisher's theory is precisely the fact that it is a nonmonetary theory of interest, and for that reason I now turn to the study of monetary theories, which can lead toward a more complete understanding of the phenomenon of interest and the determinants of the rate of interest in our society.

PART TWO

MONETARY THEORIES OF INTEREST

(Note: This key to symbols does not apply to chapter viii)

A	Real value of real assets	R	Money value of bonds
B	Balances on hand	r	Rate of interest
b	Number of bonds	S	Savings. "Gross" in the sense that depreciation reserves are included: "Net" in the sense that dissaving is deducted from saving to give S
b (subscript)	Business sector		
C	Consumption (both planned and realized)		
C_b	Consumer borrowing		
C_p	Planned consumption		
C_r	Realized consumption	S'	Gross saving of positive savers
D	Demand		
d	Notation for derivative	S_p	Planned saving
F_b	"Finance" borrowing	S_r	Realized saving
f	Functional notation	Sy	Supply
H	Hoarding (net): i.e., net increase in hoards	SI curve	Locus of combinations of r and Y that equate saving with investment
H'	Hoarding of those whose hoards increase	SI–LM curve	Locus of combinations of price and income that simultaneously equate supply with demand for money, and saving with investment
h	Household sector		
I	Investment (gross): i.e., replacement plus new investment		
I_n	New investment, or "net" investment	s (subscript)	Supply
		V	Income velocity of money
I_p	Planned investment	W	Real wages
I_r	Realized investment	We	Real value of wealth
I_{rp}	Replacement investment	$WwPp$ curve	Locus of combinations of price and income that equate real wage with marginal product of labor for assumed money wage
L	Demand for money		
L_1	Demand for transactions balances		
L_{1a}	Anticipated demand for transactions balances		
L_2	Demand for speculative balances	w	Money wage level
LF_d	Demand for loanable funds	w curve	Locus of combinations of price and real wage that correspond to a given money wage
LF_s	Supply of loanable funds		
LM curve	Locus of combinations of r and Y that equate the supply and demand for money		
		x	Quantity of goods
		Y	Real income
M	Money supply	Y_a	Anticipated (expected) income
M_1	Supply of active money		
M_2	Supply of money available for speculative balances	Y_d	Disposable income
		Y_e	Earned income
m	Functional notation for hoarding	Y_r	Realized income
		Δ	Positive change
N	Employment	ϱ	Notation for partial derivative
p	Price level		

Subscript numbers generally refer to time periods, though context will show some cases where these relate to active money (1) and to speculative money (2).

Overlining of letters refers to parameters.

MONEY RATES, OWN-RATES, AND REAL RATES OF INTEREST

BASIC CONCEPTS

Before entering upon the problems introduced by hoarding and by changes in the quantity of money, further insight concerning the nature of interest may be gained by studying the relations between the "money rate" of interest, with which we conventionally deal, and the so-called "own-rates" of interest on commodities. Keynes' analysis, which I shall follow, discusses two somewhat distinct issues in connection with these various rates. The first concerns the meaning of own-rates in relation to the rate on money, and the second examines more complex problems concerning the relation of these rates to the level of employment. Anyone wishing to move on rapidly with the main development of my analysis may either omit this entire chapter without loss of continuity, or may read the part concerning the meaning of own rates and the section on Fisher's "Real Rates of Interest" skipping over the more complex analysis which Keynes builds upon his discussion of own-rates.

Keynes describes the conceptions of money rates and own-rates concisely.

The money-rate of interest . . . is nothing more than the percentage excess of a sum of money contracted for forward delivery, e.g. a year hence, over what we may call the 'spot' or cash price of the sum thus contracted for forward delivery. It would seem therefore, that for every kind of capital-asset there must be an analogue of the rate of interest on money. For there is a definite quantity of (e.g.) wheat to be delivered a year hence which has the same exchange value today as 100 quarters of wheat for 'spot' delivery. If the former quantity is 105 quarters, we may say that the wheat-rate of interest is 5 per cent per annum; and if it is 95 quarters it is a *minus* 5 per cent per annum. Thus for every durable commodity we have a rate of interest in terms of itself.[1]

The problems immediately presented by these considerations are the following. If assets other than money "have a rate of interest," will all

---

[1] J. M. Keynes, *The General Theory of Employment, Interest and Money* (New York: Harcourt, Brace, 1936), p. 222.

such rates be equal? If not, do we err when we direct our attention almost exclusively to the money rate? Keynes states that these rates are not the same, even in equilibrium. Next, he indicates that there is one sense in which the money rate has no special significance, but that there is another sense in which the money-rate has unique qualities. I shall proceed by first examining more fully the meaning of own-rates, after which I shall test Keynes' views concerning the senses in which the money-rate is, and those in which it is not, unique.

The understanding of this problem has been greatly complicated by the inadequacy of attention given to the precise meaning of terms used in its discussion. As already indicated, the issue involved is that of relations between present and future values of assets. The most fundamental relationship underlying the entire analysis is that described in the review of Fisher's theory in chapter iv, namely, the marginal rate of return over cost. It will be remembered that this term as used by Fisher meant:

$$\frac{\text{Future income} - \text{Present income}}{\text{Present income}}$$

where the amounts of "present" and "future" income indicate the amount of future income that could be secured in return for a given amount of present income. Since this analysis is in terms of assets rather than of income, the reference here will be to the amount of an asset which could be secured at some future time in return for a given present amount. I say "amount" of an asset only provisionally, and I shall define that term in the paragraphs immediately following.

Measurement versus "Conversion"

The present study is inherently complex for several reasons, two of which are these: (a) The "amounts" of an asset just referred to may be *measured* in different ways, and (b) present assets may be converted into future assets by various *procedures*. The rate of return which we label "interest rates" is that associated with one such procedure, namely, borrowing and lending. Other procedures, which provide other types of rate of return, will be analyzed in the second part of this chapter.

For the present, then, we are concerned with various *ways of measuring* the rate of return achieved by only one procedure, namely, by lending assets. Such a return may be earned, however, for lending any of many varieties of assets, including money. Furthermore, it must be noted that buying futures in exchange for spot claims is really nothing other than lending. If I "lend" money I am selling an immediate claim to funds in return for the acquisition of a future claim. Conversely, if I borrow wheat I am merely buying a spot claim and selling a future claim. In summary, then, the problem of clarifying the relations between money rates and own-rates involves analysis of (1) the relations between different ways of measuring rates of return, and (2) the problem of relating to one another the rates of return achieved by dealing in various types of assets, including money. With respect to each of these issues the rate of interest is that rate of return which arises in connection with borrowing and lending, or its equivalent, making exchanges between spot and future claims.

METHODS OF MEASUREMENT

Two general methods of measurement may be described:

First, the amount of any asset may be measured directly in terms of itself, that is, as the quantity — pounds, bushels, square feet, or what-not — of that asset. An example of the rate of return secured by measuring amounts in this way would be the following. If a claim to 10 bushels of wheat deliverable now exchanges for a claim to 11 deliverable next year, then the marginal rate of return over cost of wheat measured in terms of wheat is simply $(11 - 10)/10 = 10$ per cent. In cases like this, where the rate of return on an asset is defined in terms of the asset itself, we shall call the rate an own-rate. If the *procedure* for acquiring this return is by lending (or transactions on the futures market), we shall call the resulting rate of return an "own-rate of interest." [2]

Second, it may be decided to measure all amounts of assets in terms of some common standard. In that event the amount of wheat at any time would be represented by the quantity of the standard asset which could be secured at that time through exchange on the market. In the previous illustration, suppose that 10 units of wheat are worth $10 today, and 11 units of wheat will be worth $12 next year. Then the marginal rate of return over cost for wheat, when measured in dollars as the standard of value, is $(12 - 10)/10 = 20$ per cent. In sum, it is possible to measure the rates of return on assets in terms of themselves *or* in terms of some other asset selected as a standard of measure; the most common such measure, of course, is money.

I have referred above to the present amounts and future amounts of assets. It seems more general, and therefore more appropriate, to use the term "value" instead of "amount." The term "amount" would appear to be truly appropriate only when the good is measured in terms of itself, whereas "value" may apply to any standard of measure. It is important, however, to avoid two possible misinterpretations of this term. (1) By using the word "value" we do not necessarily mean dollar value, and we

---

[2] This is the terminology used by A. P. Lerner, "Essential Properties of Interest and Money," *Quarterly Journal of Economics*, 66 (1952), 172–193. I agree with Lerner that this is the most appropriate use of the term "own-rate." In my view this is also Keynes' intended use of the term, though Lerner believes otherwise. (See p. 129, n. 8, for further comment.) This article by Lerner is exceedingly valuable, and I owe much of the basic thought that enters this chapter to Lerner's analysis.

do include, as one possible kind of value, the value in terms of itself, or the quantity, of the asset. (2) When we contrast present value and future value, we are contrasting present quantities of the good (or equivalent quantities of the standard) with corresponding quantities to be delivered at a future date. In other words we must note carefully that "future value" does *not* mean the present value of a claim to future assets, but refers rather to what that claim entitles its holder to receive at a future time.

TRANSFORMATION OF OWN-RATES INTO RATES IN TERMS OF A COMMON STANDARD

It is useful for some purposes to be able to transform rates of return that are given in "own" terms into rates of return as expressed in terms of some common standard of measure. Keynes suggests that this may be done by adding to the own-rate an adjustment factor which he designates by the letter a.[3] He states that this adjustment factor shows simply the "expected percentage appreciation" of the asset in terms of the standard, but it would appear that proper calculation of a is more complex than this, its value being derived as follows.

Since values in "own" terms are really just quantities of the asset being studied, I shall represent them by the letter Q. I shall let P stand for the price of the asset in terms of the standard asset. Subscripts 1 and 2 represent "this year" and "next year" respectively. My aim is to find the adjustment factor a which represents the difference between the rate of return by the common standard and the own-rate of return. In terms of the symbols just defined, we may write:

$$\text{Own-rate of return} = \frac{Q_2 - Q_1}{Q_1}.$$

$$\text{Rate of return by common standard} = \frac{P_2 Q_2 - P_1 Q_1}{P_1 Q_1},$$

$$\therefore a = \frac{P_2 Q_2 - P_1 Q_1}{P_1 Q_1} - \frac{Q_2 - Q_1}{Q_1} = \frac{P_2 Q_2 - P_1 Q_1 - (P_1 Q_2 - P_1 Q_1)}{P_1 Q_1}$$

$$= \frac{P_2 Q_2 - P_1 Q_2}{P_1 Q_1} = \left(\frac{P_2 - P_1}{P_1}\right)\left(\frac{Q_2}{Q_1}\right).$$

This computation[4] shows that the adjustment factor is the product of the expected proportionate appreciation of the asset price in terms of the

---

[3] *Ibid.*, p. 227. I shall show later in this chapter that Fisher's "real rates" are identical with money rates in terms of the standard of real goods. His mathematical analysis therefore provides a solution to the problem described here. See his *Appreciation and Interest* (American Economic Association, Third Series, Vol. XI, No. 4, Aug., 1896), pp. 331–342; also, *The Rate of Interest* (New York: Macmillan, 1907), appendix to chapter v, pp. 356–374.

[4] The logic of this derivation may be explained as follows. (1) Our objective is first to measure the value of the price change resulting from the changed value of the good

standard multiplied by the ratio of the future to the present quantity of the asset in question. The use of the factor a may be illustrated in relation to the previous example, where the own-rate of return on wheat was 10 per cent. The initial price of wheat in that example was $1 per unit, and the price in the second years was $12/11. Given these data, our adjustment factor may be calculated as follows:

$$a = \left(\frac{P_2 - P_1}{P_1}\right)\left(\frac{Q_2}{Q_1}\right) = \frac{(12/11) - 1}{1} \cdot \frac{11}{10} = 10 \text{ per cent.}$$

We may, therefore, transform the own-rate on wheat (10 per cent) into the rate in terms of money by adding the adjustment factor 10 per cent, giving 20 per cent as the solution, which is the same as the result derived by direct calculation.

RATES OF INTEREST ON MONEY AND ON GOODS BY VARIOUS STANDARDS

Equilibrium Relationships

It is clear from the definitions given at the start of this chapter that all assets, not just money, may be said to have a rate of interest. The first question, then, is whether these assets all have *the same* rate of interest at any given time. Keynes states that rates on different assets vary greatly even in equilibrium, and he illustrates this view by hypothetical illustrations. I believe that his terminology is unfortunate, and that a more complete vocabulary permits more complex but less misleading statements which may give a different impression from that of Keynes. Table 3 presents my hypothetical relationships.

In this table it is presumed that amounts of each good supplied, both this year and next year, are fully determined, as well as the demand, and that the resulting price changes are those shown in columns 5 and 6. The underlying assumption might be, for example, that weather predictions make it inevitable that food output will be far less next year than this year, and that storage costs are equal to 20 per cent of any food stored. The demand for food next year makes it profitable to store it despite this cost, and so 100 units of food now will exchange on the market for a promise of 80 next year. Clothing production is taking place so rapidly, on the other hand, that next year's market will be very amply supplied,

---

in terms of the standard, and then to express this value as a percentage of the original value of the good. (2) The value of the price change per unit will be equal to the proportion by which the price has changed, multiplied by the original price. The total value of the price change will, therefore, be equal to the proportionate price change times the original price times the final quantity of the good. This equals $[(P_2 - P_1)/P_1] \cdot P_1 \cdot Q_2$. (3) In order to express this value as a proportion of the original value, we must divide it by that original value, which $= P_1 Q_1$. This gives the result derived algebraically above, $a = [(P_2 - P_1)/P_1] \cdot (Q_2/Q_1)$.

TABLE 3

A. QUANTITY AND PRICE RELATIONS ON SPOT AND FUTURES MARKETS

1	2	3	4	5	6	7	8
Time	Quantity equivalents			Implied money prices		Percentage increase in price	
	Money	Food	Clothing	Food	Clothing	Food	Clothing
This year	100	100	100	$1.00	$1.00	+30%	−20%
Next year	104	80	130	1.30	.80		

B. IMPLIED INTEREST RATES FOR INTERVENING YEAR

9	10	11
Money rate in terms of money	Food rate in terms of food	Clothing rate in terms of clothing
+4%	−20%	+30%

and therefore a promise of 130 units next year will exchange for only 100 now. We assume that the interest rate on money is 4 per cent (for reasons not yet known), so that $100 now will exchange for a promise of $104 next year.

Since we have presumed that there is a market for futures in commodities as well as in money, "arbitrage" will force present and future prices into some consistent relationship with each other. The fact that the situation described in the table represents such a market equilibrium may be demonstrated as follows. If a person invests $100 today on the money market, the $104 he receives next year will buy him only 80 units of food at the then-price of $1.30 (80 × $1.30 = $104). But that is precisely what he would secure by using his $100 today to buy futures on food, as shown by column 3. Similarly his $104 next year could buy him 130 units of clothing at a price of 80¢, and that is precisely the amount of clothing he could obtain in return for 100 units of clothing today on the futures market (column 4).

Any price relations other than those just described would cause "arbitrage" and would therefore be disequilibrium prices. The characteristics of this kind of "arbitrage" must be carefully noted, however. Suppose that the clothing futures market provides 140 units instead of 130 for 100 now, and that other relations are as shown. Persons could then borrow 100 food units for a promise to pay 80 next year, buy 100 clothing units now with the food so borrowed, exchange for 140 clothing futures, wait a year, exchange 130 of their clothing units for the 80 food units required to repay their debt, and profit to the extent of 10 clothing units (abstracting from costs of effecting the transactions involved). The crucial facts illustrated by this description of the "arbitrage" process are these. (1) The term "arbitrage" must be quoted, for a true arbitrage would be represented here only if future price relationships are given with absolute certainty. Otherwise the "arbitrager" runs the risk that his 140 clothing units will not sell for more than 80 food units next year. (2) No storage of any good was required by the process of "arbitrage" here described. (3) Partly because of "2" the process can go in either direction, and equilibrium requires complete consistency of price relations of the kind we have described.

Consider now the question of what rate of interest is implied by the data provided above. If one observed only the money column (2), he would say that the interest rate implied is 4 per cent. If he looked only at the food column (3), however, he would say that the interest rate is −20 per cent, and if he looked only at the clothing column he would say it is +30 per cent. The question with which we opened this discussion is immediately raised: why should we say that the rate of interest is 4 per cent any more than to say it is −20 per cent or +30 per cent? Furthermore, if we assume that one will invest until the marginal efficiency of investment is no longer above the rate of interest, why is the money rate the one by which we should be guided?

In dealing with these questions the first point to note is that in the most fundamental sense this illustration does *not* reveal three rates of interest, but rather three ways of describing a single rate of interest.[5] So far as the rate of exchange between present and future is concerned here, *the issue is not what one borrows or lends, but rather by what measuring stick one evaluates the result of borrowing or lending.* Thus if I measure initial and final quantities in terms of money, I shall find that the investment of $100 yields me the same return in money values ($104) whether I buy food futures, clothing futures, or securities, selling either asset at year's end. This fundamental equality of all rates *when measured in the same units* is precisely the relationship which the possibility of arbitrage made a necessary condition of equilibrium.

If, now, we measure the rate of return in terms of food, we shall secure a different value from the one obtained by measurement in terms of money. But once again we shall find that consistent use of the food yardstick gives equal results as between the different assets whose interest rate is being measured. Column 3 shows us directly that the rate on food in terms of food is −20 per cent. Suppose we decided instead to invest in clothing. Our original 100 units of food will buy 100 units of clothing.

---

[5] This is a major point contributed by Lerner, "Essential Properties of Interest and Money."

This can then be exchanged for 130 units of clothing futures. This clothing will sell for $104 next year, which will buy 80 units of food, representing a 20 per cent decline in food quantity at the then-price of $1.30. Thus we see that investment in clothing yields the same −20 per cent as investment in food so long as we measure each in terms of food.

Examples could be multiplied, but the conclusion is already clear. If markets are in equilibrium, then the rates of interest on different commodities will be identical with one another when measured in terms of any single standard; but the set of equal rates found by use of any one standard will not be the same as the corresponding set of equal rates found by another standard. In the illustration, the money rate, the food rate, and the clothing rate are all 4 per cent if measured in money; they are all −20 per cent if measured in food; and they are all +30 per cent if measured in clothing. So long as we assume that "arbitrage" is permitted to establish market equilibrium, as it will quickly do, each of the columns in part B of the table could be given any one of three equally appropriate titles. The first could be "money rate," "food rate," or "clothing rate" so long as each is written in terms of money. Corresponding titles could be submitted for the other two columns. Thus the difference in own-rates, which will normally exist even in full equilibrium, does not represent fundamentally different rates on the different assets, but arises instead from the fact that these rates are all measured in different standards one from another.

In the light of these observations I may rephrase my previous questions (p. 125) to read, "Why is it more appropriate to quote interest rates in terms of money than in terms of commodities?" Or again, "In determining the equilibrium level of investment, why should we be concerned with interest rates quoted in terms of money instead of those quoted in terms of food or clothing?" Once the question is phrased in this way the answer becomes obvious. One measuring rod is *not* more "right" than any other so long as measuring rods are not changed in the middle of the problem. The money rod is more convenient for a number of reasons, including the fact that we are accustomed to using it for other value measures. But it is not more correct. Moreover, if we are trying to decide whether to invest further in the production of some third good, X, and if we assume that table 3 describes ultimate equilibrium values for the items shown there, then we may legitimately say that investment should take place up to the point where its marginal efficiency equals −20 per cent in food, or to the point where it equals +30 per cent in clothing. This means simply that if current income equal in value to 100 units of food is invested in X, then the resulting X a year hence, together with its net yield, must be worth at least 80 units of food to justify the investment. Alternatively one could say that current investment in X of value equal to 100 units of clothing must yield enough by next year to exchange for at least 130 units of clothing or the investment should not have been undertaken. As the table shows, the meaning of these two statements is precisely the same as to say that the return from $100 invested in X must next year be worth $104 in order to make the investment profitable.

The major conclusions of this section may now be summarized. (1) With given and uniform expectations the rates of interest on different commodities are identical in equilibrium, provided only that they be measured by the same standard. (2) Differences in own-rates may well exist, even in equilibrium, but these differences arise, not because the rate on X differs from the rate on Y, but only from the fact that own-rates measure the rate on X *by one standard* (i.e., relative to X) and the rate on Y *by another standard* (i.e., relative to Y). (3) It therefore follows that under the circumstances described here, as Keynes himself says, ". . . the money rate of interest has no uniqueness compared with other rates of interest, but is on precisely the same footing."[6] (4) Likewise, as Keynes again agrees, one rate of interest is no better than another for measuring the marginal efficiency of investment (called "capital" by him). "Now each of these commodity standards offers us the same facility as money for measuring the marginal efficiency of capital."[7] (5) It is important to note these essential ways in which Keynes agrees that money rates are not unique, for in discussing rates of return other than interest we will find major ways in which he believed that money rates do have a significance not attributable to other rates.

Disequilibrium Relationships

It has been indicated above that one consequence of the possibility of "arbitrage" is to force upon the market a kind of internal consistency within the structure of present prices, expected future prices, and rates of interest. This consistency is one which assures that an individual will expect to gain the same total amount of X next year whether he buys futures now in exchange for his present stock or, instead, sells that stock, lends the proceeds for a year, and then spends principal and interest to buy X at the end of the time. Furthermore, the kind of equilibrium that assures this outcome is one that will normally be very closely approximated wherever future markets exist, because frictions in these markets are small and "arbitragers" are always active. In these comments I abstract from problems raised by diversity of expectations.

Despite this close approximation to equilibrium which may normally be assumed on the futures markets, it is useful to note the relations among various kinds of interest rates which may exist in a time of *dis*equilibrium.

---

[6] J. M. Keynes, *The General Theory* . . . , p. 225.
[7] *Ibid.*, p. 224.

For this purpose let us suppose that table 4 describes present and expected prices, together with the ruling exchange ratios between spot and future quantities of money and clothing. The only difference between this table and table 3 is that I assume the clothing futures market and the money futures market are now out of touch with each other, so that, with the price expectations shown, they are inconsistent with one another.

TABLE 4

QUANTITY AND PRICE RELATIONS ON SPOT AND FUTURES MARKETS

1	2	3	4	5	6
Time	Quantity equivalents		Assumed money price of clothing	Rate of return on clothing	
	Money	Clothing		In terms of clothing	In terms of money
This year	100	100	$1.00	...	...
Next year	104	180	.80	$\dfrac{180 - 100}{100}$ $= 80\%$	$\dfrac{(180 \times .80) - 100}{100}$ $= 44\%$

The first comment that may be made about this disequilibrium model is that the rate on clothing no longer equals the rate on money even when both are measured in the same standard. Indeed, four statements of the rate of interest may now be distinguished:

1. The rate of interest on clothing in terms of clothing is 80 per cent (column 5).

2. The rate of interest on money in terms of money is 4 per cent (analogous to statement 1: column 1).

3. The rate of interest on clothing in terms of money is 44 per cent (column 6).

4. The rate of interest on money in terms of clothing is 30 per cent. [(104/.80) − 100 ÷ 100].

The logic of statement 3 is that one can earn 44 per cent in money value if he buys clothing, lends it (i.e., sells spot for futures) and sells the clothing when it is delivered to him at the end of the year. This figure represents the interest rate *on clothing* because it is clothing that is loaned. It is 44 per cent in *terms of money* because $100 buys him 100 units of clothing, which he trades for a promise of 180 next year, knowing that the latter can be sold at 80¢ per unit, returning him $144 and yielding him $44 gain on the $100 investment. The logic of statement 4 is similar. One can earn 30 per cent in clothing by a process of lending money (hence it is the interest rate on money, in terms of clothing). By selling 100 clothing units and investing the proceeds one obtains $104 next year, which can then be used to buy 130 units of clothing at the then-price of 80¢, providing a gain of 30 units on the 100.

The second comment that may be made about table 4 is that market forces will obviously operate to end the disequilibrium. The highest rate of return is 80 per cent, available to those who buy clothing futures. The lowest, 4 per cent, is paid to those who lend money. If the only information available were that given in this table shifts in prices should be expected all along the line, but since I have introduced the hypothesis that the money rate is already at equilibrium and that the 80¢ future price of clothing is an appropriate expectation, the equilibrating process will take place through changes in the futures market for clothing. The great demand there will cause sellers of futures to offer less and less for a present unit until the rate of exchange becomes 130 future for 100 present, at which time the equilibrium illustrated in table 3 will have been reëstablished. With this exchange ratio of future to spot clothing the four interest rates described above have merged into two. Both the interest on clothing and that on money are 30 per cent if measured in terms of clothing (statement 1, derived in column 5, becomes equal to statement 4), and both are 4 per cent if measured in terms of money (statement 3 becomes equal to statement 2).

Conclusions from this brief exploration are as follows. The four concepts of interest are distinct, and the values may even be different in disequilibrium. But this variety of disequilibrium will be minor in extent and brief in duration so long as markets are fairly well integrated and "arbitragers" are active. In a world of uniform and confident expectations it will generally be true that there is at any one time a single rate of interest observable on any commodities that enter into trading in futures, though the quantitative expression for this rate will vary according to the standard of measure used for its evaluation.[8]

---

[8] Only with the background of this analysis is it possible to comment on a minor difference with Lerner referred to earlier. Lerner argues that Keynes meant by "own-rates" the rate on money in terms of other goods. I believe that he meant precisely what both Lerner and I mean, the rate on a good in terms of itself. Lerner's interpretation of Keynes is based on a passage in *The General Theory* (p. 223) in which Keynes manipulates a table similar to our table 3 where equilibrium on the futures market is already assumed, and where for this reason the rate on money in terms of wheat is the same as the rate on wheat in terms of wheat. Part of this Keynesian explanation of the meaning of "own-rate" is based on an operation in which money is loaned, and the returns are measured in wheat, giving basis for Lerner's interpretation. On the other hand, part of the same illustration assumes the lending of wheat, supporting my view. Since the two are here equal, it would seem to me impossible to deduce Keynes' definition from this example. In other references, however, Keynes seems clearly to support my view. (1) On page 227 he speaks of "the own-rate of houses, wheat, and money *in terms of themselves*" (italics mine). (2) On page 226 Keynes specifically says ". . . $q - c + l$ is the own-rate of interest of any commodity, where q, c, and l are measured in terms of itself as the standard." Here he makes his typical confusion between MEH and rates of interest (see p. 136, n. 13), but the "own" relationship seems to be very clearly stated.

This section really completes the analysis of relations between own-rates and rates in terms of money or other common standards of measure. By showing the strong tendency toward equality between own-rates on money and rates on other assets in terms of money, it demonstrates that the convenience of referring in future chapters to the money rate of interest without discussion of other rates is permissible. In order to follow the subsequent analysis of the theory of interest it is not essential to read the remaining parts of this chapter. Furthermore, those who wish may turn to the discussion of Fisher's "Real Rate of Interest" (p. 140) without covering the intervening sections. Keynes' discussion of own-rates, however, led him much farther than we have thus far gone into the implications of money in our economy. His analysis is intimately related to the theory of interest and the problem of underemployment. The insights it offers seem worthy of the time required to gain them. In order to follow his argument, however, it is necessary to examine further the equilibrium relations between MEH, MEI, and r. To these relations we now turn.

RATES OF RETURN OTHER THAN
THE RATE OF INTEREST

Keynes' Attribution of Special Importance
to the Money Rate

Table 3 and the accompanying discussion explained and supported Keynes' assertion that ". . . the money rate of interest has no uniqueness compared with other rates of interest, but is on precisely the same footing." [9] The following sections will attempt to explain, and to reconcile with this statement, Keynes' apparently conflicting view to the effect that the money rate has "predominating practical importance," and that "the volume of output and employment [are] more intimately bound up with the money rate of interest than with the wheat rate of interest or the house rate of interest." [10]

In analyzing this paradoxical position it must first be recognized that so long as equilibrium exists between various futures markets (as I shall assume it does in this analysis) there is only one rate of interest, not many.[11] Therefore Keynes' assertion that the money rate has unique qualities must be transformed into the statement that there is something unique about the rate of interest *when measured in terms of money*. But this way of putting his statement strongly suggests that the "uniqueness" cannot have very profound qualities. To say that distances measured in

---

[9] *Ibid.*, p. 225.

[10] These quotations are taken from questions, but the questions are so worded as to imply clearly that the inference given above is legitimate. See *ibid.*, p. 225.

[11] As described in the closing page of this chapter, this generalization does not apply to the different "rates of interest" yielded by securities of different term or risk. That problem is examined in Part Three of this book.

feet have a uniqueness not possessed by distances measured in meters suggests a kind of triviality to this uniqueness. The unique character of the money measure is that in that measure interest rates tend to be much more stable than rates measured in terms of other standards. This adds to the convenience of the money measure, but it does little more than that.

If this conclusion were the only valid element in Keynes' analysis the discussion could be dropped at this point. However, in his effort to show unique qualities attributable to the money rate Keynes has brought out a number of interesting characteristics of money that may present special problems for any money economy. In order to understand and evaluate his argument, I must first introduce a number of concepts not previously discussed in this book.

Alternative Procedures for Transforming Present into Future Claims

In the introduction to this chapter it was pointed out that one reason for the complexity of the issues here discussed is the fact that different procedures may be followed for converting present assets into future assets. The procedure thus far discussed is the one in which a rate of interest occurs — borrowing and lending, or its equivalent, exchange between spot and future claims to assets through transactions on the futures market. There are, however, three other procedures by which one may transform present into future assets. The study of these three additional methods is directly relevant to the study of interest rates because the ratio between the present values of present and future claims (which directly determines the rate of interest) is obviously influenced by all the elements affecting expectations concerning supply and demand in the future, and by all elements affecting actual present supply and demand. An important element affecting both present and future supplies and demands will be the degree to which people employ any or all of the different methods of converting present into future assets.

Finally, the study of converting assets from present to future is important not only because of its influence on interest rates, but also because it reveals some of the peculiar characteristics of money which, in Keynes' view, increase the danger that a money economy may find the maintenance of full employment especially difficult.

As one would expect, the rate of return provided by any procedure of transforming present into future assets will equal that of any other if the economy is in equilibrium and if both procedures are actually being applied. Despite this equality, the procedures are entirely distinct, and hence a different name has been devised for each rate of return according to the procedure involved (except for one such procedure which we shall find to be essentially identical to another, making a separate label redundant).

One method of converting present into future claims (other than lending) is merely to hold the assets, either in storage or in use. When this procedure is employed the marginal rate of return over cost is called *the marginal efficiency of holding assets* (MEH). There are a number of reasons for the fact that 100 units of an asset held from now until next year will not make available to the holder precisely 100 units of the asset next year. Some considerations tend to make next year's equivalent quantity greater, some to make it less. Keynes has classified these consequences of holding an asset in three categories. In the first place, the asset may provide a *yield,* as a house provides shelter and a machine assists in production. In the second, there may be *costs,* such as storage and wastage. Finally, the holder will benefit during the period to the degree that the power of disposal over the asset provides him with an element of *liquidity.* Thus the person who elects to hold an asset may have at the end of a year a slightly smaller amount of the asset itself because there was wastage or necessity of paying part of it as a cost of storage, but he may also have received benefits equivalent in value to several units of this asset resulting from its provision of yield and liquidity. It may be noted in passing that because the benefits and costs may not be quantities of the good being held, a problem of evaluation arises even when the MEH is measured in terms of the good itself, to the extent that these benefits must be measured by the equivalent quantity of the good involved.

It will be convenient to recognize the identity of two alternative ways to express the marginal rate of return over cost for holding assets. The first is simple and direct as derived from Fisher's approach:

$$\text{MEH} = \frac{\text{Future value} - \text{Present value}}{\text{Present value}},$$

where conversion is achieved through holding the present asset, and where the future value is considered to rest not only on what will then remain of the present asset, but also on the yield from its use and the benefit from the liquidity it will have offered, minus storage cost.

The second alternative way of expressing MEH may be derived directly from analysis of the first. I have shown that the future asset value is equal to the present value, plus yield, minus carrying cost and wastage, plus liquidity premium. The numerator, therefore, reduces simply to the last three of these terms. If we let q represent the ratio of yield to present value, and let c represent carrying cost and wastage as a proportion of present value, and let l represent the liquidity premium as a percentage of present value, then the preceding expression reduces to: MEH $= q - c + l$. This last expression is the one which Keynes uses to describe the marginal efficiency of holding assets. However, Keynes also speaks of this same expression as if it defined the rate of interest on assets measured in terms of themselves. As Lerner has pointed out[12] Keynes makes the mistake, when he does this, of identifying two expressions which are actually equal only under some equilibrium conditions, but which are conceptually not identical, and which will not even be equal under all equilibrium situations.

I shall speak of the "own-MEH" of an asset when both present and future values are measured in terms of the asset itself, and of the "MEH in terms of money" when the measure of both present and future assets is in terms of money. As indicated earlier, it would be equally possible to measure in terms of any asset, but we shall have use for only these two standards.

THE PRODUCTION OF ASSETS

Another way of converting present into future goods (other than lending or holding) is to produce (and hold) assets. This procedure is called the *marginal efficiency of investing in assets* (MEI). It introduces still one more problem of evaluation. When we speak of the marginal efficiency of investing in an asset (let us say X), then the future value consists not only of X, but, as in MEH, it includes also the value, in terms of X, of q, $- c$, and l. In MEI, however, even the present value does not represent an initial stock of X, as it does in the measure of MEH. Rather it represents the value, in terms of X, of the cost elements going into the production of X. To represent the elements in MEI, when expressed as a ratio in terms of itself, I shall use the same symbols as in MEH except that I shall add a prime to them. Thus: MEI $= q' - c' + l'$ when expressed in terms of the asset being measured. Using the Fisherian expression, MEI still equals (Future value $-$ Present value)/Present value, with the assumption in this case, however, that the conversion is via producing (and holding) the asset, and that present value represents cost of production.

I shall speak of the "own-MEI" of an asset when both present and future values are measured in terms of the asset itself, and of the "MEI in terms of money" when the measure of both present and future values is in terms of money.

---

[12] See Keynes, *The General Theory* . . . , p. 227, and Lerner, "Essential Properties of Interest and Money," p. 181.

EXCHANGE AND PURCHASE OF FUTURES COMBINED

A fourth method of converting present into future assets is to exchange them for some second asset, sell that in exchange for the purchase of a future in it, await the future date, and then exchange again for the same kind of asset originally held. This is a method which we shall have occasion to study shortly, but we shall not give its rate of return a special title, for a system which included the first three methods applied to all assets would have already included this one. In other words, the result of converting X to Y, holding Y, and then converting back to X would give the same rate of return over cost as would be obtained by finding the MEH of Y and then measuring it in terms of X. Since this procedure (in the "opposite direction") was covered under "The Storage of Assets," the assignment to it of an additional title now would be redundant.

RECAPITULATION OF BASIC CONCEPTS

For purposes of convenience in future reference I shall now review briefly the major relations described in the chapter thus far.

1. The effective conversion of present into future assets may be achieved by various means. Three of these are so important that the marginal rate of return secured by each method is given a distinctive title, as follows:

a) *The rate of interest* (r) is the name given to the rate of return for conversion by borrowing and lending or for transactions on the spot-futures market, these expressions being, in fact, nothing more than two ways of describing a single type of procedure.

b) *The marginal efficiency of holding assets* (MEH) is the name given to the rate of return for conversion by holding present assets, either through use or storage. This return includes not only the value of the original asset which may remain, but also the value of the yield and the liquidity benefit minus storage costs, obsolescence, and wastage.

c) *The marginal efficiency of investing in assets* (MEI) is the name given to the rate of return for conversion by *producing* (and holding) assets. The return is calculated as in b above, but the base on which the rate is calculated (the present value) is in this case the cost of producing the asset.

2. A fourth means of converting present into future assets will be examined, but its return is not given a special name because it proves to be nothing other than MEH applied to some other asset and measured in terms of this one. This method consists of selling the present asset in exchange for another, holding the latter, and reconverting later to the original form of asset.

3. The rate of return achieved by any of these methods may be measured by different standards. It may be measured in terms of the asset whose return is being studied, in which case the return is called an "own-rate," or it may be measured in terms of any other asset chosen as a common standard for purposes of comparing rates of return on different assets. The most common of these standards is, of course, money, and the return in terms of money will be called the "money-rate."

4. Fisher's expression for the marginal rate of return over cost provides a formula which may be employed for the measure of rates of return by all three methods and by each type of measure. The expression is (Future value — Present value)/Present value. To secure any desired type of rate of return (e.g., r, MEH, or MEI) one simply employs in this formula the future value that could be acquired by that particular method of conversion. To secure a measure by any desired standard of measure, one need only be sure to measure both present and future values in those terms. When own-rates are desired, therefore, these values appear as quantities of the asset whose return is being studied, and it is in this form that they appeared in our earlier discussion of Fisher's theory, for he was there examining the own-rate on money.

5. An alternative formula for deriving rates of return wherever assets are held, as in MEH and MEI, is revealing and useful for some purposes. This method utilizes the following symbols:

q = the yield of any asset as a proportion of initial value.
c = the carrying cost of any asset as a proportion of intitial value.
l = the "liquidity premium" of any asset as a proportion of initial value.
a = an adjustment factor (to be used additively) for converting own-rates into rates measured by some other standard. The value of a depends partly upon the rate at which the value of the asset being measured changes relative to that of the standard in which the new measure is sought: $a = [(P_2 - P_1)/P_1]\ (Q_2/Q_1)$ as shown on pp. 122–123.

6. Own-rates may be derived by use of the above symbols as follows:

MEH $= q - c + l$, where the base used is the present market value of the asset.
MEI $= q' - c' + l'$, where the prime indicates that the base is the cost of producing the asset.

7. Rates on the basis of a common standard are derived by simply adding a to the own-rate.

8. Equilibrium and disequilibrium relationships will be developed in the following discussion.

EQUILIBRIUM RELATIONS BETWEEN
INTEREST RATES AND OTHER
RATES OF RETURN

Interest Rates and the Marginal Efficiency of
Holding Assets

As in the discussion of relations between spot and futures markets, I shall examine relations between MEH and r by asking about the nature of equilibrium and the degree to which it is likely to be approximated in the market. A somewhat longer lag may be expected here than within the structure of spot and future markets, for storage plans may involve greater complications, but the lag should not be great, and relations close to those of equilibrium should normally be realized. It may be this fact that led Keynes erroneously to identify the rate of return on holding assets and the rate of interest on them (see p. 129, n. 8). But the error is made especially important because *even equilibrium may not involve equal rates*. An explanation of this follows.

The principle upon which equilibrium is based is that whenever the rate of return is higher by conversion from present to future by one channel than by another, persons will expand the profitable process and contract the less profitable one until rates of return are equal. Now it is always possible, when rates of return for holding are higher than those for buying futures, to sell futures, buy spot, and hold. The converse, however, does not follow. When the rate of return on the futures market is higher than the rate for storing, then storing will, of course, be reduced. But the time may well come when storing is reduced to zero and the yield on the futures market is still the higher of the two. An equilibrium will be established with zero holding and with unequal rates of return for the two procedures of converting present to future assets. The theoretical principle here is a simple one: if any procedure cannot be carried on in negative amounts, then its rate may be lower even in equilibrium than the alternative rate, since the only operations that could restore equality are impossible. Futures transactions can operate in either direction (purchase or sale) but holding is estopped at zero in the downward direction.

In our example (see p. 123) the rate of return on holding food is exactly equal to the rate of return on the futures market, for conditions are such that it pays to undertake some holding. In the clothing industry, however, it is clear that simple holding of present clothing will not take place, for the price will be lower next year than now, and storage costs will undoubtedly be greater than any yield or liquidity premium for holding clothing. For clothing, $q - c + l$ is presumably far less than the rate of interest in terms of clothing.

Lerner states that this kind of situation represents an extreme case, and he therefore abstracts from it, assuming that in equilibrium MEH will equal r. Assuming that one regards the employment of working inventories as storing or holding assets, his position seems convincing: the inventories provide a yield q, and in equilibrium the size of these holdings would be such as to equate MEH (including q) with r at the margin. On the other hand, if we abstract from inventories used in the normal process of business, I should expect that the own-rate on many commodities would often be greater than MEH, and no storing could be said to take place.

Interest Rates and the Marginal Efficiency
of Investing

Next I turn to the equilibrium condition in relation to investment activity, specific reference in this case being to the relation between r and MEI. Here again asymmetry may occur, this time because of the impossibility of negative gross investment. It would be entirely possible for the marginal efficiency of investing in every asset to be less than the rate of interest, each measured by a common standard, but in this event no investment activity would be taking place even in gross terms. Since there is no stop to changes in the other direction, however, equilibrium would not be established with MEI higher than the rate of interest, for investment activity would expand until the gap was closed.

Marginal Efficiency of Investing and of Holding

This last relationship is somewhat complex but quite important. Equilibrium may be established with MEI either higher or lower than MEH under certain conditions. (a) If there is no storing taking place, indicating that MEH may be less than the rate of interest, then investment activity will continue until MEI is forced down to the rate of interest but not to MEH. (b) If high costs and low yields should prevent any gross investment from taking place, then it is conceivable that storage would be occurring, with MEH equal to the rate of interest and both higher than MEI.

A major point concerning MEI is the sluggishness that may impede its movement toward equilibrium. Much time may elapse between an invention whose profitability seems sure and the actual application of that new technique on a scale large enough to produce equilibrium. Since innovation of one kind or another is regularly taking place, the economy may seldom, if ever, be in full equilibrium so far as MEI and r are concerned. Yet the movement toward the level of investment so described is strong, and the equilibrium concept is as important here as it is elsewhere.

COMPARATIVE RATES OF RETURN AND
THE LEVEL OF EMPLOYMENT

The remaining part of Keynes' argument is inherently difficult and it is made more so by some apparent confusions on his own part, including inconsistent use of terminology. In the appendix to this chapter I spell out the apparent intent of Keynes' argument, adding my own comments at each step: here in the text only an outline of Keynes' major points is given.

The preceding analysis demonstrates that so long as the MEI on any good exceeds the rate of interest (both measured in any common standard) there will be a tendency for the production of that good to expand until the difference between the two rates is eliminated. While this expansion persists, any underemployment will thereby be reduced. The threat of underemployment equilibrium may be said to arise from the danger that all MEI's become equal to the corresponding own-rate of interest at levels of activity that do not imply full employment.

In general the expanded production of an asset will tend to reduce not only its MEI, but also its own-rate of interest, and therefore expansion does not quickly become choked off by its own consequences through elimination of the spread between MEI and r. Any asset that has the characteristics possessed by money in our economy, however, will display an own-rate that does not tend to fall, or at best falls very sluggishly, as expansion takes place. Furthermore, since all rates of interest, so long as they are measured in a common standard, will be forced by arbitrage toward equality, the incapacity of the money rate to fall significantly must imply the incapacity of all other rates to fall. For this reason Keynes' argument leads to the conclusion that the peculiar characteristics of money tend to keep its rate, and hence all other rates, so high that expansion of production may be quickly choked off as the consequent reduction of MEI eliminates the gap between MEI and r.

The crucial issue in this argument concerns the forces whereby expanded production would tend to reduce own-rates of interest on normal assets but not on money. Keynes supports his position at this point by two major arguments. (a) When unemployment exists, any tendency for money wages to fall relative to the price of finished goods would increase the profitability of producing the latter, and this increased production would lower own-rates on the commodities by increasing their stocks and thereby reducing the net yields from holding them.[13] Money, however, cannot in general be thus "produced" at will, and hence this cause of a declining own-rate would not exist for money as it does for other goods. (b) As production of commodities expands, and as increasing out-

---

[13] Keynes, *ibid.*, p. 230.

put brings higher prices because of higher costs, consumers shift purchases to other goods, thus increasing aggregate output through this channel. But a corresponding substitution of other assets for money does not take place as its value rises (i.e., as prices fall), because its sole ultimate function is to buy other goods, so that its value to the holder rises *pari passu* with the cost of acquiring it.[14]

Although the preceding arguments would appear to explain why the production of additional money does not take place, thereby reducing the own-rate on it, Keynes recognizes that there is a sense in which the *effective* quantity of money is, indeed, increased when prices drop. This results from the lowered requirement for transactions purposes. But he goes on to argue that even this consideration does not permit the own-rate on money to fall as does the own-rate on other commodities. The reason that even an increase in the effective quantity of money can have only a limited tendency to reduce its own-rate is, first, that this rate cannot (in equilibrium) lie below the marginal efficiency of holding money (its MEH), and, second, that a virtual floor exists at a positive level in relation to the MEH on money. In explanation of this floor, it must first be remembered that the MEH of an asset is equal to $q - c + l$ as described on pages 132–133. Except for working balances the yield on money (q) is zero. Because of its nature, the cost of storing money (c) is virtually zero. The liquidity premium on money cannot readily fall below some presumably positive value for familiar Keynesian reasons (see chapter ix). This means that even though the effective quantity of money is increased by lower prices, its MEH cannot be reduced beyond definable limits by the forces affecting most assets.

Any brief summary of this analysis is subject to important qualifications, and reference to the appendix to this chapter (if not also to Keynes and Lerner) should precede any detailed appraisal. Furthermore, my effort to correct for what are fairly obvious Keynesian errors runs the risk of misinterpreting his intended analysis as well. This discussion does, however, seem to throw light on some of the peculiarities of money which enable it to become "a bottomless sink for purchasing power" under some circumstances. But it should be emphasized, as Keynes recognizes explicitly, that, in the absence of conventional money, other assets — such as land — can acquire similar characteristics. They, too, may be bought and held merely as a means of storing wealth until their prices have little relation to their current use in either production or consumption, so that their economic function becomes similar to that of money.

---

[14] As explained in the appendix to this chapter (p. 152), it seems to me that this argument by Keynes does not adequately recognize the possible effect of falling prices on the quantity of goods bought.

FISHER'S REAL RATE OF INTEREST

In my previous discussion of Fisher's theory of interest I accepted the assumption, which he carries through most of his analysis, that prices remain constant. As is obvious, this assumption makes rates of return by all standards equal to one another.[15] Fisher was thus justified in abstracting from the problem of differing own-rates in the model with which he worked. He was well aware of the complications introduced by price changes, however, and he devoted extensive study to this problem, both theoretically and empirically.[16] The conclusions that he reached may be summarized briefly in two steps. The first concerns the concept of the real rate of interest, and the relation between this rate and the money rate. The second concerns the effect of expected price changes upon the levels of these two rates (unforeseen price changes will have little direct effect upon money rates).[17]

In his first step, Fisher argues that "income is the most fundamental factor in our economic lives. . . . Consequently a rate of interest in terms of fundamental income itself would seem to come as near as we can practically come to any basic standard in which to express a real rate of interest. . . . By means of [a cost of living index] we may translate the nominal, or money rate of interest, into a goods rate or real rate of interest, just as we translate money wages into real wages." [18] Here we have Fisher's concept of the real rate, and in the definition itself the general means of determining the relation between this real rate and the money rate: for every 1 per cent that prices have risen the real rate will be 1 per cent lower than the money rate. If prices rise 5 per cent during the year in which I invested funds at 5 per cent, my real return is obviously zero.[19]

In his second step, Fisher argues as follows. Falling prices, of course, hurt the debtor and help the creditor, since loan contracts are typically made in money terms. If prices are expected to fall when the loan contract is made, therefore, it would stand to reason that the debtor cannot afford to pay so much as he otherwise would, and the creditor need not demand so much. Consequently the effect will be to make money rates lower than they would otherwise have been.[20] Fisher emphasizes that this analysis

---

[15] One may readily check this conclusion by reference to the fact that the "adjustment factor," or a, described on pages 122–123 would here equal zero, since the numerator of one factor $(P_2 - P_1)$ equals zero.

[16] See Irving Fisher, *The Theory of Interest* (New York: Macmillan, 1930), pp. 37–44 and pp. 411–431; also his *The Rate of Interest*, appendix to chapter v.

[17] Fisher, *The Theory of Interest*, p. 37.

[18] *Ibid.*, p. 42.

[19] *Ibid.*, p. 39. See also p. 122, n. 3, and p. 142, n. 24.

[20] *Ibid.*, p. 37.

implies low (not falling) rates when prices are expected to fall (not simply "remain low"). Thus the *level* of the rate is related to the *rate of change* of the expected prices.[21] Fisher's empirical evidence, which was drawn from experience in many countries and over many years — often going well back into the early part of the nineteenth century — led him to the following conclusion concerning the relation between fact and theory. "The evidence . . . indicates that there is a very apparent though feeble tendency for the interest rate to be high when prices are rising, and the reverse. The adjustment is imperfect and rather irregular, but in a great majority of the cases the tendency is evident." [22]

I shall now examine further these two steps in Fisher's analysis, and relate them to the preceding work in this chapter. So far as the first step is concerned, it is quite obvious that his illustration is an important special case of the general theory I have been developing. The real rate is simply the rate on money in terms of goods. Fisher's outline is subject to the criticism which Lerner made of Keynes, namely, that it may appear to indicate that there is more than one rate in equilibrium. He is sufficiently ambiguous that he might be interpreted to mean only that different figures will describe the rate if different yardsticks are used. Note how fully his statement is subject to either interpretation: "There are, therefore, theoretically just as many rates of interest expressed in terms of goods as there are kinds of goods diverging from one another in value." [23] In any event the term "real rate" is convenient, and I shall continue to use it subject to this initial warning that it implies a difference only in standard of measure, not a different rate on different assets.

Once this point is clarified, the concept of Fisher's real rate is straightforward and fits neatly into the theory developed here. As stated above, it represents simply the rate of interest on money in terms of goods, where goods are treated as a single element by the use of a price index to measure their combined change in value relative to money. In order to convert money rates into real rates, therefore, we need only add the adjustment factor a described on pages 122–123. In this context the "price" appearing in the formula for a is the "price of money in terms of goods" and the "quantity" represents the quantity of money. Thus the equation may be adapted as follows:

$$a = \left(\frac{P_2 - P_1}{P_1}\right)\left(\frac{Q_2}{Q_1}\right) = \left(\frac{1/p_2 - 1/p_1}{1/p_1}\right)\left(\frac{M_2}{M_1}\right) = \left(\frac{p_1 - p_2}{p_2}\right)\left(\frac{M_2}{M_1}\right)$$

where p represents the price index and M_2 represents the quantity of next year's money that will exchange for M_1 of money now. For example, sup-

[21] *Ibid.*, p. 411.
[22] *Ibid.*
[23] *Ibid.*, p. 42.

pose the rate of interest in money terms is now 5 per cent and $M_1 = 100$ so that $M_2 = 105$. If prices rise 5 per cent during the year, the real rate equals the money rate (5 per cent) plus a $(-5\%) = 0$.[24] Had prices risen more, the adjustment factor would have been a larger negative number, and the real rate would be negative.

Fisher's second step presents more of a problem. To repeat his conclusion in his own words, "If perfect foresight existed, continuously rising prices would be associated . . . with a continuing high rate of interest, and falling prices would be associated . . . with a continuing low rate of interest . . . *assuming in each case that other influences than price changes remained the same.*" [25] The difficulty for me in this passage concerns the meaning of the *ceteris paribus* reservation. If prices change, some reason must be presumed, and what that reason is may entirely alter the conclusion. A much more satisfactory analysis is suggested by Fisher's own theory as developed elsewhere and described in Part One of this book. To simplify, let us suppose that there are no durable commodities, but only perishables and money. Word suddenly comes that predicted hurricanes make it certain that the output of these goods must be less by one half next year than this year. We should like to store goods for the lean year ahead, but that possibility is ruled out by the hypothesis of perishability. Under these conditions I should find myself willing to exchange two apples today for a promise of one next year. Suppose that the supply of money remains constant. Then prices next year may be double those of this year (admittedly abstracting from much of reality, but not thereby destroying the point illustrated here). One dollar would buy me 10 apples now. One dollar next year will buy me 5 apples. But I am perfectly willing to exchange 10 apples now for a promise of 5 next year, and therefore I am willing to exchange one dollar now for a promise of one dollar next year. The money rate of interest is zero, the real rate is —50 per cent. Despite the expected price rise, the money rate is not high, as indicated by Fisher's second step.

On the other hand we can readily illustrate the point Fisher presumably had in mind. Instead of assuming a severe shortage of next year's output, suppose we presume unchanging needs and unchanging supplies of goods, but that monetary authorities plan to double the amount of money, again resulting in expected prices next year double those of this year. What now will happen? Assuming myopia is zero and needs constant, the

---

[24] In this example: $a = (100 - 105)/105 \times 105/100 = -5/100 = -5\%$. This illustration may seem to imply that the price-adjustment factor could be stated simply to equal minus the percentage change in the price of the standard as measured by the asset under study, i.e., in this example, the price of goods measured in money. This is not true, however, except in special instances of which the example in the text is one. The particular circumstance which permits this solution here is the fact that the percentage price change and the rate of interest were identical.

[25] *The Theory of Interest*, pp. 411–412. Italics supplied.

interest rate in real terms will be zero, for I should be indifferent to another apple this year or next. The money rate, on the other hand, will be 100 per cent, for my indifference as between an apple now and one next year is equivalent to indifference between 10¢ now and 20¢ then in view of the expected price change.

Fisher's statement would have to imply that in the second illustration there was no disturbance other than the price change, whereas in the first there was. I find this interpretation considerably less than clear, but we need not argue about semantics so long as we note that one cannot determine the levels at which interest rates in terms of money will settle by reference only to price changes without asking about the cause of these price changes.

What does the theory of this chapter offer to aid us in relation to what we have called the second step of Fisher's analysis, which has to do, not with the relations between real and money rates, but the effects of price expectations on the equilibrium levels of these rates? In the first place the implications of the two cases just described can be made clear by the simple tables of quantity equivalents which have been used in this chapter.

TABLE 5

Time	Assumption I Goods become scarce during second year; quantity of money is unchanged.			Assumption II Supplies of goods are unchanged in second year; quantity of money is doubled.		
	Money	Goods	Prices	Money	Goods	Prices
Year 1	100	100	$1.00	100	100	$1.00
Year 2	100	50	2.00	200	100	2.00

Table 5 makes it obvious that the money rate of interest will be zero under assumption I, and 100 per cent under assumption II, though prices of goods rise 100 per cent in each. By use of the adjustment term derived above we note that the real rate of interest proves to be −50 per cent under assumption I and 0 under assumption II.[26]

[26] Calculations follow:

Item	Formula	Value of item shown on left	
		Case I	Case II
Money rate	$\dfrac{M_2 - M_1}{M_1}$	$\dfrac{100 - 100}{100} = 0\%$	$\dfrac{200 - 100}{100} = 100\%$
Adjustment factor (a)	$\dfrac{p_1 - p_2}{p_2} \cdot \dfrac{M_2}{M_1}$	$\dfrac{1-2}{2} \cdot \dfrac{100}{100} = -50\%$	$\dfrac{1-2}{2} \cdot \dfrac{200}{100} = -100\%$
Real rate	Money rate + adjustment factor	$0\% - 50\% = -50\%$	$100\% - 100\% = 0\%$

This chapter has been concerned with the essential properties of interest. I have unavoidably discussed elements in the determination of interest rates, but I have not examined these elements systematically or thoroughly. I now turn, therefore, to a more complete analysis of the determinants of the rate of interest in a monetary economy. Since the relation between rates by various standards has been clarified, it is no longer important in what standard the analysis proceeds, and I shall define the rate of interest as the own-rate on money, i.e., the rate on money in terms of itself.

It is important to indicate at this point, however, that the entire problem of a multiplicity of rates has not been eliminated. When the fact of risk is introduced it will become apparent that the rate on money in terms of money will not be the same if the loan is made to an unreliable borrower as it will if it is made to the United States Government; we shall find likewise that risks arise from the possibility of changing prices on outstanding loan contracts, and that for this reason rates will be found to differ also, in part, according to the maturity term of the contract. These problems of "structure of rates" are in a different dimension from those discussed above, in which it was assumed that all uncertainty was removed in order to prove that the apparent diversity of rates on different assets in equilibrium is illusory.

In order to clarify my argument I have recapitulated ideas many times, and it would seem redundant to do so once more at this point. I shall, therefore, in the next chapter proceed directly to the two major partial-equilibrium models for monetary theories of interest: the loanable-funds theory and the liquidity-preference theory.

APPENDIX: RELATIONS BETWEEN r, MEH, AND MEI

This appendix is intended to clarify the relations described on pages 138–139. In my own attempt to understand the complex relations between the rate of interest, the marginal efficiency of holding assets, and the marginal efficiency of investing in assets, I found it necessary to work out a numerical illustration applied to changing economic circumstances. I shall first present this numerical example, after which I shall use it to illustrate Keynes' analysis and my comments on that analysis. The table on page 146 presents the basic data and derivations of my illustration.

Panel I describes an equilibrium situation essentially similar to that of table 3 (page 124), but we here omit clothing and add instead columns for MEH, MEI, and the rate of interest. In this initial period carrying costs on food are 10 per cent (column 6), and the own-rate of interest on food is −10 per cent (columns 2 and 8). It is next assumed that this equilibrium is disturbed by an innovation that raises productivity in food by 30 per cent. Panel II shows this situation when the first innovator is just starting to function, and when prices have not yet reflected the consequences of the new knowledge: 100 units of food can now purchase resources capable of producing 130 units at going prices (columns 2 and 3), providing a 30 per cent profit to food producers. Provision of food for next year via production now yields 17 per cent net return in terms of food (column 9) since the food profit more than covers the 10 per cent carrying cost. Food production for next year is profitable because this MEI of +17 per cent in terms of food greatly exceeds the own-rate of interest on food, which is still −10 per cent (column 8). This profitability of producing food for next year is revealed equally well by examining the gains in terms of money. The MEI in food measured by money is +35 per cent (column 11), as compared with a food rate of interest in terms of money equal to 4 per cent (column 10).

Panel III of the table shows a new equilibrium based on the following assumptions: As food production expanded, the costs of production rose so that at the new rate of output, productivity (in terms of ultimate resources as measured by their money value) is only 20 per cent higher than before the innovation (columns 1 and 2) instead of being 30 per cent higher as at first impact. Storage costs have risen from 10 per cent to 20 per cent (column 6) so that the 120 units that can now be produced for $100, when stored, yield only 96 units (column 3) a year hence. Since an equilibrium has been established again, cost equals price, and spot-futures relations are the same for trading on the market as by way of production (column 2 equals column 3). Columns 8 to 11 show the equality again of MEI, MEH, and r whether measured in terms of food (−20 per cent) or in money (+4 per cent).

The explanation of this adjustment process is essentially the familiar one. An innovation raises the marginal efficiency of investment relative to the rate of interest. As investment expands, the cost of investment goods rises, their yield declines, and therefore MEI falls until it no longer exceeds the interest rate. This equality sets the rate of investment that maximizes profits. The chief difficulty with this traditional explanation is that it begs the central question that now concerns us, for it assumes that the interest rate in terms of money remains constant while other rates of return in terms of money adjust to it. The same relationship is portrayed in the familiar simplified Keynesian model, where the interest rate is assumed to be given (from the supply and demand for money, M and l), and this r, together with MEC, determines the quantity of I. The table illustrates just such a result by showing that both the food rate and the money rate, when measured in terms of money, remained at 4 per cent throughout the entire process (columns 7 and 10). The own-rate of interest on food, however, dropped from −10 to −20 per cent as the new

Basic Data and Derivations

	(1)	(2)	(3)	(4)	(5)	(6)	(7)	(8)	(9)	(10)	(11)
	Quantity equivalents			Prices and costs			Rates of return on food				
							Money rates	In terms of food		In terms of money	
	Money (M)	Food on market (Q)	Food via production (I)	\$ price per unit of food (P)	\$ cost per unit of food (K)	Storage costs[a] (C)	Own-r (=MEH)[c]	Own-r (=MEH)[d]	MEI	r (=MEH)[d]	MEI
	Assumed	Assumed	Assumed			Percentage Assumed	$\dfrac{M_2 - M_1}{M_1}$	$\dfrac{Q_2 - Q_1}{Q_1}$	$\dfrac{I_1 - C_p - Q_1}{Q_1}$	$\dfrac{P_2Q_2 - P_1Q_1}{P_1Q_1}$	$\dfrac{P_2I_2 - P_1Q_1}{P_1Q_1}$

DERIVATION[b]

Panel I

	(1) M	(2) Q	(3) I	(4) P	(5) K	(6) C	(7)	(8)	(9)	(10)	(11)
Year 1	100	100	100	\$1.00	\$1.00	10% $C_h=10$ $C_p=10$	$\dfrac{104-100}{100}=4\%$	$\dfrac{90-100}{100}=-10\%$	$\dfrac{100-10-100}{100}=-10\%$	$\dfrac{(1.16)(90)-(1.00)(100)}{(1.00)(100)}=4\%$	$\dfrac{(1.16)(90)-(1.00)(100)}{(1.00)(100)}=4\%$
Year 2	104	90	90	1.16	1.16						

M/Q: 1.00, 1.16 ; M/I: 1.00, 1.16

Panel II

	(1) M	(2) Q	(3) I	(4) P	(5) K	(6) C	(7)	(8)	(9)	(10)	(11)
Year 1	100	100	130	1.00	.77	10% $C_h=10$ $C_p=13$	$\dfrac{104-100}{100}=4\%$	$\dfrac{90-100}{100}=-10\%$	$\dfrac{130-13-100}{100}=+17\%$	$\dfrac{(1.16)(90)-(1.00)(100)}{(1.00)(100)}=4\%$	$\dfrac{(1.16)(117)-(1.00)(100)}{(1.00)(100)}=35\%$
Year 2	104	90	117	1.16	.89						

M/Q: 1.00, 1.16 ; M/I: .77, .89

Panel III

	(1) M	(2) Q	(3) I	(4) P	(5) K	(6) C	(7)	(8)	(9)	(10)	(11)
Year 1	100	120	120	.83	.83	20% $C_h=24$ $C_p=24$	$\dfrac{104-100}{100}=4\%$	$\dfrac{96-120}{120}=-20\%$	$\dfrac{120-24-120}{120}=-20\%$	$\dfrac{(1.08)(96)-(.83)(120)}{(.83)(120)}=\dfrac{104-100}{100}=4\%$	$\dfrac{(1.08)(96)-(.83)(120)}{(.83)(120)}=\dfrac{104-100}{100}=4\%$
Year 2	104	96	96	1.08	1.08						

M/Q: .83, 1.08 ; M/I: .83, 1.08

NOTES: Panel I shows initial equilibrium. Panel II shows relations at the margin when productivity has risen 30 per cent but market adjustments to this possibility have not occurred. Panel III shows relations at the margin in the new equilibrium, with productivity only 20 per cent above that in Panel I (production costs rose with output) and with storage costs risen from 10 to 20 per cent.

[a] C_h and C_p represent total carrying costs for food, measured in terms of food, referred to the quantities "held" (column 2) or "produced" (column 3) respectively.

[b] The meaning of the letters M, Q, I, P, K, and C, is indicated by the columns which they head from 1 to 6.

[c] Subscripts 1 and 2 indicate Year 1 and Year 2.

[d] Equality of r and MEH is by hypothesis, not identity.

1. *Quantity equivalents:* Within any one panel each quantity in columns 1 and 2 will exchange on the market for any other quantity shown in either of those two columns. For example, in Panel I it is possible to exchange $100 now for a promise of $104 next year, or for 100 units of food now or for a promise of 90 units of food next year. Year 1 rows of column 3 give the amount of food that can be produced with resources of value equal to those shown in columns 1 and 2.

2. *Rates of return:* (a) The basic method of calculating rates of return is described on pp. 120 ff. and 134 ff. above. The "master" formula is:

$$\frac{\text{Future Quantity} - \text{Present Quantity}}{\text{Present Quantity}}$$

(b) The own-rate of interest on any asset is calculated directly from this formula by reference to quantity equivalents as shown on the market (columns 1 and 2). These are shown for money and for food in columns 7 and 8 respectively.

(c) The own-MEH could be calculated by the following substitution in the master formula:

Future quantity = Present quantity + Yield − Carrying cost + Liquidity premium.

Since the table assumes zero yield and zero liquidity premium on food, this gives:

$$\text{Own-MEH} = \frac{Q_1 - C_A - Q_1}{Q_1} = -\frac{C_A}{Q_1}$$

Since MEH = r by hypothesis in our example, we have not calculated MEH separately in the table but the method of derivation is confirmed by independent derivation according to this formula as shown in column 1 of the table below.

(d) The own-MEI (column 9) follows a principle similar to that of MEH, except that in this case:

Future Quantity = Present *Productive Possibility* − C_p.

The equation is therefore

$$\text{Own-MEI} = \frac{I_1 - C_p - Q_1}{Q_1}$$

(e) Measures of food-rates in terms of dollars may be secured either by using dollar values in the master formula, or by adding the price adjustment factor (a) to the corresponding own-rates of return. The former method is used in the main table, and confirmation by the other method is shown in columns 2 and 3 of the table below, where results prove to be the same as those derived in the main table.

ALTERNATIVE METHODS OF DERIVING COLUMNS 8, 10, AND 11 OF TABLE

	(1)	(2)	(3)
	Own-MEH on food	Rate of interest on food in terms of dollars	MEI on food in terms of dollars
		DERIVATION	
	$-\dfrac{C_A}{Q_1}$	Own-rate on food $+ a$, where $a = \left(\dfrac{P_2 - P_1}{P_1}\right)\left(\dfrac{Q_2}{Q_1}\right)$	Own-MEI on food $+ a$, where $a = \left(\dfrac{P_2 - P_1}{P_1}\right)\left(\dfrac{I_2}{Q_1}\right)$
Panel I	$\dfrac{10}{100} = -10\%$	$-10\% + \left(\dfrac{.16}{1.00}\right)\left(\dfrac{90}{100}\right) = -10\% + 14\% = +4\%$	$-10\% + \left(\dfrac{.16}{1.00}\right)\left(\dfrac{90}{100}\right) = +4\%$
Panel II	$\dfrac{10}{100} = -10\%$	$-10\% + \left(\dfrac{.16}{1.00}\right)\left(\dfrac{90}{100}\right) = +4\%$	$+17\% + \left(\dfrac{.16}{1.00}\right)\left(\dfrac{117}{100}\right) = 17\% + 18\% = +35\%$
Panel III	$\dfrac{24}{120} = -20\%$	$-20\% + \left(\dfrac{.25}{.83}\right)\left(\dfrac{96}{120}\right) = -20\% + 24\% = +4\%$	$-20\% + \left(\dfrac{.25}{.83}\right)\left(\dfrac{96}{120}\right) = +4\%$

equilibrium position was approached, because the net yield ($-c$ in this case) fell. Keynes' first task is to show why he believes that this is approximately what will occur. His second is to describe the implications of that fact for the level of employment.

I shall now summarize the steps in what I believe to be the Keynesian argument when corrected for Keynes' inconsistencies in the use of his own terms.[1] Comments on his analysis will be made point by point as the argument proceeds. For the sake of completeness some points already described will be repeated.

1. Beginning in a disequilibrium situation, production will expand in those assets whose MEI, in terms of any common standard, exceeds the rate of interest as measured by the same standard. This follows because it would then pay to borrow the standard asset and invest the proceeds in producing the other.

Comment. — In relation to our illustration the profitability of such a procedure has already been demonstrated in Panel II by comparison of MEI and r on food, both as measured in money and as measured in terms of food itself. An even more direct way to show the same conclusion is facilitated by the table, assuming either that money or food is borrowed. (*a*) Panel II shows that one could borrow $100, produce 130 units of food, store the product at a cost of 13 units, sell the remaining 117 units at a price of $1.16 a year later, grossing $135.72 and netting $31.72 after paying the $104 interest and principal on the loan. (*b*) Alternatively one might borrow 100 units of food (i.e., sell 90 futures in exchange for 100 spot), exchange the spot food for productive resources that would provide 117 units of food next year by the same process as before, permitting delivery on the 90 futures contract and leaving a profit of 27 food units, having a value, at $1.16 each, of $31.72.

2. As production of each good expands, its marginal efficiency of investment falls for the familiar reasons already given: cost of production rises, and net yield falls.

Comment. — In the illustration costs of production rose from 77¢ to 83¢ as equilibrium was approached (column 5), and net yield in terms of food fell (here, because storage costs rose) from -10 per cent to -20 per cent (column 8).

---

[1] In order to give any meaning to his analysis, we have been forced to make adjustments for Keynes' failure to distinguish between terms he uses, sometimes interchangeably, in ways that appear to be clearly incorrect. Lerner describes some, but I think not all, of the points where the presentation in the *General Theory* is confused by these errors, but I shall not attempt to review them here. Lerner's discussion is in his article, "Essential Properties of Interest and Money," *Quarterly Journal of Economics*, 66 (1952). Keynes' discussion is in his *The General Theory of Employment, Interest, and Money* (New York: Harcourt, Brace, 1936), chapter 17, pp. 222–245.

3. Because of statements 1 and 2 a point will come for each asset when further expansion of production is no longer profitable, *unless* the rate of interest falls *pari passu*.

Comment. — In our example the rate of interest *when measured in dollars* did not fall (columns 7 and 10), and investment stabilized when the MEI on food had fallen to that level (4 per cent, as seen in column 11). Correspondingly the rate of interest in *terms of food* did fall, and investment did not stop when MEI in terms of food reached the initial r in terms of food (-10 per cent, column 8), but continued to expand until MEI dropped to the more slowly declining r at -20 per cent (columns 8 and 9, Panel III).

4. The obviously crucial question raised for Keynes by statement 3 is this: *will* the rate of interest fall *pari passu*, either indefinitely or at least until full employment is reached? Keynes presumes that investment will be expanding in assets generally, and that for this reason own-rates will be declining all across the board (i.e., everywhere except for the own-rate on money!).

Comment. — Under the assumptions of this model it is true that both own-MEH and own-rates of interest will be likely, in general, to decline on any asset in which investment is expanding as equilibrium is being approached. This conclusion rests on the assumption that net yields will fall as output increases. In our illustration the own-rate on food fell from -10 per cent to -20 per cent (column 8) because of increasing storage costs. Two further comments are required at this point, however.

a. In the first place, our illustration is a limited one because the asset we have been examining was a consumers good with peculiar supply expectations. A more representative type of investment activity is in producers equipment. The chief active determinant of own-rates for these assets is not storage costs, but yields; i.e., not c, but q. As pointed out earlier, q will tend to fall as investment expands both because the most attractive opportunities are used first (MEI is a function of the quantity of capital) and because the costs of producing capital goods rise with increasing output (MEI is a function of the rate of investment). If the asset in our example were a machine instead of food a positive q would appear in the calculation of MEI. Future quantities would typically be greater than present quantities instead of less, and declining own-rates would be governed by falling q rather than by rising c. In this model it would be assumed that the market value of capital goods is determined by the discounted value of their expected contribution to future production, and the profitability of real investment lies in the excess of this value over costs of producing the capital goods in question. The essentials of the process by which equilibrium is approached would be similar to that described in this section.

b. This discussion suggests that Keynes' fourth point is valid so far as he is correct in assuming that investment will be taking place all across the board. In an expanding economy this should normally be the case in typical industries, but not in all. Some assets will always grow obsolete, and though gross investment is still positive, net investment in these will be negative. At zero net investment, r for these assets will typically be higher than MEI and MEH. As disinvestment takes place both own-rates and MEI may be rising because of increasing q or declining c. Since Keynes was painting in broad strokes and made no point of his assumption that own-rates would be generally declining throughout the economy, the purpose of this comment is not to take any major issue with his position. But the observation has importance, especially when we turn to money, for it is highly possible that an individual's positive investment in producible assets may be at the expense of "disinvestment in money." As persons try to shift out of money into other assets own-rates on money may not simply fall slowly as Keynes suggests — they may actually rise. Indeed, that is precisely what we observe when we say that an increase in the investment demand for funds pushes up the rate of interest. In terms of Keynes' model, the l on money should rise as more is drawn into transactions balances and less remains to satisfy the liquidity need.

In sum, so far as statement 4 is concerned my criticism strengthens rather than weakens Keynes' concern that money may be the culprit. For I have said that the reason the MEI of produced assets in terms of money may reach the own-rate on money rapidly as the former declines is not merely that the own-rate on money may fall slowly (as Keynes said), but that it may even rise.

5. On the basis of statement 4, Keynes' argument continues, it becomes clear that the crucial rate of interest for determining the level of investment is that rate which declines most slowly,[2] for it is this rate that will set the limit below which the marginal efficiency of other assets cannot fall: ". . . that asset's rate of interest which declines most slowly as the stock of assets in general increases . . . eventually knocks out the profitable production of each of the others." [3] Now it happens that in our kind of economy there is one asset with peculiar characteristics of a kind which almost assure that its own-rate will normally fall more slowly than all others. This unique asset is money, and it is for this reason that its rate knocks out the profitable production of other assets.

Comment. — So far as this point is concerned, the first thing to note is the previous observation that the own-rate on money has been no more stubborn in refusal to decline than has the rate on food in terms of money: the latter rate also stuck at 4 per cent (column 10). Yet there is surely a sense in which it is primarily a semantic issue to criticize Keynes

---

[2] I here revert to the idea that all rates are declining, because I am now returning to a paraphrase of the Keynesian argument rather than to my amendment of it.

[3] Keynes, *The General Theory* . . . , p. 229.

on this point, for it is the behavior of money which was postulated in this illustration that kept both rates, measured in money, from falling. Suppose, for instance, that a process similar to that which caused an increase in food production also operated on money, as a result of which its storage costs were raised until its own-rate was zero. We should then have $100 spot exchanging for $100 futures instead of for $104 as in column 1. "Arbitrage" on the futures markets would require that under present estimates of future prices 120 units of spot food would exchange for 92+ future units instead of 96 (whereas $104 would buy 96 at $1.08 each, $100 will buy only 92+). This would reduce the own-rate on food to −23 per cent without affecting the own MEI (see derivations for columns 8 and 9), and thus further investment in food would be profitable. Alternatively, if one chose to measure in terms of money, the r on food would be reduced to zero without causing a change in MEI, and consequently further investment would be profitable (see derivations for columns 10 and 11).

6. As his final step in the argument, Keynes gives three major reasons for his view that the own-rate on money may be expected to be especially sticky.

a. Whereas declining costs of labor in terms of reproducible commodities tend to increase the profitability of producing those goods[4] (unless demand is equally weakened), falling money wages cannot draw labor to the production of money (except in gold-producing countries where this process does, indeed, take place). Thus there is no normal tendency for the quantity of money to increase if and when unemployment reduces the level of wages. Since it is the increased production of assets which lowers their own-rates by augmenting their stocks and reducing the net yields from holding them, the zero elasticity of production for money removes a factor tending to reduce its own-rate.

b. When the value of a commodity rises, the increased output caused by the greater profitability to producers is not the only consequence. Consumers as well as producers respond to the change. Consumers in part shift their purchases to substitutes. Thus the increased value of typical goods results not only in the expansion of their own output, but also in some expansion of the output of other goods. But an increase in the value of money resulting from falling prices in depression does not cause the substitution of other assets for money. This fact follows primarily because money does not significantly satisfy a final consumer need as do other commodities, but finds its value only in its capacity to be exchanged for these other goods. In Keynes' words, because ". . . its utility is solely derived from its exchange value, so that the two rise and fall *pari passu* . . . as the exchange value of money rises there is no motive or

---

[4] This seems like a somewhat un-Keynesian argument, but it is the only way I can interpret pp. 230 ff. in *The General Theory.*

tendency to substitute some other factor for it." [5] Unlike other goods, money provides a "bottomless sink for purchasing power" when the demand for it increases, both because no labor can be employed in producing more of it, and because "there is no value for it at which the demand is diverted — as in the case of other rent factors — so as to slop over into the demand for other things." [6]

Comment. — Keynes does not relate this part of his argument directly to the issue of rates of return which led him to introduce it. The transformation of his argument to that frame of reference would appear to be as follows. As the low demand for goods that characterizes depression reduces the MEI of other assets than money, the resulting shift to money with its higher MEH never sets in motion the forces required to terminate the shift: it does not reduce the MEH on money because of money's near-zero elasticity of production, and it does not raise the MEI of other assets because of money's low elasticity of substitution. This argument is characteristic of Keynes' frequent treatment of money exclusively as an asset to hold. In fact the increase in the quantities of goods purchased which might result from falling prices would be a kind of substitution of goods for money resulting from the increased value of money. By omitting this consideration Keynes makes his case stronger than appears to be justified.

c. Keynes recognizes that falling prices may increase the effective quantity of money even though they do not change its absolute quantity, for they release funds from active circulation to satisfy the liquidity motive. Of course this process does not directly provide employment as does the actual output of commodities which results from increased demand for them, but it might still appear that the *virtual* increase of money would reduce its own-rate of interest just as the actual increase in output of other goods reduces their own-rates. Keynes admits the possibility of such a decline in money's own-rate, but argues that under circumstances common in an economy like ours, such a decline will be far less than in relation to other goods, and will possibly reach a floor below which it cannot drop farther. To recapitulate the reasons for this view as described on pages 138–139, an important reason that the money rate cannot fall is the fact that the carrying cost on money, c, is virtually zero. With q also zero, the only element remaining in the determination of the own-rate on money is l. The determination of l provides a central and familiar feature in Keynes' explanation of the rate of interest. At this point the relevance of that analysis is his conclusion that l cannot readily fall below some definable level. Since c cannot increase, and l cannot decrease, and q is zero, the MEH of money $(q - c + l)$ cannot fall as it can on other goods even though the quantity of it is effectively increased by falling prices.

---

[5] *Ibid.*, p. 231.
[6] *Loc. cit.*

Comment. — Without at this point entering the general discussion of Keynes' horizontal liquidity preference curve, this issue cannot now be wholly settled. But it is true, as Keynes asserts, that the liquidity premium is not *per se* changed by an accomplished fall in prices.[7] Such a change already effected can hardly alter one's preferences for present as compared with future money except in indirect and somewhat unpredictable ways.

Lerner argues, too concisely for my full understanding, that Keynes is wrong at this point, and that the case for the peculiarity of money's own-rate must depend exclusively upon the stickiness of money prices. My own interpretation of the issue would be as follows. If by "stickiness" we mean the tendency of prices to "stay put" at any achieved level, in contrast to price stability, which would imply a tendency to return to some given level if temporarily disturbed, then Lerner's basic argument is correct but it is not contrary to Keynes', as he alleges it to be. If, on the other hand, Lerner attributes some other meaning to the term "sticky," then he does differ with Keynes, as he alleges he does, but Keynes is apparently correct. In any event the discussion of Lerner's position will shed light on the entire issue, and I shall state what I believe it to be.

First, Lerner rules out the significance of Keynes' argument that the quantity of money will not be automatically increased by a fall in money wages (see *a* above) by pointing out that money is effectively increased if money prices fall. We have just shown that Keynes explicitly recognized this consideration. Next Lerner reraises the question Keynes himself posed: Why is it that people do not permit land to serve as a bottomless pit for purchasing power since it, like money, cannot be produced directly? A possible answer is, as Lerner points out, that the price of land rises in relation to other goods, thereby causing shifts in purchases to them. Keynes correctly goes on to add that if the price of land did *not* so rise in terms of other goods, then it *would* serve as a bottomless pit.

Thus far Lerner's argument would appear to be that the unique quality of money is the tendency for its purchasing power to change less than does the exchange value of other assets. Keynes' explicit statements in the *General Theory* show that he would fully agree that this characteristic is one of the attributes that tends to make money unique. But he goes on to describe another. It is a fact, he states, that the value of money, like that of land, is not always unchanging. It is when we admit this fact that we discover the unique quality of money even as compared with rent factors. For people tend to think of land's appropriate value as being such that its marginal utility in use or its marginal efficiency in production will be equal, per dollar's worth, to that of other goods. Therefore when land

---

[7] This statement does not contradict the fact that each dollar will have greater buying power if prices fall, and that it will in this sense have more liquidity than before. The liquidity premium referred to in this analysis refers to the liquidity to be enjoyed during the period considered, *as a ratio* to present value (see pp. 133 ff). Hence an accomplished price fall will influence numerator and denominator in equal proportions and leave the full fraction unchanged. It is because an *expected* change in price affects only the numerator that l is affected by such expectations.

values rise rapidly in relation to other goods without any evidence of increase in its productivity as a commodity, people expect its price to fall again and hence they hesitate to invest further in it. Money is unique in that, unlike other assets it has virtually no direct utility. Its only utility is that which arises from its purchasing power, and this utility rises right along with any increase in its value. Therefore nobody can be expected to assume that the value will drop back to its former level again; there is no reason to assume that, in general, a price decline (rise in value of money) will be followed by a rise again.

Having sketched this defense of his conclusions, Keynes could add that he explicitly recognized in his text the possibility of some conditions which could make money no different from land.[8] If and when land acquires a value in the public mind that is not based on its service as a commodity, so that its relative value can stay at any level indefinitely, then it is behaving precisely like money. Indeed, economic history reveals that this tendency for land speculation to siphon off purchasing power is an exceedingly important phenomenon. Conversely, if the public ever assumes that a fall in money prices will be followed by a rise, money will cease to be a bottomless sink for purchasing power.[9] But because the two conditions sketched in this paragraph are seldom realized, money is unique.

If this is what Lerner meant by his statement, then, as I argue above, he would appear to be correct. But in that event he seems to me to be in complete agreement with Keynes. In any case the point which justifies the discussion is that according to the argument presented here money as we know it will generally be, at least to some degree, unique, not only because prices in terms of it do not readily change downward (especially prices of labor and other costs), but also because when they do, there is no general basis for assuming that they will spring up again. It is for this reason that when prices do fall persons may not run from money by purchasing assets that must be produced by labor, and money tends to become a bottomless sink.

I shall leave this phase of the discussion without implying that I have settled the issue concerning underemployment equilibrium. That issue still rests in part upon the nature of the liquidity-preference function, to be examined later, and upon the reactions of consumption and investment to effective increases in the quantity of money, and upon relative price changes with their differential effects upon the marginal efficiency of investment. Thus far all I have done is to show that money does seem to have characteristics which may impede any automatic tendency toward full-employment equilibrium.

---

[8] Keynes, *The General Theory . . . ,* pp. 241 ff.
[9] *Ibid.,* p. 231.

SKETCH OF LOANABLE-FUNDS AND
LIQUIDITY-PREFERENCE THEORIES OF INTEREST

In the first chapter of this book it was noted that monetary theories are not new to the history of economic doctrine: they substantially out-date the "real" theories of the classical economists. It is true, however, that following their eclipse in the early nineteenth century they attained little prominence in the English-speaking tradition until the depression of the 1930's and the Keynesian controversy that began with the publication of his *General Theory* in 1936.

In the present era monetary theories of interest have had three major roots. One grows out of the Swedish approach that was initiated largely by Knut Wicksell in his *Geldzins und Güterpreise*,[1] and developed later by a group of eminent economists that includes Bertil Ohlin, Eric Lindahl, Gunnar Myrdal, and Bent Hansen. Another, which follows the English neoclassical tradition, is perhaps most fully represented in the writings of D. H. Robertson. A third is, of course, that found in the school of John Maynard Keynes and his followers. It is convenient to group together the Swedish and the Robertsonian theories under the head of *loanable-funds theories;* the Keynesian theory is best known as the *liquidity-preference theory.*

There is a sense in which Wicksell explicitly synthesizes monetary and nonmonetary theories, for his "natural" rate of interest is that of a non-monetary theory, and his money rate is that of a monetary theory. Wicksell, like Ricardo, regarded the money rate as a kind of aberration from the rate determined by nonmonetary theory (except in those instances when the two were identical), the true character and importance of the latter being well revealed by its title, "natural," or "normal." Yet Wicksell, unlike Ricardo, did not brush aside the monetary theory as unimportant because ephemeral. Instead, he made the divergence between the two the central feature of his dynamic analysis.

Although contemporary economists, including those of Sweden, tend to be quite critical of Wicksell's concept of a natural rate, there is a sense in

---

[1] Knut Wicksell, *Geldzins und Güterpreise,* translated as *Interest and Prices* (London: Macmillan, 1936).

which all three types of contemporary interest theory lead to a similar synthesis. Consistent with each is a market equilibrium that is likely to be achieved rapidly, with its interest rate determined by the forces described in monetary theory; and there is a longer-run and more-complete equilibrium, which is achieved more slowly, as adjustment takes place in slow-moving variables like the level of income, and in which the rate of interest is consistent with that described in nonmonetary theories. Wicksell's analysis was, of course, dynamic, and in his frame of reference the system did not even tend toward rest at the "equilibrium" here described (see page 186 below).

This generalization will be clarified in the analysis ahead, but two qualifying comments are required now to avoid misinterpretation. In the first place, theories which I shall describe as "monetary" do not describe only monetary phenomena: rather, they include both real and monetary elements in their structure. Although at times Keynes appears to pay little attention to real elements like productivity and thrift, I do not use the term "monetary theory" to describe only such narrow interpretations as that, and I shall discuss below the question of how far Keynes himself thought in such terms. The second qualification is that I do not wish to imply that the equilibrium of the nonmonetary theories is ever reached, nor do I even mean to say that such an equilibrium is not influenced by monetary phenomena. In short, the nonmonetary equilibrium that is in a sense "approached" is one in which saving equals investment — as with Fisher — but one in which the saving and investment functions may themselves be influenced by monetary phenomena of the preequilibrium periods.

LOANABLE-FUNDS THEORY

According to the loanable-funds theory, as sometimes stated, the equilibrium rate of interest is that rate which equates the supply of and demand for "claims," or interest-bearing securities.[2] At other times this theory is so stated as to hold, as its name implies, that the interest rate will be in equilibrium when it is at the level which equates the demand for and the supply of "loanable funds." On examination these are seen to be essentially two ways of saying the same thing, for the supply of loanable funds may be thought of as being the demand for claims, and the demand for loanable funds may be regarded as the offer of claims. It is common for loanable-funds theorists, however, to go behind the functions describing supply and demand for claims and seek underlying com-

---

[2] See Bertil Ohlin, "Some Notes on the Stockholm Theory of Savings and Investment," *Economic Journal*, 47 (1937): 53–69 and 221–240; reprinted in American Economic Association, *Readings in Business Cycle Theory* (Philadelphia and Toronto: Blakiston, 1944), pp. 87–130. For this specific reference, see especially pp. 107–112 in the reprint.

ponents. When this is done it often proves convenient to consolidate items in such a way that the result represents an equation of demand and supply in which neither represents the same quantity as the original and fundamental supply of claims and demand for them. Part of this process was shown when Fisher's theory was converted into one which is written in terms of saving and investment.[3] Fisher's original formulation made the interest rate so adjust as to equate desired lending and desired borrowing. It was a pure form of nonmonetary loanable-funds theory. But the transformation of this equation into the familiar saving-investment relation involved subtraction of all disinvestment from investment, and the subtraction of dissaving from saving. The resulting equation was as accurate as the first, and it gave the same rate of interest, but the supply and demand figures were each lower than in the original expression. These and other changes will be encountered when monetary theories drawn up in terms of supply and demand for claims are transformed into theories drawn in terms of demand and supply of loanable funds as typically presented. Such a translation will be spelled out shortly.

I have just referred to Fisher's theory as a nonmonetary loanable-funds theory. It was this structure of theory, it will be remembered, that Keynes attacked as the "classical" theory of interest. Robertson, among others, was quick to argue that loanable-funds theorists could, and often did, include in their concepts of supply and demand monetary as well as nonmonetary elements.[4] To be more specific, these supply and demand functions can well include, in addition to saving and investment, net hoarding and net changes in the quantity of money. I shall not concern myself here with the long debate that ensued, including its many terminological confusions. In my judgment, both sides of the controversy contributed essential elements to the present synthesis. Surely much pre-Keynesian writing did not adequately reckon with monetary elements; and surely much that Keynes wrote tends to underplay nonmonetary aspects, though his system as a whole certainly includes them.

The remaining part of this section will be devoted to a review of the contemporary presentation of the loanable-funds theory, including monetary elements. This review, like the one of the liquidity-preference theory which will follow, will be brief, since the ground is generally familiar and my main purpose is to lay the basis for a more thorough analysis of the similarities and differences between these theories.[5]

---

[3] See above, chapter iv, p. 52–53.

[4] D. H. Robertson, "Alternative Theories of the Rate of Interest," *Economic Journal*, 47 (1937): 428.

[5] More detailed presentations of the monetary loanable-funds theory may be found in Joe Bain, *Pricing, Distribution and Employment* (New York: Henry Holt, 1953), pp. 626–691. A somewhat different exposition is given by E. S. Shaw, *Money, Income and Monetary Policy* (Chicago: Irwin, 1950), esp. pp. 274–330. Earlier expositions may be

I shall begin with the formulation of the loanable-funds theory according to which the rate of interest is said to be determined at that level which equates the supply of securities and the demand for them. This is exactly the same as saying that the price of securities will so adjust that supply equals demand in the market; for the price of any security — given its coupon rate and its term to maturity — determines a unique yield. The proposition would appear to be such a simple example of the most basic tenet in competitive-price theory that it should arouse no controversy. In one crucial respect, however, the pricing of securities presents problems different from those in competitive price theory. Demand and supply curves in conventional price theory are drawn *ceteris paribus*. This procedure is legitimate in dealing with any individual good whose production and price have relatively little effect on the output and prices of other goods. It is the very essence of the problem of interest theory, however, that aggregate income, among other variables, is affected by interest rates — i.e., by the prices of securities. This does not alter the conditions essential for equilibrium, but it raises substantial problems in the construction of supply and demand curves. I shall deal with these difficulties in due time, but for the present shall abstract from them in order to present the conventional loanable-funds theory, which is typically drawn on the explicit or implicit assumption of given prices and income.

One of the virtues of the loanable-funds theory when stated in terms of the supply and demand for securities is that it does not require the existence of a single rate of interest on all securities, regardless of risk or term. Each security may have its own supply and demand, and its own resulting yield. Another interesting feature of the theory when thus stated is that the supplies and demands involved may be conceived in terms of either stock or flow. That is, one may think of the demand and the supply for securities at a moment of time, or may think in terms of the quantities that would be bought and offered over a period of time.

Unfortunately the problems for which theory is created are not solved merely by definitions of supply and demand curves. Loanable-funds theorists rightly wished to examine the sources of supply and demand in order to understand their determinants. The process they followed immediately lost for them some of the advantages characteristic of the simple theory just described. In the first place, they adopted the frame of reference of a flow analysis, directing attention to a period of time and examining supply and demand by inquiring: From what sources do the funds

found in Gottfried von Haberler, *Prosperity and Depression* (Geneva: League of Nations, 1937), pp. 191 ff., and in D. H. Robertson, "Mr. Keynes and the Rate of Interest," in *Essays in Monetary Theory* (London: P. S. King, 1940), pp. 1–38; reprinted in American Economic Association, *Readings in the Theory of Income Distribution* (Philadelphia and Toronto: Blakiston, 1946), pp. 425–460.

being offered for securities during this period arise, and what are the sources of securities in search of funds? In the second place, they answered these questions in terms of securities in general rather than securities in particular, and thus the structure of rates was abstracted away. This is not the only approach that might be used, and the issue will be discussed somewhat more fully in Part Three of this book, but it is not an unreasonable approach in view of the great difficulty of defining the demand for any given type of security. The analysis based on individual securities would involve all the complexities of cross-elasticities among highly substitutable products (i.e., securities of different term and risk). In view of these difficulties the simplification made in the conventional loanable-funds theory may be justified, at least for reaching rough conclusions, but the price paid, however appropriately, must be acknowledged: we find ourselves abstracting from the structure of rates.

What, then, are the sources of demand for loanable funds? In other words, what kinds of borrowers may be listed? (1) First, there are the borrowers of nonmonetary theory, who wish to use funds for new investment, and whose demand may be represented by I_n. (2) A second group of borrowers, the importance of which has grown sharply since World War II, is represented by consumer borrowers. We shall call their demand C_b. (3) Another source of demand for loanable funds is that arising from those who borrow with the result that their balances are built up. This borrowing may be a deliberate recognition of need for additional working balances, or it may represent borrowing for investment that does not actually take place during the time period under review. This group, like the preceding one, is of considerable importance today. Both corporations and municipalities, for example, may sell a large block of securities, even though the actual expenditure of the money received can take place only over an appreciable period of time. The demand of this group will be called F_b, since their borrowing is in response to what has often been called the finance motive. The demand items may now be brought together to define the demand (D) for loanable funds:

$$D = I_n + C_b + F_b.$$

Next we may ask: What are the sources of the supply of loanable funds? The nonmonetary theories suggest the first source, namely, saving. This term may be usefully broken down, for analytical purposes, into the following elements. First, there is the positive saving of those who save, which I shall designate S'. From this supply must be deducted, however, the dissaving of those who dissave, DS'. One complication must now be recognized. Consumer borrowing, which I have included on the demand side of my formulation, is in fact a part of dissaving. Since this item is added to the demand side it cannot also be deducted from the supply side without thereby representing double counting. The elements of supply thus far discussed may, therefore, be written $[S' - (DS' - C_b)]$, or $(S' - DS' + C_b)$. Before leaving the saving term one further issue must be considered. If saving is presumed to be gross in the sense that it includes depreciation allowances, then replacement investment, to be called I_{rp}, must be deducted, since saving so employed does not reach the loan market. The entire saving term may now be brought together in the expression $(S' - DS' + C_b - I_{rp})$.

A second element in the supply of loanable funds is the dishoarding of those who dishoard, which we shall call DH'. From this supply must be deducted, however, the hoarding of those who hoard (H'). But again one complication must be recognized. I have included explicitly on the demand side the item F_b, which represented borrowing that increased hoards. It would be double counting to include this item on the demand side and then also to deduct it from the supply side. If it is to be retained as part of demand, therefore, there must be deducted from supply, not all hoarding, but hoarding minus F_b. In conclusion, then, the second item in the supply of loanable funds is $[DH' - (H' - F_b)]$, or $(DH' - H' + F_b)$.

A third source of supply of loanable funds is newly created money. I shall designate the increase in money supply by the term ΔM, which will be a negative quantity in any period during which the money supply is reduced.

Finally, there are three items that cancel each other out entirely and which may be disregarded. Two of these arise from the exchange of existing assets. (a) Transactions in old securities may be regarded as representing elements of both supply and demand for loanable funds, hence balancing one another. (b) Transactions in other existing assets — i.e., real assets as opposed to claims — might be regarded as a supply of funds to the seller but they are simultaneously a deduction from the supply of funds available to the buyer, and hence also cancel one another. The third self-canceling item (c) arises because of the reinvestment of saving by business. These funds represent a part of saving that is not actually supplied to the loan market, and should, therefore, be deducted from S on the supply side. On the other hand, they also represent a part of investment demand that does not enter the loan market, and should for this reason be deducted from I on the demand side. This item may therefore be omitted entirely, since it would cancel out anyway when supply is equated to demand.

It is now possible to state symbolically the condition of equilibrium in the market for loanable funds. The rate of interest must rest at such a level that the demand for these funds (or, put otherwise, the supply of claims) must equal the supply of loanable funds (demand for claims). I shall repeat the elements in the demand side on the left, and assemble the supply terms on the right. This equation will then be simplified by cancellation of identical terms on the two sides.

Demand for
Loanable Funds =   Supply of Loanable Funds

$$I_n + C_b + F_b = S' - DS' + C_b - I_{rp} + DH' - H' + F_b + \Delta M. \qquad (1)$$

$$I_n + I_{rp} + H' = S' - DS' + DH' + \Delta M. \qquad (2)$$

If, now, we let H represent net hoarding (i.e., $H' - DH'$), and let S represent the saving of savers minus the dissaving of those who dissave (i.e., $S' - DS'$), and let I represent gross investment (i.e., $I_n + I_{rp}$) we may write:

$$I + H = S + \Delta M. \qquad (3)$$

Another familiar form of this equation does not consolidate the hoarding elements, and is written:

$$I + H' = S + DH' + \Delta M. \qquad (4)$$

The last two expressions, equations (3) and (4), are the two most familiar representations of the loanable-funds theory. The preceding analysis should show how these equations do, in general, describe the equality of supply and demand for loanable funds, or, put otherwise, the demand and supply of claims. This derivation also demonstrates two further points which we shall now make explicit.

In the first place, one should note that the simple, final equations include implicit allowance for the demand of consumer borrowers and borrowers for finance motives. These demands for funds may not now be added to the demand side as an additional element without breaking the equality. On the other hand, there are times when it becomes desirable to include such items as these explicitly. The fact that C_b must appear on both sides if it appears on either does not mean, as it might appear to, that there is no point in reckoning it. Often a forecaster is concerned with the direction of movement in major variables. An increase in consumer borrowing normally implies a simultaneous increase in aggregate dissaving. In this case the result of such an increase in C_b is to raise the demand side more than the supply side, since only C_b is affected in the former, but simultaneous increases in DS' and C_b on the supply side cancel each other.

The second point concerns the possibility of changes in the velocity of active money — i.e., changes in velocity not like those commonly regarded as changes in hoards, but changes arising from increased efficiency in means of payment, from integration of industry, or from other gradual institutional adjustments with similar effects. An increase in this velocity clearly releases funds for the loan market: but how would the preceding formulation account for this phenomenon? One might argue that these changes release funds from active circulation, thereby swelling idle funds and permitting dishoarding despite the absence of any change in the desired size of inactive balances. This procedure is not incorrect, but one must recognize that if he uses it he cannot identify "net hoarding" with "changes in the size of idle balances." Thus an increase in active velocity would be an instance in which net dishoarding took place but in which there was no change in the size of hoards. My own preference would be to preserve the identity of "change in hoards" and "net hoarding," either arguing that this theory abstracts from changes in the velocity of active money, or adding another element to the supply of loanable funds to represent such changes.

The conventional forms of the loanable-funds theory have now been derived from the fundamental statement that in equilibrium the interest rate will be determined at that level which equates the supply of and demand for claims. One familiar graphical illustration of this theory as expressed in equation (4) is presented in figure IIa, where the equilibrium rate of interest proves to be 2.7 per cent. Brief consideration will make it clear that under normal assumptions about behavior both elements in the demand curve should be negatively sloped, though it is commonly argued that the elasticity of the investment curve may be very low. The shape of functions on the supply side is less clear. ΔM is assumed to be autonomous and is typically drawn vertical, though this need not be so, since monetary authorities might be assumed to determine their action as a function of the rate of interest.[6] Furthermore, the saving curve might be either positively or negatively sloped, as discussed above (chapter iv, pp. 58–63). I have drawn it in the conventional way, however, and the dishoarding curve may readily be presumed to be positively sloped as well.

The assumption that the aggregate supply curve and the aggregate demand curve will cross at some positive rate of interest appears to be generally accepted by economists of all schools, though the Keynesians in particular do not assume that I and S would necessarily intersect at positive rates of interest under conditions of full employment.

This brief review gives a picture of the loanable-funds theory of interest as commonly presented. It is a partial-equilibrium theory, for such important variables as income and prices are assumed to be given. The implications of this feature will be discussed in succeeding chapters. Furthermore, I have proceeded without reference to the definition of either saving or hoarding. I have done this deliberately, because, as stated above, there are at least two major definitional systems used, and the implications of equilibrium under each are not identical. One system is that of Robertson, the other is that of the Swedish economists. In the following

---

[6] In figure IIa I have not drawn in ΔM, but have indicated its effect by shifting the saving curve uniformly to the right by this amount.

chapter I shall outline these two approaches to the loanable-funds theory, but in the meantime I shall present an introductory sketch of the liquidity-preference theory of interest.

LIQUIDITY-PREFERENCE THEORY

In his *General Theory of Interest, Employment and Money,* John Maynard Keynes launched a vigorous attack on what he called the "classical" theory of interest, and presented what appeared to be an entirely new theory in its stead. The apparent novelty[7] of this new theory is derived from features like these: (1) Whereas earlier theories had made the investment-demand curve a central feature of the determination of interest rates, Keynes generally appeared to regard that function as merely the determinant of the quantity of investment that would take place, interest rates having been already determined elsewhere: "The schedule of the marginal efficiency of capital [read 'investment'] may be said to govern the terms on which loanable funds are demanded for the purpose of new investment; whilst the rate of interest governs the terms on which funds are being currently supplied."[8] (2) Whereas the second major determinant of interest rates in previous theories was the saving curve, which was assumed to be elastic to the interest rate, Keynes appeared in some contexts to divorce this function also from the determination of interest rates. The rate of interest ". . . cannot be a return to saving or waiting . . ." but is rather ". . . the reward for parting with liquidity."[9] (3) Summarizing points 1 and 2 Keynes presents this contrast between his and earlier theories: "The rate of interest is not the price which brings into equilibrium the demand for resources to invest with the readiness to abstain from present consumption. It is the price which equilibrates the desire to hold wealth in the form of cash with the available quantity of cash."[10]

In the succeeding analysis Keynes therefore sets himself the task of examining the determinants of the demand for and the supply of cash. The latter question is readily solved, for, in his theory, the banking system determines the amount of money outstanding at any one time. The demand, in Keynes' analysis, can best be examined by studying the various motives which lead people to hold cash. Two of these are insensitive to the rate of interest, and may be regarded graphically as essentially verti-

---

[7] I say "apparent" novelty because the characterization given here is not a complete one and for this reason gives more appearance of novelty than is suggested by a fuller exposition, as will be shown in the latter part of this section.

[8] J. M. Keynes, *The General Theory of Employment, Interest, and Money* (New York: Harcourt, Brace, 1936), p. 165. Figure IIc shows the way these "demand" and "supply" curves determine *I*.

[9] *Ibid.*, p. 167.

[10] *Loc. cit.*

cal lines. They are the transactions motive and the precautionary motive, the former representing the need for working balances, the latter the need to be prepared for unforeseen opportunities or necessities of expenditure.[11]

In addition to these two interest-inelastic motives for holding cash there are two other motives that are interest elastic. The first of these interest-elastic motives, the speculative motive, bears the major responsibility for the determination of the rate of interest in Keynes' theory. This is the desire of persons to hold cash because of uncertainty concerning future rates of interest. As rates fall, two "speculative" considerations increase the desirability of holding balances:[12] (1) the reward for giving up cash in order to buy securities is reduced; and (2) the danger of capital loss from investing in securities is increased, because in any given historical and institutional setting, a relatively low rate implies increased probability that future movements may be upward — i.e., that security prices may fall. At low rates of interest the possibility of capital loss could well outweigh the prospect of all interest income for some years to come. Thus the speculative motive increases the desire to hold cash as interest rates fall, and gives to the demand curve for cash a marked sensitivity to the rate of interest. The slope of the curve will be generally negative, but may flatten out well above zero.[13]

The second interest-elastic motive for holding cash was not included in *The General Theory* but was added later in answer to criticism. It is called the finance motive.[14] Keynes' descriptions of this motive and its operations are not entirely consistent with one another,[15] but the most satisfactory interpretation appears to be this: If interest rates fall, then enterprise will borrow for investment activity even though the project cannot be carried out in the immediate time period. Furthermore, consumers will respond to the same changes in rates by witholding funds

---

[11] It seems to me that a strong case could be made for the view that the demand for precautionary balances would be subject to influences from the rate of interest essentially similar to those affecting the demand for speculative balances. If rates are high one would tend to keep more of his "rainy day" reserves in securities both because of the high return and because the probability of securing cash without capital loss would then be great.

[12] *The General Theory*, pp. 201–202.

[13] See Appendix B to this chapter for further discussion.

[14] See J. M. Keynes, "Alternative Theories of the Rate of Interest," *Economic Journal*, 47 (1937): 246 ff.; J. M. Keynes, "The 'Ex-Ante' Theory of the Rate of Interest," *Economic Journal*, 47 (1937): 663 ff.; D. H. Robertson, "Mr. Keynes and Finance: A Note," *Economic Journal*, 48 (1938): 314–318; J. M. Keynes, "Mr. Keynes and Finance: Comment," *Economic Journal*, 48 (1938): 318–322; D. H. Robertson, "Mr. Keynes and the Rate of Interest."

[15] See discussion in D. H. Robertson, "Mr. Keynes and the Rate of Interest," pp. 436–440 in reprint. For a more complete discussion of the finance curve, including my reasons for defining it as I have done here, see pp. 210–212 below.

for consumption that cannot be carried out instantaneously. Thus the demand for idle funds in any given period must include these two elements beyond those described under the speculative and precautionary motives. The intensity of this demand would rise with increased investment plans and with reduced saving plans. The finance curve should, therefore, exhibit negative elasticity that increases with the absolute amount of the elasticity of the saving and investment curves. Keynes, although admitting this motive for holding cash to his system, argued at times that it was not of great consequence, being simply a "revolving fund" from which money flows out into actual investment at one end as it flows in at the other end from savers or enterprise. Robertson, on the other hand, argues that the size of this fund may fluctuate significantly in response to interest rates because of changes in unfulfilled plans to expand investment and consumption when changes occur in the rate of interest, thus introducing in the Keynesian model of interest-rate determination an element that reflects the influence of interest rates on saving and investment.[16] In figure IIb the demand for cash in response to these four motives is aggregated to form the L curve, which intersects with the supply curve, M, to determine the rate of interest in the familiar liquidity-preference graph.

This outline of the liquidity-preference theory is sharply drawn in order to emphasize the revolutionary appearance of the theory. Quotations from Keynes have been given to show that he also at times presented his theory in this kind of bold relief wherein the rate of interest appears to be determined without reference to either saving or investment demand. Robertson and others have sharply criticized him for appearing to hold just such ideas as these. In defense of Keynes, however, it should be pointed out that in many passages which seem to conflict with some of those quoted above, Keynes appears to grasp much more fully than these statements imply the bearing of saving and investment on interest theory.[17]

This recognition is especially clear in relation to the influence of thrift, or time preference. Keynes states clearly here that his objective is not to remove the relevance of the desire to save and replace it with the desire to hoard, but rather to include both in his scheme.

The psychological time preferences of an individual require two distinct sets of decisions to carry them out completely. The first . . . determines for each individual how much of his income he will consume and how

---

[16] *Ibid.*, p. 436. This issue is further examined in chapter xii, p. 210.

[17] The literature describing and discussing this theory is too abundant to cite, but statements of the theory may be found in J. M. Keynes, *The General Theory*, chapters 13–15 and 18, pp. 165–194 and 245–257; Dudley Dillard, *The Economics of John Maynard Keynes* (New York: Prentice-Hall, 1949), chapter 8, pp. 161–206; Alvin Hansen, *A Guide to Keynes* (New York, Toronto, and London: McGraw-Hill, 1953), chapters

much he will reserve in *some* form of command over future consumption. But this decision having been made there is a further decision which awaits him, namely, in what form he will hold the command over future consumption which he has reserved. . . . We shall find that the mistake in the accepted theories of the rate of interest lies in their attempting to derive the rate of interest from the first of these two constituents of psychological time preference to the neglect of the second; and it is this neglect which we must endeavor to repair.[18]

We note here that Keynes does not reject the "classical" aspect of time preference, but intends only to add a forgotten feature to the analysis.

It may also be argued, though somewhat less convincingly, that Keynes did not wish to rule out the investment curve in the determination of interest rates. In discussing the "classical" theory, for instance, he says he would not dispute the classical statement that *if we assume the level of income to be given,* then "we can infer that the current rate of interest must lie at the point where the demand curve for capital corresponding to different rates of interest cuts the curve of the amounts saved out of the given income corresponding to the different rates of interest." [19]

In the light of the comments made in the last two paragraphs, one may ask where, then, allowance is made in the simplified Keynesian model of interest theory as depicted in figure II*b* for the influence of these two important classical elements in the determination of interest rates: saving and investment. The answer is complex, and it is hoped that chapter xii will clarify it, but two comments now may suggest its general nature. In the first place figure II*b* may be drawn under the assumption that the finance demand (included in *L*) is elastic enough to influence the rate of interest in the same way that the elasticity of saving and investment curves would have done. A second alternative would be to permit the transaction demand (also included in *L*) to show interest elasticity. Either of these two procedures would permit the use of figure II*b* as an illustration of a partial equilibrium model of the liquidity-preference theory of interest. A third alternative would be to modify figure II*b* by drawing a family of *L* curves similar to the one shown, each corresponding to a particular level of income and therefore including a particular transactions demand. This figure would then be used in relation to II*c* and II*d* as part of a general-equilibrium model. This procedure would emphasize, as did Keynes,[20] the complete interdependence of the various functions in his system. In

6–9, pp. 126–165; and Lawrence Klein, *The Keynesian Revolution* (New York: Macmillan, 1947), chapter 3, pp. 56–91.

[18] *The General Theory,* p. 166.

[19] *Ibid.,* p. 178. Italics mine.

[20] See, for example, *ibid.,* the opening pages of chapter 18, or pp. 200–201 in chapter 15.

equilibrium, then, the L curve appropriate to the equilibrium level of income would intersect with M in IIb to determine the rate of interest. In IIc a horizontal representing this rate would intersect with the investment demand curve (MEC) to determine the level of investment. In IId that level of investment is added vertically to the consumption function to determine the aggregate demand for output. The equilibrium level of income is thus determined as that level which evokes a demand for income equal to itself. This simplified model of general (aggregative) equilibrium will be referred to subsequently as the "Keynesian three-graph model."

These comments show that when the Keynesian system includes the finance motive, or when it is made part of a general-equilibrium system, it provides for the influence on interest rates of not only strictly monetary variables, but also the saving and investment demands which formed the heart of the "classical" theory of interest, and which are shown explicitly in the loanable-funds theory. But once we look at the Keynesian theory of interest in this way we rob it of much that gave it an appearance of novelty. On the other hand, the emphasis which it placed upon monetary elements in the determination of interest rates is sharply highlighted in the way the theory is presented, both geometrically and in words, with the result that Keynes himself at times seemed to forget the bearing of nonmonetary considerations and provided grist for the mills of those who supposed that the liquidity-preference theory omitted them entirely as shown in quotations cited above and perhaps most explicitly in this one: "Thus the functions used by the classical theory, namely, the response of investment and the response of the amount saved out of a given income to changes in the rate of interest, do not furnish material for a theory of the rate of interest; but they could be used to tell us what the level of income will be, given *(from some other source)*, the rate of interest . . ." [21]

APPENDIX A: TESTS OF LOANABLE-FUNDS
EQUATIONS AS OUTLINED IN TEXT

The method I have followed for deriving the loanable-funds relations was used because it seemed logically direct and relatively easy to follow. It should be recognized that even the most complete form here presented — equation (1), p. 161 — already assumes some considerable consolidation of accounts as among people, and it does not show either the total supply of loanable funds actually offered on the market or those "conceptually" offered, in the sense of being offered to oneself or in other nonmarket ways. If John Doe saves and offers his funds for securities while Elizabeth Roe dissaves and tries to maintain her balances by selling securities, then there is both a supply and demand in the market for claims, but my equation (1) would show zero on both sides, since S' and

---
[21] *Ibid.*, p. 181. The italics are mine, but the statement in this context is not qualified.

DS' are netted against each other on the supply side. On the other hand, if we try to secure a "grosser" figure by placing DS' on the demand side, we may still give false impressions. For John Doe may both save and hoard while Elizabeth Roe dissaves and dishoards. No demand for securities, and no supply, enters the market, yet both would appear to be present if we followed this procedure. This entire issue is irrelevant so far as determination of interest rates is concerned, but it seems useful to note that none of my expressions really represents actual quantities of funds offered for, or demanded by, security transactions.

Recognizing, then, the arbitrary nature of the process followed in "netting" positive and negative items against one another, we may note the way in which the listing of items as carried out here does properly account for all sides of certain types of transaction in such a way as to give ex post equalities between realized supply and demand, as it must give if it is not in error. I shall list a few hypothetical events and record the items affected under supply and under demand.

For convenience in reference I restate equation (1) from page 161:

$$D\,[=I_n + F_b + C_b]$$
$$= Sy\,[=S' - DS' + C_b - I_{rp} + DH' - H' + F_b + \Delta M].$$

In the table below the sign shown in parentheses indicates whether the term adds to ($+$) or reduces ($-$) the total amount on the side of the equation in which it appears. Thus in event 1, the increase of A's F_b adds to the demand side. The supply side is increased by both this amount (F_b) and by B's DH; it is also reduced by B's H'. The net addition to the demand side equals that to the supply side, as required.

Event	Demand side		Supply side
A borrows from B and adds to his balances	A:	F_b (+)	H' (−); F_b (+)
	B:	(o)	DH' (+)
A gets haircut on credit from B	A:	C_b (+)	DS' (−); C_b (+)
	B:	(o)	S' (+)
A builds house with mortgage finance selling mortgage to B	A:	I_n (+)	(o)
	B:	(o)	DH' (+)
GM replaces outworn machine by drawing down balances	GM:	(o)	DH' (+); I_r (−)
GM buys new machine with funds borrowed from A, who saved them in this same time period	GM: I_n (+)		(o)
	A:	(o)	S' (+)
GM borrows from bank and adds to balances for early need	GM: F_b (+)		H' (−); F_b (+)
	Bk:	(o)	ΔM (+)

APPENDIX B: THE KEYNESIAN L CURVE

Controversy is endemic over the Keynesian curve showing demand for speculative balances. One question concerns Keynes' view about the shape of this curve, another concerns the true shape, and a third concerns its significance. A few brief comments are offered here on the first and third of these questions.

I gave in the text (page 164) Keynes' explanation of the reason that one might expect the L curve to be interest elastic and to approach the horizontal as rates fall. The first question is whether he believed it would really flatten out, or *might* flatten out, or what he did believe. The two major passages in the *General Theory* that refer most explicitly to this question give somewhat different impressions, and I shall quote them in full. The first, on page 207, reads as follows:

There is the possibility, for the reasons discussed above, that after the rate of interest has fallen to a certain level, liquidity-preference may become virtually absolute in the sense that almost everyone prefers cash to holding a debt which yields so low a rate of interest. . . . whilst this limiting case might become practically important in future, I know of no example of it hitherto. Indeed, owing to the unwillingness of most monetary authorities to deal boldly in debts of long term, there has not been much opportunity for a test.

Immediately after this passage in which Keynes says he knows of no past example of a flat liquidity-preference curve, he proceeds to describe two instances in which there was "a complete breakdown of stability in the rate of interest, due to the liquidity function flattening out in one direction or the other." He refers to these, however, as having "occurred in very abnormal circumstances." One was in Russia following World War I, when all persons ran *away* from money, refusing to retain either money or debts. The second, of the opposite kind, and the one of relevance here, when people ran *to* money, was in the United States in 1932, "when scarcely any one could be induced to part with holdings of money on any reasonable terms."

Keynes' next reference to this issue is in his chapter, "The Nature of Capital," (pp. 218–219). Having commented upon the fact that money rates cannot fall below zero because of the zero storage costs on money, he adds:

In fact, however, institutional and psychological factors are present which set a limit much above zero to the practicable decline in the rate of interest. In particular, the costs of bringing borrowers and lenders together, and uncertainty as to the future of the rate of interest . . . set a lower limit which in present circumstances may perhaps be as high as

2 or 2½ per cent on long term. If this should prove correct, the awkward possibilities of an increasing stock of wealth, in conditions where the rate of interest can fall no further under laissez-faire, may soon be realized in actual experience.

I shall not attempt to state further what Keynes' view on this matter "really was," but a few comments will be offered concerning the *implications* of such a "liquidity trap" in case it should exist. The first issue is related directly to monetary policy. If the supply curve for money intersects the liquidity-preference curve at a point where the latter is horizontal, then it would appear to be impossible to expand output by using monetary policy to affect the rate of interest. Two qualifying comments are required, however. One is that despite the general implications of the Keynesian system to the effect that monetary policy can influence the economy only through the rate of interest, Keynes does at a few points open the door to a road which economists like Robertson and Pigou would believe to be important: it is possible, he recognizes, that an increase of money in relation to securities may so increase the sense of liquidity that consumption will be encouraged. The second comment in qualification of the impotence of monetary policy in the context of a horizontal liquidity-preference curve takes us beyond the simplifying assumptions of this study, but should be mentioned none the less. If monetary policy can include devices for loosening credit for risky ventures, it may do much to encourage economic activity even when "pure" rates of interest cannot be lowered because they are already near zero.

Monetary policy is not the only issue involved in appraising the significance of the shape of the *L* curve. The question of underemployment equilibrium under laissez-faire is also involved. One of the avenues through which it is assumed by some that underemployment may tend to set in motion forces which eliminate it, is the effective increase in the money supply which results from falling wages and prices. This mechanism, like that of monetary policy, may be thought to operate both on the consumption function and on the rate of interest, but its efficacy in the second respect is obviously limited by the degree to which the *L* curve flattens out.

A third suggestion concerns the possible *un*importance of a lower limit of money rates "around 2 or 2½ per cent." If we presume that in any event the interest rate could not well fall below zero, then why does it matter so very much whether there is some other limit at a slightly higher level? Many Keynesians and non-Keynesians would agree that the generally accepted validity of the zero-level trap may greatly reduce the importance of the argument over a 2 per cent trap. Keynes himself, in passages like the following (page 219), suggests that this is really just a matter of degree: "Moreover, if the minimum level to which it is practicable to bring the rate of interest is appreciably above zero, there is less likelihood of the desire to accumulate wealth being satiated before the rate of interest has reached its minimum level."

In summary, regarding the significance of the question whether L flattens out in the neighborhood of 2 or 2½ per cent, these comments may be made: (1) The existence of such a trap provides a check to one (but not necessarily the only) means by which monetary policy may be made effective in combatting underemployment. (2) Such a trap may also provide part of the basis for the view that unemployment may not set in motion forces to bring its own elimination. (3) In the broadest theoretical context the argument over a horizontal L curve in the neighborhood of 2 or 2½ per cent is less crucial than might be supposed, because there are many reasons to believe that even if such a region does not exist at these rates, it will still exist at or above zero. Thus the problems noted in comments 1 and 2 may exist in any event, though the likelihood of their actually arising would of course be greater the higher the level of the "liquidity trap."

X

AN APPARENT DIGRESSON
ON SWEDISH AND ROBERTSONIAN CONCEPTS

It is clear that the loanable-funds theory in its classical, nonmonetary form, wherein the interest rate is that rate which equates saving and investment, is entirely inadequate as an explanation of realized rates in a world with money. Changes in the velocity of money (or, alternatively put, changes in hoards) and changes in the quantity of money must be included in the analysis. It is equally clear that the liquidity-preference theory in its simplest form is incomplete: the level of income must be given a prominent place along with the rate of interest in the equation depicting the demand for money. Each theory as defended in the early days of the debates that followed the publication of *The General Theory* contributed its important elements to the synthesis that is taught today. The loanable-funds theory as now presented always includes a function for hoarding and a datum for changes in the quantity of money. The liquidity-preference theory as presented today always includes emphatic reference to the transactions demand as a function of income and as an essential part of the total demand for money. The question now before us does not concern the old controversy over incomplete theories. Rather the issue now is whether, in their present familiar forms, these two theories come to the same thing.

Robertson has stated emphatically that when the liquidity-preference theory is corrected for its omissions it leads us right back where we were in the first place, with a good loanable-funds theory. "Essentially they are two different ways of saying the same thing. Mr. Keynes' long-maintained determination to treat them as 'radically opposed' has been to me from the beginning the most baffling feature of this whole controversy." [1]

[1] D. H. Robertson, "Mr. Keynes and the Rate of Interest," in *Essays in Monetary Theory* (London: P. S. King, 1940), reprinted in American Economic Association, *Readings in the Theory of Income Distribution* (Philadelphia: Blakiston, 1946), p. 433. Robertson had reached this conclusion much earlier, as indicated by the following quotation from "Notes on Mr. Keynes' General Theory of Employment," *Quarterly Journal of Economics*, 61 (1936): 183. "Ultimately, therefore, it is not as a refutation of a common sense account of events in terms of loanable funds, but as an altered version of it, that Mr. Keynes' account as finally developed must be regarded."

Many other writers have agreed with him, and have set out to prove him right. Others have differed and still do so. It is one of the purposes of this Part of my book to examine this controversy and to try to translate from mathematics into simple English the essential content of those parts of the argument which require such a translation. Before this examination can be adequately carried on, however, it is necessary to study two other issues. In the first place, as I have suggested earlier, the loanable-funds theory itself cannot be understood without describing its two major variants, the Robertsonian and the Swedish. It will be helpful also to compare these variants not only with each other, but with a familiar and highly simplified form of the Keynesian saving-investment analysis. This chapter will review briefly the similarities and differences in these three approaches to the study of monetary equilibrium. It should be emphasized that I do not pretend to summarize fully the monetary theories referred to, but only to examine highly simplified versions of one aspect of these schools of thought.

The second study that will provide essential background for an understanding of the liquidity-preference–loanable-funds controversy is one which places interest theory in the setting of a very simple general equilibrium model. That analysis will be presented in the next chapter.

The following symbols will be used throughout this chapter.

B_1 = Balance at start of Day 1
C = Consumption (planned and realized)
I_p = Planned investment
I_r = Realized investment
LF_s = Loanable funds supplied
LF_d = Loanable funds demanded

S_p = Planned saving
S_r = Realized saving
Y_a = Anticipated (expected) income
Y_d = Disposable income
Y_e = Earned income
Y_r = Realized income

Subscript numbers indicate the "day" to which the symbol refers. If variables are not defined as "anticipated" or "realized," then "realized" values should be assumed. If Y is not defined as "disposable" or "earned," then "earned" should be assumed.

DEFINITIONS

As noted on page 162, the term "saving" was not defined in the construction of the loanable-funds theory, the reason being that various concepts may be applied to this theory. In all cases the basic notion is similar: saving = income − consumption. But even under this definition at least three major conceptions may be distinguished.

1. Robertson makes the behavioral assumption that persons receive today the income earned yesterday, and that they decide how much to consume today largely on the basis of the income earned yesterday and

disposable today. Given this conceptual framework, it is natural and convenient to define saving as that part of today's disposable income (yesterday's earned income) which is not consumed today. This concept not only suggests a convenient definition of saving, but it also defines the "day" as any period of such length that the income earned therein is not spent, but is available for spending during the next one. For convenience in analysis I shall follow Bain in adding also the assumptions that (a) this day is short enough that income, employment and prices do not change significantly during it, and that (b) the income velocity of active money is unity during one day.[2] It is not realistic to presume that these three conditions will actually define days of equal length, and hence the simplified analysis will require subsequent qualification. The second assumption — unit income velocity of active money — is one of convenience only, and will not alter the conclusions of the analysis in any important way. The assumption of constant income and prices is of central importance, and its implications will be discussed at some length in succeeding chapters.

An important consequence of Robertson's definition of saving is the fact that equality of saving and investment in his system implies equality of today's and yesterday's earned income. Similarly, an excess of saving over investment implies that income has fallen. This result, it should be noted, does not depend upon any behavioral assumption, but rests entirely on Robertsonian definitions. It may be simply demonstrated as follows:

$$Y_{e1} = C_1 + I_1, \qquad \text{by all definitions examined here.} \tag{1}$$

$$S_1 = Y_{d1} - C_1 = Y_{e0} - C_1, \qquad \text{by Robertsonian definition.} \tag{2}$$

$$\therefore Y_{e0} = C_1 + S_1, \qquad \text{by rearrangement of equation (2).} \tag{3}$$

$$\therefore S_1 - I_1 = Y_{e0} - Y_{e1}, \qquad \text{by subtraction of (1) from (3).} \tag{4}$$

2. A second concept of saving is that which the Swedish economists call "ex post" saving. Keynes' concept in the *General Theory* is of this type.[3] In it, saving is defined as the difference between the income earned in any period and the consumption of the same period. Under this definition saving is always by necessity equal to investment. In contrast to the Robertsonian system in which saving-investment equality occurs only when income is the same as in the previous period, the Keynesian and Swedish ex post saving must equal investment in times of changing as well as stable income, in disequilibrium as well as in equilibrium. The demonstration of this conclusion is simple. All symbols here refer to the same time period.

[2] Joe Bain, *Pricing, Distribution, and Employment* (New York: Henry Holt, 1953), pp. 627–628.
[3] J. M. Keynes, *The General Theory of Employment, Interest, and Money* (New York: Harcourt, Brace, 1936), pp. 61–64.

$$Y = C + I, \qquad \text{by all definitions examined here.} \qquad (5)$$

$$S = Y - C, \qquad \text{by Swedish ex post and by Keynesian definition.} \quad (6)$$

$$\therefore Y = C + S, \qquad \text{by rearrangement of equation (6).} \qquad (7)$$

$$\therefore S = I, \qquad \text{by comparison of (5) and (7).} \qquad (8)$$

3. The third concept of saving is the Swedish *ex ante* or "planned" saving. As in the Swedish *ex post* concept, income, consumption and saving all refer to the same time period. It therefore follows that if expectations were fulfilled in all respects, then ex post and ex ante values would be identical, and planned saving would necessarily equal planned investment since the corresponding realized values must always be equal. The converse statement, however, does not follow: equality of planned saving and investment does not necessarily imply equality of all expected and realized values. Just what such an equality does imply may be shown by a simple but important derivation that can be developed subject to a number of assumptions commonly made in American expositions of the Swedish system. Ohlin has made these same simplifications in his analysis, but Lindahl and Hansen reject them and therefore operate with much more complex systems.[4]

The Swedish system assumes that all variables may be viewed either ex ante or ex post. The simplification referred to above, which I shall make here, is this: it is assumed that all persons are able to purchase what they plan to purchase, and since the "day" in their system is too short to permit changes in plans, this means that realized purchases equal planned purchases.[5] In consequence, planned consumption always equals realized consumption, and planned investment differs from realized investment only because and to the extent that inventories change in unplanned ways. The implications of equality or inequality between planned saving and investment in the simplified Swedish system may now be readily derived as follows:

---

[4] Eric Lindahl, *Studies in the Theory of Money and Capital* (London: Allen and Unwin, 1939), and Bent Hansen, *A Study in the Theory of Inflation* (London: Allen and Unwin, 1951).

[5] The Robertsonian "day" differs from the time period of Swedish analysis both conceptually and clockwise. As stated earlier, the former is of such a length that "yesterday's" earned income is spent "today," and is thus closely related to the intervals of income receipts. The Swedish period is of such duration that plans are made at the end of each "day" but not changed during a "day." In Keynesian analysis a still different time period is often convenient because of multiplier analysis. Roughly this period is that necessary for money to pass from one income receiver through the productive process and back to another ultimate income receiver. Obviously all of these "days" are crude concepts of averages, since they will differ among individuals and over time. A fairly lengthy literature discusses them, but this issue does not seem crucial to our analysis. If we wished to refine our study we should have to examine this question in detail.

$$S_p = Y_a - C, \qquad \text{by definition.} \tag{9}$$

$$Y_r = I_r + C, \qquad \text{by definition.} \tag{10}$$

$$\therefore C = Y_r - I_r, \qquad \text{by rearranging (10).} \tag{11}$$

$$S_p - I_p = (Y_a - C) - I_p, \qquad \text{by subtracting } I_p \text{ from both sides of}$$
$$\text{equation (9)} \tag{12}$$

$$= [Y_a - (Y_r - I_r)] - I_p, \qquad \text{by substitution for } C \text{ from (11)} \tag{13}$$

$$= (Y_a - Y_r) + (I_r - I_p), \qquad \text{by regrouping (13)} \tag{14}$$

$$= (Y_a - Y_r) + \textit{unintended inventory increase}, \qquad \text{by the simpli-}$$
$$\text{fying assumption described in text above.} \tag{15}$$

Putting the final equation in words, we may conclude that an excess of planned saving over planned investment implies either (a) a deficiency of realized as compared with expected income, or (b) an unintended increase of inventories, or (c) a combination of the two, or possibly (d) a value of one of these two which is high enough to more than compensate for a negative value of the other (e.g., a small unexpected decrease in inventories might be more than compensated by a larger deficiency of realized over expected income).

The implications of the saving-investment relations revealed in this brief review of the three systems will be seen more fully in the following discussion of monetary equilibrium and in the further analysis of the relations between the three approaches to equilibrium. In the next section I shall follow the general pattern of a simple Keynesian analysis of saving-investment equilibrium in which abstraction is made from both (a) the rate of interest, together with the effects of its changes, and (b) prices of goods and services, together with the effects of changes in these. Since the purpose of this study is to examine the theory of interest, it may seem digressive to examine models that abstract from interest rates. The relevance of this step will become obvious, however, when we study general equilibrium solutions in which the factors which I now isolate become essential parts in the determination of interest rates.

THREE SIMPLE MODELS

Keynes emphasized the idea that equality of saving and investment is not achieved primarily through changes in the rate of interest, but rather through changes in the level of income. The adjustment process under even this limiting assumption has been explained in many ways. Three rather familiar simplified expositions will be analyzed here, both because their frequent use makes it important to understand assumptions on which they rest that are not always explicit, and because they provide a convenient means of presenting major elements in adjustment toward equilibrium. These models also provide a convenient way of showing the meaning of the Swedish equations developed above, which in a sense provide a parent model from which each of the other two may be derived by adding limiting assumptions.

Model 1

Figure IIe represents a conventional picture of Keynesian saving-investment equilibrium. In this model it is assumed that both saving and investment are functions of income, but, as is typical in the Keynesian system, saving is much more elastic to income than is investment. The income that equates saving with investment is OR,[6] as may be seen directly from the saving-investment intersection at W or from the intersection of $C + I$ with the 45 degree line at Q. Some of the implicit assumptions of this model as commonly presented are these:

1. Planned consumption equals realized consumption, as in all models here presented.

2. Realized income always equals anticipated income, accepting the common interpretation of anticipated income as that anticipated by consumer-savers. The fact that familiar presentations of this model do make this implicit assumption may be demonstrated by considering the way the figure is used. (a) The level of consumption is said to be functionally related to income because of psychological propensities, and each point on the consumption function is said to be psychologically related to the corresponding level of income. Thus it is clear that values on the x-axis must represent *expected* income, since it is in relation to these that the C-curve is drawn. (b) The distance AF, for example, is "realized income," being made up of actual consumption (AB), planned investment (BE), and unplanned investment (EF). (c) But AF is deliberately made equal to OA by the construction of OF at a 45 degree angle with the x-axis. (d) Therefore realized income (AF) and anticipated income (OA) are clearly assumed to be equal in this elementary model.

3. Planned saving equals realized saving (equals BF). This follows directly from the fact that saving equals income minus consumption, and planned values have been shown equal to realized values in each of the latter two.

4. The only expectations or plans that are frustrated in this model are those of entrepreneurs, who find that realized investment differs from planned investment to the extent of unintended accumulation or decumulation of inventories. This fact follows from (a) the identity of realized and planned magnitudes in all other variables than investment, from (b)

---

[6] Throughout this chapter and the following ones letters referring to points on the figures are printed in roman type in order to distinguish them from letters that have direct symbolic meaning (such as C for "consumption") and are printed in italic.

the assumption made in this and the other models that planned investment purchases are all carried out successfully, and from (c) the assumption that prices are constant.

5. Keynes would have said that "saving equals investment" in this
model whether or not equilibrium has been achieved. He would mean by
this that realized saving of BF equals realized investment of BF. Most
contemporary expositions of Keynes would say that in any disequilibrium
with income greater than OR, such as OA, saving exceeds investment.
They would mean by this that *ex ante,* or planned saving of BF exceeds
ex ante, or planned investment of BE.

6. The process which moves the system toward equilibrium is the unintended increase or decrease of inventories, represented in this case by
EF, which may be equally well described as the excess of realized investment over planned investment or as the excess of planned saving over
planned investment. The former expression $(I_r - I_p)$ is a direct expression of the fact of unintended growth of inventories, whereas the latter
$(S_p - I_p)$ leads us to the cause of the trouble in the relation between the
propensity to consume and the determinants of planned investment.

7. The working-out of this model might be described by some such
process as the following. A previous equilibrium at F may have been
disturbed by a sudden downward shift of *C* or *I* or both as a result of
changed expectations or attitudes toward thrift. Production plans do not
immediately adjust wholly to the change, and hence income produced =
OA = AF in the immediately succeeding period. The undesired increase
of inventories EF causes business to reduce output in the following period. This model is static. It does not describe the path to equilibrium,
but only indicates that there will always be a tendency to move in that
direction from any displacement on either side of it.

8. It may be indicated in passing that if we measure these variables in
money values, and if we then relax the assumption of constant prices, the
discrepancy between planned saving and investment may not represent
an increase in inventories, but may instead indicate that unwanted inventories were cleared by price cuts. In both this event and the one where
constant prices were assumed, the distance EF represents an excess of out-
payments made by business over sales and results in a consequent reduction of business outlays during the succeeding period. In this case, however, business has suffered a straight loss (or, in a noncompetitive model,
perhaps only a deficiency of realized compared with expected profits),
with consumers securing the same goods as anticipated but at a lower
price, whereas in the other instance enterprise retained the goods represented by EF.

9. The identity of realized income with that expected by consumers,

as implied by this model, is admittedly unrealistic. Two comments should be added, however. One is that the lack of realism may not be quantitatively serious if the time period involved is long enough that consumption plans can adjust to emerging evidence about income as the period passes. This rationalization would, of course, be inconsistent with the assumption of the Robertsonian "day," but Keynes did not define his time periods in those terms. The second comment is that this unrealistic assumption of identity between expected and realized values is not novel, but characterizes most equilibrium systems. The Walrasian system for example, avoids cobwebs by presuming a somewhat similar identity in relation to prices assumed by suppliers.

10. If we refer back to equation (14), i.e. $(S_p - I_p) = (Y_a - Y_r) + (I_r - I_p)$, we may now note that the simple Keynesian model just described is a special case of the more general Swedish model. Indeed, if we merely add to the latter the assumption that realized and expected income are always equal, the second term drops out, and we secure precisely the relations just illustrated by Model 1. An excess of saving over investment implies an equal excess of realized over planned investment — that is, an equal growth of undesired inventories. If S_p equals I_p, on the other hand, then all expected values equal all realized values, and there is no reason within the system to expect a change in the level of income in the next period.

Model 2

The same figure (IIe) which illustrated Model 1 may also be used to illustrate a second kind of approach to equilibrium of saving and investment. Whereas the former was drawn in Keynesian terminology and fairly well represents a simplified Keynesian analysis, the second model is drawn with Robertsonian terminology. For this reason, although we shall use the same figure, given points and distances now have very different connotations from those of Model 1. Furthermore, by admitting to this model the Robertsonian behavioral assumption that today's consumption is a function of yesterday's income, we shall find that successive time periods are much more clearly tied together in the second than in the first model.

If we again permit OA to represent income earned in period 1, then C and I (i.e., AB and BE) represent consumption and investment as actually realized in period 2. Similarly BF represents Robertsonian saving for period 2, not for period 1, since $S_2 = Y_1 - C_2$ (i.e., AF − AB). No distinction is now required between planned and realized magnitudes, because income refers to the previous period and is known, while consumption and investment plans do not have time to be changed during the "day" being studied. In this description of the model it may be noted that the Robertsonian behavioral assumption is indicated by the fact that the levels of consumption and investment in day 2 are determined by the income of day 1.

The path toward equilibrium is now clearly defined. Income in day 2 equals $C_2 + I_2$, i.e., AB + BE, or AE. By marking off OH equal to Y_2 as thus determined, we may measure $C_3 = HJ$, $I_3 = HT = JK$, and $Y_3 = HK$. We now draw NP so that ON, and hence NP, = HK, and continue the process until equilibrium is reached at Q.

We demonstrated in paragraph 10 of the preceding section that Model 1 may be regarded as a special case of the Swedish system. If we now add to Model 2 the assumption that today's expected income (Y_a) is always equal to yesterday's realized income (Y_r), then Model 2 also becomes a special case of the Swedish system. Indeed, it becomes precisely the complementary case to that presented in Model 1. In Model 2 we abstracted from any difference between realized and planned investment, thus making the third term of the Swedish equation equal to zero. Introducing this assumption, the Swedish equation becomes

$$S_p - I = Y_a - Y_r. \tag{16}$$

But precisely the same equation may be derived from the Robertsonian saving-investment equation when we admit to it the assumption that Y_{a1} equals Y_{r0}. The Robertsonian equation was:

$$S_1 - I_1 = Y_{e0} - Y_{e1}, \qquad \text{(equation (4), p. 174).}$$

But the Robertsonian definition of saving, together with the identity of realized and earned income, permits us to write this as:

$$(Y_{r0} - C_1) - I_1 = Y_{r0} - Y_{r1},$$

and the assumption described above that Y_{a1} always equals Y_{r0} transforms this equation to:

$$(Y_{a1} - C_1) - I_1 = Y_{a1} - Y_{r1},$$

or, in Swedish vocabulary:

$$S_p - I = Y_a - Y_r,$$

which is precisely equation (16).

Comments on Models 1 and 2

In summary it may be said that Model 1, a familiar presentation of Keynesian saving-investment equilibrium, is a special case of the Swedish system. The major feature that must be added to the Swedish system in order to obtain Model 1 is the assumption that expected and realized *income* are always equal to one another. Similarly Model 2, which is sometimes used to illustrate Keynesian equilibrium in terms of Robertsonian analysis, can be transformed into a complementary special case of the Swedish system by assuming that expected and realized *investment* are always equal to one another. The dynamics of these two special cases may be readily contrasted by consideration of these differences in special assumption. In Model 1 consumers are not frustrated, for they consumed and saved in each day the desired amounts with given income; but entrepreneurs were frustrated by an unintended inventory change, and they therefore so acted as to change the level of income the succeeding day. In Model 2, on the other hand, entrepreneurs were not frustrated (no divergence appeared between I_p and I_r), but consumers' realized income turned out to be different from expected income so that their consumption did not bear the desired relation to income; in consequence, consumers revised their expectations concerning income for the next period, and altered their consumption plans accordingly. Thus the major dynamic force that moves the system toward equilibrium in Model 1 arises from frustrated expectations of producers, that in Model 2 arises from frustrated expectations of consumers.

I have deliberately labeled these models Model 1 and Model 2 rather than Keynesian and Robertsonian models because neither one adequately represents the whole thinking of either author, and because the points of contrast I have drawn do not properly emphasize the basic differences between the Keynesian and Robertsonian approaches. Nor does this discussion appropriately focus attention on the central differences between the Swedish and Robertsonian systems. In short, the contrast just presented is useful because it reveals important characteristics of familiar models of analysis, not because it is an adequate characterization of these schools of thought. In order to avoid misinterpretation brief additional comments should be given on the emphases of these three approaches.

The Keynesian system as presented in *The General Theory* is essentially a static-equilibrium model, and it is fairly represented in Model 1 so far as the partial-equilibrium system of saving-investment equality is concerned, though Keynes emphasizes the interdependence of the equations examined here with others in his general-equilibrium system. As is typical of static equilibrium models, the analysis cannot describe the path to equilibrium, though it does describe the kind of forces that will tend to move the system toward equilibrium in case of disturbance. As Model 1 implies, Keynes' emphasis is on changes in entrepreneurial behavior as a result of unfulfilled expectations rather than upon any divergence between the expected and realized income of consumers.

The Robertsonian line of thought does not emphasize explicitly the idea that consumer expectations rather than business expectations are the moving elements in adjustment to equilibrium, though Model 2 is so drawn as to give this emphasis. The central emphasis of Robertsonian methods is to describe today's behavior in terms of yesterday's events rather than in terms of today's. The Robertsonian system is therefore a dynamic one with the aid of which a clear path toward equilibrium may be traced, and this is its basic difference from the Keynesian model. It seems to me more a coincidence than an intention that Robertson's model as sometimes presented places such special emphasis on the consumption function that its exposition neglects possible frustration of entrepreneurs arising from unintended changes in inventories.

We turn now to the Swedish system. I believe that the model given here represents a fair presentation of that system as commonly described in America as well as by Ohlin, though it greatly oversimplifies the analyses of Lindahl or Hansen. The contrast between the Swedish and the Robertsonian theory is not adequately described, however, by what has been emphasized thus far in our presentation of Model 2 as a special case of the Swedish. I have already shown that the central feature of Model 2 emphasized above — its abstraction from unintended inventory changes — is not intended to be a characteristic of the Robertsonian system. A second assumption that was made in order to transform the Swedish model into Model 2 was that today's expected income is determined by and equal to yesterday's realized income. The absence of this assumption in the Swedish model comes much closer to describing the real difference between the Robertsonian and Swedish systems. Yet I cannot go quite all the way with the idea frequently voiced that the Robertsonian system can be regarded as a special case of the Swedish by merely adding this assumption. I should prefer to say that in addition to permitting no unintended inventory change, we may transform the Robertsonian and Swedish systems into a single integrated theory by admitting two further assumptions, of which this is only one. Thus we would need to add to the Swedish theory the idea that persons' expectations of today's income are determined by and equal to yesterday's realized income; and we would need to add to the Robertsonian system the assumption that the reason people spend today on the basis of yesterday's income is because this determines their expectations. This integration of theories would greatly facilitate the application and testing of the Swedish system (though it might make the theory less valid!) by describing an objective determinant of expectations, and it would provide a single, clear psychological basis (but not the only possible one) for the Robertsonian behavioral assumptions.

It may be added that the numerical results of the two systems would be equal without admitting both of the special assumptions made above. The assumption that yesterday's realized values determine equal expected values for today is sufficient for this numerical identity, since Y_{r0} could then always be substituted for Y_{a1} and the transformation described above following the statement of equation (16) could always be made.

But it does not seem to me legitimate to say that this means the theories are the same. Robertson might well believe, for instance, that the reason today's consumption is determined by yesterday's realized income is not exclusively because of the influence this datum has upon expectations; it might be even more crucial that means of payment are not available today from today's income, either expected or realized, but only from yesterday's income. In this event the identical numerical result of the two theories follows for reasons that are entirely different one from the other. The identity of Y_{r0} and Y_{a1} would then become at least in part an unimportant coincidence in the Robertsonian explanation, whereas it remains the central explanatory element in the Swedish system. It is for this reason that I am reluctant to accept the view that the Robertsonian theory is merely a special case of the Swedish system: in order to make the two theories identical it is really necessary to admit qualifying assumptions to both theories, not just to the Swedish one.

Model 3

Although the central feature of the Swedish system is its emphasis upon divergences between expected and realized values of economic variables, the system of equations I have derived above to represent that theory has made it possible to show another sense in which it exhibits a breadth which is lacking in Models 1 and 2. It permits adjustment from disequilibrium because of frustrated expectations of both enterprise and consumers. This model may now be presented by diagram as were Models 1 and 2.

Figure II*f* illustrates this analysis. Since adjustment now takes place in two ways rather than one, the solution is more complex. And since expectations need not be wholly explained by objective features of previous realized values, the path to equilibrium is not wholly defined in this system. I shall proceed, as in Model 1, by describing the direction of movements that might be expected in consequence of unrealized expectations, and then by arbitrarily selecting values that are consistent with this direction of change.

The x-axis now measures both expected and realized income, but the two are not identified with each other as in Model 1. In this illustration we begin by assuming that anticipated income for day 1 is indicated on the x-axis by Y_{a1} (= OA). Realized income cannot be inferred from this assumption as it could in Model 1, where it was assumed equal to expected income, and hence some figure will have to be hypothesized: let us say OH. Our objective is now to describe the process that leads toward equilibrium and also to relate this to the difference between planned saving and planned investment. I first repeat in tabular form the relations described above for the first time period, and then derive additional ones.

Anticipated income $\equiv Y_a = \text{OA} = \text{AF}$

Planned consumption (C_p) $\equiv C = f_1(Y_a) = \text{AB}$
  = Realized consump-
    tion (C_r)

Planned investment $\equiv I_p = f_2(Y_a) = \text{AT} = \text{BE}$

Planned saving $\equiv S_p = Y_a - C = \text{AF} - \text{AB} = \text{BF}$

Realized income $\equiv Y_r = \text{OH (by hypothesis)} = \text{HM} = \text{AD}$

Realized investment $\equiv I_r = Y_r - C = \text{AD} - \text{AB} = \text{BD}$

Realized saving $\equiv S_r = Y_r - C = \text{BD} = $ Realized investment

The way in which figure II*f* illustrates equation (14) may be demonstrated as follows:

Equation (14) is: $S_p - I_p = (Y_a - Y_r) + (I_r - I_p).$

Corresponding elements
  in figure II*f* are: $\text{BF} - \text{BE} = (\text{AF} - \text{AD}) + (\text{BD} - \text{BE}),$

                         $\text{EF} \quad = \quad \text{DF} \quad + \quad \text{ED}$

   In the tabulation above, realized income was said to have been determined arbitrarily. This is true in the sense that it cannot be derived from the other variables shown. Yet it is, of course, "determined" in some way. Indeed, I shall assume that it is equal to the total amount that producing enterprises expect to be the demand for their output, both of consumer and of investment goods. This follows in part because I assume that enterprise is able to buy what productive services it wishes, just as I assume that consumers can do the same with consumer goods. Furthermore, by defining inventories as capital goods, not as consumer goods, this formulation permits deliberate changes in the size of inventories despite the statement that the production of consumer goods equals enterprise expectations of demand for these. The crucial point is that there is no reason to presume that enterprise expectations of C must equal the level of C shown in figure II*f*, which represents plans of consumers, not of enterprise; and there is no reason to presume that expectations of I by enterprises producing these goods need equal the value of I in figure II*f*, which represents demand for investment goods by buyers.

   The following relations may now be summarized with respect to the level of realized income assumed in figure II*f*.

   1. Unlike the assumptions of Model 1, realized income does not here equal income anticipated by consumers. Under my assumption it turns out that realized income is less than was anticipated, by the amount DF.

   2. Unlike the assumption of Model 2, realized income does not equal $C + I$, since both of these elements describe demands based on income

expectations of the demanders, whereas realized income is determined by the expectations of each producer regarding sales of his particular product. Under my assumptions it turns out that realized income is greater than $C + I$, indicating that expectations and hence output of producers exceeds actual sales by the amount ED, which represents unintended growth of inventories.

3. The difference between output demanded and anticipated income (EF) is thus made up of two components: (a) The unintended increase in inventories (ED), which corresponds to the gap between $C + I$ and Y in Model 1; and (b), the discrepancy between anticipated income and realized income (DF), which corresponds to the gap between $C + I$ and Y in Model 2.

In order to move from day 1 to day 2 we must either assume some new arbitrary set of expected values or some principle for their determination. We might choose a model in which expectations are determined by previous levels of realized values; or we might assume that rates of change of variables determine expectations; or we might relate business expectations to profit rates, or to election returns, or to news from the Middle East. The Swedish framework leaves room for a great variety of dynamic and other determinants of current expectations. In the model I have drawn in figure IIf, I make the arbitrary assumption that buyers' income expectations are based on, and equal to, previous income, with the result that the new Y_a (i.e., OH, or HM) equals AD. On the other hand I have not derived sellers' expectations (which determine realized income of HR in day 2) directly from any previous variables shown in the figure. The direction of change in enterprise expectations is assumed to be downward because of the entrepreneurs' discovery that previous expectations exceeded actual demand, with a consequent undesired increase of inventories; hence HR is assumed to be less than AD. But the exact location of R is not fully determined by the values that emerged during day 1.

Given the functions as drawn and the assumptions just described concerning expectations, it is now possible to describe the values of all variables in day 2. C and I reflect buyers' expectations as shown by Y_{a2} and they are therefore determined by the intersections of HM with the consumption and investment functions. Thus $C = HJ$, $I_p = HU = JK$. Aggregate demand for output equals HK. Other values are as shown in the figure. This process for moving from one day to the next may continue so long as we have means of determining relevant expectations. Consumption continues to drop so long as realized income, and hence the next period's anticipated income, is less than this period's expectations. This is the adjustment process described also in Model 2. Investment continues to decline so long as demand $(C + I)$ proves to be less than producers' expectations, with consequent undesired increases of inventories. This is the process of adjustment described in Model 1.

It may be observed in passing that we could readily convert Model 3 into Model 2 by assuming that each period's expectations are in all respects equal to previous realized values. Business expectations in day 2 would then equal previous $C + I$, or AE. MD is thus moved down to the position of a horizontal from E, just as in figure IIe. Similarly, buyer expectations for day 2 are based on an expected income of AE, determining a new C and I by the intersections of the respective functions with a vertical from the new M, which corresponds precisely to the M of figure IIe. This graphical demonstration illustrates the conclusions reached earlier regarding the relation between Swedish and Robertsonian models.

A Note on the Stability of Equilibrium

One final feature of these systems should be mentioned before we move on to examine the relation of interest rates to these constructions. As I have presented these systems, each equilibrium had the general quality of stability. A disturbance tended to cause movement toward a new equilibrium. Yet it is characteristic of the Wicksellian analysis that disequilibrium generates cumulative forces moving away from equilibrium! Myrdal emphasizes this view and gives it his own support: "The monetary equilibrium has the nature of being labile instead of stable as in the general price theory . . . and the monetary equilibrium position is, therefore, not a tendency at all but just the contrary. The equilibrium position is a state of the system which must be upheld by incessantly counteracting the influence of all intervening primary changes, if the system shall not start rolling." [7] To be sure, the cumulative movements are not envisaged as going on indefinitely, and "Wicksell gave the reasons why the banking system would sooner or later stop such a process by changing the conditions under which credit could be obtained." [8]

The apparent contradiction between the models given above and Myrdal's model of highly unstable equilibrium may be explained partly by the fact that I have here abstracted from the effects of the rate of interest, the behavior of which provides the setting for the cumulative movements just described, and partly because I have abstracted from price changes and the effects of these on further price expectations. Since the focus of this book is not on monetary equilibrium, I shall not examine these issues further here, but the subsequent analysis of interest rates will offer some added elements to this sketch.

---

[7] Gunnar Myrdal, *Monetary Equilibrium* (London: Hodge, 1939), p. 36.
[8] *Ibid.*, p. 29.

CONCEPTS OF SAVING IN RELATION TO
THE THEORY OF INTEREST

The major part of this chapter has been devoted to a review of the way in which a Swedish, a Robertsonian, and a simple Keynesian definitional system, together with corresponding behavioral assumptions, may be applied to an aspect of equilibrium theory that abstracts from the rate of interest (among other things). The question now is whether one system of thought is more appropriate than another to the analysis of interest rates. Which concept of saving is appropriate for the saving curve used in the determination of these rates?

In the first place it is obvious that ex post saving cannot be used for this purpose. Ex post saving is a datum, not a schedule. Furthermore, ex post saving must equal ex post investment regardless of the rate of interest and regardless of whether or not the system is in equilibrium, whereas no such equality should in general characterize the kinds of saving and investment schedules used in determining interest rates.

Both ex ante saving and Robertsonian saving are schedules of the kind required for the determination of an equilibrium. The curves depicting them would normally intersect investment curves at only one rate of interest. Which is the appropriate schedule would appear to depend entirely upon the findings of behavioral observations: does the level of saving by economic entities depend upon previous levels of income, as implied by Robertson, or upon expectations regarding current income as suggested by the Swedish model?

A number of criticisms that have been leveled at the Swedish approach may be mentioned though they do not appear valid. D. H. Robertson, for example, objects because expected values are always nebulous and imprecise.[9] It would be helpful, to be sure, if some way could be found to relate these expectations, or their results on the rate of interest, to some objective quantitative measure or some familiar economic function. Without some such direct relation to other economic variables one feels tempted to suggest the application here of Robertson's well-known reference to the determinants of the rate of interest in Keynes' system as "a grin without a cat." [10] Much as this criticism appeals to our desire for a more manageable theory than the Swedish, it seems to me to miss the essential point. The true issue is not whether expectations are vague, but whether they are, in fact, determinants of saving decisions. At this point I share Rothschild's preference for being vaguely right rather than precisely wrong. It is not their precision but their relevance

---

[9] "Mr. Keynes and the Rate of Interest," p. 431.
[10] *Ibid.*, p. 448.

to decision-making that must determine their appropriateness for a theory of interest.

Another objection to the Swedish system is that market prices must be objectively determined, and saving which has not yet occurred but is merely expected cannot enter a loan market as a part of demand. In reply it may be said that whatever funds enter the loan market come from balances, only indirectly from income. Those balances may have been built up by excesses of income over expenditures over many past periods. The real issue is what determines how much of these balances will be offered for securities. Ohlin provides a good solution in his suggestion that the amount offered will depend upon both the *possible* supplies — the balances available — and the supplies that lenders *desire* to make available. Possibilities are greatly influenced by earnings of the immediate past, but ultimately by balances. Desirabilities are very likely influenced by expectations over many future periods, and to some extent by past income, especially through the habits it has engendered.[11] Furthermore, since most persons' expected income for today is close to yesterday's realized income, that figure gives a good bench mark for the objective determination of future expectations. We have already observed that all one needs to do in order to make the Swedish system yield results identical with those of Robertson is to introduce the hypothesis that persons always expect today's income to equal that of yesterday: then today's expected income becomes the same as today's disposable income — yesterday's earned income.

In this proposal lies a compromise which appropriately recognizes the influence on saving decisions of both yesterday's realized income and today's expected income — both the Robertsonian and the Swedish models — together with the possibility of circumstances which would cause each to give identical results. The suggestion comes from Sweden. And Robertson likewise recognizes the appropriateness of a solution that encompasses both kinds of influence: "I am far from denying that people's current expenditure on consumption is influenced by their expectations as regards future income." [12] A real-world saving function, we may conclude, will take something from Robertson and something from the Swedes.

One final comment concerns the implication for concepts of hoarding that follow from the various definitions of saving discussed in this chapter. The definitional distinction drawn here between Robertsonian and

---

[11] Bertil Ohlin, "The Stockholm Theory of Savings and Investment," *Economic Journal,* 47 (1937), reprinted in American Economic Association, *Readings in Business Cycle Theory* (Philadelphia and Toronto: Blakiston, 1944), 87–130. For this reference see p. 100 in the reprint.

[12] D. H. Robertson, "Mr. Keynes and the Rate of Interest," p. 430.

Swedish saving is a familiar one. It appears less widely recognized, however, that these contrasting concepts of saving are necessarily associated with correspondingly different concepts of hoarding.

The question that forces this recognition upon us is this: Where simultaneous saving and Robertsonian saving are unequal, how can it be possible that the rate of interest equates $S + \Delta M$ to $H + I$ according to each definition simultaneously? If the loanable-funds theory of interest is valid when used in relation to Robertsonian analysis, then the equilibrium rate of interest must be such as to satisfy this equality, according to Robertsonian terminology. But the Swedish system would imply that it must also hold both ex ante and ex post in the equilibrium they envisage. Suppose interest rates are in equilibrium, but income is gradually rising (or falling) so that ex post saving $(Y_{r1} - C_1)$ does not equal Robertsonian saving $(Y_{r0} - C_1)$. How, in this case, can both statements of the loanable-funds theory be valid?

A detailed analysis of the processes envisaged by these two approaches will show that a perfect reconciliation is achieved if one recognizes the different concept of hoarding appropriate to each of the two views of saving. In the appendix at the end of this chapter this question is examined, and a numerical example is used to illustrate this and other relations discussed above. Briefly, the conclusion is that Robertsonian definitions require that hoards at the end of a day be conceived as the difference between the money supply then and the money in active circulation on that day. This view is essentially consistent with our popular conception of the term. Swedish (or Keynesian) terminology, on the other hand, results in a definition of hoarding which identifies it with the entire money supply, so that changes in hoards occur only when the quantity of money changes. All money held is hoarded by this set of definitions. Keynes was not arbitrary, therefore, but was consistent with his use of the meaning of saving when he said that "it is impossible for the actual amount of hoarding to change as a result of decisions on the part of the public, so long as we mean by 'hoarding' the actual holding of cash. For [by this view] the amount of hoarding must be equal to the quantity of money." [13]

APPENDIX: CONCEPTS OF HOARDING

At the close of the preceding chapter I have shown that a problem may arise if, in applying the loanable-funds equation to a given circumstance, one wishes to reconcile the implications of the Robertsonian system with those of the Swedish. The difficulty occurs because it seems reasonable to suppose that an equilibrium rate of interest would be possible under

---

[13] *The General Theory*, p. 174.

conditions wherein the values of saving by these two approaches would not be equal. If that were true, how could each equation hold at the same time? If both do not hold, which definition permits a consistent loanable-funds theory?

The following considerations and examples suggest that the loanable-funds equation may legitimately be applied under either set of definitions, and that both can be simultaneously true even with different values of S, because the appropriate concept of hoarding will differ in a compensatory way between the two systems. In the table on page 191 I have developed a hypothetical example of a community made up of two individuals. Values of the crucial variables are shown at a succession of time periods. The appropriate concepts of saving and hoarding according to the Robertsonian and Swedish approaches will be clarified by study of this example.

It will be necessary to trace the processes described here by examination of the table, since I shall not recapitulate the full analysis in the text. The following general features of the example should be noted in order to interpret the table. Numbered subscripts on symbols for flows refer to the time period of the flow; those on the symbols for stocks refer to the start of the period in question. B (balances) will be boldface when referring to the measure appropriate for the Robertsonian analysis. This differs from the balance used in the simultaneous analysis for the following reason. Robertson's "day" is one in which yesterday's earned income is first received and then spent; dawn therefore precedes the receipt of this income. The simultaneous approach assumes that the expenditure of today is drawn from today's earned income, and therefore today's change in balances must reflect today's income rather than yesterday's. The opening balance must already incorporate the receipts of yesterday's earned income, and the closing balance must reflect the receipt of to-day's income. This argument is supported by the fact that, as the illustration shows, no other accounting will satisfy the loanable funds equation in each of the two systems simultaneously.

In this example I have abstracted from the shifts of functions which would result from changes in interest rates as time passes. That issue will be examined in the next chapter. Because of this abstraction, the following illustration provides a numerical example consistent with the sequence analysis described earlier in this chapter in which the interest rate does not appear.

I assume for the purposes of this illustration that the entire community is made up of two individuals, A and B. During period 1, B uses 200 units of his investment expenditure to hire A, and 100 to pay himself imputed wages. During period 2 he again pays 200 to A, but this time he pays only 90 to himself. Since A's entire income is derived

HYPOTHETICAL EXAMPLE

Date or time period	Item	Symbols used		Amounts		
		Robert-sonian	Simul-taneous	Mr. A	Mr. B	Aggre-gate
Jan. 1	Balance excluding Y_{e0}	B_1	...	300	100	400
Jan. 1	Previous earned income[a]	$Y_{e0} = Y_{d1}$	Y_0	800	800	1600
Jan. 1	Balance including Y_{e0}	...	B_1	1100	900	2000
Jan. 1–31	Consumption (assumed)	C_1	C_1	700	500	1200
Jan. 1–31	B sells bonds valued at 200 to A, and "buys" 100 himself	LF_{s1} LF_{d1}	LF_{s1} LF_{d1}	200 0	100 300	300 300
Jan. 1–31	B spends on capital goods	I_1	I_1	0	300	300
Feb. 1	Balance excluding Y_{e1}	B_2	...	200	300	500
Feb. 1	Previous earned income[a]	$Y_{e1} = Y_{d2}$	Y_1	700	800	1500
Feb. 1	Balance including Y_{e1}	...	B_2	900	1100	2000
Feb. 1–28	Consumption (assumed)	C_2	C_2	620	530	1150
Feb. 1–28	B sells bonds valued at 200 to A, and "buys" 90 himself	LF_{s2} LF_{d2}	LF_{s2} LF_{d2}	200 0	90 290	290 290
Feb. 1–28	B spends on capital goods	I_2	I_2	0	290	290
Mar. 1	Balance excluding Y_{e2}	B_3	...	80	480	560
Mar. 1	Previous earned income[a]	$Y_{e2} = Y_{d3}$	Y_2	730	710	1440
Mar. 1	Balance including Y_{e2}	...	B_3	810	1190	2000

MEMORANDA DERIVED FROM ABOVE DATA

Date or time period	Item	Robert-sonian	Simul-taneous	Mr. A	Mr. B	Aggre-gate
Period 1:	Robertsonian saving	$Y_{d1} - C_1$		100	300	400
	Simultaneous saving		$Y_1 - C_1$	0	300	300
	Robertsonian Δ hoards	$B_2 - B_1$		−100	+200	+100
	Simultaneous Δ hoards		$B_2 - B_1$	−200	+200	0
Period 2:	Robertsonian saving	$Y_{d2} - C_2$		80	270	350
	Simultaneous saving		$Y_2 - C_2$	110	180	290
	Robertsonian Δ hoards	$B_3 - B_2$		−120	+180	+60
	Simultaneous Δ hoards		$B_3 - B_2$	−90	+90	0

NOTE: Periods 0, 1, 2, and 3 refer to December, January, February, and March respectively.

[a] Earning of income represents a flow, of course, but the payment in models like this one may be regarded as occurring at a moment of time.

from B's consumption plus this employment in investment activity, A's income in period 1 = 200 + B's consumption = 200 + 500 = 700. Similarly B's income = A's consumption plus the 100 investment paid to himself (A incurs no investment expenditure), or 700 + 100 = 800. Period 2 income of A and B are similarly interrelated.

As stated earlier, the chief purpose of this illustration is to clarify the

concepts of hoards required by the Robertsonian system in contrast to
that of the Keynesian and the Swedish systems. I have indicated verbally
above why the balances must be measured at different points of time in
order to give values appropriate to these two approaches. If the "hoarding" term in the loanable-funds equation represents "increase in balances," then the conditions of this equation are consistently satisfied by
methods used here in computing these balances, as shown below.

General loanable-funds equation [(3), chap. ix]		$I + H = S + \Delta M$
Robertsonian concepts	Period 1	$300 + 100 = 400 + 0$
applied to above	Period 2	$290 + 60 = 350 + 0$
Ex post concepts	Period 1	$300 + 0 = 300 + 0$
applied to above	Period 2	$290 + 0 = 290 + 0$

Using these definitions of hoards and balances, the hoards for the community must always equal the money supply in the simultaneous system,
so that the change in hoards had to equal zero in the illustration, where
M was held constant. In the Robertsonian system, on the other hand,
hoards at sunset (shown in the table as Robertsonian balances at the
following dawn) are equal to the difference between the money supply
then and the money in active circulation during the day just past; the
change in hoards is not zero even though M was constant. It may be
noted also that for individuals net hoarding does not equal zero even
in the simultaneous terminology.

This numerical example illustrates a number of conclusions reached
throughout this chapter and the previous one. For some persons the
previous discussion will be clarified by tracing through these relations,
and a few examples follow.

1. For the entire community, ex-post saving must equal ex-post investment in every time period. Thus in period 1, investment (I_1) and simultaneous saving (see Memoranda at bottom of the table) both equal 300.
Similarly I_2 equals 290 equals simultaneous S_2. It will be noted that this
equality does not hold for individuals.

2. The difference between Robertsonian saving and investment always
equals the change in income from the previous period. Thus $S - I$ in
period 1 equals $400 - 300$, or 100, and $Y_0 - Y_1 = 1600 - 1500 = 100$.
Similarly $S - I$ in period 2 equals $350 - 290 = 60$, and $Y_1 - Y_2 = 1500
- 1440 = 60$.

3. In the Robertsonian system we may say that the excess of saving
over investment was absorbed in hoards. That is, the change in Robertsonian hoards was not equal to zero as was the change in Swedish hoards.
As the Memoranda of Table 7 show, Robertsonian hoards increased by

100 in period 1, and by 60 in period 2, corresponding with the excess of saving over investment as shown in paragraph 2.

4. If behavioral patterns of the kind described by Robertson are assumed, then the average propensity to consume would be 75 per cent in period 1 (1200/1600) and 76.6 per cent in period 2 (1150/1500). If one assumes that behavior is determined by simultaneous income, then the average propensity to consume in these two periods would be about 80 per cent in both years (1200/1500 and 1150/1440 respectively).

THE RATE OF INTEREST
AND GENERAL EQUILIBRIUM: A KEYNESIAN
MODEL ASSUMING CONSTANT PRICES

The equilibrium models described in the preceding chapter are incomplete in a number of respects, two of which consist of their abstraction from the effects of changing interest rates and changing prices.[1] In this chapter I shall continue to abstract from changing prices, but I shall admit the role of interest into the analysis.

Any analysis, such as that of the familiar multiplier, which rests upon models like those just presented, will have to be substantially modified in order to give results consistent with even the simplified structure of Keynesian theory. Essentially I have been using only Graph 3 in the three-graph Keynesian model of general equilibrium.[2] To admit Graphs 1 and 2 is to admit the role of the interest rate, which is determined by the forces described in Graph 1, and which enters through Graph 2 into the determination of the level of investment.

One way to describe some of the central characteristics of Keynes' attack on what he called classical theory is as follows. Classical economists presumed that adjustments of relative prices would provide full-employment levels of income, and that saving-investment equality would determine the rate of interest. Keynes argued that price adjustments would not or could not assure full-employment income, and that the saving-investment equality would be attained chiefly by adjustments in income rather than through changes in the rate of interest. The latter was determined for Keynes by the equality of the supply and demand for money. It will be useful to note that each of these systems is consistent with the assumption that in full equilibrium there will be equality *both* between saving and investment, *and* between the supply of and demand for cash. When we admit to our theory all the functional relationships that both approaches recognize, we shall see that both the level of income and

---

[1] In addition these models abstract from uncertainty and maintain the familiar assumptions of static theory that tastes, resources, and production functions are unchanging.

[2] See page 166 and figures II*b* to II*d* for meaning of "three-graph model." Graph 3 refers to figure II*d*.

the rate of interest are involved in the adjustment required for equilibrium levels both of the supply and demand for cash, and of saving and
investment. J. R. Hicks has provided a convenient means of showing the
way in which equilibrium is achieved by the simultaneous adjustment
of the interest rate and the level of income in such a way as to equate
both saving and investment on the one hand, and supply and demand
for cash on the other.[3]

HICKS' *LM* AND *SI* CURVES:
A TWO-DIMENSIONAL MODEL

One way to present the essentials of Hicks' analysis[4] under simplified
Keynesian-type assumptions is illustrated in figures III*a* to III*d*. Figure
III*a* is the familiar Keynesian curve for marginal efficiency of capital
(investment) rotated one quarter turn counterclockwise. Figure III*b* is
the typical saving-income curve used in the preceding chapter and shown
as the *S* curve in figures II*e* and II*f*. Any horizontal line crossing both
figures will represent equality of investment and saving at a value shown
by the height of the line. Its intersection with the investment curve in
figure III*a* shows by its x-value the interest rate that will be consistent
with this level of investment, and its intersection with the saving curve
shows by that x-value the level of income that is consistent with that
level of saving. Thus the conditions permitting the equality of saving
and investment may be represented by any combination of income and
interest rate shown by the intersections of any horizontal line with the
saving and the investment curves of figures III*a* and III*b*. We may now
show in figure III*d* the combinations of interest rate and level of income
which equate saving with investment in our example. For instance, the
lowest horizontal line in figures III*a* and III*b* indicates an interest rate
of 6 per cent (figure III*a*) and an income of 450 (figure III*b*). Therefore
one point on the *SI* curve is A, which represents this combination of
interest and income. Other points are similarly derived. The resulting
SI curve therefore shows directly that when *r* equals 6 per cent, *S* will
equal *I* only at a level of income of 450; when *r* equals 1 per cent, then
S will equal *I* only at a level of income of 900; and so forth. The logic
of the negative slope of the *SI* curve may be briefly stated as follows:
only at a low rate of interest will investment be great enough to equal
the large saving generated by a high level of income.

[3] J. R. Hicks, "Mr. Keynes and the 'Classics'; A Suggested Interpretation," *Econometrica*, 5 (1937): 147–159. Reprinted in American Economic Association, *Readings in
the Theory of Income Distribution* (Philadelphia and Toronto: Blakiston, 1946), pp.
461–476.
[4] Hicks calls the *LM* curve the *L* curve (see *ibid.*), but I share Hansen's preference for
the designation *LM*. See Alvin Hansen, *Monetary Theory and Fiscal Policy* (New York,
Toronto, and London: McGraw Hill, 1949), chapter v, pp. 71–83; also Alvin Hansen,
A Guide to Keynes (New York, Toronto, and London: McGraw Hill, 1953), p. 144.

These three figures show the relation between income and interest rates required for saving-investment equilibrium. A similar relation may be derived for the requirements of equilibrium in the supply and demand for cash. In figure IIIc typical liquidity-preference curves are drawn for each of the four levels of income associated with horizontal lines in figures IIIa and IIIb. The precise location of the L curves has been arbitrarily chosen, but the general nature of the relation between them is not arbitrary: it reflects the fact that transactions balances will have to be higher for high than for low levels of income. Any given M determined by the banking system will intersect these liquidity curves at different rates of interest (unless they are horizontal or do not intersect at all), and these rates may be related in figure IIId to the level of income associated with the L curve in question. Thus Y_1, representing an income of 450, determines an L curve shown by L_{y1}, which intersects M at an interest rate of about 2.2 per cent; and Y_4 (= 900) determines an interest rate of 4.2 per cent. These points trace out the LM curve. The logic of its positive slope is the consideration that a high income brings with it a high demand for active balances and, with a given money supply, must be associated with a high enough interest rate to force a corresponding reduction in the demand for idle balances.

So far as saving-investment relations are concerned, equilibrium could lie anywhere along SI in figure IIId. So far as the supply and demand for cash are concerned, equilibrium could lie anywhere along LM. Only at the intersection of the two curves are both conditions satisfied. Such an intersection will presumably exist since the SI curve is negatively sloped and the LM curve is positively sloped. In all reasonable probability the intersection will lie in the upper right quadrant. The argument for this conclusion can be developed by a discussion of the probable locations of the LM and the SI curves, but it is equally convincing and much simpler to recognize merely that equilibrium at zero or negative income is scarcely conceivable as a real world phenomenon, and that negative rates of interest in terms of money are also unlikely where the costs of storing money are negligible.

One of the inadequacies of the model we have just described is the fact that it achieves its simplicity partly by assuming that investment is a function of the interest rate but not of income, and assuming also that saving is a function of income only and not of the rate of interest. These assumptions express the behavioral characteristics that Keynes wished to emphasize, and in this respect they have merit. Those who wish to relax these qualifications of the theory are forced to a more complex system of equations. It will be useful to employ a three-dimensional model in order to examine relations under these less simplified assumptions. Some effort may be involved in understanding the illustrations, and

I shall describe the figures in successive steps. Since these figures will be used extensively in the next 90 pages it is worth the time required to understand them fully.

A THREE-DIMENSIONAL MODEL OF *LM* AND *SI* CURVES

In figure IV*a* one is asked to imagine that he is looking at the inside of a box that lies in front of him and to his right. Only two sides of the box are still standing, the end of the box (EFGH)[5] and the "back" of the box (JKNR). The floor is represented by ABCD. The red surface rises to the right from its intersection with the floor at abc to a high point at g in the back near the KE corner, and rises less sharply in the front to j. As an economic diagram the front left corner represents the origin; income is measured to the right, and the rate of interest is measured from the front toward the back (rising from D to A). Any point on the floor represents a unique combination of income and the rate of interest. The height of the surface above any such point shows the amount of saving that the community would wish to carry out at the indicated combination of r and Y.

Any vertical plane parallel to the back of the box (JKNR) will intersect the saving surface in a curve which shows how saving will vary as a function of income when the rate of interest is fixed at the level indicated by the location of the vertical plane employed. Thus the back wall itself shows the saving-income curve when r equals 5 per cent. This curve is adg, and its similarity to the Keynesian saving curve shown in figures II*e* and II*f* is obvious. Had the interest rate been 3 per cent, saving would presumably be somewhat less at each level of income, so that the saving curve shifts down to the position bqh.

Any vertical plane parallel to the end of the box (EFGH) will intersect the saving surface in a curve that shows how saving will vary as a function of the rate of interest when income is fixed at the level indicated by the location of the vertical plane employed. Thus ghj at the end of the box shows the saving-interest curve of the loanable-funds theory as pictured in figure II*a*. If one visualizes the x-axis as GF and the y-axis as GH, with the origin at G, this picture should be clear. Should income be lower than DC, however, saving at all rates of interest would be lower, representing a shift of the curve toward the y-axis (i.e., toward the floor). An illustration is given by dqf which is the saving curve for an income of $1,200. The combinations of income and interest rate at which saving is reduced to zero are shown by abc. To the left of this the surface should continue below the floor of the box, but that part is not drawn in.

---

[5] It may facilitate the study of these figures to note that planes are lettered clockwise beginning from the upper left corner.

The origin and axes in figures IV*b*, IV*c*, and IV*d* are identical with those in IV*a*. Figure IV*b*, however, describes the relation of investment to income and interest rates. This surface is intended to resemble a sheet that nearly touches the floor at the back wall, but rises with increasing steepness as it comes forward toward the front of the box. Likewise, it is slightly tipped, so that the right edge is higher than the left edge. By procedures analogous to those used with reference to the saving curve, a'd'g' shows investment as a function of income when the rate of interest is 5 per cent, and b' qh' represents the slightly higher investment function associated with an interest rate of 3 per cent. This curve is similar to the investment curve in the Keynesian graphs shown as figures II*e* and II*f*.

Again we may look at the end of the box, letting GF serve as x-axis and GH as y-axis. We now see in g'h'j' the familiar investment curve of the loanable-funds theory (as in figure II*a*), where the level of investment is a function of the rate of interest, and income is assumed to be given. Were income lower, let us say $1,200 instead of $2,400, this curve would be slightly closer to the y-axis, as indicated by the relaton of d'q'f' to the floor under it.[6]

Our next task is to observe what combination of income and interest rates will equate investment and saving. This may be done readily by plotting both surfaces in the same box, as in figure IV*c*. The intersecting curve, si, shows the combinations sought. By projecting this curve vertically downward to intersect the floor at *SI* we are provided with the *SI* curve of the Hicksian analysis. Our model is more complete than before, however, because both saving and investment are now shown as functions of both income and the rate of interest. Figure IV*d* is so drawn as to emphasize the curves showing saving and investment as functions of the rate of interest at different levels of income. In this figure I have dropped a number of vertical planes, parallel to the end of the box, each representing a specific level of income. Each such plane is given three different colors: the lower part is grey, the excess of saving over investment is shown in red, and the excess of investment over saving is shown in green. The Hicksian *SI* wall is shown in blue.

We may readily compare the simple Keynesian analysis with the classical by asking what would happen if we found the economy in a disequilibrium position represented by an income of $2,400 (let us presume full employment) and interest rates of 5 per cent (see HE in the back right hand corner of IV*c*). The classical economist would state that the excess of saving over investment would force down the rate of interest to about

---

[6] The investment curve is typically drawn as if fairly inelastic to the level of income, other variables being regarded as the major determinants of the rate of investment. These other variables include the *rate of change* of income (or consumption), the rate of profit, the state of innovations, and the nature of expectations.

1¾ per cent at i, where saving and investment are equal and where full employment rules. The simplified Keynesian view would be that income would fall to $400, where saving equals investment at s. It was exclusively the latter type of adjustment that I described in the saving-investment analysis of the preceding chapter, for I abstracted there from effects of the rate of interest.

This brief contrast overstates the difference in views in order to make it clear and sharp. Actually the classical economists would all admit the possibility of temporary periods with income less than full employment. And the Keynesian illustration we have just used represents the solution in which his Graph 3 is used alone, as in the last chapter, without reference to the effects of changing income on the rate of interest and hence on investment (or even saving). In order to gain a more complete picture of the Keynesian theory, therefore, I must introduce the three-dimensional counterpart of Keynes' Graph 1 showing the supply and demand for money. This is done in figure V.

Unfortunately the shapes of the surfaces are such that it seems best to alter the axes sharply in depicting the liquidity-preference surface. In the first place our view of the box is changed. It now lies before us and to the left. The floor is JKNR, the back wall EFGH, and the end ABCD. The origin is at O, but this time the rate of interest is measured vertically, and income from front to back (R to J). It is important to notice that the end wall of figure V (ABCD) corresponds precisely with the floor of figure IV, each relating income (Y) to the rate of interest (r). The quantity of money demanded or supplied is shown by the horizontal distance of the appropriate surface from the end wall, ABCD.

In figure Va, I have drawn a surface representing the demand for inactive balances (Keynes' L_2). For any given level of income (i.e., for any plane parallel to the back wall EFGH) the surface will trace out an orthodox L_2 curve with the x-axis on the floor of the box running from left to right, and the y-axis rising vertically, as along HE. Examples of L_2 curves are given by $a_2b_2c_2$ and $d_2e_2f_2$, the former for income of $2,400 and the latter for income of $1,200. We have assumed that the demand for idle balances may be to some extent a function of income, and so we have drawn the surface slightly farther to the right in back than in front.[7]

In figure Vb the surface represents the demand for active balances (Keynes' L_1). On the Keynesian assumption that the demand for these funds is a function of income and not of the rate of interest I have drawn

---

[7] In no sense do I stress the elasticity of L^2 to the level of income. One basis for suggesting it is the assumption that persons with larger incomes are more likely to be conscious of "speculative" considerations. The analysis would proceed essentially unchanged if this elasticity were not assumed to exist.

this surface vertical.[8] For simplicity of exposition I assume the income velocity of active money to be constant and equal to the price level. The equation of exchange $(M_1 V_1 = pY)$ thus reduces to $M_1 = Y$ (where M_1 and V_1 represent the quantity and the income velocity of active money respectively), and hence our L_1 surface must cut any horizontal plane in a 45 degree line running through DA. In other words, every dollar of income must represent an equal amount of active money.

The total demand for money will equal the sum of the demand for active balances and the demand for idle ones.[9] This will be shown graphically by the horizontal sum of the surfaces of figures Va and Vb. The resulting L surface is shown in red in figure Vc. Assuming that the supply of money is determined by the banking system and is not a function of the rate of interest or the level of income, this supply may be drawn as a vertical plane parallel to the end wall at whatever distance from it the banking system determines. I have assumed the supply of M to be \$1,740, and have drawn a vertical plane colored green to represent it. The intersection of the vertical M-plane with the L-surface is the curve lm, which shows the combinations of interest rate and income that equate supply and demand for money. As with the saving-investment intersection, this curve may be projected onto the interest-income plane, which is here the end of the box. The blue surface represents the LM wall, and it traces on the end of the box the Hicksian LM curve of figure IIId.

Having now derived both the SI and the LM curves, it remains only to find their intersection and read off the implications of this equilibrium point. The mechanics of presenting the intersection point are complicated by the fact that the interest-income plane is represented by the floor of the box in the SI analysis (figure IV) and by the end of the box in the LM analysis (figure V). I have therefore derived the equilibrium intersection in two ways. In order to facilitate the understanding of both procedures I have reproduced figure IVc immediately under Vc, making comparison easy. From this figure I have transposed the SI curve to a corresponding position on the end wall (ABCD) of figure Vc. This transposition permits inspection of both SI and LM in the same diagram (Vc). The intersection of the two curves is at Q, indicating an interest rate of 3 per cent and an income of \$1,200. This combination of interest rate and level of income, and only this combination, satisfies both conditions for equilibrium: the equality of saving and investment, and the equality of

---

[8] Hansen permits this surface to bend to the left at high rates of interest because of the plausible assumption that even the velocity of active money will then be affected. I omit this refinement only because it would complicate subsequent exposition without altering the major purposes of this analysis. See A. Hansen, *Monetary Theory and Fiscal Policy*, pp. 66 ff.

[9] At this point in my analysis I abstract from both precautionary and finance balances. Each will be discussed later.

supply and demand for cash. The horizontal line from the equilibrium intersection at Q is drawn to the right in figure Vc to show the equilibrium point on the L and M surfaces at e, where M and L both equal $1,740. If similar constructions are plotted on the ends of boxes Vb and Va, the resulting points on the surfaces shown there (e$_1$ and e$_2$ respectively) will indicate a demand for active balances of $1,200 (since income equals $1,200 and the income-velocity of active money equals the price level), and a demand for idle balances of $540, the two together equaling the total demand of $1,740.

In figure IV c (see reproduction under Vc) a corresponding method enables us to observe the equilibrium solution in relation to saving and investment. Here, it must be remembered, the floor of the box corresponds to the end of the box in figure V. We now transpose to this floor the LM curve from figure Vc. The intersection with SI must, of course, be the same as before, indicating equilibrium at an interest rate of 3 per cent and an income of $1,200. We may now draw a vertical line from this intersection to the intersection of the saving and investment surfaces at q. This shows saving equal to investment at a level of $200.

ALGEBRAIC PRESENTATION

Earlier in this chapter I described the conflicting implications of the simplest presentations of the Keynesian and classical analyses, whereby the former would have found equilibrium at s and the latter at i in figure IVc. I then stated that this simplification of the Keynesian theory did not adequately present Keynes' own position because it abstracted from reference to interest rates. By now introducing the determination of these rates, an equilibrium point on the si curve is determined, lying between the classical solution (i) and the one which would be suggested by consideration of only Graph 3 in the Keynesian model (s). I have now derived a graphical presentation of Keynes' general equilibrium system under the assumption he uses throughout much of his book, namely constant prices. It will be convenient to review these relations briefly in a set of familiar equations.

One way to summarize the description given above would be to state the following relations:

$$S = f_0(Y, r). \tag{1}$$
$$I = f_1(r, Y). \tag{2}$$
$$S = I. \tag{3}$$
$$L_1 = f_2(Y). \tag{4}$$
$$L_2 = f_3(r, Y). \tag{5}$$
$$L_1 + L_2 = L. \tag{6}$$
$$L = \overline{M}, \text{ which is given.} \tag{7}$$

We now have seven equations to solve for the seven unknowns: S, I, L_1, L_2, L, r, and Y. We may, if we choose, abbreviate this statement and focus attention on the crucial variables r and Y by writing expressions which correspond to the SI and LM curves. This is done as follows. By substituting in equation (3) the values for S and I given in equations (1) and (2), we may state algebraically that saving, as a function of r and Y, is equal to investment, as another function of r and Y. This gives us the SI curve:

$$S(Y, r) = I(r, Y). \tag{8}$$

Similarly we may obtain the LM equation by substituting in equation (7) the value of L derived from equation (6) with the aid of (4) and (5). This gives us:

$$L(r, Y) = \overline{M}. \tag{9}$$

When we solve these two equations simultaneously we thereby find the values for r and Y which correspond to the intersection of the SI and LM curves.

ADJUSTMENT PERIODS

I have been discussing here equilibrium models of static systems and hence have not faced the problem of the path to equilibrium. One general comment may readily be inferred from the theoretical construction reviewed, however, and that comment will prove to be important in the following chapter. It is well known that the adjustment which equates saving with investment is time consuming. Even the simple Keynesian multiplier analysis, when presented in the form of a sequence analysis, requires a theoretically infinite time for adjustment, and some months would be needed to reach even a rough approximation of the full equilibrium.[10] The adjustment of the rate of interest in such a way as to provide equality of supply and demand for cash, on the other hand, can be as rapid as the adjustment of security prices which define that rate. With security markets as perfect as ours it is reasonable to assume, therefore, that the economy generally operates close to the LM curve, with a constant pressure toward the intersection of this curve with SI, but with the latter seldom fully achieved.

---

[10] For discussion of the multiplier period, see Gardner Ackley, "The Multiplier Time Period," *American Economic Review*, 41 (1951): 350–368, and sources cited there, including especially F. Machlup, "Period Analysis and Multiplier Theory," *Quarterly Journal of Economics*, 54 (1939): 1–27, reprinted in American Economic Association, *Readings in Business Cycle Theory* (Philadelphia and Toronto: Blakiston, 1944), pp. 203–234.

LIQUIDITY-PREFERENCE THEORY
COMPARED WITH LOANABLE-FUNDS THEORY

The analysis of the two preceding chapters enables us to continue the task of comparing loanable-funds theories with the liquidity-preference theory. Even when both types of approach have been rounded out to include all essential elements, as discussed on the first page of chapter x, a number of important issues still remain to be examined. In the first place two major differences appear between the liquidity-preference and the typical loanable-funds approach. One is that the liquidity-preference theory is drawn in terms of stock concepts: the measures of supply and demand that are used measure the supply and demand at a given moment of time. In contrast, the loanable-funds theory is typically expressed in terms of flows that describe the funds that will be supplied to the market or demanded on the market during a defined (though brief) period of time.[1] The second difference between generalized loanable-funds theories and the liquidity-preference theory is that the former are drawn in terms of the supply of and demand for securities, whereas the latter is drawn in terms of the supply of and demand for money, or cash balances. Beyond the resolution of the controversy over whether these two differences cause the theories to be essentially different three further questions stand out. One concerns the validity of the behavioral assumptions underlying the theories; a second concerns the question whether the functions as commonly drawn in these two theories have similar or very different implications; the third concerns the usefulness and convenience of the two theories — even if it should be true that both theories come to the same thing, one might be considered a more helpful instrument than the other.

HICKS' GENERAL-EQUILIBRIUM ANALYSIS

Various comparisons of these theories of interest have been made, but I know of none that have systematically examined each of the questions I have described. One approach is from the standpoint of general equilib-

---

[1] For further discussion of flow and stock concepts, see pp. 218–222.

rium theory, and Hicks' "proof" is well known.[2] I shall deal with that
briefly first. Hicks' analysis is carried out as though both theories were
built on stock concepts, and it fails to consider any of the problems described above except that of whether a basic difference between the two
theories inheres in the fact that one is presented in terms of supply and
demand for securities, the other in terms of supply and demand for
money. Hicks essentially presumes an auction market where recontracting
takes place until prices are found that will clear the market at a moment
of time. This market includes transactions in all goods and services as well
as money and credit, and in it a full Walrasian type of equilibrium is
achieved. In this situation supply will equal demand for each good, each
service, money, and securities. If we measure prices in terms of money,
we may describe $n - 1$ supply-demand equations for the $n - 1$ goods and
services envisaged. In addition there will be one equation describing
equality between the supply and demand of money-for-hire, and another equation stating the equality of supply and demand for securities,
with the interest rate representing price in each case. Since equilibrium
must equate the marginal benefit of all possible dispositions of funds,
these equations are all made interdependent by stating every quantity as
a function of all prices. Including the rate of interest as one of these
prices, we now have n prices and $n + 1$ equations. One equation is redundant, and this means that any equation in the system may be dropped.
If we follow the conventional practice of retaining all equations for goods
and services, thereby providing Walrasian equilibrium in those markets,
we may also retain either that which equates the supply and demand for
money or that which equates the supply and demand for securities. If
we keep the former, then we are operating with a liquidity-preference
theory; if the latter, then we are making use of a loanable-funds theory.
"It seems to me," says Hicks, "that either of these methods is perfectly
legitimate; the choice between them is purely a matter of convenience." [3]
Thus Hicks joins the ranks of those who say that the two theories are
essentially the same and are merely using different ways to describe the
relationships whereby the rate of interest is determined.

I believe that all parties to the controversy would agree that Hicks'
analysis is correct — so far as it goes. Most would likewise agree that it
does not go very far. First, as stated above, it faces only one of the questions raised in my opening paragraph. Second, as Fellner and Somers
point out,[4] this analysis makes the two theories of interest identical only

---

[2] J. R. Hicks, *Value and Capital*, 2d ed. (Oxford: Clarendon Press, 1948), pp. 154–155
and 160–162.

[3] *Ibid.*, p. 161.

[4] W. Fellner and H. Somers, "Alternative Monetary Approaches to Interest Theory,"
Review of Economics and Statistics, 23 (1941): 43.

in the context of a general equilibrium solution. The characteristic feature of a theory is the first approximation which it states, and the essential function of both loanable-funds and liquidity-preference theories is to serve as particular equilibrium approximations. The question at hand is whether *in this sense* they come to the same thing. Finally what seems to me the most devastating criticism of this "proof" is brought out by Klein in a simple demonstration that Hicks' general equilibrium system, if properly stated, requires neither the "cash" nor the "securities" equation to determine the rate of interest! [5] This rate will have been determined already in the supply-demand equations for goods and services. What the "cash" equation (or, alternatively, the "securities" equation) adds is not determination of the rate of interest, but determination of the absolute level of prices in terms of the numeraire money.

Klein's point is demonstrated by a system of six equations to which I shall refer again later. Two describe the supply and demand functions for goods, two describe the supply and demand functions for services, and two state the equality of supply and demand in goods and services markets. The supply and demand for both goods and services are presumed to be functions of real wages and the rate of interest. The six unknowns are, therefore, (1) quantity of goods demanded, (2) quantity of goods supplied, (3) quantity of services demanded, (4) quantity of services supplied, (5) real wages, and (6) the rate of interest. With six independent equations and six unknowns the system can normally be solved for these unknowns, one of which, it will be noted, is the rate of interest. Since real wages are stated as money wages divided by prices, the solution of this system does not determine either money wages or prices, but only their ratio. When the money equation (or the securities equation) is added, then a solution for either the price level or the wage level is provided, and the other may be derived directly. But the rate of interest will have already been determined.

In terms of the analysis given earlier, it is possible to say that the reason the rate of interest is determined in Hicks' and Walras' system without reference to the money equation is because both authors assume that relative price adjustments force the solution at full employment (i.e., along the end wall in figures IV*c* and IV*d*), with the interest rate necessarily set at the point i by the condition that S must equal I. Given such a condition, introduction of the *LM* relationship would appear to overdetermine the system, but it does not, for the present discussion no longer assumes prices given, as in the earlier presentation of this model. With variable prices the location of the *LM* curve cannot be arbitrarily determined. That is, *LM* shifts as prices change, and equilibrium will be

[5] Lawrence Klein, "Stock and Flow Analysis in Economics," *Econometrica,* 18 (1950): 238, n. 2.

achieved under these circumstances only when prices reach such a level that *LM* intersects *SI* at *I* on the full-employment end of the box. This mechanism will be explained much more fully in chapter xiii when other consequences of variable prices are also recognized.

Because of these limitations in the Hicksian proof, we must turn to other methods of examining the relations between loanable-funds and liquidity-preference theories of interest. A highly informative discussion of the issues which I shall examine in the remainder of this chapter may be found in a series of articles by Fellner, Somers, Klein, Lerner, and Brunner running from 1941 through 1950.[6] Partly because of certain inherent difficulties, however, and partly because the mathematical form of presentation does not always make it easy to see the full economic meaning of the discussion in terms of the customary simple models, my method of analyzing the question is quite different from the one developed in that series.

SINGLE-DAY ANALYSIS: ROBERTSONIAN TYPE OF LOANABLE-FUNDS THEORY

I shall begin by comparing the Robertsonian type of loanable-funds theory with the liquidity-preference theory. My method will be to presume a given set of data and functions, and then to derive the equilibrium rate of interest by each theory for a given "day." I shall then assume certain interday shifts of the functions,[7] and again compare the implications of the two theories under the new conditions of the second day. I shall make brief comparisons of this kind in relation to four different days in order to illustrate a variety of issues.

Figure VI presents the assumed functional relationships and other data for the days chosen. On the left side of the figure these data are utilized in the presentation of a liquidity-preference theory, on the right side in terms of a loanable-funds theory. Figures VI*a* and VI*b* represent one day, figures VI*c* and VI*d* another, VI*e* and VI*f* a third, and VI*g* and VI*h* a last day. The loanable-funds model used is that of equation (3), page 161 above, according to which the equilibrium rate of interest is that rate which equates investment plus net hoarding with saving plus the increase

---

[6] These sources include the following: (1) L. Klein, *The Keynesian Revolution* (New York: Macmillan, 1947), esp. pp. 121–122. (2) A. P. Lerner, "Interest Theory — Supply and Demand for Loans or Supply and Demand for Cash?" *Review of Economics and Statistics*, 26 (1944): 88 ff. (3) Fellner and Somers, "Notes on 'Stocks and Flows' in Monetary Interest Theory," *Review of Economics and Statistics*, 31 (1949): 145 ff. (4) Articles and replies by Klein, Fellner and Somers, and Karl Brunner, *Econometrica*, 18 (1950): 236–252.

[7] These interday shifts are not arbitrarily assumed, but may be derived from examination of the three-dimensional functions in figures IV and V.

(or minus the decrease) in the quantity of money: $I + H = S + \Delta M$. The symbol Δ represents a positive change. The H curve in figure VIb indicates the net amount which hoarders and dishoarders combined would like to add to their idle balances in the first time period — Day 1 — at various rates of interest. In figures VId, VIf and VIh this H curve crosses the y-axis, indicating that at or above some rate of interest dishoarders wish to reduce their balances more than hoarders wish to increase theirs. The I and S curves indicate the investment and saving that will take place in a given day as a function of the rate of interest. According to the equation referred to above, the loanable funds theory states that the equilibrium rate of interest is that rate which equates total supply and demand for loanable funds, where the demand curve (D) is drawn by adding horizontally the H and I curves; the supply curve (Sy) is derived by adding ΔM to S. For the first example I shall presume that there is no change in M. These data determine the interest rate of 5 per cent, with the \$250 excess of saving over investment being completely absorbed in hoards.

In turning to the liquidity-preference presentation it is necessary to remember that I have assumed for simplicity that active money turns over once in a day, so that the volume of active money equals income. To draw figure VIa two further assumptions must be made: $\overline{L_1}$ and $\overline{L_2}$ represent active and inactive balances respectively at the start of the day. M, the supply of money, is therefore determined as the sum of these two amounts. L_1, L_2, and L may be derived from figure VIb as follows. First, the aggregate amount people would like to add to their hoards as a function of the rate of interest is shown directly by the H curve. Since $\overline{L_2}$ shows the amount they now hold idle, the amount they would like to hold idle at day's end is indicated by adding H to this amount. If the rate of interest, r, is 5 per cent, net desired additions to hoards $(H) = +250$. Therefore at 5 per cent L_2 is 250 units to the right of $\overline{L_2}$. Similarly, at $r = 3$ per cent, $H = 500$, and L_2 lies 500 units to the right of $\overline{L_2}$. It is assumed, incidentally, that plans are carried out successfully according to whatever interest rate rules.

Similarly L_1 may be derived from L_1 by the aid of the S and I curves. It will be remembered that in the Robertsonian system an excess of S over I indicates that income in this period will be less than that of the previous period by the amount of this difference. Active balances must therefore decline from L_1 by the excess of S over I in figure VIb — or rise by the excess of I over S. It may be noted that L_1 is so drawn, intersecting $\overline{L_1}$ at $r = 2.6$ per cent, at which rate $S = I$ in figure VIb. The total demand for money equals the horizontal sum of L_1 and L_2, and it is drawn as L. The liquidity-preference theory of interest determines the rate of interest at the intersection of total demand for and supply of money, i.e., where L intersects M in VIa, which proves to be 5 per cent, precisely as in VIb.

Furthermore, this interest rate implies that persons will add to hoards during the period exactly the $250 which they withdraw from active balances, just as in figure VI*b* the excess of saving over investment was added to hoards. Indeed, this is what must occur unless the quantity of money or the velocity of active money changes.

This simple example of Day 1 illustrates the fact that with the data given here the loanable-funds theory and the liquidity-preference theory yield the same rate of interest. But it is immediately obvious that one feature of the liquidity-preference graph appears unorthodox. The L_1 curve is not vertical. Furthermore the method by which we derived it makes it impossible for this curve to be vertical unless we presume the horizontal distance between the S curve and the I curve in the loanable-funds graph to be equal for all levels of interest. Although such a condition is not inconceivable it is extremely unlikely. It would be realized if both saving and investment were believed to be totally inelastic to the rate of interest, but I doubt if any one would wish to build a theory on an assumption this extreme.

How, then, do we explain the sloping L_1 curve in terms of the logic by which I previously drew the Keynesian L_1 curve vertically? Indeed what does this L_1 curve of figure VI represent in terms of the three-dimensional model? The answer to these questions is that L_1 in figure VI represents a section of a surface not yet drawn at all. It describes the demand for active funds necessary to support the *earned* income that results from given combinations of interest rate and *disposable* income. In short, by plotting both disposable and earned income, and by not assuming them to be equal, we find it no longer possible to utilize a vertical L_1 surface as in the simple Keynesian presentation. If our three-dimensional model is to represent a Robertsonian loanable-funds analysis, then the income measure by which the floor of the LM box is calibrated from front to back must refer to *disposable* income, and the active balances demanded for any given level of disposable income will not be invariant to the rate of interest unless "saving minus investment," and hence the corresponding *earned* income, is likewise invariant to r. In order to illustrate the Robertsonian version of the loanable-funds theory in our three-dimensional system, therefore, we must draw a new L_1 surface. This may be done with the aid of figure IV by simply noting that the demand for active balances equals current earned income in our model, and that this equals disposable income plus $(I - S)$. The L_1 surface is constructed, therefore, by placing each point a distance from the end wall that equals its distance from the front of the same box (disposable income) plus the value of $(I - S)$ for that combination of disposable income and interest rate, as shown in figure IV*c* (or IV*d*). In figure VII I have drawn a model based on this assumption, VII*b* showing the new L_1 surface, and VII*c* showing the new total L surface. For convenience in study I have redrawn the L_2 surface in figure VIIa, though it is left identical to that of Va since there is nothing which requires it to be of a shape other than that previously assumed.

An over-all rationalization of the shape of this L_1 surface as contrasted with that of the surface shown in figure Vb would run as follows. Whereas the Vb surface is vertical, this one has a negative slope, because for any level of disposable income, investment falls and saving rises as interest rates increase, so that the demand for active balances at any given disposable income falls with rising rates. Second, whereas the other surface cuts the floor and other horizontal planes in a line that forms a 45-degree angle with the x-axis, this L_1 surface cuts such planes with a curve whose slope is at all times greater than 45 degrees. The reason is, that as disposable income increases, saving rises more rapidly than does investment, so that earned income and the corresponding demand for active balances rises less rapidly than does disposable income. In the figure the intersection with the floor always lies to the right of a 45-degree line through the origin, because, in figure IV, when $r = 0$, investment exceeds saving at all levels of disposable income. This is a purely arbitrary assumption used in the construction of these figures, and need not always hold.

The question now raised is whether the need for this new construction of the L_1 surface implies a significant difference between loanable-funds and liquidity-preferences theories of interest. The answer requires an analysis of the various interpretations that might be given to the vertical L_1 curve in the latter theory. Such a curve would seem legitimate under either of two types of assumptions: (1) If the investment and saving curves are assumed to be virtually interest inelastic (or parallel at some other slope than vertical), then the rate of interest would have no significant effect on the level of income, and no problem is presented in drawing L_1 vertical. (2) If the graph showing the demand and supply of money is presented as an integral part of a full general-equilibrium model, as in the model of the Keynesian system shown in figures IIb to IId, then a vertical L_1 curve is legitimate even though saving, investment, and hence income are presumed to be interest elastic. This is because shifts in income resulting from changed levels of interest rates will feed back from the rest of the system into the money equations and cause appropriate shifts in L_1. Without the general-equilibrium model it would not be appropriate to draw a vertical L_1 under the assumptions of this example, because the money equations would then be drawn on *ceteris paribus* assumptions although the influence of the dependent variable r on the functions is so great that only a *mutatis mutandis* equation would be appropriate.

The first set of assumptions described above would clearly not provide a satisfactory reconciliation of the liquidity-preference model with the loanable-funds model, since it would deny to the determination of the rate of interest precisely those functions that the loanable-funds theory places in a position of central importance — saving and investment. The second set of assumptions would be entirely consistent with a reconciliation of the two theories as blocks in a general-equilibrium framework, but it would be unsatisfactory as a presentation of a particular equilibrium theory of interest because of the illicit *ceteris paribus* assumptions.

One implication of these comments is illustrated by the fact that figures V and VII give precisely the same general-equilibrium solution for all variables, since the values of the L surfaces in these two figures are equal for all points corresponding to solutions along the SI curve. This follows from the fact that the demand for money in figure VII equals that of figure V plus $(I - S)$, and $(I - S)$ equals zero for all points along the SI curve. In summary, then, either figure V or figure VII will give appropriate solutions for full equilibrium, but only figure VII will give appropriate interest equilibrium under conditions when income has not so adjusted as to equate saving with investment.

Keynes himself, partly in an effort to bridge the gap between his theory and that of Robertson, proposed a procedure that could, under proper interpretations, make the two theories consistent with one another even while L_1 is drawn with zero interest elasticity. His procedure makes two general assumptions. In the first place it is a special case of (1) above in which saving and investment are not functions of current interest rates — hence the vertical L_1 curve — but are functions of yesterday's rate of interest. Second, it assumes that there is a "finance" motive for holding funds in addition to the three motives described in *The General Theory*. Keynes' statements about this motive are inconsistent with one another or ambiguous, and it is not clear how far he felt it would go to provide a full reconciliation between the two theories. But Robertson and others have taken the opportunity to argue that some such curve as this must be drawn to make the Keynesian theory valid, and they have maintained that when it is properly drawn it can provide a reconciliation between loanable-funds and liquidity-preference theories despite the inelasticity of the transactions curve to the rate of interest.

Keynes describes the finance curve in this way. "I introduced this term to mean the cash temporarily held by entrepreneurs to provide against the outgoings in respect of an impending new activity." [8] Under this assumption low rates of interest, by raising the volume of "impending new activity" (i.e., investment), increase the amount of funds demanded for finance. Thus even though it is assumed that actual investment in real assets exhibits only a lagged response to interest rates, the effect of a

---

[8] "Mr. Keynes and Finance: Comment," *Economic Journal*, 48 (1938): 319.

sloping investment curve on the demand for money, and hence on interest rates, is felt immediately, as in the loanable-funds theory, and a reconciliation between the two theories is achieved on the side of investment, since the horizontal sum of a vertical transactions curve and the interest-elastic finance curve provides the same elasticity of demand for funds as required by the investment curve of the loanable-funds theory.

A problem still remains on the side of saving. It would seem to me that the only way for the finance curve to provide a full reconciliation between the two theories would be to presume that, just as enterprise builds up a finance balance in immediate response to a fall in interest rates for the purpose of later real investment, so also consumers sell securities and thereby build up their balances in immediate response to a fall in interest rates and in advance of the actual increase of consumption which the lower rate encourages them to make, the latter being carried out only in the following period. Under these assumptions the finance curve will have a negative slope equal to that of one measuring $(I - S)$.

An examination of Robertsonian assumptions in conjunction with this analysis of the transactions demand in the Keynesian system suggests the following conclusions. (1) The Robertsonian version of the loanable-funds theory is built on the assumption that saving and investment are functions of yesterday's income but of today's interest rates, and that they have significant elasticity with respect to these rates. Under these assumptions a reconciliation with the liquidity-preference theory would require that the transactions curve not be vertical but exhibit slope equal to that of an $(I - S)$ curve. This procedure is not consistent with the Keynesian presentation, but I see nothing in it which in any basic way contradicts the fundamental character of a liquidity-preference theory of interest. When the latter is presented as a particular equilibrium theory for the determination of interest rates without assuming full general equilibrium, it seems to me that the sloping L_1 curve would be a useful and convenient feature to include, and one which would make it consistent with the loanable-funds theory. (2) Reconciliation of these two theories by means which retain the vertical slope of L_1 is also possible. Since interest-elastic saving and investment curves are basic assumptions of the loanable-funds theory in general they must be retained. The Keynesian determination of interest rates can be reconciled with this theory while retaining vertical L_1 only by adding a finance curve that reflects the elasticity of $(I - S)$ but does not imply that these curves are reflected in simultaneous changes of income. The use of this finance curve as defined in the preceding paragraphs does permit the liquidity-preference model to give the same rate of interest as the loanable-funds theory despite the employment of a vertical L_1 curve. This reconciliation would require a basic reconstruction of the income relations in the Robertsonian system because of its implication that the impact of changing interest rates on income is a lagged one, but such a change need not be contradictory to the essential character of a loanable-funds theory of interest.[9] (3) If interest theory is used as part of a set of general equilibrium relations, then the same general-equilibrium solution will result whether L_1 is vertical or not, and whether a finance curve does or does not supplement a vertical L_1.

Having now compared loanable-funds and liquidity-preference constructions of the analysis of interest rates in a single "day" of sequence analysis, we next move on to the succeeding "day" in order to study the adjustment of interest rates over time. Figures VIa and VIb provide some of the information required for this transition, but not all. A set of behavioral assumptions adequate to determine the entire shift to equilibrium will require three-dimensional functions, and we may utilize the three-dimensional models of figures IV and VII for that purpose. First, however, the consistency between those models and the drawing I have made of Day 1 in figure VI should be noted. (1) Both figures VIa and VIIc show an interest rate of 5 per cent resulting from an M of $1,740 and a disposable income of $1,600 (point l' in both figures). (2) Under these circumstances the demand for active balances is $1,350 (Fk in VIa and L'k in VIIb), the difference between this and disposable income implying a $250 decline in income ($1,600 − $1,350). (3) This fall in income may be regarded as having resulted from a $250 excess of saving over investment (VIb and IVd), together with corresponding increases in hoards (Pj in VIb and in VIa). (4) Fj in VIa corresponds with L'k' in VIIa, both being equal to $390.

On the basis of information from our three-dimensional graphs and from the outcome of Day 1, we may now derive the curves for Day 2 as shown in figures VIc and VId.

1. $\overline{L_1}$ and $\overline{L_2}$ must, by definition, represent the active and inactive balances respectively at the close of the preceding day. They are therefore drawn as continuations downward of kC and jB from figure VIa. The shift of these curves from the start of the first day reflects the transfer of $250 from active to inactive balances which has already been noted.

2. L_2 may be read directly from figure VIIa in the light of the fact that disposable income is now $1,350.

3. L_1 may be drawn by the same method as in Day 1, its value at all levels of r being equal to $\overline{L_1}$ plus $(I − S)$, this last term being represented by the difference between the green and red surfaces corresponding to a disposable income of $1,350 in figures IVc and IVd. Alternatively we may read L_1 directly from VIIb for a disposable income of $1,350.

---

[9] In the preceding discussion I have been aided by discussion with Ronald Jones of the University of Rochester.

4. L is now drawn by adding L_1 and L_2 horizontally. Assuming no change in the money supply, M is drawn vertically below the corresponding curve in VIa, and this completes the drawing of the liquidity-preference figure (VIc) for the second day. The rate of interest is determined at 3.6 per cent.

5. I and S in figure VId may be drawn directly from the corresponding surfaces in figures IVc or IVd assuming disposable income of \$1,350.

6. H can be drawn readily with the aid of figure VIc, being equal to $L_2 - \overline{L}_2$.

7. Assuming no change in the quantity of money we may now regard the supply of loanable funds as identical with the S curve; the demand is drawn as the sum of I and H; the intersection shows an interest rate of 3.6 per cent, just as did the liquidity-preference construction.

There is no need to trace through the derivation of the rate on subsequent days, as it is entirely analogous to that of the previous two periods. The process continues to approach as a limit the full equilibrium pictured in figures VIe and VIf. Here the amount of active balances is \$1,200 and the rate of interest is 3 per cent, at which rate saving equals investment, net hoarding equals zero, and both L curves cross their respective $\overline{L}$ curves. The fact that this situation provides equilibrium is shown similarly in the three-dimensional models. In figure VIIc, an M of \$1,740 provides equilibrium at an interest rate of 3 per cent and disposable income of \$1,200 (intersection of SI and LM at Q). In figure IVc we find that this combination of income and interest rate provides equality of saving and investment at a level of \$200, just as shown in VIf.

By our previous assumptions, however, an income of \$1,200 is far from the one required to provide full employment. The banking authorities therefore decide to increase the money supply drastically — e.g., by \$1,260, raising the amount supplied from \$1,740 to \$3,000. The new situation is shown in figures VIe and VIf by the shift of M to M' in the former and the shift of the supply curve to Sy' in the latter. The immediate effect is to reduce interest rates to about 1 per cent and develop a marked excess of investment over saving (about \$300 as seen in either figure VIf or IVd). The resulting expansion of income is shown by the excess of L_1 over $\overline{L}_1$ at a 1 per cent rate of interest (figure VIe). Now a process of income expansion is set in motion. As income rises interest rates are forced upward by expanding demand for transactions balances, but the rate never reaches its former equilibrium. Rather it approaches as a limit the level shown in figures VIg and VIh, where it equals 2 per cent, inducing active balances of \$2,000, with saving equal to investment at a higher level than before, namely, \$400 per day. The lower interest rate encourages the larger investment, and the higher income produces the higher level of saving. As in the previous equilibrium, this solution was derived from figures IV and VII. The latter shows that with a money supply of $3,000 equilibrium will be achieved at T, with a disposable income of $2,000 and an interest rate of 2 per cent. Similarly T and u in figure IVc show that this combination of income and interest result in equality of saving and investment at $400.

AN ALGEBRAIC RESTATEMENT

A simple translation into algebra will provide a check on the arguments advanced above. This section may be omitted without loss of continuity, but the mathematics is elementary, and I believe it will further clarify the relations discussed.

The system I have been presenting may be related to four sets of equations. The first set describes saving-investment relations; it is an integral part of both the loanable-funds and the liquidity-preference presentations. The second set consists of equations for the supply of and demand for cash; this set is used in presenting only the liquidity-preference interpretation. The third set consists of equations describing the supply of and demand for loanable funds in terms of saving, investment, hoarding, and changes in the supply of money; this set is, of course, used in the loanable-funds interpretation of the system. The fourth set of equations describes the interrelationships between the second and third sets of equations that provide the resulting equivalence of the two systems when applied to one day and/or when applied to the entire sequence analysis, assuming that interday shifts are related in each system to the same underlying three-dimensional functions. These four sets of equations will now be described. The headings for the columns in each presentation are indicated by letters, as follows: (*a*) Equation number used for reference; (*b*) Number of equations; (*c*) Number of equations excluding equation 3; (*d*) Unknowns; (*e*) Sometimes unknown; (*f*) Assumed data. Columns *d* and *e* include both the symbols for the variables and numbers showing the cumulative total of unknowns to that point.

1. *Equations for both theories*

a	b	c	Equations	d	e	f
1	1	1	$S_t = f(Y_{t-1}, r_t)$	$\begin{cases} S_t & (1) \\ r_t & (2) \end{cases}$	Y_{t-1} (3)	...
2	2	2	$I_t = g(Y_{t-1}, r_t)$	I_t (3)	(4)	...
3	3	2	$S_t = I_t$	... (3)	(4)	...

Notes. — (i) If *full employment* is assumed, then Y_{t-1} is a datum in this system (determined by the production function for labor and the labor supply). The system of equations is then solved for saving, invest ment, and the rate of interest by aid of the 3 equations in this set alone. For number of equations and number of unknowns, see columns b and d respectively. Similarly, in our graphs, figure IVc provides the full solution, that being determined at I.

ii) For any day in *sequence analysis,* Y_{t-1} is given, but does not necessarily equal \$2,400. In the sequence analysis presented here, saving does not equal investment until ultimate equilibrium is reached, and therefore equation 3 is dropped. This leaves us 2 equations (column c) with 3 unknowns (column d), and the system is not solved. Indeed, what we have now is the S and the I curves of traditional theory, with the location of these curves determined by the assumed value of Y_{t-1}, but with*out* the assumption that the solution for the rate of interest will lie at their intersection. Figure IVd illustrates a number of such pairs of curves.

iii) For *full equilibrium not assuming full employment* we use all 3 equations and assume Y_{t-1} to be unknown. The system now has 3 equations (column b) and 4 unknowns (column e). It is therefore unsolved, and, indeed, defines our Hicksian type of SI curve (Figure IVc).

2. *Money Equations added to Equations of Set 1*

a	b	c	Equations	d	e	f
4	4	3	$L_{1,t} = h(Y_{t-1}, r_t)$	$L_{1,t}$ (4)	5	$\ldots$
5	5	4	$L_{2,t} = j(Y_{t-1}, r_t)$	$L_{2,t}$ (5)	6	$\ldots$
6	6	5	$L_{1,t} + L_{2,t} = M_t$	$\ldots$ (5)	6	M_t

Notes. — (i) If *full employment* is assumed, so that Y_{t-1} is given *and* equation 3 retained, then the system is now overdetermined. Column b shows 6 equations and column d shows 5 unknowns. Graphically, LM might not intersect SI under i in figure IV, in which case two conflicting solutions would be suggested. A way to avoid overdetermination is to admit prices as a variable and assume that they will so adjust as to make LM intersect SI at a point corresponding to I. This is the classical system, and it indicates that the function of the LM relations is to determine prices, not interest rates.[10]

ii). For any day in *sequence analysis,* with Y_{t-1} given but equation 3 omitted, the system is now complete with 5 equations and 5 unknowns as shown by columns c and d respectively. As in our one-day solutions of figure VI, S does not equal I except in ultimate equilibrium. This solution would correspond to a point on the LM curve, with the specific point determined by the given Y_{t-1}.

iii) For *full equilibrium not assuming full employment* the solution is now complete, with all equations included (6 by column b) and with 6

[10] See chapter xiii below.

unknowns including Y_{t-1} as shown in column e. With M equal to \$1,740, the solution would be at Q in figures IVc and VIIc; with M equal to \$3,000, it would be at T in these figures.

3. *Loanable-Funds Equations added to Equations of Set 1, now omitting Set 2. (R^S and R^D represent the supply and demand for new securities respectively.)*

a	b	c	Equations	d	e	f
7	4	3	$R_t{}^S = I_t + \Delta H_t$	$\begin{cases} R_t{}^S \ (4) \\ \Delta H_t \ (5) \end{cases}$	5 6	... ...
8	5	4	$R_t{}^D = S_t + \Delta M_t$ $= S_t + M_t - M_{t-1}$	$R_t{}^D \ (6)$	7	M_t, M_{t-1}
9	6	5	$\Delta H_t = h(Y_{t-1}, r_t)$	... (6)	7	...
10	7	6	$R_t{}^D = R_t{}^S$	... (6)	7	...

Notes. — (i) If *full employment* is assumed, then the system is overdetermined as shown by the 7 equations of column b and the 6 unknowns of column d.

ii) For any day in *sequence analysis* columns c and d show the system determined, with 6 equations and 6 unknowns.

iii) For *full equilibrium not assuming full employment,* columns b and e show the system determined, with 7 unknowns and 7 equations.

4. *Relations between Equations of Set 2 and those of Set 3.*

i) Sets 1 and 2 and 1 and 3, representing the liquidity-preference and the loanable-funds theories respectively, give quite parallel results. In both cases the assumption of full employment yields overdetermined systems, whereas the study of a single day in a sequence analysis and the study of full equilibrium without assuming full employment both provide systems which are neither over- nor underdetermined.

ii) The above systems, however, do not imply each other. Set 3 cannot be derived from 1 and 2, and 2 cannot be derived from 1 and 3. There is no reason to presume that they would yield the same equilibrium solutions unless more restrictions are provided than are stated in the systems as thus far described. In other words, more relations must be stated before we can say that loanable-funds and liquidity-preference theories yield identical results in terms of equilibrium values.

iii) It will be remembered that in drawing figure VI I related the loanable-funds and the liquidity-preference systems to one another in ways which were made necessary by the economic relations assumed in the Robertsonian system. The relations utilized may be stated in a set of equations, a study of which reveals that:

Equation 11 shows how we drew L_1 in relation to $\overline{L_1}$, I, and S.

Equation 12 shows how we drew ΔH in relation to L_2 and $\overline{L_2}$.

Equation 13 for period $t-1$ corresponds to equation 6 for period t.

The equations referred to follow:

a	b	c	Equations	d	e	f
11	8	7	$L_{1,t} = L_{1,t-1} + I_t - S_t$	$L_{1,t}$ (7)	$L_{1,t-1}$ (9)	...
12	9	8	$\Delta H_t = L_{2,t} - L_{2,t-1}$	$L_{2,t}$ (8)	$L_{2,t-1}$ (11)	...
13	10	9	$M_{t-1} = L_{1,t-1} + L_{2,t-1}$	... (8)	... (11)	...

iv) Just as my method of deriving figure VI resulted in identity between loanable-funds and liquidity-preference analyses, so these additional equations demonstrate a similar identity. If we add them to sets 1 and 2, they will enable us to show that the equality between supply and demand for money defined in equation 6 necessarily implies also equality between the supply and demand for securities. Conversely, if we add them to sets 1 and 3 they will enable us to show that the equality between supply and demand for securities expressed by equation 10 necessarily implies also equality between supply and demand for money. I shall demonstrate this fact for the second case only, but the first is equally simple.

$R_t^S = R_t^D$. Equation 10.

$\therefore I_t + \Delta H_t = S_t + M_t - M_{t-1}$. Substituting from equations 7 and 8.

$(I_t - S_t) + (M_{t-1} - M_t) + (L_{2,t} - L_{2,t-1}) = 0$. Transposing and substituting from 12.

$(L_{1,t} - L_{1,t-1}) + (M_{t-1} - M_t) + (L_{2,t} - L_{2,t-1}) = 0$. Substituting from 11.

$[(L_{1,t} + L_{2,t}) - M_t] - [(L_{1,t-1} + L_{2,t-1}) - M_{t-1}] = 0$. Regrouping.

$\therefore L_{1,t} + L_{2,t} = M_t$, since the second term above equals zero by equation 13.
Q.E.D.

v) The equations above permit the proof given there concerning equivalence of the two types of interest theory, but they are not sufficient to provide a solution for all the variables that have now been introduced. For full solution we must introduce two more equations:

a	b	c	Equations	d	e	f
14	11	10	$Y_{t-1} = L_{1,t-1}$	... (8)	... (11)	...
15	12	11	$Y_t = L_{1,t}$	Y_t (9)	... (12)	...

The *full employment* equilibrium system is still overdetermined. It includes the unknowns of column e except for Y_{t-1}, making 11 in all, and it utilizes all 12 equations of column b. Only by introducing variable prices can it become an acceptable system. For any single day in *sequence analysis* the system is precisely determined. There are 9 unknowns as in column d; there are also 9 equations — the 11 of column c minus equations 13 and 14, the latter merely describing relations among terms that were assumed as given in the sequence analysis. The *full equilibrium* system, not assuming full employment, is wholly determined but not overdetermined, with 12 equations and 12 unknowns as shown by columns b and e.

STOCK CONCEPTS VERSUS FLOW CONCEPTS

I shall now utilize figure VI to help clarify two major controversies over the similarity or difference between loanable-funds and liquidity-preference theories of interest. The first of these, to be discussed in this section, concerns the meaning and implications of the fact that the loanable-funds theory is couched in flow terms, the liquidity-preference theory in terms of stocks. The second, to be discussed in the subsequent section, concerns the implications of the fact that the loanable-funds theory is drawn in terms of supply and demand for securities, whereas the liquidity-preference theory is drawn in terms of demand and supply for cash.

The distinction between a flow concept and a stock concept is familiar and unambiguous, but the distinction between a flow theory and a stock theory is subject to quite different interpretations. An economic analogy commonly used to illustrate the two *concepts* is the reference to balance sheets and earnings statements. A balance sheet uses stock concepts because it describes quantities in existence at a moment of time; the earnings statement deals with flow concepts because it refers to flows of economic variables over a period of time. A physical analogy would be the measure of water in a reservoir at a moment of time (stock), compared with the flow of water into or out of the reservoir during a period of time (flow). The relation between these two concepts is also familiar: the change in stock as between two moments of time must equal the net flow in or out during the interval between the two moments at which the stocks are recorded.

These elementary relations between stocks and flows are illustrated in figure VI. The change in stock of idle funds between the beginning and the end of the period studied in the left-hand panels (dotted vertical red line in VI*a* minus solid vertical red line) is equal to the net inflow of hoards as shown in the right-hand panels (H) assuming an interest rate of 5 per cent. Similarly the decline in the stock of active balances as shown in the left-hand panels is equal to the excess of the flow of saving over the flow of investment as shown in the right-hand panels. These brief references serve not only to illustrate the use of stock and flow concepts in interest theory, but also to show how the conventional statement of the loanable-funds theory is, indeed, drawn in terms of flow concepts, and how the liquidity-preference theory utilizes stock concepts.

In his excellent analysis of the controversy between loanable-funds and liquidity-preference theorists, Karl Brunner draws the following conclusions regarding the "flow-stock" aspect of the discussion.[11] "By analysing observable phenomena as if they were solutions of a succession of static equational systems, the flow and stock theories of interest coincide." But, Brunner continues, "stock and flow theory will differ essentially as soon as observable phenomena are treated as solutions of dynamic equational systems describing the structure of adjustment processes." The first of these two statements is precisely what we have observed in relation to the Robertsonian version of the loanable-funds theory. The various days examined, when viewed as problems in static equilibrium, showed exactly the same interest rate by the two theories. The second statement is equally valid, but its meaning requires considerably more elucidation. I shall begin an explanation of what it does and does not mean by raising a question which might appear at first sight to contradict it.

Surely our model is a "dynamic system describing the structure of adjustment processes." Indeed, the Robertsonian formulation is, by its nature, a dynamic one, with each day defining the circumstances of the next, and the system as a whole determining not only ultimate equilibrium, but also the path by which it is approached. Yet did we not find that the two theoretical systems — the stock and the flow — described the same path to equilibrium in this dynamic framework? What does Brunner mean when he denies the identity of the two types of approach under the circumstances of his second statement?

The answer to this question is to be found in further study of the meaning of flow and stock theories in contrast to flow and stock concepts. Brunner and Klein would say that one does not create a flow theory merely by using flow concepts. A flow theory would have to assume that ultimate behavioral patterns are defined in terms of flows. To be specific, figure VIb tells us that under the given circumstances people would like to add $250 net to their hoards if interest rates were 5 per cent. Figure VIa shows the same fact. But the crucial question is *why* people wish to add $250. Is it because they desire a stock of $390 and happen to have a stock of only $140; or is it because under the circumstances of income and interest rate they would like to see their idle balances regularly rising by $250 per time period? If their basic attitudes can best be described by the

---

[11] Karl Brunner, "Stock and Flow Analysis: Discussion," *Econometrica*, 18 (1950): 247.

first of these explanations, then Brunner would say we have a stock theory; if the second statement best explains behavior, then we have a flow theory. For the purpose of analyzing one day only it is clearly irrelevant which explanation is accepted, and hence the two theories would yield identical results in this context. But the second day would be entirely different by one theory from what it would be by the other. If income were unchanged, then the stock theory would indicate that idle balances need not change further in the second day: hoarders' goals would have already been achieved. The flow theory, on the other hand, would indicate a need to add $250 more the second day, and the third, and so on indefinitely.

Figure VI was derived by use of the underlying three-dimensional models of figures IV and V. These underlying models assume that hoarding behavior is directed toward the achievement of desired levels of stocks, not of flows. Had these underlying behavioral assumptions been based on flow goals, then the red surface in figure Va would have been forced to shift outward to the right every time-period by the amount of the desired flow.

Now it is clearly a matter of choice what one wishes to define as a flow, or a stock, theory. Fellner and Somers choose to regard the loanable-funds theory as a flow theory because the variables are flow variables. Brunner and Klein would prefer to say that whether it is a flow theory in a more fundamental sense depends upon the underlying behavioral assumptions, and they would say that my presentation is really a stock theory whether I choose to express its day-to-day adjustments in loanable-funds terminology as in the right-hand panels of figure VI, or in the liquidity preference terminology as in the left-hand panels. Although I believe that Fellner and Somers are right in suggesting that past practice would support their terminology, I agree with Brunner and Klein that theirs serves an important function.

It may be useful to note that if the system was in disequilibrium at the close of "yesterday," then there is a sense in which the flow and stock theories would yield different results even for the analysis of a single day. If today's objective is determined by goals conceived exclusively in terms of stocks, then the amount of funds we wish to add today will depend in part upon yesterday's actual stock. If, on the other hand, today's objective is determined by goals conceived exclusively in terms of flows, yesterday's stock is irrelevant to the determination of today's desired flow. A somewhat different way of expressing this idea would be to suppose that the stock desired today must be equal to the net sum of all desired flows since the beginning of time. If the sum of these desired flows up to yesterday was not achieved, and if the desired stock defines demand, then today's desired flow must be larger than it would have been if we started the day from equilibrium. Fellner and Somers of course recognize that in this sense stock and flow theories do not yield identical results if yesterday is assumed to have ended in disequilibrium.[12]

The controversy over stocks and flows may now be summarized. Loanable-funds theories are stated in flow terminology, liquidity-preference theories in stock terminology. So long as the difference is merely one of terminology there can be no difference between the results found by the two theories, because a flow concept can be directly translated into stock concepts by noting that the flow during a day is equal to the difference between yesterday's and today's closing stocks. Those authors who choose to define loanable-funds theories as flow theories exclusively because of the terminology used, are correct in noting that no difference in results inheres in the fact that loanable-funds is a flow theory and liquidity-preference a stock theory. Other authors emphasize the fact that there is a further sense in which stock and flow analyses may differ. They say that a theory does not become a flow theory merely by using flow terminology. A true flow theory **must define behavior in terms** of flow goals, and a stock theory in terms of stock goals. Given this terminology, all would agree that there can be a substantial difference between stock and flow theories. One circumstance that brings about a difference is the existence of disequilibrium at the close of the day preceding the day being examined. Another basis of difference between the two theories would be revealed by an attempt to describe the way in which a succession of time periods are related to one another.

Thus far I have spoken only of idle balances (the L_2 and the H functions). The analysis of the L_1, I, and S functions might be expected to be analogous but converse, since the underlying assumptions I made in this connection were flow concepts, as shown by the saving and investment surfaces of figure IV. Happily that is not so, for, as we shall see, no difference between the two theories exists in connection with active funds. So long as we retain the simplifying assumption of constant velocity of active money, any given *flow* of income corresponds to, and requires, a constant *stock* of active balances. Similarly, an increase in income flow requires a corresponding increase in active stocks. Returning to the physical analogy, it might be said that the kind of flow represented by income is like a circular flow of water within a reservoir, that, to remain constant, requires a constant, not a growing, stock of water in the reservoir. Whereas a constant "daily" flow of new hoarding implies a daily change in idle stocks, a constant daily flow of income does not imply a change in the stock of active balances. For this reason behavioral assumptions defined in terms of desired levels of flow in income are entirely consistent

[12] W. Fellner and H. Somers, "Stock and Flow Analysis: Comment," *Econometrica,* 18 (1950): 242 ff.

with desired levels of stock in active balances. We can, therefore, draw saving and investment surfaces in figure IV which are stable and also consistent with a stable L_1 surface as in figure VIIb. We could not have drawn a stable "hoarding" surface to correspond to a stable L_2 surface.

DEMAND AND SUPPLY OF SECURITIES VERSUS SUPPLY AND DEMAND FOR CASH

The second major controversy over the characteristics which may cause a loanable-funds theory to differ from a liquidity-preference theory concerns the implications of the fact that the former is drawn in terms of demand and supply for securities, the latter in terms of supply and demand for cash. Klein has presented an analysis which indicates that these two theories are consistent with one another only if there is equilibrium in the market for goods and services. Since our comparison of these two theories revealed no such problem, a study of Klein's model is required to find whether our earlier presentation needs modification.

The heart of Klein's argument may be seen by manipulation of two budget restrictions which he sets up, one for households and the other for business. These two equations — (1) and (2) below — are his, but I have somewhat modified the manipulation of them, and the interpretation is largely mine. I believe, however, that this presentation of the possible difference between cash theories and security theories is essentially true to Klein's position.

The following symbols will be used:

b = business sector	R = values of securities
D = demand	r = rate of interest
h = household sector	S = supply
L = demand for money	t = "today"
M = supply of money	$t - 1$ = "yesterday"
N = quantity of employment	w = money wages
p = price of goods	x = quantity of goods

The budget restriction equations reflect the assumption that the demands of members of both the household and business sectors for resources to be held at the end of the day must be consistent with their holdings of resources at the end of yesterday together with expected income and planned expenditures for the day. No behavioral assumptions are made here. Desires concerning purchase and sale of goods or services, desires regarding the allocation of income to expenditure, or to money balances, or to the acquisition of securities — questions of this kind depend upon choices that are influenced by the rate of interest and the prices of goods and services. Klein provides other equations to describe these relations and thereby permits an equilibrium solution. But the analysis at hand requires only the budget restrictions.

Equation (1) below, the household-budget restriction, states that households' demand for holdings of money and securities at the end of today must equal their holdings at the end of yesterday, plus today's income from securities and from the labor they plan to sell, minus the expenditures they wish to incur in payment for goods purchased. Equation (2), the business-budget restriction, states that business demand for net wealth at the end of today, so far as that is represented by cash minus securities owed, must equal yesterday's holdings of money minus securities then owed, plus receipts from goods it expects to sell, minus planned expenditures of interest and wages. It is obviously assumed that all securities represent debt owed by business to households. Equation (3), representing the combined business and household sectors, is obtained by adding equations (1) and (2).

$$L_{h,t} + R_t^D = M_{h,t-1} + (1 + r_{t-1})(R_{t-1}) + w_t N_t^S - p_t x_t^D \qquad (1)$$

$$L_{b,t} - R_t^S = M_{b,t-1} - (1 + r_{t-1})(R_{t-1}) - w_t N_t^P + p_t x_t^S \qquad (2)$$

$$(L_h + L_b)_t + (R^D - R^S)_t = (M_h + M_b)_{t-1} + w_t(N^S - N^D)_t + p_t(x^S - x^D)_t. \qquad (3)$$

Klein's budget restrictions as drawn above assume no change in the quantity of money between yesterday and today. Since our models allow for such a possibility we can relate his to ours by simply adding ΔM, (i.e., $M_t - M_{t-1}$) to the right-hand side of equation (3), thereby indicating that the "money + securities" at the end of the period will be greater than otherwise by ΔM (i.e., $M_t - M_{t-1}$). Correspondingly we would have to add ΔM_h and ΔM_b to the right-hand sides of equations (1) and (2) respectively. This treatment raises some problems that I do not discuss because they are not germane to the issue under examination. I shall now make this adjustment to equation (3) while consolidating business and household sectors:

$$L_t + (R^D - R^S)_t = (M_{t-1} + M_t - M_{t-1}) + w_t(N^S - N^D)_t + p_t(x^S - x^D)_t.$$

By combining and rearranging terms we have:

$$(M - L)_t = (R^D - R^S)_t + [w_t(N^D - N^S)_t + p_t(x^D - x^S)_t]. \qquad (4)$$

Klein now suggests that a useful dynamic equation for the rate of interest would be one that describes how interest rates will change during a period because of inequality between supply and demand for cash (or for securities) at going interest rates. One who holds a theory of interest based on supply and demand for cash would then write:

$$r_t - r_{t-1} = f(M - L)_t, \qquad (5)$$

with the restriction that $f(0) = 0$. This restriction simply states that if the supply and demand for money are equal, then the interest rate is in equilibrium and will not change.

From the standpoint of our immediate purpose, which is to compare loanable-funds and liquidity-preference theories of interest, Klein's major conclusion from this analysis is revealed by study of equations (4) and (5). Dynamic equations of the kind sketched here would indicate that a theory of interest based on supply and demand for cash would not be equivalent to one based on supply and demand for securities unless $(M - L)_t$ in equation (5) could be replaced by $[R^D - R^S]_t$. But equation (4) shows that this cannot be done unless the right-hand bracket in equation (4) equals zero. If there is equilibrium in the markets for goods and services, then this condition is fulfilled, but not otherwise (unless by coincidence the two terms in brackets cancel each other). In short, then, equation (4) shows that a theory which describes changes in the rate of interest as a function of the difference between supply and demand for cash (i.e., $M - L$) is not equivalent to one that describes those changes as a function of the difference between the demand and supply for securities (i.e., $R^D - R^S$) unless the market for goods and services is in equilibrium.

For one who has just completed my demonstration of the equivalence between interest theories drawn in terms of cash and those drawn in terms of securities Klein's proof presents a number of questions. What is the basic element in this last approach which makes it appear to yield a different result? Does it indeed contradict or qualify our analysis? When a difference of this kind arises between securities theories and cash theories, which has the stronger claim to validity?

These questions require further interpretation of the meaning of Klein's model in order to see the relation between it and the somewhat different one I have presented. What is the essential feature that leads to the disparity Klein has noted? In the first place, I do not believe the dynamic formulation used here is central to the conclusion. Even if we drop the relationship which describes changes in the rate of interest as a function of discrepancies between demands and supplies, and make instead the familiar statement that the rate of interest is determined at the level which equates supplies and demands, equation (4) shows us that securities and cash equations may yield different results: equality of supply and demand for cash does not imply equality of demand and supply of securities unless equilibrium has been achieved in the market for goods and services.

The real reason for the discrepancy which Klein finds seems to me to reside in the concept of "demand for money" which is implicit in his model. L in his equation refers to the size of balances desired on the basis of anticipated income and expenditures. So far as the loan market is concerned, however, funds will not be offered for securities if they are required either to meet L or in anticipation of purchases that cannot be financed from expected income. Thus any excess of demand over supply for goods and services will represent a tying up of funds which must be added to the demand expressed by L in order to find what funds are offered for securities. This is precisely what Klein's equation (4) states, as can be seen by transposing the bracket from the right side and rebracketing it with L on the left side. In other words, the effective demand for money represents the sum of the desired balances and money tied up in an unsatisfied demand for goods and services.[13]

In pointing out that these two types of theory may give different results Klein does not contend that one is superior to the other. Fellner and Somers had argued that whatever forces may bear on the rate of interest, they must operate through the supply and demand for securities, the implied reason being that interest is the reward for buying securties.[14] Klein replies that it is quite as legitimate to argue that interest is the reward for being illiquid, implying that the equation for supply and demand for money has an equal claim to being the determinant of interest rates.[15] At this point I agree with Fellner and Somers for several reasons. In the first place I have already given my reasons for defining the rate of interest as the return for lending money, for which I regard the purchase of securities as an equivalent. Second, if we do regard all loan contracts as equivalent to the purchase of securities, then I do not know what else one can mean by the reward for illiquidity in the context of this controversy except the return on securities. Third, if the interpretation I have given above regarding the bracketed term in equation (4) is legitimate, then it seems to me that one need only transpose the term, join it with L, and then redefine the meaning of demand for money, in order to make a liquidity-preference approach entirely consistent with one based on the loanable-funds theory.

Before drawing conclusions from this discussion it may be useful to remark upon a sense in which it parallels my earlier analysis of a single day and of the "finance" motive for holding funds. If one assumes in the

---

[13] This addition to demand could, of course, be negative, as it would if the demand for goods and services was less than the value of these goods and services offered for sale. In this event the supply of funds offered for securities would be larger than if equilibrium were assumed, since persons expecting to receive income will demand fewer funds from other sources by this amount.

[14] Articles and replies by Klein, Fellner and Somers, and Karl Brunner, *Econometrica*, 18 (1950): 244.

[15] *Ibid.*, p. 246.

Klein model that all investment activity is carried on through the business sector, then if the last two terms of equation (1) taken together have a positive value, this indicates an excess of income over expenditures, and hence represents planned saving. And if wages paid exceed receipts from sales, as shown by the last two terms of equation (2), this represents planned investment. Under this interpretation, equation (4) states that the excess of supply over demand for money in any period must equal the excess of demand over supply of securities plus $(I - S)$. Put another way, as implied by the transposition of terms proposed above, one need only add $(I - S)$ to the demand for money as expressed in L in order to make the liquidity-preference formulation give the same results as those given by the loanable-funds statement. This corresponds quite directly to the fact that our analysis of a single day required a sloping L_1 curve, the slope being determined by $(I - S)$. And it corresponds also to the fact that in a model where L_1 is drawn vertical it becomes necessary to include a finance curve whose slope is that of $(I - S)$. The difference between the Klein formulation and the others is that his is drawn in terms of simultaneous variables relating planned saving to planned investment, whereas our previous analysis employed the Robertsonian concept of saving, hence introducing a lagged income variable. Corresponding with this difference in definitions there is a difference in the meaning of the equations. In the Robertsonian model the $(I - S)$-slope resulted because income for the period studied is itself a function of the interest rate in that period, so that the transactions demand had to slope. In the vertical-L_1 model current income did not respond to current interest rates, and so the slope of the finance curve refers to a demand for funds related to income behavior planned for the next period. In the Klein model as interpreted here the excess of I over S represents demand that is unsatisfied and ties up money (i.e., holds it off the market for securities) in addition to that desired for transactions and idle balances. This is, of course, not the only possible interpretation of Klein's equations, but it is one which seems reasonable, and it gives what seems to me to be the valid implication of Klein's analysis. This implication for our immediate problem is that the single-day analysis presented above does not require modification, because it includes in its sloping L_1 curve the effects on the securities market of $(I - S)$, which in turn reflects the disequilibrium in the commodities markets that could, were this not shown, introduce a discrepancy between the two theories.

This completes the examination of the comparison between the Robertsonian type of loanable-funds theory and the liquidity-preference theory. I shall recapitulate my findings after a brief section in which a similar comparison is made between a Swedish type of loanable-funds theory and the liquidity-preference approach.

SWEDISH TYPE OF
LOANABLE-FUNDS THEORY

My object now is to see whether a loanable-funds theory based on Swedish ex-ante and ex-post concepts can be translated into a liquidity-preference theory as was that of Robertson. The essentials of the analytical procedure will be the same as before, and I can therefore proceed rapidly. Indeed, I shall begin with a simple algebraic transformation that describes a process analogous to the one followed in deriving figures VIa and VIb. When that has been completed I shall illustrate the results graphically in figures VIj and VIk.

As before, $\overline{L_1}$ and $\overline{L_2}$ represent active and inactive balances at the start of the day. These are data, not functions. The L_1 function, defined as the demand for active balances, will be equal to the sum of the demand for consumers goods and that for investment goods. Anticipated income, previously symbolized by Y_a, will be represented here by the expression L_{1a}.

The relations among the variables of the system may be described by the following equations. The first three represent definitions:

$$L_1 = C_p + I_p = (Y_a - S_p) + I_p = Y_a + (I_p - S_p) = \overline{L_{1a}} + (I_p - S_p). \quad (1)$$

$$L_2 = \overline{L_2} + H. \quad (2)$$

$$M = \overline{L_1} + \overline{L_2} + \Delta M. \quad (3)$$

According to the loanable-funds theory the interest rate will so adjust as to equate the supply and demand for loanable funds according to the formula previously derived.

$$I + H = S + \Delta M,$$

or

$$(I_p - S_p) + H - \Delta M = 0. \quad (4)$$

By the aid of equations (1) to (3) above, substitutions for each term in equation (4) may be made, with the following results:

$$(L_1 - \overline{L_{1a}}) + (L_2 - \overline{L_2}) - (M - \overline{L_1} - \overline{L_2}) = 0, \quad (5)$$

or

$$L_1 + L_2 = M + (\overline{L_{1a}} - \overline{L_1}). \quad (6)$$

For some purposes we shall find it convenient to use an alternative expression which may be obtained by substituting in (6) the value for M found in equation (3). Making this substitution we may write:

$$L_1 + L_2 = \overline{L_{1a}} + \overline{L_2} + \Delta M, \quad (7)$$

where the left side represents demand and the right side supply.

The following conclusions may now be noted. In the first place, this expression of the loanable-funds theory, like that of the Robertsonian model examined above, requires for its liquidity-preference equivalent the use of a sloping rather than a vertical L_1 surface. This fact follows because, as equation (1) shows, the demand for active balances is found by adding $I_p - S_p$ to anticipated income, just as in the previous example it was found by adding $I - S$ to disposable income. Secondly, however, we find a new complication not characteristic of the Robertsonian model. This form of loanable-funds theory is not equivalent to the liquidity-preference statement, in which $L_1 + L_2 = M$, but rather to the modification of that relationship as shown in equation (6) above. The two theories become fully equivalent of one another only if the last term in equation (6) vanishes, which occurs precisely when anticipated income equals previous realized income. We have seen earlier that this last relationship is just the one that is required to make the Robertsonian and Swedish models give similar results, and so this finding is entirely consistent with our previous analysis. But these equations also show that unless this assumption is made the loanable-funds theory based on Swedish concepts differs from the liquidity-preference expression in this way beyond the ways in which the Robertsonian model differs from the liquidity-preference model.

The graphical illustration of this transformation is shown in figures VIj and VIk. It is analogous to that applied to the Robertsonian type of theory. Underlying functional relationships are derived from our three-dimensional system of figures IV and VIIa. In this case, however, the income dimension of these figures refers to expected income rather than to disposable income, since the Swedish system makes its variables functions of expected income.

The derivation of the functions and data in figures VIj and VIk are as follows.

Data which must be assumed as given are:

$\overline{L_{1a}}$ (expected, or anticipated, income) is assumed to equal \$2,400.
$\overline{L_1}$ (previous realized income) is assumed to equal \$2,600.
M (money supply in this period) is assumed to equal \$2,740.
ΔM (change in money from previous period) is assumed to equal 0.

Data and functions which may be derived on the basis of the above assumptions, in conjunction with figures IV and VIIa, are:

$\overline{L_2} = M - \Delta M - \overline{L_1}$ (by equation (3) above) = \$140.

L_1 is derived from figure IV (or taken directly from figure VIIb) by the aid of equation (1) above: $L_1 = \overline{L_{1a}} + (I_p - S_p)$.

It will be noted that L_1 also equals $C_p + I_p$, as stated earlier. The consistency of these two statements is shown by remembering that by definition $S_p = Y_a - C_p$, or $\overline{L_{1a}} - C_p$, and by substituting this value for S_p in the first of the two expressions.

L_2 is derived directly from figure VIIa.

Sy is the supply curve implied by equation (7) above, in which demand on the left equals supply on the right. By this, $Sy = L_{1a} + L_2 + \Delta M = \$2,540$.

$L = L_1 + L_2$ (by definition of L). This is the demand for money.

I and S in figure VIk are derived from figure IV, assuming Y_a equals $\$2,400$.

$H = L_2 - \overline{L_2}$ [by equation (2)].

Sy in figure VIk equals $S + \Delta M$ (as n the general loanable-funds equation) which equals S here, since $\Delta M = 0$.

D in figure VIk equals $H + I$ (as in the general loanable funds equaton).

According to the liquidity-preference theory the equilibrium rate of interest is that rate which equates the supply and demand for money. But the quantity of money supplied ($\$2,740$) equals the demand for money (L) at a rate of interest of 4 per cent as seen in figure VIj whereas the interest rate determined by the loanable-funds theory, in figure VIk, is 5 per cent. The supply curve in figure VIj which would give a rate of interest consistent with that of the loanable-funds theory is not M, but Sy as given in the derivation from equation (7) above. We therefore observe, in the graphical presentation, the same difference between loanable-funds and liquidity-preference theories that was expressed earlier in algebra. Just what is the meaning of this difference, and how is it explained?

The relation between the liquidity-preference formulation and the Swedish type of loanable-funds theory may be readily interpreted by noting the difference between M, the supply curve of the liquidity-preference theory, and Sy, the supply curve required in that structure to yield results identical with those of the loanable-funds theory. Equation (3) tells us that $M = \overline{L_1} + \overline{L_2} + \Delta M$. But we have found by equation (7) that $Sy = \overline{L_{1a}} + \overline{L_2} + \Delta M$. The difference, then, between these two theories is simply that the loanable-funds formulation implies the substitution of anticipated transactions needs $(\overline{L_{1a}})$ for previous realized transactions needs $(\overline{L_1})$ in the supply function of the liquidity-preference set of variables. On reflection, this is merely the liquidity-preference counterpart of the fact that in the Swedish theory the supply of loanable funds is dependent upon *expected* saving, rather than upon realized saving of the Robertsonian variety. Thus the supply function is not an objective datum such as the quantity of money, but is based on subjective considerations. I have commented on the adequacy of this kind of assumption earlier (see p. 187–188).

This example illustrates the way in which the loanable-funds theory may be graphically and algebraically related to the liquidity-preference theory when the former is developed according to the Swedish analysis. By the use of Sy in place of M in the latter these constructions yield identical results, just as they did when the loanable-funds model used was of the Robertsonian type. But it is important to remember that figures VIj and VIk describe relations between very different variables from those depicted in figures VIa and VIh, as the comparison of Robertsonian with Swedish terminology makes clear. Furthermore we cannot read from figures VIj and VIk the actual, realized income that emerges; only the rate of interest is clearly determined. The level of realized income depends upon the expectation of enterprise concerning total demand, as well as upon enterprise decisions concerning investment purchases (I). Similarly, the actual level of hoards is not now determined by the intersection of the 5 per cent horizontal with the L_2 curve since the desires depicted by that curve may prove to have been thwarted by mistaken expectations. Those who wish to pursue this illustration further may do so with the aid of the following paragraphs and the application of figure IIf in addition to that of figures VIj and VIk. Others may move on to the summary of our comparison of loanable-funds and liquidity-preference theories (p. 232).

In our earlier discussion of the Swedish system we utilized figure IIf, which is in a sense the complement of figures VIj and VIk. The former figure assumed interest rates to be determined at 5 per cent and abstracted from the shifts of function that would result as the movement toward equilibrium changed these rates. Thus it depicted saving and investment as functions of the level of income but not of interest rates. Figures VIj and VIk, on the other hand, assume a given level of (anticipated) income, and show their variables only as a function of the rate of interest. Justification of the latter procedure rests upon the fact that we are now considering a "one day" picture, in which interest rates can adjust but income cannot. By using these two illustrations together we can show the consistency of their implications.

In the first place it will be noted that when one assumes expected income to be $2,400 in II$f$ (the underlying assumption of VIj and VIk), and when one assumes interest rates of 5 per cent in VIj and VIk (the underlying assumption of IIf), then variables in the two figures have identical values. I shall mention only a few key instances, but others may be readily traced:

The demand for active balances:

In IIf, this equals $C + I = \$1,690 + \$250 = \$1,940$.
In VIj, L_1 intersects the 5 per cent horizontal at $\$1,940$.

Planned saving:

In IIf, S_p equals CF $= \$710$.
In VIk, $S = \$710$ at its intersection with the horizontal at $r = 5$ per cent.

Planned Investment:

In IIf, I_p equals BE $= \$250$.
In VIk, $I = \$250$ at its intersection with the horizontal at $r = 5$ per cent.

Realized income:

In IIf the determination of realized income depended upon assumptions not made explicit by the general framework of the theory. In our example we assumed that enterprise expects consumers and enterprise together to absorb, through purchases of consumers goods and investment goods respectively, an output of $\$2,100$. Business therefore produced that amount, and realized income was depicted by making AD equal to $\$2,100$. In figure VI$j$, as in figure II$f$, an additional assumption had to be made in order to draw $\overline{L_{1r}}$, which we have similarly located at $\$2,100$.

The realized level of $\overline{L_2}$ will have been determined by $\overline{L_{1r}}$, since the two together must equal the total money supply of $\$2,740$. The vertical L_{2r} line is therefore drawn at a level of $\$640$. As indicated above, this result is based on the assumption that idle balances are a residual, not necessarily equal to the desired amount ($\$600$), but diverging from these values in whatever way is made necessary by unrealized expectations.

As in the construction of figure IIf, anticipated income for the second day cannot be derived directly from the relations thus far described without further assumptions. Once these assumptions are made, $\overline{L_{1a}}$ may be drawn for the second day.

Referring back to the original set of relations used in deriving the values for the first day, we have now made sufficient assumptions about expectations that, with the quantity of money given, figures IV and VIIa

provide all the information required to complete the construction for the second day. Once again we will find that the loanable-funds and the liquidity-preference constructions will give us identical rates of interest if, and only if, we alter the supply curve in the liquidity-preference formulation as described above.

The major conclusion from this model is that if one accepts what I believe to be a fairly general interpretation of Swedish analysis, then the application of these ideas to the theory of interest yields a loanable-funds concept which is not identical to the liquidity-preference theory. The latter can be readily modified to remove the difference, but at least the modification should be noted. Either, one must use the conventional L_1 and L_2 curves in conjunction with a new supply curve — not the quantity of money — or one may continue to use the quantity of money for a supply curve and make an adjustment on the demand side. One would need to add to the supply curve, or deduct from the demand curve, an amount equal to the excess of anticipated over preceding realized income.

SUMMARY AND CONCLUSIONS

The long debate over whether the loanable-funds and the liquidity-preference theories are equivalent or not is an important one. If the theories are contradictory then they cannot both be correct as general theories. Either one must be rejected, or else each must be used in a context for which it is appropriate and the other is not. It happens that in certain respects each has convenience which the other lacks, and therefore the issue of their validity and appropriateness is crucial.

There are three major differences between conventional forms of loanable-funds theories and liquidity-preference theories, regardless of whether the former are stated in Swedish or Robertsonian terms. One is that the loanable-funds theories are typically described with reference to flows over a period of time, whereas liquidity-preference theories are stated in terms of stocks at a moment of time. A second is that loanable-funds theories are usually stated in terms of supply and demand for securities, whereas liquidity-preference theories are stated in terms of demand and supply for cash balances. Finally, the loanable-funds theories generally analyze the supply and demand for securities in terms of the sources of these supplies and demands classified into four types: investment, saving, net hoarding, and changes in the supply of money; the liquidity-preference theory, on the other hand, proceeds by setting the supply of money as a datum against the demand, where the latter is broken down into categories according to the motives for holding balances: transactions, precautionary, speculative, and finance. A comparison of these two types of interest theory can be best made by considering each of these aspects of the theories in turn.

The fact that one theory is described in terms of flows and the other in terms of stocks has the following results. (a) If a given set of functions adequate for general equilibrium is provided, and if one is prepared to break up time into discrete intervals, as is conventionally done in period analysis, then the Robertsonian loanable-funds theory will give the same result as the liquidity-preference theory. In this context the "same result" applies both to the analysis of a single day and to the analysis of the sequence by which a more general equilibrium is approached. (b) If the underlying functions imply demands for flows, then the results are entirely different from those that would follow if these underlying demands are for stocks. This difference occurs only in relation to the L_2 function, where I believe that a stock theory is more reasonable. (c) In the sequence analysis this difference shows itself in the nature of the interday shifts of the L_2 function as contrasted with those of the H function. (d) Since the interday shifts are different according to the nature of the underlying theory, any set of dynamic equations will give different results according to whether it is based on behavioral assumptions related to flow or to stock concepts. (e) Since the loanable-funds theory is stated in flow terms it may suggest behavioral assumptions of a flow type. If such behavioral assumptions necessarily followed, I should prefer the liquidity-preference theory so far as this point is concerned, because I believe people are more likely to hold objectives in terms of the size of balances desired than to hold them in terms of regular changes in size per unit of time. (f) However, there is no necessary reason to associate the type of ultimate behavioral assumptions with the form of short-period terminology used. In figure VI we used both flow terminology, as in the loanable-funds presentation, and stock terminology, as in the liquidity-preference theory; yet each of these models was drawn on the same underlying (stock) behavioral assumptions regarding idle balances, as described by figure Va. (g) So long as a theory of interest is to serve the purpose of partial-equilibrium analysis, therefore, either loanable-funds or liquidity-preference formulation may be used.

The fact that one theory is based on the supply of and demand for securities, while the other is based on the demand for and supply of cash, has no effect on the outcome in the models we have studied. It has been argued that when the markets for goods and services are out of equilibrium a theory built on supply and demand for securities will give a different interest rate, or different changes in the rate over time, from one built on the demand and supply of cash. Our analysis would suggest that this discrepancy arises because the effective demand for funds includes not only the amounts persons desire to hold at the end of the day, but also funds that are tied up in the unsatisfied demand for goods and services. The implication is that the two theories may be made equivalent again so far as this issue is concerned by adding to the deliberate demand for money an amount representing these other funds that do not enter the market for securities. Under simplified assumptions appropriate to our models, this difference is equal to the excess of planned investment over planned saving. The model we used in figure VI, because it makes the slope of L_1 inversely proportional to the difference between I and S, needs no further correction. Where L_1 is drawn vertically the use of a finance curve as reviewed below accomplishes a similar purpose.

These paragraphs summarize my answers to the two primary questions raised at the start of this chapter, namely: What is the significance of the stock-flow controversy? What is the significance of the securities-cash controversy? This analysis also makes it easy to state briefly my response to the three other questions raised at the beginning of the chapter. (1) An adequate discussion of the validity of the underlying behavioral assumptions of the two types of interest theory here discussed must rest upon empirical work which I have not attempted. However, it would appear that so far as active balances are concerned there is no difference between the behavioral assumptions implicit in the loanable-funds theory and those of the liquidity-preference theory. There may or may not be a difference concerning idle balances depending upon what one means by the "flow" quality of the loanable-funds theory. If a difference does exist here, then it would be attributable to the implication of underlying flow behavioral assumptions in the loanable-funds theory, and in that event I believe the liquidity-preference theory would rest on the more realistic empirical hypothesis. (2) Whether the functions as commonly drawn in the two presentations of interest theory have similar or different implications depends in part upon the resolution of the flow-stock controversy just described. Beyond this, our analysis suggests that the implications of the two theories are not identical unless the transactions curve in the liquidity-preference formulation is given sufficient interest elasticity to reflect the horizontal distance between the saving and the investment curves of the loanable-funds formulation. I would suggest that it be so drawn. This procedure implies, of course, that the independent income variable is yesterday's earned income, not that of today. A *somewhat* similar method of reconciling the two theories at this point is the use of the familiar finance curve. This method would cause the two types of theory to give the same interest rate in any "day" being analyzed, but it would imply a lag in the response of income to interest rates by implying that any excess of investment over saving (positive or negative) would first tie up (or release) funds in idle balances called "finance" instead of utilizing them in income transactions.

(3) The final question concerned the relative usefulness of the two types of interest theory, and this must await further studies. My present

view is that each has convenience that the other lacks. To the extent that one wishes to fit his theory into a dynamic or general-equilibrium framework of the Keynesian variety, the liquidity-preference theory obviously has special convenience. On the other hand to the extent that one is interested in partial-equilibrium theory the loanable-funds approach has the advantage arising from its use of saving and investment relations. Especially now that the Federal Reserve is supplying regular data on "sources and uses" of funds, the practical applicability of the loanable-funds view is greatly facilitated.

Thus far my review has been concerned only with the Robertsonian approach to the loanable-funds theory. An important alternative type of loanable-funds theory is that of the Swedish school. The choice between this and the Robertsonian version can be made only with the aid of empirical study, since the two theories rest upon different behavioral assumptions. These differences show themselves in a number of ways. In the first place the meaning of the functions differs, and the dynamics of the movement over time differ. This aspect of the question requires no further review at this point. We may still compare the loanable-funds theories with the liquidity-preference theory in ways quite similar to the way the comparison involving the Robertsonian theory was made. To do so, however, we must change the meaning of the functions in both systems — both loanable-funds and liquidity-preference — and instead of analyzing the differences between past and present income we must analyze the differences between expected and realized variables for the same time period. One new difference emerges, however, when we shift from Robertsonian to Swedish analysis. In the Robertsonian loanable-funds system the analysis of any given "day" proves identical to that in the liquidity-preference system if the latter's curves are properly inclusive. In the Swedish system, however, differences between anticipated and realized income cause the emergence of an influence on the size of idle balances not present in the Robertsonian theory: funds entering the securities market in this system could well be influenced directly by anticipations of income rather than by realized values. As a result persons might be forced to fill commitments made in the securities market by drawing on their idle balances until they fell below their intended level; or conversely, these balances might rise more than desired. Thus the supply curve in the liquidity-preference model would no longer be merely the quantity of money, but it would be this plus the excess of anticipated over realized income.

XIII

INTEREST THEORY
AND PRICE VARIABILITY

COMPLETING THE GENERAL
EQUILIBRIUM SYSTEM

The Problem Outlined

In these introductory paragraphs I shall give a very brief outline of the problems with which this chapter will be concerned. We have already admitted variable prices into the discussion of a number of specific questions, but we have not systematically included this element in our general-equilibrium model. A theory of interest built on the assumption of rigid prices is especially convenient for the presentation and interpretation of the Keynesian system, because the first approximation used by Keynes makes this simplifying assumption at many points. Furthermore, the partial-equilibrium systems we have discussed — both loanable-funds and liquidity-preference — consider prices to be given. For the more general purposes of this book, however, the introduction of variable prices is of paramount importance. In the first place, even the Keynesian system is not complete if left at the constant-price stage of approximation. In the second place, it is impossible adequately to compare classical and Keynesian interest theories without introducing prices. Finally, our most fundamental purpose is to derive a theory of interest which aids us in understanding the real world, and price changes are among the most important variables actually involved.[1]

I have shown both algebraically and geometrically (see pp. 205, 215) that the system which determines equilibrium at the intersection of the *SI* and the *LM* curves would appear to be overdetermined if we also added the condition of full employment, thereby requiring that equilibrium lie at a specific income which might not be consistent with the *SI–LM* intersection. Full employment was assumed to lie along the "end wall" of figure V*d*, which is the "back wall" of figures V*c* and VII*c* (EFGH in all 3 figures). The classical economists combined the full-employment assump-

---

[1] It may be noted that Patinkin, whose orientation and point of departure is closer to the classical school, introduces price variability at the start and emphasizes influences of changing prices that are often unrecognized or only half-recognized. See Don Patinkin, *Money, Interest and Prices* (Evanston, Illinois, and White Plains, New York: Row, Peterson, 1956).

tion with the avoidance of overdetermination by adding two elements that are omitted from our models, and both of these elements have to do with price variability. First, they assumed that *relative* prices would so vary as to clear all markets, including the labor market, thus providing full employment and introducing the possibility of overdetermination into the system. Second, they also admitted variability of the *general* price level, and by thus introducing an additional unknown without adding an additional equation they avoided overdetermination. In geometry the introduction of the general price level into the system of equilibrium equations permits both the *SI* and the *LM* curves to shift until their intersection is on the full-employment wall (for simplicity we have heretofore referred only to the shift of *LM*).

Classical analysis always included prices in the money equation and, in terms of our model, thereby permitted changing prices to shift the *LM* curve. Keynes also described a process, though a different one, by which price changes *might* cause *LM* to shift toward a full-employment intersection with *SI*. He had little faith in the efficacy of this mechanism, however, and gave strong reasons for hoping that full employment would be sought by other means.

A. C. Pigou placed emphasis on forces which should make the *S* surface and hence the *SI* curve shift under the impact of changing prices, again moving the system toward full employment. Patinkin has added considerable emphasis to the forces described by Pigou, has applied them to the investment function as well as to the saving function, and has shown that these forces were a necessary part of even the familiar classical analysis, though not generally so recognized.

The full meaning of these general statements cannot be clear until we examine them further. Our purpose, in short, is to add variable prices to the system I have been describing, to show the major ways by which this new element may move the system toward equilibrium at full employment, and to discuss the relevance of these considerations to economic analysis.

This discussion outlines the tasks of the rest of this section. We shall first admit to our system the functions which show how classical economists believed that relative prices would so adjust as to cause full employment. We shall next observe two ways — the classical and the Keynesian — by which the absolute price level might shift the *LM* curve until its intersection with *SI* would be consistent with this full-employment equilibrium. Third, we shall show how Pigou and Patinkin suggest that this same changing absolute price level might cause the *SI* curve to shift in the direction of a full-employment intersection with *LM*.

"CLASSICAL" FULL-EMPLOYMENT EQUILIBRIUM

The three interrelated classical functions which determine equilibrium at full employment are pictured in figures VIIIa and VIIIb.[2] Figure VIIIa presents a production function with the level of employment measured horizontally and the resulting output measured vertically. It is here assumed that the marginal product of labor falls very little until full employment is nearly reached, but thereafter declines rapidly, as indicated by the leveling off of the production curve. Finally, when employment reaches OD'', output cannot be further increased by the addition of more man-hours. The declining marginal product of labor reflects both the law of diminishing returns and the fact that labor efficiency declines when hours exceed reasonable limits. The possibility of employment beyond full employment reflects our concept of full employment as a level determined by the willingness to work at given wages in contrast to the maximum number of hours that could be obtained by forced labor.

Figure VIIIb presents the demand curve for labor, together with the classical supply curve. The demand curve is obtained directly from figure VIIIa by plotting the derivative (slope) of the production function for each level of employment. This assumes that the demand curve for labor in real terms is the marginal product of its services. Keynes accepted this classical demand curve.[3] The supply curve drawn here assumes that labor will continue to work until the marginal utility of the real wage is no longer greater than the marginal disutility of labor. Any solution on this curve implies full employment, because it implies that any worker wishing employment at going real wages can secure a job. Keynes rejected the view that this curve would be effective in determining the level of realized employment, though he essentially retains it as a bench mark for the definition of full employment.

As indicated above, the classical analysis assumes that equilibrium will be determined by the intersection of Sy and D for labor as at F' in figure VIIIb. The level of employment is thus determined directly and is equal to OF''. The corresponding level of real income is shown by VIIIa to be $2,400, just as assumed in the three-dimensional figures.

THE PRICE LEVEL AND THE LIQUIDITY SURFACE

Before continuing it should be emphasized that from this point on all values in our three-dimensional figures except M will represent "real" levels, being measured in constant dollars of the value indicated by base

---

[2] Although the following analysis was developed independently, it is essentially similar to that presented by Joseph McKenna, *Aggregate Economic Analysis* (New York: Dryden Press, 1955).

[3] J. M. Keynes, *The General Theory of Interest, Employment and Money* (New York: Harcourt, Brace, 1936), pp. 17 ff.

prices, the level of which is symbolized by p_0. Money is the only exception to this rule, being measured in actual dollars, not in "real balances" (M/p) as is often done.

Speculative Demand. — It will be remembered that Keynes' "speculative" demand for cash is the demand for cash that is to be held as an asset in contrast to cash intended for current use or precautionary reserves on the one hand, and in contrast to the holding of bonds on the other. Actually we might make the list more complete by including another major alternative — holding real assets. It seems reasonable to presume that people who choose among these alternative uses of resources will decide upon some proportion in which they wish to divide their purchasing power. When I say "purchasing power" here, I imply that their consideration will be in terms of the "real" value of each asset. In other words they will seek a desirable ratio between these three quantities: (1) M/p, or the real value of cash balances; (2) R/p, or the real value of their bonds, where "R" represents the money value of these bonds; and (3) A, or the real value of their real assets.[4] With reference to the second category, R/p, a useful substitution may now be made. If we assume all bonds to be perpetuities with a coupon of one dollar per year, then the money value of these perpetuities (i.e., R) will be equal to the number of bonds (which equals the number of dollars of annual income) divided by the rate of interest. By designating as b the number of bonds we may replace R by b/r, and hence the real value of bonds may be represented by the expression b/rp.

The total demand for cash balances may be subdivided into two major components: the demand for money held for the mechanics of income transactions and that for money held as an asset for the purpose of storing wealth. The first need for holding money — the requirement for transactions balances — will be examined on pages 245–248. The second general reason for holding money — to store wealth — consists of holding money for "precautionary" purposes, to be discussed on pages 244–245 below; holding it for finance, discussed on page 245; and holding it for "speculative" purposes, to be discussed forthwith.

The amount of real cash balances demanded for speculative purposes will depend in part upon the total resources available, and in part upon the way in which it is desired to allocate these resources between the

---

[4] This analysis, like other important elements in the chapter closely parallels or follows that of Patinkin's *Money, Interest and Prices.* The first draft of this chapter was finished before Patinkin's book became available, and it has been encouraging to note at how many places my conclusions proved to be identical with those he reached by a different route. The present revision of my analysis has, nonetheless, been substantially improved by the aid of his book, and I should like to recognize at this point the important debt I owe to it. See footnote 1 for full reference on Patinkin's *Money, Interest and Prices.*

various kinds of assets. As indicated above, the three types of wealth considered in this analysis may be measured by the three expressions: M/p, b/rp, and A. Among the elements determining the desired allocation of assets between these three forms we now single out for study the rate of interest. The comments of this paragraph may be summarized by the algebraic statements:

$$\left(\frac{M_2}{p}\right)^D = L_2(r, We) \tag{1}$$

where We represents the real value of wealth, which is constituted as follows:

$$We = \frac{M}{p} + \frac{b}{rp} + A. \tag{2}$$

In order to relate the demand for money to the actual supply in terms of dollars (i.e., not in purchasing power) it will be convenient to rewrite equation (1) in the form:

$$M_2^D = p \cdot L_2(r, We). \tag{3}$$

To clarify the influences operating on the rate of interest it will now be useful to comment on three elements in the above set of equations: M/p, b/rp, and the multiplicative p of equation (3).

1) Discussion of M/p: The presence of M/p implies that the demand for speculative balances is influenced by what we may call a "real balance effect." That is, the higher the value of real balances supplied the greater will be the demand for speculative balances, *ceteris paribus*.[5] This interdependence between supply and demand presents a complication not commonly troubling supply-demand analysis and not recognized in the conventional presentation of the money equation. Consideration of the nature of the demand for money forces us to admit it, however. In common-sense terms the view that such interdependence exists may be supported by arguments like the following. If one wishes to keep about half of his spending power in speculative balances and half in real assets (abstracting from transactions needs for the moment), and if a drop in prices or an increase in M raises the value of these balances (M/p) substantially, then he will be in a situation of disequilibrium until he has reapportioned his assets in such a way that he still holds half his purchasing power in cash and half in real assets. This implies a desire to hold more purchasing power in cash than originally (though less than immediately after the price drop or the increase in M), and more in real assets as well. In short, for any given level of income and interest rates, the purchasing power desired to be held in each asset will be an increasing

---

[5] Patinkin suggests the same conclusion, *ibid.*, chapter iii, esp. p. 43.

function of the total purchasing power of all assets held. When that total rises (measured in real terms), then the value demanded of each component will also be larger than before.

If additional M is injected into the economy directly without changing R (we thus exclude open-market purchases from the public and new private borrowing from the banks), the desired holdings of M are also increased so long as prices are constant or rise less than proportionately with M. These considerations complicate the analysis of the effects that are produced by changing M, but they do not basically invalidate the conventional analysis whereby the vertical M line is simply shifted along the L curve, because it is still true that L will not move so far in either direction as does M. This fact may be explained in either of two ways. Perhaps the simplest explanation is that since people would, at going interest rates, want to hold part of the new assets in other forms than cash, the demand for M shifts less than the full amount of the new assets — i.e., the additional supply of money. The second way by which to see the logic of this conclusion is to note that the new equilibrium after an increase of M must be one in which people are content to hold a larger M, together with the same number of bonds as before. The only way for this to be possible at any given Y and P is for the rate of interest to drop, and this means that the M surface must have shifted farther to the right than did L.

2) Discussion of b/rp: The term b/rp carries two implications. One is that the rate of interest will influence the value of bonds and thus indirectly influence the demand for other assets, including speculative balances. High rates reduce capital values, and thus an additional restrictive impact of tight money may be noted: the lower security values caused by tight money lead persons to shift funds from transactions balances to asset accounts. The second implication of the term b/rp is that there will be a "real bond" effect of changing prices, just as there is a "real balance" effect: the higher the real value of bonds the greater will be the demand for the real value of all other assets, including speculative balances.

3) Discussion of the multiplicative p: In first deriving the function for speculative balances (p. 239) we argued in a kind of common-sense way that the demand for these balances had to be in real terms. Since the supply of money as determined by the banking system is directly measured not in real but monetary terms, we next converted the expression for demand into money terms by multiplying the L function by p (equation 3). Since Keynes did not include this term in his speculative function it may be useful briefly to discuss the reasons it must be present.

A good way to test the appropriateness of the inclusion of p as a multiplier of L is suggested by Patinkin's analysis.[6] Consider the expected con-

---

[6] For this and other references in the paragraph, see *ibid.*, pp. 54 and 174.

sequences of doubling simultaneously the price level (including wages), the amount of everybody's cash balances, and the number of bonds possessed by everybody. Clearly all real values in the system are now unchanged. Nothing has happened to real income or real wealth: the former because the prices of the goods bought and the services sold are doubled; the latter because the purchasing power of cash balances and of assets, as well as of the total supply of bonds and their coupons, are all unchanged. With no changes in any of these real elements, it is difficult to conceive of any reason for now seeking to hold speculative balances of only half the previous purchasing power. Indeed, it seems probable that persons would now wish to retain an unchanged real value of these balances by holding twice the number of speculative dollars formerly held (in view of the doubled price level). Thus the demand for speculative balances must include p as a multiplicative factor. This argument may be summarized by Patinkin's statement that the omission of p at this point would imply a money illusion in reference to the demand for speculative balances, since it would imply that our demand for these balances is altered by changes in nominal prices when all real values are unchanged.

This conclusion contradicts the impression that may easily be drawn by following Keynes' discussion of the issue. His emphasis upon holding speculative balances as alternatives to bonds certainly suggests that the price level is irrelevant to the level of speculative demand: surely there would be no reason to shift from cash to bonds merely because of a change in commodity prices, since bonds and money are both denominated in the same unit, dollars. Why, then, does p have to appear as a multiplier in the speculative function? The answer lies in the fact that speculative balances are held as alternatives not only to bonds, but also to real assets and to the use of funds for transactions. A rise in prices will reduce the real value of both money and bonds, but will not affect (*per se*) the real value of real assets. *Ceteris paribus,* then, people will wish to rebuild the amount of their purchasing power stored in both money and bonds at the expense of transactions and real assets.

Summarizing and relating the multiplicative p to the p in the denominator of the terms M/p and b/rp we may conclude as follows: The multiplicative p just described shows that if prices (and money incomes) double, people would tend to want to double the size of all monetary balances (i.e., to retain the same "real" size). But the p in the denominators of the money and bond terms show that people will feel poorer because of the price rise to the extent that they hold assets denominated in money, and therefore their demand for all types will be less than implied by the doubling of prices and income — i.e., they will demand less than double the former monetary value of these assets.

4) Further extensions of the speculative demand function: It is possible, of course, to continue almost indefinitely adding relevant considerations to our analysis. New elements may be included, or old elements may be broken down into significant subheads. The former procedure is illustrated in figure V, where I have shown a slight influence of income on speculative demand. The latter — the breakdown of variables into subcategories — may be carried out according to the nature of assets or claims, or it may be done according to the type of holder. Empirical work must consider all influences and try to find which are sufficiently important to retain in the equations used. The answer will, of course, depend in part upon the purposes for which the equations are being employed at any particular time. We shall not introduce more complexity into the speculative demand function than that of functions 1 to 3 above. Indeed, I believe that for many pedagogical purposes one might usefully operate with the much more simple structure, $M_2^D = p \cdot L_2 (r)$. If this is done, however, it should be remembered that a more complete statement will be required for the discussion of a number of issues such as those described in the preceding paragraphs.

Patinkin's analysis of the problem discussed here raises an interesting point regarding aggregation.[7] He rightly emphasizes that the *distribution* of changes in holdings of money and bonds, from which we have abstracted, may be quite important. This is essentially an illustration of the "breakdown of variables" referred to in the preceding paragraph. Furthermore, he points out that if perfect symmetry in the response of lenders and borrowers to changes in the real value of debt owed and of payments receivable could be assumed, then the process of aggregation would permit the term b/rp to be dropped. This conclusion follows from the fact that under the assumption of such symmetrical response, the stimulating effect of falling prices on creditors would be precisely balanced by the depressive effect on debtors. In point of fact, however, this symmetry of response is not realized for at least two reasons. One is that even in the private sector a loss to one individual may have greater (or less) influence on behavior than would an equal gain to another. A second is that much debt is governmental, and governmental behavior cannot be expected to be guided by the maximizing behavior of individuals in the private economy. It might be added, incidentally, though Patinkin does not make this point, that a similar argument could be advanced concerning the relevance of the term M/p. Under a fractional reserve banking system such as ours a major part of the money supply represents private debt mediated through the banking system. The argument for inclusion of the term M/p stands on very much the same grounds as that for in-

[7] *Ibid.,* esp. pp. 200 ff.

cluding b/rp: it rests on the fact that much money is governmental, together with the fact that even in the private sector the attitude toward debt is asymmetrical to that toward receivables.

Precautionary Demand. — I now turn to precautionary balances, from which I have abstracted almost entirely up to this point. The demand for these is extremely important, and shifts in this element of demand may even go far to explain the empirical evidence that is often used to support the idea of a horizontal L curve at low rates of interest.[8] I have omitted reference to this important element heretofore for two reasons. One is that their chief role is seen only in dynamic analysis, and its study is thus reserved for subsequent work. A second is that this demand seems to have some characteristics of the transactions demand, some of the speculative. It can, therefore, best be described after each of these has been explored.

Precautionary balances are those held for the unforeseen rainy day, or for the unforeseen opportunity. Like transactions balances, they will presumably be influenced by the level of income, though even the direction of this influence may be hard to judge: if one's income is large he need not set aside the balances for small emergencies that a man with small income may require; on the other hand, if one's income is large the kind of emergencies and of opportunities that may arise can in all likelihood be met only by larger balances than can those facing the man of modest income.

Precautionary balances are obviously and directly influenced by the price level, since appendectomies rise in price quite as much as do foreseeable expenditures. In this sense, precautionary demand will be measured in real terms, as are the transactions and the speculative demand.

Patinkin suggests that persons are uncertain about the time when they must pay out their transactions balances, and that in this sense the so-called "transactions" demand contains a combination of transactions and precautionary elements.[9] With this I agree, and in my treatment below I shall lump the two together, as Patinkin has done. On the other hand one important difference between the two types of balances may be noted. When, instead of a motivational classification, one that classes money as "active" or "idle" is used, then the precautionary balances must be grouped with speculative balances in the latter category, rather than with the transactions component in the active balances.

In static analysis no important revision in our over-all functional forms is imposed by the existence of precautionary balances, and therefore none

[8] See William Fellner, *Monetary Policies and Full Employment* (Berkeley and Los Angeles: University of California Press, 1946), pp. 146 ff.

[9] Patinkin, *Money, Interest and Prices*, p. 17.

is made — but, I repeat, in a dynamic analysis this issue looms much larger.

Demand for Finance. — The "finance" demand has been discussed in some detail above (pp. 210–212), and nothing need be added now except a note concerning the method of treating it in this chapter. In general, I shall hereafter refer to the functions of figure VII instead of those of figure V, and in this way obtain results that are similar, so far as determination of interest rates is concerned, to those that would follow if I introduced this motive for holding cash. Figure VII*b* may be regarded as a presentation of both the transactions demand and the finance demand.

Having now examined the three motives for holding cash as a store of wealth — speculative, precautionary, and finance — there remains the task of examining the behavior and method of portraying the transactions demand.

Transactions Demand. — When figure V*b* was first introduced (p. 200), the assumption was made that the income velocity of active money equals the price level, as a result of which the equation of exchange reduces from $M_1 V_1 = pY$ to $M_1 = Y$. This assumption could be readily made because the quantity units in which goods are measured can be made any arbitrary size, thus permitting p to assume any desired value. Now that variable prices have been introduced to the analysis, however, this procedure must be modified. We may again make the same assumption for the level of prices chosen as base (p_0) but so long as we assume the velocity of active money to be constant, the M_1 associated with any given Y will have to vary directly and proportionately with prices. This may be demonstrated simply by returning to the equation of exchange, replacing V_1 with its equivalent p_0 and transposing this to the right-hand side. This gives $M_1 = (Y)(p/p_0)$. If M_1 is interpreted as the demand for funds to finance a desired level of income at given prices, this expression becomes the demand function for transactions balances:

$$M_1^D = (Y)(p/p_0). \tag{4}$$

That is, the demand for active balances equals real income multiplied by the ratio of the going price level to the base price level. For some purposes we shall later find it convenient to use another form of this expression:

$$M_1^D = p \cdot L_1(Y) \tag{5}$$

where the function $L_1(Y)$ is Y/V_1, or the equivalent, Y/p_0. The expression M^D used here is equivalent to L as used earlier.

Equation (4) supports the procedure used in drawing figure V*b* wherein the demand for transactions balances was shown always equal to the level of real income because prices were held constant and equal to p_0. If prices were double this level, however, the red plane representing demand for M_1 would have to rotate clock-wise around DA so that every point on it would be twice as far from the end wall as before. The base would then lie along OP instead of Oc_1. Similarly if prices were halved the red plane would rotate counterclockwise until its base lay along OW_1, where OW_1 equals one-half Oc_1.

Figure Vb may now be used to illustrate a difference between the Keynesian and classical interpretation of the characteristics of equilibrium. To illustrate this, assume first a full employment equilibrium compatible with each theory, with the quantity of transactions balances available equal to \$2,400 so that this supply is equal to the demand at an income of \$2,400 and price equal to p_0, indicating equilibrium along the line a′c′ in figure Vb. Suppose, now, that this equilibrium is disturbed by monetary action reducing the quantity of money available for transactions to \$1,200, the amount actually indicated by the position of the green surface in figure Vb. In this event Keynesians would point out that the assumption of full employment imposes an internal contradiction on the system, since the requirements for transactions balances at that level (Hc_1) greatly exceeds the actual supply (HW_1). Viewed another way and still abstracting from inactive balances, the contradiction is shown by the fact that the LM curve (i.e., the projection of d_1f_1 on the end wall, ABCD) intersects SI at Q, indicating an income of \$1,200, instead of at I, where it would represent full employment. With the given supply of M_1, and with prices given at p_0, a higher level of Y than \$1,200 simply cannot be financed. A Keynesian type of approach would, therefore, assume just such an underemployment level of income to exist.

A typical classical explanation of events would be quite different. In this view figure Vb shows that if M_1 were reduced from \$2,400 to \$1,200, the L_1 surface could not remain where it is. The same internal contradiction which forced the Keynesian equilibrium from full employment to underemployment while retaining the former L_1, leads the classical economist to expect falling prices to cause a counterclockwise rotation of the L_1 surface around DA until its base lies along OW_1 and equilibrium is reestablished along the full-employment wall, now at V_1W_1 instead of at a′c′. The reason for these falling prices may be read from figure Vb just as readily as were the reasons for the Keynesian decline of income and employment. The classical economist would note that along the full employment wall the demand for transactions balances at p_0 exceeds the supply by the amount $W_1c′$. This unsatisfied demand for money leads people to try to sell goods and services in order to secure funds, and the attempted sales force prices down. The process continues until the red surface rotates to the position described above with its base along RW_1.

Two conclusions from the preceding discussion may now be summarized. First, the effect of changing price levels on the demand for transactions balances may be indicated by rotation of the L_1 surface about the DA axis. This rotation will be clockwise for price increases and counterclockwise for price reductions. Second, the classical school was able to deny the necessity for underemployment equilibrium at such points as Q in figure Vb by assuming that price changes would cause rotation of the L_1 surface as just described.

Probably the most important of all the characteristics of the Keynesian system is its solution at Q, with the unemployment implied by this level of income, yet Keynes recognized the possibility that the conditions of this position *might* move the system in the direction of full employment. As in the classical adjustment this movement would take place by a counterclockwise rotation of the L surface caused by falling prices. Yet the process was significantly different from that described by the classical analysis. Keynes would expect the price decline (if it occurred) to be the result of falling money wages caused by the quest of the unemployed for jobs. And the consequence of rotating the L surface in the Keynesian interpretation is seen by noting that, as the LM curve moves "back" along the end wall, its intersection with SI shifts from Q toward I. This movement along SI means that interest rates are falling, and the resultant rise in income may be attributed to this change in the rate of interest. At lower rates investment rises and saving declines, both facts causing a multiplier effect on income. The significance of the difference between these two explanations (classical and Keynesian) of the tendency toward full-employment equilibrium will be seen later when we examine possible impediments to the movement. For the moment, however, we note the similarity: each suggests the possibility that changing levels of prices might make full-employment equilibrium internally consistent by shifting the LM curve until it intersects SI at the full-employment wall.

In the preceding discussion we have characterized as "classical" the disequilibrium in which full employment is maintained, and as "Keynesian" the tendency for disequilibrium to show itself in the form of unemployment. This characterization seems legitimate as a means of emphasizing the common interpretations of these two approaches. It should be recognized, however, that the classical school does not assume that unemployment may not occur in disequilibrium, and in this sense it is not accurate to identify their analysis wholly with this interpretation of the economy's response to disequilibrium. Our identification of Keynes with the second type of system, where rigid prices cause the impact of disequilibrium to fall upon employment, may be subject to less objection, but the assumption of no price change represents a limiting case in his position too.

THE PRICE LEVEL AND THE SAVING AND
INVESTMENT SURFACES

Pigou fully recognizes that declining prices can well have the results described by Keynes — i.e., by increasing the effective supply of money, interest rates are reduced, and a tendency toward full employment is felt. He has added to this, however, a type of response that has been dubbed the "Pigou effect," pointing out that persons holding either cash or bonds payable in fixed amounts of cash will enjoy increased claims to real wealth when prices drop, and in consequence will spend more readily than before. The result may be illustrated by a fall of the saving surface in figure IVc; this causes the SI curve to move "back" in figure IV and "up" in figure VII. The implications of this shift will be examined shortly when Patinkin's additions have been included. In the meantime it may be noted, however, that in an analysis like that depicted in figures Vc, VIIc, or VIIb a rise of SI will tend to move equilibrium toward full employment. If the LM curve were at L″M″ in VIIc, for instance, it is clear that SI would not have to rise much before it intersected the LM curve at the full-employment wall.

Patinkin also describes the response emphasized by Pigou, but he now gives it the more instructive title of "real-balance effect." [10] By recognizing that firms may respond to increases in their real balances quite as much as do private households, Patinkin is led to include the effect of changing M/p in the investment function as well as in the saving function. Thus the same fall in prices which shifts the saving surface downward, also shifts the investment surface up. The impact on SI is reinforcing, causing it to shift "back" in figure IV ("up" in figure VII) even more than if the effect on consumption alone were involved, and thus the adjustment toward full employment is still further facilitated.

Another important clarification introduced by Patinkin is the observation that this real-balance effect, was implicit though generally unrecognized in the classical analysis whereby a change in prices caused a shift of the LM curve. In other words the direct monetary consequences of changing prices were clearly seen and analyzed, but the effects on saving-investment relations, though logically an entirely necessary part of the same phenomena, were seldom fully recognized. The monetary aspect of the analysis, whereby the effort to build up cash balances following a reduction of M and hence of M/p would show itself in price declines caused by the desire to sell goods, has been described in relation to the demand for transactions balances of figure V above (p. 246). This was, indeed, the process by which the quantity theory of money worked itself out. Patin-

[10] The more familiar title, "Pigou effect," is apparently from an earlier article by Patinkin himself. *Ibid.*, p. 21, n. 11.

kin's contribution at this point is to note that since the process just described results from a change in attitudes concerning the holding of money *versus the purchase of output,* its effects must be reflected in the functions describing the demand for goods as well as in those describing the demand for money. To picture these results in our model the saving and investment surfaces must be shifted.

Remembering that the disturbance described here was an inappropriate relation between M and p — i.e., a disequilibrium value of M/p — the conclusion may be drawn that since a change in either M or p which alters the value of M/p results in changed levels of spending, the effects of this change must be recognized not only in the money relations of figure V, but also in shifts of the saving and investment surfaces of figure IV.

The operation of this effect on the S and I surface in response to an arbitrary reduction of M from an equilibrium situation, as assumed in the preceding illustration (p. 246) could be traced as follows. We retain the classical assumption that disequilibrium need not push us off the full-employment wall — i.e., the end wall of figure IVc (or, perhaps more clearly, IVd). If we imagine that the saving and investment surfaces as drawn there had been appropriate in the equilibrium enjoyed when $M = \$2,400$, and $p = p_0$, then the decline in real balances implied by the sudden reduction of M to \$1,200 will shift the S curve up the end wall in figure IVc (or IVd), and the I curve down. This means that at the going rate of interest, saving greatly exceeds investment, setting off deflationary movements. (This is simply to state in terms of saving-investment relations the process that is described above in terms of money functions.) The result in classical analysis is a decline in prices. But the decline in prices raises real balances again, and shifts the S and I surfaces back toward their original positions. If there were no real-bond effect, full-employment equilibrium would be ultimately reëstablished when prices had fallen to half their former level, so that with M also at half its former amount real balances (m/p) would be restored to their original value, and the S and I surfaces would likewise be back to the position from which they started.

Given the existence of government bonds, however, halved M and halved p will leave a higher level of real-bond holdings, b/rp. The effort to restore desired relations between these and other variables will force a shift from bonds to both income and cash balances, SI shifts up slightly, LM shifts up, and hence the new equilibrium must be at a higher rate of interest than before the reduction of M.

As stated above, one of Patinkin's important points in this discussion is his recognition that the real-balance effect on the commodity markets is an essential element in the classical process of adjustment. One reason that it has often been overlooked is that so long as one abstracted from government bonds, this real-balance effect was a temporary phenomenon, since in the new equilibrium M/p would be at its former level, and hence there would be no occasion for any persisting real-balance effect.

A quick glance backward at what we have done may now be useful. This restatement will first abstract from real-bond effects. For analytical purposes we have viewed in isolation different parts of an adjustment process which will in fact be simultaneous. We have also seen these adjustments under different kinds of assumptions about the nature of the economy following a disturbance of equilibrium. To some extent both the Keynesian and the classical mechanisms have been caricatured in order to highlight their major emphases. The resulting picture is something like this: Assume that M is suddenly reduced from a position of full-employment equilibrium. Before adjustments can take place disequilibrium will appear in one or more markets. It is convenient to picture the classical adjustment process by imagining that this disequilibrium does not occur in the labor market, but that full employment persists. The disequilibrium exists instead in the markets for money and for commodities. The resulting adjustment may then be visualized by examining either of these two markets. The classical economist typically looked at the money market, and saw the excess of demand for money forcing an attempted sale of goods until prices were halved in accord with the halving of M. In figure Vb, the base of the L surface shifts from Oc_1 to OW_1, where equilibrium is reëstablished at prices that are half of what they were formerly. Although the classical economists scarcely realized it (and most of the rest of us did not either), Patinkin has shown that this same process may be described in relation to the commodity market in terms of real-balance effects. The drop in M and hence in M/p forces the S surface up and the I surface down, causing an excess of saving over investment, and bringing about a decline in the demand for goods and hence in prices. The latter, by raising M/p again, gradually return the S and I surfaces to their original positions, with the new equilibrium showing itself only in a lowered price level.

Keynes would emphasize a different response to the decrease of M, namely, one which expresses itself in the labor market through unemployment, rather than expressing itself in the money market. Indeed, for him the economy would shift fairly quickly to the state of underemployment described by Q in figures IV and VII. If equilibrium forces were to function effectively, as he doubted for reasons to be explored later, they would do so through the downward pressure of unemployment on wages and, through these, on the general level of prices. The L surface would rotate counterclockwise, as in the classical case. But the result of this adjustment would be a movement of Q along SI toward I instead of along the back wall as in the classical picture. As the adjustment toward full employment takes place (if it does), this adjustment represents primarily the response of stable saving and investment functions to changing interest rates, where these changes in interest result from the release of money previously tied up in transactions requirements but now freed by falling prices.

Finally it may be remembered that because of real-bond effects, the result of decreases in the money supply will be a permanent, if slight, rise in interest rates even if full employment is restored by falling prices. The L surface will be shifted slightly to the right, and the SI surface to the left, by the real-bond effect of these falling prices.

AN APPLICATION: OPEN MARKET OPERATIONS

The preceding analysis may be used to compare the effects of changes in the money supply through direct increase in M (e.g., via deficit spending financed by Federal Reserve Banks), with the effects of an equal volume of open-market purchases. In this analysis it will be assumed that wages and prices are sticky, so that underemployment equilibrium occurs, as in the analysis in previous chapters. Furthermore, abstraction is made from the differing effects of these two policies during the interim in which impact effects are felt, as they are following an injection of spending, when the multiplier temporarily raises the level of income.

It is conventional to depict the effect of open-market operations by a simple shift of M to the right, without any change in L. An increase of M by direct injection would typically be shown the same way. If our analysis is correct this procedure turns out to be legitimate for open-market operations but not for the direct injection of M. The open-market purchase actually involves two changes in the economy whose effect on the location of the L surface cancel each other. Thus the increase in M would, by itself, shift L to the right because it indicates an increase in the real value of total assets (prices being held constant by hypothesis), but the concomitant reduction of bonds outstanding serves to reduce the real value of assets by an equal amount, causing L to shift back to its original position again (or, more accurately, removing any tendency for it to shift in the first place). On the other hand, our analysis would suggest that a mere injection of M without reduction of bonds outstanding would shift L to the right without any counteracting effect. The implication is that if only these considerations obtain, open-market operations would be more expansionary (after impact effects) than the injection of an equal amount of money unassociated with changes in b. The logic of this result is that when the real value of wealth increases (as in the second case but not the first) people will wish to hold more idle funds.

This conclusion, however, rests on incomplete analysis. The difficulty is that we have abstracted from the real-balance effects of changes in wealth on the saving and investment surfaces. Just as the real-balance effects of the open-market operations on L cancelled out, so they also cancel out in their effects on S and I; however, the real-balance effect of the direct injection of M is not cancelled, but results in an expansionary shift of all three of these surfaces. If we believe it probable that the expansionary effects of increased real balances on spending will normally exceed the deflationary effects of these increased balances on the demand for idle funds, the conclusion of the preceding paragraph is reversed: a direct increase of M will be more expansionary than open-market purchases of equal volume. But the point of importance to note on the theoretical level is that this conclusion rests upon real-balance effects on spending decisions, effects of which much conventional theory has overlooked.

An additional consequence of open-market operations is revealed by consideration of the term b/rp in the functions describing S, I, and the demand for money. The presence of r in this term expresses the fact that changes in capital values associated with variations in the rate of interest will amplify the effects of increased money, whether by direct injection or open-market operations. Since the latter, by directly changing the number of bonds outstanding, will have more effect on r than direct injection of M, the aid to policy provided by the effects of changing capital values will be greater in response to open-market operations.

Finally, it may be useful to contrast the effects of financing government spending by new money with the effect of securing funds from sale of bonds to the public. The final results of the former (after impacts have worn off) is an increase in M with the number of bonds unchanged; of the latter, an increase in the number of bonds with M unchanged. The real-balance effects would, therefore, be the same in this model, which does not differentiate between the influences of different types of wealth. The increase in M, however, would cause a reduction of interest rates, whereas the increase of b would increase these rates. For these reasons, despite similar real-balance effects, the use of new money would be clearly more expansionary than would the sale of new bonds to the public.

An Algebraic Summary

The equilibrium system with which we have been working geometrically may be readily summarized by a system of equations, the elements of which were developed by Lawrence Klein and expanded by Patinkin.

Money Equation   (Figs. V*c* and $\overline{M} = p \cdot L\left(r, Y, \overline{A}, \dfrac{\overline{M}}{p}, \dfrac{b}{rp}\right)$ (1)
                              VII*c*)

Saving   (Fig. IV*a*) $S = f_1\left(r, Y, \overline{A}, \dfrac{\overline{M}}{p}, \dfrac{b}{rp}\right)$ (2)

Investment	(Fig. IV*b*)	$I = f_2\left(r, Y, \overline{A}, \dfrac{\overline{M}}{p}, \dfrac{\overline{b}}{rp}\right)$	(3)
Keynesian Equilibrium	(Fig. IV*c*)	$S = I$	(4)
Production Function	(Fig. VIII*a*)	$Y = \phi(N, \overline{A})$	(5)
Demand for Labor	(Fig. VIII*b*)	$W = \dfrac{\partial \phi}{\partial N} = \dfrac{\partial Y}{\partial N}$	(6)
Supply of Labor	(Fig. VIII*b*)	$N = \theta(W)$	(7)
Supply of Labor	(Fig. VIII*c*)	$\overline{w} = Wp, \quad \overline{w}$ given	(7')
Supply of Labor		$W = \overline{Z}, \quad \overline{Z}$ given	(7'')

A recapitulation of the meaning of symbols used is given on page 118. Equations (7') and (7'') will be explained later. In the meantime the rest of the set will provide a convenient basis for summarizing the conclusions developed in the graphical analysis.[11]

1. The three-dimensional model used earlier and often given as the Keynesian system omits the multiplicative p from equation (1), and omits the three last terms from equations (1) to (3). In consequence a full determination of the equilibrium level of income may then be obtained from equations (1) to (4), the unknowns being r, Y, S and I. This solution represents the intersection of SI and LM, and involves no implication of full employment. The associated level of employment may then be determined by the aid of equation (5) or figure VIII*a*, and the real wage by equation (6) or figure VIII*b*. If equation (7) is added, (the supply curve in figure VIII*b*), the system is overdetermined, having only 6 unknowns. This corresponds to the fact that, before variable prices were admitted to the system, SI might intersect LM at some other level than that of full employment.

---

[11] Tobin has shown a number of advantages in a different statement of this system more closely following the equation used earlier in relation to the demand for speculative balances. Such a system might run as follows:

(1) $\overline{M} = p \cdot L(r, Y, We)$ (5) $We = \overline{A} + (\overline{M}/p) + (\overline{b}/rp)$
(2) $S = f_1(r, Y, We)$ (6) $Y = \phi(N, \overline{A})$
(3) $I = f_2(r, Y, We, \overline{A})$ (7) $W = \partial\phi/\partial N$
(4) $S = I$ (8) $N = \theta(W)$

The advantages of this system include these: (*a*) To a mathematician the expression in equation (1) of the text is awkward or worse because the term M/p in the L function appears redundant. (*b*) The textual expression does not show that the sum of the three wealth terms may be used as a single variable in equations (1) through (3), as in our textual exposition. Despite these admitted advantages of a reformulation, I have retained the system as shown for two reasons. In the first place this formulation is more general, permitting one to go beyond the simplifying assumptions of the text and to assume functions according to which wealth of different liquidity affects behavior differently. In the second place, this formulation facilitates comparison with other systems to which reference is made in the following paragraphs.

2. When the multiplicative p is introduced into equation (1) it becomes impossible to solve any of the first four equations without the aid of the entire system, number (7) of which implies full employment. Geometrically, this means that, since no solution for p is possible without the use of all equations, the location of the L surface cannot be known without this full solution. On the other hand we can begin at the bottom of the set and solve for real income, real wages, and the level of employment with the aid of only equations (5) to (7). Equilibrium values of these key real variables are thus entirely independent of the saving and investment equation, the rate of interest, the quantity of money and the level of prices. Saving and investment relations simply indicate how much of the full-employment output will be devoted to current and how much to future consumption. They do determine the rate of interest, however, which is not influenced by the quantity of money. The latter influences only the price level. These same conclusions may be shown geometrically by the fact that figures VIIIa and VIIIb together determine Y, W, and N, without any reference to the rest of the system. Figure Vd then, together with this Y, which equals \$2,400, determines r, S, and I. The L surface of figure V (or VII) then shifts as a reflection of changing prices until LM passes through I.

3. There are three important comments to be made about the implication of introducing M/p to equations (2) and (3). First, this amendment is the one that brings into operation the Pigou, or real-balance effect on spending decisions: it permits changing prices to shift the S and I surfaces, and hence the SI curve, to facilitate the movement toward equilibrium on the full-employment wall. Second, it should be noted that even this fairly complete and familiar model implies the same conclusion concerning the relation of prices to money supply which was taught by the crude quantity theory. So long as neither M nor p appear in the system except in the ratio M/p, a change in either one must, *ceteris paribus*, force a proportionate change in the other, since the equilibrium conditions determine the ratio between them. Thus I agree with Patinkin's statement that "the propositions of the quantity theory of money hold under conditions much less restrictive than those usually considered necessary . . ." [12] I shall comment much more fully on the quantity theory below (see pp. 268–270). The third fact that should be noted about the implications of our model when it includes all elements except b/rp is that the quantity of money, although determining the level of prices, has no influence whatever on the rate of interest. With income determined by equations (5) to (7) along the full-employment wall, and with equations (2) to (4) determining that the solution lies along SI, the rate of interest is necessarily set at the intersection of SI with the full-employment wall.

[12] Patinkin, *Money, Interest and Prices*, p. 3.

That is, equations (2) to (7) fully determine the rate of interest without reference to equation (1), the price level, or the quantity of money. On this last point Patinkin would rightly warn us that these equations describe equilibrium, and that the classical economists were well aware of the temporary effects that changes in the money supply could have on the rate of interest. Only when M and p have returned to their equilibrium ratio would the classical economist argue that interest rates would also revert to their former levels.

4. Once we admit b/rp to the system (or even b/p) all of the preceding generalizations break down. Now a change in M associated with a proportionate change in p would not preserve but would destroy equilibrium unless we assume a simultaneous and exactly proportionate exogenous change also in the number of securities outstanding, for a change in p would otherwise alter the ratio of b to p.

5. The familiar model of aggregative equilibrium which includes equations (1) to (7) but omits $\overline{b}/rp$ and $\overline{A}$ exemplifies several features which identify it with what Keynes would call a "classical" system, although the general structure utilizes a clearly Keynesian type of formulation. The classical features of this system include these. (i) Full employment is a necessary condition of equilibrium. (ii) The quantity of money influences only prices, not the rate of interest. (iii) Propensities to save and to invest have no influence on the current level of employment or income, but simply determine how much of current output goes into consumption and how much goes into capital goods for future consumption.

Having now constructed a Keynesian type of model to describe the classical conclusions, we can readily note the essential Keynesian assumptions that permit him to reach his own conflicting view. The model will also be used to suggest the general nature of possible answers to questions that Keynes did not emphasize.

The SI–LM Curve

The preceding analysis gives emphasis to the fact that the familiar presentation of the Keynesian system — which is, if anything, even simpler than the three-dimensional model we used before introducing flexible prices — is not sufficient to demonstrate the Keynesian conclusion of underemployment equilibrium. A full demonstration really requires the Keynesian reply to a full model like the one which includes figure VIII.

Keynes' analysis proceeds on at least two levels. In the first place he argues that prices are not flexible downward, which in a sense does return us to the earlier models we have used. But he also argues that even if they were flexible, this would be of no help, because full-employment equilibrium might still be impossible. This last step is really essential, because even the classical economists would admit that if unions held wages at too high a level, underemployment could follow. The ultimate issue which Keynes wished to urge was that unions could not solve the problem by simply accepting wage cuts.

In light of these observations I shall divide the analysis of the Keynesian solution into two parts. The first concerns the nature of equilibrium in a world where money wages behave as Keynes suggested they actually do behave. The second examines the consequences that he believed might follow if wages were flexible.

The following analysis, in both this and succeeding sections, will rest heavily on the use of a somewhat complex but highly important curve, the *SI–LM* curve of figure VIII*d*. The importance of the relations described by this function justifies our spending some time to understand it clearly. It is derived entirely from figures IV and VII, which represent equations (1) to (4) on page 253.

I have already shown that with given *M* each possible price level implies a given position for the *L* surface of figure VII*c* (as indicated by the rotation of that surface with changing prices), and a given position of the *S* and *I* surfaces (according to the real-balance and real-bond effects). But each position of *L*, in relation to any given *M*, determines a unique *LM* curve; and each position of *S* and of *I* determines a unique *SI* curve. Finally, each pair of *LM* and *SI* curves determines a unique equilibrium solution (e.g. at Q), for *Y*, *r*, *S* and *I*. We shall now direct our attention to only one of these determined values, the level of real income (*Y*). To summarize, with *M* and the functions described by equations (1) to (4) given (illustrated by figures IV and VII) each level of prices determines a unique equilibrium level of income by determining a unique location of the *L*, *S*, and *I* surfaces. In figure VIII*d* I have drawn the curve showing this relationship between prices and income.[13]

_____

[13] A note on this construction may be useful. We take as our point of departure the point N_0 since that assumes base-level prices and a money supply of $1,740 together with equilibrium of *SI* and *LM* at a real income of $1,200, as shown in figures IV, V, and VII. One may then superimpose new *L* surfaces in VII*c* to represent different possible price levels. Next an arbitrary assumption must be made regarding the shifts of *SI* in response to real-balance and real-bond effects. For each possible price level a location for Q may then be determined, and the *Y* (income) value of that Q, together with the price level that produced it, give the coordinates of a point on the *SI–LM* curve.

In order to visualize the consequences of all these changes at once, we may employ the following device. Suppose our object is to find the location of the point on *SI–LM* corresponding to prices equal to $\frac{1}{2} p_0$. First we may note that, beginning with equilibrium at N_0, by simultaneously halving prices, money, and bonds outstanding no changes would take place in any real values of the system. Viewing figure VII*c*, no change occurs except in the units on the money axis. Now we may double *M* (thereby restoring it to its former level) by shifting the green wall to the right. This gives an *LM* curve which, abstracting from real-balance effects, virtually passes through *I* on *SI*. The level of income has risen to about $2,400. If we admit real balance effects, the increased size of real balances will raise *SI*, and, by shifting *L* to the right (as described on pp. 245 ff.)

I call it the SI–LM curve because it shows the combinations of prices and income which, with any given M, determine simultaneous equality between saving and investment on the one hand, between supply and demand for money on the other.

Those who find three-dimensional geometry difficult can readily follow the rest of the analysis by recognizing that a similar SI–LM curve may be derived from the Hicksian model given on pp. 195 ff. and illustrated by the two-dimensional drawings of figure III. Here also SI and LM will shift in response to changing prices or changing supply of money, so that with any given M the income levels represented by their intersection may be plotted against various price levels, forming an SI–LM curve entirely analogous to that of figure VIII. The only difference between these two derivations is that the three-dimensional one recognizes more variables in the S and the I functions. When the SI–LM curve is derived from the two-dimensional model it becomes essentially identical with McKenna's aggregate demand curve.[14]

In the drawing I have presumed relations such that a halving of p from p_0 would double the level of income. This is shown by a shift of equilibrium from N_0 to H_3. It should be emphasized that this relationship is not a general one (see footnote 13), but depends upon the shape of the liquidity surface in the relevant range and upon other special assumptions.

The scale for real income is shown on the y-axis with values based on a price level equal to p_0. Price levels are measured on the x-axis. The basic

will raise LM as well. Thus the intersection of SI and LM may still be at or near the full-employment wall, though at a higher rate of interest.

Next, consider the consequences of doubling the number of bonds and thus restoring them to their initial level. The effect will be, again, to make people feel better off, and hence to accentuate the rise of SI and LM caused by the increase in M. If we arbitrarily assume that the vertical shifts of SI and of LM resulting from both the real-balance and the real-bond effects are equal, then equilibrium will still be at the full-employment wall, but at a higher rate of interest than before, because of the shifts of SI and LM.

We have now located the point on SI–LM corresponding to a price level of $\frac{1}{2} p_0$, for our three successive operations were first to halve simultaneously prices, money supply, and bonds; then to double money supply; and finally to double bonds, thus restoring everything to the *status quo ante* except prices, which remain at $\frac{1}{2} p_0$. The derived point on SI–LM is at H_3, in figure VIIId, where this price level corresponds to a full-employment real income of $2,400.

It should be emphasized, as stated in the text below, that the shape of the SI–LM curve in our figure is the result of the special assumptions made in our model regarding the shapes and shifts of all surfaces. The fact that in figure VIIId a halving of prices has the effect of exactly doubling income (moving from N_0 to H_3) is not general, but is a coincidence.

It may be mentioned in passing that a somewhat related analysis by Patinkin (*Money, Interest and Prices*, p. 206) shows that if M is changed by the monetary authorities, then the new equilibrium rate of interest, even after all price adjustments have been completed, will differ from the old because of real bond effects. The rate of interest will increase when M is reduced, and vice versa. This conclusion and the nature of the explanation are essentially parallel to the relevant part of the argument above.

[14] McKenna, *Aggregative Economic Analysis*, chapter 11, pp. 171–187.

unit of measure here is p_0, which is seen by the *SI–LM* curve to be associated with a real income of \$1,200. This means that if prices were at the base level, and *M* were equal to \$1,740 the *SI* curve would intersect the *LM* curve at an income of \$1,200, as indeed it does in figures IV*c* and VII*c*.

Before leaving the description of the *SI–LM* curve, it will be useful to consider the way it would be affected by a number of events that might occur. (1) Suppose the banking system increases *M*. Then for any given price level the *LM* curve in VII*c* will shift "down and back," causing Q to shift downward along *SI*, and implying lower interest rates and higher income. *SI–LM* in VIII*d* will therefore shift upward, showing that at each price level (x value) real income (y value) will be higher than before. (2) Suppose the propensity to consume rises. Then the saving surface of figure IV*c* shifts downward, *SI* moves up to the right, forcing Q to slide along *L'M'* in the same direction. This implies that for any assumed price level both income and interest rates will be higher than before. Once again, *SI–LM* in VIII*d* shifts upward. (3) Suppose optimism raises the marginal efficiency of investment. Again *SI* in IV*c* moves in the same general direction as before, this time because the investment surface rises vertically. And again we find *SI–LM* in VIII*d* rising. In short, any of the events which our simple Keynesian analysis would lead us to regard as a means of increasing income, will raise the *SI–LM* curve in VIII*d*.

ALTERNATIVE MODELS

Full-Employment Equilibrium

It is now possible to relate the classical full-employment equilibrium described eariler in this chapter to the *SI–LM* curve. Figure VIII*b* shows the intersection of the classical supply and demand curves for labor, indicating employment of OF″. Figure VIII*a* shows that this level of employment determines a real income of \$2,400. *SI–LM* in figure VIII*d* now permits us to see that this equilibrium can be achieved only by an adjustment of the price level to ½ p_0, since the \$2,400-income line (H_3H) intersects *SI–LM* at a p-value of ½ p_0.

If we wish to go further and discover other features of this equilibrium we must use figures IV and VII, together with information on how their surfaces shift under the impact of real-balance and real-bond effects. For example, if the surfaces used in these figures are drawn for *M* = \$1,740 and $p = p_0$, then the equilibrium value found at $p = ½ \ p_0$ would represent a situation where real balances were higher than assumed in the figures, and the surfaces would have to be shifted somewhat from their positions as pictured. A similar modification would have to be introduced because of the real-bond effects of the price change just described. The nature of these shifts is indicated in footnote 13.

The Keynesian Solution

The Keyensian solution is more complex. Keynes argued that because of the money illusion a cut in money wages would tend to cause a general withdrawal of labor from the market. The implication is that money wages are effectively rigid against downward movement. Furthermore, so long as there are appreciable numbers of unemployed workers an increase in effective demand can cause greater employment without producing a noticeable rise in money wages. In short, then, under conditions of marked unemployment, money wages are approximately constant. As full employment is closely approached, however, further labor can be secured only by marked rises in money wages.[15] When full employment is actually achieved, any further increase in the quantity of labor supplied will be obtained only if these money wage increases are at least proportional to the simultaneous price rise. From this point on, therefore, one may regard the supply curve as being drawn in real terms and representing constant (or rising) real wages.

This description of the supply curve for labor seems a reasonably accurate statement of Keynes' general position. It also seems to present a fairly realistic hypothesis concerning the relation between the supply of labor and money wages. It is admittedly more schematic than either Keynes or the real world, but even in this form its graphic presentation is slightly complex. This portrayal of a Keynesian system will be described in two steps. The first will illustrate the consequences of constant money wages. In the second this assumption will be modified by permitting these money wages to rise sharply near full employment, and, from the latter point to rise proportionately with prices, so that real wages are constant.

GEOMETRIC PRESENTATION OF CONSTANT
MONEY WAGE ASSUMPTION

Since real wages are by definition money wages divided by prices, we may write $W = w/p$, or, as in equation (7') on page 253, $w = Wp$. In this last form it is easy to see that any constant money wage may be depicted by a rectangular hyperbola on a graph with the two axes representing real wages and the price index. In figure VIIIc I have drawn such curves for each of four possible levels of money wages. These are labeled w_0, w_1, w_2, and w_3.[16]

---

[15] *The General Theory*, p. 301.

[16] For some purposes it may be useful to find the relation between the money wage level implied by one w curve and that of another. This relation will be found to be precisely the same as the relation between the p-values of the intersections of the respective w curves with any horizontal line. For example, draw G_1G. Its intersection with w_3 is at $\frac{1}{2} p_0$, and its intersection with w_1 is at $\frac{3}{4} p_0$, indicating that the ratio of the wage level represented by w_3 to that of w_1 is $\frac{1}{2} \div \frac{3}{4}$, or $\frac{2}{3}$. The reason this procedure may be

Our task now is to construct in figure VIIId, for each possible money wage, a curve that will show the relation between real income and the price level that is required to equate real wages with the marginal product of labor. Each w curve in VIIIc permits the drawing of just such a curve in VIIId, and I have labeled these latter curves $WwPp$ because it is their function to relate real income to the four elements, real wages (W), money wages (w), productivity (P), and prices (p). Each assumed money wage yields its own $WwPp$ curve. First the construction of these curves will be described, then their fuller meaning will be considered.

Any given level of real income (e.g., \$2,000) may be represented by a horizontal line at that level in VIIId. Extending this line to the left gives an intersection with the production function of VIIIa (e.g., at B) showing that employment of OB" is required to produce the real income assumed. Continuing vertically downward, figure VIIIb shows that the real wage offered for this level of employment would be 19, as indicated by B'. But figure VIIIc tells us that at this real wage and with money wages equal to w_0, the price level would have to be that shown by J_0. We have now derived the level of prices consistent with the assumed money wage (w_0) and a real income of \$2,000. By drawing a line vertically upward from J_0 to the \$2,000 income level in VIIId we locate K_0, which shows this price-income relation and which is, therefore, one point on the desired $WwPp$ curve corresponding with the w_0 money-wage curve. To derive a second point we assume a different level of real income and locate the corresponding price level by the same procedure. If we choose the income \$1,200, for instance, we draw a horizontal in VIIId at that level, extend it to form the intersection A in VIIIa, continue downward to A' in VIIIb, move horizontally again to M_0 in VIIIc, and finally rise vertically to the initial \$1,200-income line in VIIId. This gives the intersection N_0 as a second point on $WwPp_0$. By a similar process the rest of this and the other $WwPp$ curves may be drawn. Each such curve gives us the combinations of real income and price level that satisfy the equilibrium requirements imposed by the assumed money wage, the production function, and the theory of marginal productivity. These curves correspond to McKenna's aggregate supply curve. It is important to note that they in no way reflect the implications of the three-dimensional functions described previously. Equilibrium requirements of the latter are described by the SI–LM curve.

To summarize, then, full equilibrium for any given money wage is described by the intersection of SI–LM with the appropriate $WwPp$ curve.[17] This combination of price and real income satisfies all the con-

---

used is as follows. The money wage level represented by any point on a w curve is the area subtended by the curve at that point. The money wage levels represented by a series of points whose w/p values are equal must, therefore, be proportional to the p values.

[17] To the extent that there is unemployment the term "equilibrium" may be questionable. See page 267 below.

ditions of our system, where we assume that (1) behavioral functions for saving, investment and demand for cash are as depicted in figures IV and VII (subject to known shifts from real-balance and real-bond effects); (2) that the quantity of money supplied by the banking system is $1,740; (3) that the production function and the resulting real demand for labor are as shown in figures VIIIa and VIIIb; (4) that the classical (full-employment) supply curve for labor is ineffective and is replaced by an institutionally determined money wage as shown at w_0 in VIIIc; and (5) that prices other than wages are competitively determined.

A number of inferences may now be drawn from figure VIII. (1) With institutionally determined money wage levels there is nothing in the system to assure full employment. Only if these wages were set as low as w_3 (yielding $WwPp_3$ in figure VIIId) would full employment be achieved. (2) With given money wages, any expansionary force that may take place, including a shift of the marginal efficiency of investment, an increase of money supply, or a reduction of the propensity to save will shift SI–LM outward. Its changing intersections with any given $WwPp$ curve indicate that there will be great changes in employment but very little price change until full employment is nearly reached. Thereafter the effect will shift rapidly to inflationary price effects, first because of bottlenecks at particular points in the economy (not shown here), and then for all the other reasons that sharply reduce the marginal product of labor. (3) In this model a reduction in money wages has an effect similar to that of an increase in the money supply. Consider, for example, the unemployment equilibrium at N_0 resulting from rigid money wages at w_0 and $M =$ $1,740. The money supply might be increased until SI–LM rose to intersect $WwPp_0$ at H_0. Real wages would drop from 20 to 16 as shown by the comparison of A' with F' in figure VIIIb, the mechanism of this drop being the rise of prices from p_0 to $5/4 \, p_0$. Had the money supply remained constant, with labor accepting cuts in money wages, the same real result could have been achieved by a fall of the money wage to w_3 (two-fifths of w_0) and a corresponding fall in prices to $\frac{1}{2} \, p_0$ as shown by H_3 in figure VIIId.[18]

The algebra of the equilibrium solution for given money wages may be briefly stated. It is necessary only to replace equation (7) on page 253 with

---

[18] The fall in real wages is 20 per cent by whichever method full employment is sought. If M is expanded, the new level of real wages (W') will be:

$$W' = \frac{w'}{p'} = \frac{w_0}{\frac{5}{4} p_0} = \left(\frac{4}{5}\right)\left(\frac{w_0}{p_0}\right) = \frac{4}{5} W_0.$$

If, instead of expanding M, money wages are permitted to fall, the new real wage will be the same:

$$W'' = \frac{w''}{p''} = \frac{\frac{2}{5} w_0}{\frac{1}{2} p_0} = \frac{4}{5} W_0.$$

equation $(7')$: $Wp = \overline{w}$, with $\overline{w}$ given by the wage contract. As indicated graphically by our need for both $WwPp$ and $SI\text{--}LM$, no solution for the level of income and employment is now possible without use of all the functions in the system. The addition of p to the last equation makes it impossible to solve the final three equations by themselves. Secondly, there is now nothing in the system that implies a necessary full-employment equilibrium.

KEYNESIAN QUALIFICATION OF THE CONSTANT

MONEY WAGE ASSUMPTION

The outline just completed shows the implications of the assumption that money wages are rigid in contrast to the situation where labor is willing to accept cuts in money wages. As stated at the beginning of this section Keynes' behavioral assumption requires a modification of the rigid-wage analysis because he suggests that after full employment is reached, the rise in money wages must be at least proportionate to any rise in prices.[19] In short, real wages become constant under full employment (or possibly even rise), whereas money wages were roughly constant with marked underemployment. This modification may be introduced in figure VIIIc by drawing each w curve horizontal (i.e., constant real wages) to the right of that point where the real wage reaches the full-employment level of 16 (or it might even rise to the right of this point). Assuming real wages to be constant, for example, w_0 will be replaced by the curve M_0G_0G; w_1 will be replaced by the curve J_1G_1G; and so on for the other w curves. The result of this reconstruction is to make all the $WwPp$ curves in figure VIIId become horizontal when, as one moves up them, he reaches the full employment line (H_3H). Thus $WwPp_0$ becomes $N_0K_0H_0H$; and $WwPp_1$ becomes $N_1K_1H_1H$.

A third and final modification is easily added, though the curves have not been redrawn to illustrate it. Since Keynes admits rising money wages even before full employment is actually reached, the $WwPp$ curve could bend to the right somewhat more rapidly than in our figure, and there might be no sharp discontinuity in slope at the full-employment horizontal.

Inspection of figure VIII now permits the following conclusions. If money wages are rigid under all circumstances and there is no level of real wages below which labor refuses to work, then any expansionary forces which might occur in the economy would raise $SI\text{--}LM$ and cause its effect to be felt almost exclusively on the level of employment until the marginal product of labor begins to fall off. At that point the impact of further expansion is rapidly shifted from increases in real income and employment to inflationary price movements. If we introduce the Keynes-

---

[19] *The General Theory,* p. 301.

ian modification of this constant wage assumption for high levels of employment and argue that workers refuse to accept lower real wages than those of some full-employment levels, then the preceding generalization is only made the stronger. When full employment is reached the expansion is wholly transferred from real income to the price level. This conclusion is precisely the one described by Keynes.

A Note on the Demand Curve for Labor

The preceding analysis assumes that equilibrium, whether at full employment or at underemployment, will lie along the demand curve for labor in figure VIII*b*. Underemployment therefore implies a real wage in excess of that which would achieve full employment. I believe there is no question that this is the position taken by Keynes.[20] Patinkin raises an interesting criticism, however, which requires comment. He suggests that the solution may better be represented as lying at some such point as R in figure VIII*b*, on neither the demand nor the supply curve.[21] It is not entirely clear whether he reaches his conclusion by rejecting the assumption of perfect competition or by admitting dynamic considerations while retaining the perfectly competitive analysis.

Patinkin's argument is that low levels of aggregate demand causes inventories to accumulate in the hands of firms, and thus forces them to curtail labor input even though the going price of output would more than cover the cost of additional production. He seems to argue that perfect competition does not really mean that firms can sell all they want to at going prices, but only that they think they can. When they produce on the basis of this hope, they are disappointed by inadequate sales, and for this reason they lay men off. Patinkin admits that there is "a basic analytical problem here whose full solution is still not clear to me." He is disturbed by the implication of his argument that unsold inventories can accumulate under perfect competition.

In my view Keynes is correct and Patinkin is in error so long as the assumptions of perfect competition are accepted. Unless markets break down and fail to function entirely, the underemployment equilibrium solution for perfect competition must lie on the marginal-product curve. My reasons for this view follow.

There are essentially two ways in which we may interpret the marginal-product curve. We may regard it as representing real product, or as the value of the real product. A moment of reflection suggests that the only way to avoid the use of value concepts would be to assume that no exchange takes place, and that the worker is paid in units of his own output.

---

[20] *Ibid.*, p. 17.

[21] For Patinkin's discussion of this point see *Money, Interest and Prices*, esp. pp. 213 and 216–221, including his footnote 9 on page 220.

In this crude and unrealistic view it seems clear that expansion would continue in the production of any but free goods so long as the marginal product was greater than the wage of the worker, and this would be consistent with Keynes' conclusion.

In order to be more realistic we must admit exchange and regard the Keynesian demand curve for labor as being the value of the marginal product. As noted earlier, a recognized characteristic of perfect competition is that any firm can sell unlimited amounts at the going price. I share the misgivings that beset Patinkin because his analysis contradicts this assumption. So long as a competitive firm can hire an additional worker for an amount that is less than the value of the additional product, and so long as perfect competition assures the sale of that product at going prices, the worker will be hired.

For these reasons I have retained the Keynesian underemployment solution in this model. But I hasten to add that what I believe to be Patinkin's error arises from his recognition that the real world is not one of perfect competition. His conclusions are surely valid for the real world, and my only difference with him would be that I see here no theoretical dilemma, since the results he describes are wholly consistent with the theory of imperfect competition. Any element of monopoly destroys the assumption that workers will receive a wage equal to the value of their marginal product. It is the marginal revenue product function which becomes the demand curve in this context, and that curve may well drop off vertically in many industries. These consequences may follow from kinked oligopolistic demand curves, from short-run discontinuities in physical production functions, and from other causes such as uncertainty. In these noncompetitive situations which characterize the real world it is surely true that the underemployment solution may typically lie on neither the Keynesian (and classical) demand curve (the marginal-product curve) nor the supply curve of labor.

The Shapes of Functions

Despite the implication of underemployment in this analysis there is still nothing here that settles the ultimate theoretical issue between Keynes and the classical economists. As pointed out above, even they would admit underemployment under assumptions of rigid wages at rates above equilibrium levels. This analysis is useful, for it does indeed describe the conditions which form an important part of the Keynesian underemployment argument. But the question with which we are still left is what would happen if labor unions would accept wage cuts and permit competitive wages to emerge. The implication of this model, as described above, is that full employment would be achieved, though at a lower price level than before. Keynes argues explicitly that in some cases this result might follow, but he adds that it cannot be assumed, and that in any event an increase in the money supply could achieve the same end with a far less drastic set of consequences than those that would be associated with sharp declines in wages and prices all across the economy. For policy decisions the last consideration is probably the crucial one, and it is powerful enough that Pigou and other classically oriented theorists readily assent to it. But the theoretical argument concerning the possibility of underemployment equilibrium directs attention to the doubt Keynes expresses about the view that falling wages, if permitted by the unions, would necessarily have the desired result, despite his admission that they might.

One very important reason which Keynes gives for the belief that falling prices may not achieve the full-employment goal is the unpredictable and possibly perverse response of expectations to change. Another element in his analysis, however, and the one that is appropriate for the static equilibrium model with which we are now working, concerns the shapes of the functions involved. Thus far we have assumed that all the surfaces were of a shape to provide intersections as required for the simultaneous solution of the system. Keynes describes two types of behavior which could well prevent such a simultaneous solution, and he contends, furthermore, that such behavioral response may be extremely probable under many or most real-world situations, especially in mature economies. I shall describe these possibilities and then examine their consequences.

First, suppose the saving and investment surfaces are just as we have drawn them, but the L_2 surface (figure VIIa) is such that its intersection with the full-employment wall ($a_2b_2c_2$) becomes horizontal at some such level as $2\frac{1}{2}$ per cent. Keynes' reasons for the view that desires for speculative balances might behave in this way were discussed above on pages 164 and 169–171.[22] The consequence in terms of our three-dimensional

---

[22] Patinkin questions the reasonableness of the horizontal L curve for reasons which I find only partly convincing. His argument, highly simplified, reduces to this. A falling rate of interest has three effects on the demand for money: (a) it reduces the demand of households and business to hold money by increasing planned expenditures for consumer goods and investment commodities, (b) it increases the demand for money obtained through borrowing by households and business, and (c) it increases the demand for money in contrast to bonds as a stored asset. Patinkin argues that Keynes' horizontal liquidity-preference curve is possible only because Keynes overlooks the first two implications of falling interest rates. Even if it is true that when interest rates drop to some low but positive level persons would be willing to sell all the bonds they hold in order to acquire money — even in this case the demand for money does not become infinitely elastic unless, at the same interest rate, reasons a and b happen exactly to cancel each other. In other words, according to Patinkin, even if one component of the demand for money — that described by c — becomes infinitely elastic, the total demand for money does not become infinitely elastic unless other components cancel each other out. This argument seems to be in error. If the demand for money for any purpose becomes infinitely elastic over a region, then the total demand must

model is readily seen. The L″ end of the *LM* curve in figure VIIc is never capable of falling as far as I, no matter how much *M* is increased unless real balance or real bond effects on the *SI* curve are introduced. Similarly, it can never fall to I from a counterclockwise "rotation" of the *L* surface, however far falling prices may cause that rotation to take place. Thus a major requirement of equilibrium — the intersection of *SI* and *LM* — can never occur at the level of income generated by full employment.

A second kind of behavioral assumption made by Keynes might have a similar result. Suppose that in figure IVc the propensity to save is so great that the trace of the red surface on the end wall intersects the investment curve at rates of interest less than zero. That is, the intersection does not show in our figure at all, but lies toward the reader from the front of the box. This means that *SI* is steep and its right end (*I*) lies below the floor of figure VIIc. Since the cost of storing money is negligible, the *L* surface can never fall far below zero. This means that even if it is drawn as in our figures, reaching very low levels when one moves far to the right, *LM* cannot fall to the level required for an intersection with the *SI* curve at full employment if the latter is drawn as just described. The likelihood that the saving surface might take some such position as this was increased, in Keynes' view, both by the alleged high saving of mature economies and by the belief that low rates of interest may have very little influence on the volume of saving. Thus the ghj trace of the saving curve on the end wall of figure IVc is, in Keynes' view, nearly parallel to BC, and high above the floor.

Still a third factor, one that Keynes did not emphasize as much as some of his followers have done (e.g., Klein), is the possibility that the *I* surface may also be nearly interest-inelastic. In this case the *S* and *I* curves traced on the end of figure IVc become virtually parallel lines and no rate

---

become so also unless some other component becomes negatively infinitely elastic for at least the same size of interval and at exactly the same rate.

A closely related further point of Patinkin's seems valid and interesting. The typical Keynesian *L* curve is so drawn as to imply infinite elasticity for an indefinite distance to the right. Patinkin demonstrates that such a curve is not acceptable, since persons will at some point run out of bonds, whereupon they cannot demand still more money by continued sales of these. If it should be suggested that when persons run out of bonds, they can issue more themselves (i.e., borrow), then Patinkin's reply seems wholly sound: it is not reasonable to suppose that persons will borrow infinite amounts at the rate of interest at which they become indifferent to holding stored wealth in bonds or in cash.

In summary, I find no reason to reject Keynes' assumption that the liquidity curve may become horizontal at some positive rate of interest, but I believe that this horizontal section would be limited in length. Thereafter it is difficult to generalize about the continuation of the curve.

For Patinkin's views see *ibid.*, pp. 54, 76, 138–150, and 245–249, but especially 145–149.

of interest, however, low, can make them cross. Once again, the intersection of SI and LM cannot be moved to the full-employment wall no matter how much the supply of money is increased and no matter how far prices drop.

This is equivalent to saying that the SI–LM curve of figure VIIId is so low and so nearly horizontal that even its left end is too low to intersect H_3H. The equilibrium conditions of figures IV and VII are simply inconsistent with those of VIIIa and VIIIb. What will happen now? Clearly some wishes will not be attained — some price will be unable to equate supply with demand. Where in the economy will desires be frustrated? The answer to this question cannot be read from graphs but must refer back to the real world. At this point the Keynesian insight appears to me to be essentially valid. Security prices can, after all, adjust rapidly to equate supply and demand for money. Consumers can rapidly cut back consumer expenditures if they decide they would like to save. Business can cut its purchases of new capital goods. Both the action of savers and that of business will thus be effective in reducing the level of income, and forcing the equilibrium away from the full-employment wall. Meanwhile the process by which labor may seek to find desired work by accepting lower money wages is frustrated in hosts of ways. Fundamentally there is great difficulty in convincing business that it can afford to expand beyond the capacity of its existing labor force even at lower wages. It is not the purpose of this study to examine the dynamic and institutional realities that lie beyond the simple models here presented, but considerations like these make the underemployment solution appear highly likely in cases where SI and LM fail to intersect at the full-employment wall. In other words, the frustration caused by the inconsistency that arises from the peculiar shapes that the functions may well take will in all probability rest largely upon the shoulders of workers who would gladly labor for going wages but cannot find jobs.

Whether a situation of this kind should be called equilibrium is another question. If one is willing to let the w curves and the resulting $WwPp$ curves take the place of an effective Sy curve such as that of VIIIb, then the resulting underemployment may quite properly be called underemployment equilibrium. From the standpoint of his fundamental policy interests in this problem, Keynes would presumably have been content with this conclusion. From the standpoint of much theoretical argument, however, the case for underemployment equilibrium appears to be weaker, and "chronic underemployment" would be a better term. To the extent that Keynes' theoretical task was to show that underemployment equilibrium does not depend upon the rigid wage policy of unions — to this extent his thesis cannot rest upon the constant money-wage equation. It is difficult for me to believe that persistent unemployment would not ultimately bring about falling money wages. If the functions do not permit these and the consequent falling prices to restore full employment, it would be hard to deny that significant changes will be taking place, however unpredictable, while the declines continue. This situation is hardly consistent with our general understanding of the meaning of equilibrium.

A Note on Two "Strong" Models

A common though seriously over-simplified version of the quantity theory of money may be readily illustrated by use of the models we have now built. The way to state this version algebraically would be to modify equation (1) on page 253 to read $M/p = kY$. Geometrically this is equivalent to defining the L surface in figure Vb (transactions demand) to represent the entire demand for cash. The LM curve is then necessarily vertical, being a projection of d_1f_1 on the end wall. Equations (5) to (7), by assuring full employment, cause prices so to adjust that the L surface rotates until a_1c_1 lies precisely on V_1W_1, thereby making LM lie along the BC edge of the box, intersecting SI at I. If, now, the quantity of money were to double, the only way for equilibrium to be maintained would be for prices also to double, so that the a_1c_1 curve would continue to be coincident with the newly located V_1W_1.

The explanation just given seems to me to represent the general line of thinking on which the quantity theory in its simplest form has been commonly presented. It is often suggested that the crude quantity theory — in which prices are exactly proportional to the quantity of money — necessarily rests on such extreme assumptions as these. I have shown on page 254 above that this is not so. For example, despite commonly held views, the existence of idle balances for which the demand is a function of the rate of interest need in no way conflict with the quantity theory. So long as the demand for these funds is drawn in real terms and includes no element in which M or p appear other than in the ratio M/p, the strict proportionality between money supply and prices in equilibrium is maintained.

The question immediately posed is: What conditions would invalidate the implications of the quantity theory in simplified models? It seems to me that there are three major types of consideration that open the door for denial of quantity theory conclusions.

1. In the first place, any element of money illusion, that is, any market in which people express their demands or supplies in simple money terms without reference to the real value of these balances, introduces such a denial. Two familiar types of money illusion have often been written into simplified equilibrium systems. Keynes described the demand for speculative balances by writing $M_2^D = L_2(r)$ instead of $M_2^D = p \cdot L_2(r)$. I have

discussed above my reasons for suggesting that Patinkin is right in using the second of these equations instead of the first (see pp. 241–243). Although people may be as irrational in this as in other matters I see no reason to assume that the Keynesian equation describes a more probable behavioral response than does the Patinkin form. Keynes' description of the supply curve of labor as a function of money wages rather than real wages is a second illustration of money illusion, and this assumption would also, of course, deny the conclusion of the quantity theory. This money illusion introduces p without M in equation (7) on page 253 (see 7′). Although increasing use of escalator clauses leads us to reject the simplest interpretation of the Keynesian assumptions here, the labor resistance to money-wage cuts even if prices have fallen might be regarded as behavior reflecting money illusion, in which case the conclusions of the quantity theory would be negated by this kind of labor supply curve.

2. The labor response to reduced money wages which I have just described is not really in a class by itself, but actually represents one of many kinds of institutional stickiness of prices to declines. This element is common not only in the labor market, but also in any other market with administered prices. Such action may not be consistent with short-run maximizing behavior but may still be entirely rational in the context of institutional realities. Whenever it exists we have a case in which demand or supply is not responsive exclusively to "real" considerations, and in which there is no longer any reason to suppose that prices will be proportional to the supply of money. Psychologically it would be quite inappropriate to dub all these cases of sticky prices "money illusion," but their appearance would often be similar to that of money illusion if they were written into an equational system that operates on the assumptions of short-run maximizing behavior.

Stickiness of prices represents only one of many situations in which frictions or other dynamic considerations enter real-world relations. Clearly, from our analysis above, M/p will shift during the process by which the system responds to change. We may, therefore, lump together sticky prices and other dynamic elements as a second type of condition (in addition to strict, psychological money illusion) which would belie the assumption of a constant ratio between the quantity of money and the price level.

3. A third consideration which would force us to drop the conclusions of the crude quantity theory would be the inclusion in the model of a term representing the real value of bonds held. I have argued (p. 255) that the value of M/p will not be independent of M or of p individually if we admit the term b/rp, for then p appears without M. In general one is not justified in writing a function for speculative balances without including such a term, partly because the outstanding supply of govern-

ment securities is too crucial an element in this picture to permit abstraction from its effects.

In conclusion, I agree with Patinkin that the requirements for the validity of the quantity theory are not nearly so restrictive or so unreasonable as is commonly supposed. But I would add that his point, also, could mislead any who fail to recognize the qualifications imposed by a world of uncertainty and change. Even in the static model, I believe, the necessary inclusion of real-bond effects invalidates the conclusions of the quantity theory. Aside from that, all the elements which may tend to produce persistent underemployment tend also to invalidate the quantity theory. This conclusion is most simply suggested in the familiar equation of exchange in which a change in M can be reflected in altered Y as well as in altered p; it is described in our system by the second category listed above, namely, cases in which dynamics or rigidities prevent the kind of complete equilibrium that is posited by the full-employment assumption.

The oversimplified version of the quantity theory with which this section began is an extreme case in the sense that it yields a vertical LM curve. An opposite extreme is suggested by a "strong" Keynesian position in which it is assumed that saving and investment are virtually inelastic to the rate of interest, with the result that the SI curve is vertical (see figure VIId). Furthermore, the L surface and the LM curve may, according to this view, be virtually horizontal in the region of M (see figure VIIe): It is obvious from study of figures VIId and VIIe that if SI is vertical no shift of LM can alter the level of income. All that monetary policy can do is to shift Q up the vertical SI curve, raising the rate of interest and affecting nothing else. Correspondingly, so long as the economy remains in the horizontal region of the L surface, shifts of saving and investment propensities can have no influence on the rate of interest, but can only move Q to the right or left along LM.

These comments on two "strong" systems should help to clarify the contrast sometimes drawn between classical and Keynesian interpretations of the function of the money equation. The classical view was that the money equation determines the equilibrium values of prices and has no influence on the equilibrium value of the rate of interest. The latter is wholly determined by the intersection of the SI curve with the full-employment wall; this intersection is not influenced by the quantity of money, since only real balances (i.e., M/p) influence S and I; and the equilibrium level of real balances is not affected by the quantity of money, since the equilibrium price level will vary in direct proportion with it. By contrast, a "strong" Keynesian system, with the supply curve of labor a function of money wages, gives almost exactly the opposite results. The quantity of money determines the rate of interest, but has no influence on the level of prices, which are determined by the rest of the system. This may be explained as follows. Saving and investment in figure VIId determine the level of real income; VIIIa shows the level of employment associated with this income, VIIIb shows the resulting real wage, and VIIIc, with the money wage contract given, shows the price level. Thus with p and Y determined, the money equation determines r.

The contrast between the "strong" systems can be reviewed algebraically by stating mathematically the simplifying assumptions on which they rest.

Simplest Quantity Theory Model	*"Strong" Keynesian Model*	
$\dfrac{M}{p} = kY$	$\overline{M} = L_1(Y, r, p)$	(1)
$S = f_1(r)$	$S = f_1(Y)$	(2)
$I = f_2(r)$	$I = f_2(Y)$	(3)
$S = I$	$S = I$	(4)
$Y = \phi(N)$	$Y = \phi(N)$	(5)
$W = \dfrac{dY}{dN}$	$W = \dfrac{dY}{dN}$	(6)
$N = \theta(W)$	$N = \theta(Wp)$	(7)

(2) to (4) determine r.
(5) to (7) determine Y.
(1) with Y and M determines p.

(2) to (4) determine Y.
(5) with Y determines N.
(6) with Y and N determines W.
(7) with N and W determines p.
(1) with M, Y and p determines r.

Although it is not likely that anybody would argue the strict applicability of either of these "limiting" models, the study of their implications emphasizes an important point. We have noted that the equational system of page 253, and the corresponding graphs of figures IV, V and VII, make the classical and the Keynesian models look very much alike. The limiting models show that, despite the similarity of over-all structure, a very great difference between the two inheres in, first, the acceptance or rejection of equation (7); and second, the underlying behavioral assumptions as reflected in the shapes of the functions. A major advantage of the graphical exposition is that it provides a way to visualize contrasting assumptions regarding the nature of the functions. These limiting models, even though admittedly oversimplified, indicate positions that might be closely approached if the parameters take values which may at times be fairly realistic. And some of these values would force the decision to renounce the classical equation (7). It is, therefore, important to recognize that we have thus far provided only a structure for analysis, and that practical conclusions for either description of the economy or policy prescription must rest on extensive empirical observation. This group of functions does, however, provide a convenient framework within which to examine contending views and to define questions for empirical testing.

Thus far the structure of analysis described here has been applied to the comparison of various classical and Keynesian theories, with emphasis on the issue of underemployment equilibrium. In this context I have compared the classical supply curve of labor with one that assumes that money wages are given by contract for all levels of income, together with a modification that limits the downward movement of real wages when full employment is reached. I now turn to apply my analysis very briefly to four other problems: (a) What if, because of escalator clauses, real wages instead of money wages are contractually determined? (b) Can this model help with the analysis of inflation caused by cost-push phenomena? (c) Can it help with the analysis of inflation caused by excessive demand? (d) Would the analysis of unemployment in underdeveloped countries reflect similar causes and call for policies similar to those described above for mature economies?

APPLICATIONS

Real-Wage Contracts

Even close followers of Keynes suggest that he may have overemphasized the money illusion of labor. The increasing popularity of escalator clauses in union wage contracts verifies the fact that, regardless of how labor may have thought in 1936, it now thinks in terms of real as well as money wages. The fear that is generally raised in people's minds by the spread of this type of contract is that inflation may be an almost inevitable consequence: that a union demand for higher money wages may be explosive, pushing up prices, which then bring into play the escalator clause, causing still higher money wages, and thus higher prices, with an unending spiral of inflation. The model I have developed provides some insight into the process that might be expected if escalator clauses spread, though its abstraction from dynamics and expectations obviously calls for subsequent modification. The analysis will be presented by exploring the consequences of a hypothetical example.

Suppose the economy is at first in full-employment equilibrium, as indicated by H_3 in figure VIIId, with money wages as shown by w_3. The trade unions now wish to raise their real wages from 16 (as shown in VIIIb) to 19. They do so by demanding an increase of this proportion (i.e., $\frac{3}{16}$) in money wages, associated with an escalator clause providing subsequent increases equal to any increase in prices. We shall presume that other prices are competitively determined.

The result of this action may be developed in either of two ways. Just as in the familiar multiplier process, we may find directly what the ultimate equilibrium position will be, or, alternatively, we may trace the nature of the steps which cause the economy to approach this equilibrium asymptotically. I shall first show the new equilibrium position. The geometric exposition is extremely simple. Since the real wage is to be at the height of B' in figure VIIIb, the resulting level of employment must be OB'', and the real income is shown in figure VIIIa to be \$2,000. At this income, figure VIIId shows equilibrium at K_1, indicating a price level of $\frac{5}{8}$ p_0. The level of money wages is shown by the hyperbola passing through J_1 in figure VIIIc (i.e., relating a real wage of 19, as demanded by the unions, to prices of $\frac{5}{8}$ p_0). The curve is w_1. With prices at this level the L surface in VIIc takes such a position that LM intersects SI just above T (SI having shifted upward because of the falling prices and consequent increase in real balances) where income equals \$2,000 as shown in figure VIIIa and the rate of interest is slightly over 2 per cent. The same solution may also be traced in IVc or IVd, where we have only to recognize that equilibrium will be at the point where the shifted SI curve intersects the \$2,000-income level. This again gives the solution near T, with interest rates just above 2 per cent, and with saving equal to investment in the neighborhood of the \$400 level.

Our second approach to this problem is to study the steps by which this new equilibrium will be approached. This analysis may be described by reference to the same geometric figures, though I have not drawn in all the details. The first act to be pictured is the increase in money wages by $\frac{3}{16}$. This would be shown by a shift of the w hyperbola in figure VIIIc to the right, from w_3 to w_2, indicating a new equilibrium in prices and income at u in figure VIIId, where $WwPp_2$ intersects SI–LM. This implies a rise in prices appreciably less than the initiating rise in money wages, and the succeeding wage increase required by the escalator clause is therefore less than the first one. This procedure continues, and the final equilibrium described in the preceding paragraph is approached as a limit.

The implications of this analysis are these: (1) The result of the demand by labor for an increase of money wages equalling only $\frac{3}{16}$ of the going wage, because associated with an escalator clause, resulted in a 25 per cent increase in prices (from $\frac{1}{2}$ p_0 to $\frac{5}{8}$ p_0) and an increase in money wages of nearly 50 per cent.[23] (2) Under our assumptions the workers

---

[23] More precisely, by 31/64. The ratio of the new real wage to the old one is 19/16. Let w_1 and p_1 represent the new money wage and price level respectively; w_3 and p_3 the initial money wage and price level; x the ratio of the new money wage to the initial one, i.e., w_1/w_3. Noting that $W = w/p$ by definition and that $p_1 = (5/4) p_3$, we may write:

$$\frac{19}{16} = \frac{W_1}{W_3} = \left[\frac{w_1}{p_1}\right] \bigg/ \left[\frac{w_3}{p_3}\right] = \left[\frac{x\,w_3}{(5/4)\,p_3}\right] \bigg/ \left[\frac{w_3}{p_3}\right] \cdot x = \frac{5}{4} \cdot \frac{19}{16} = \frac{95}{64}$$

which represents an increase of 31/64 times the former level.

were able to secure their increase in real wages, but only at the cost of unemployment, the new solution being at B. (3) The spiral of price-wage increases was cumulative but not explosive. It did, after all, approach a new equilibrium. (4) After the first increase in money wages the monetary authorities could have reduced the money supply so that SI–LM intersected the horizontal from B at K_2. This would have eliminated the inflationary impact, since this new intersection would lie precisely under H_8. But it would have appeared to the world, and especially to the trade unions, that the monetary policy was responsible for the sharp decline in employment that would follow, as the number of workers dropped from OF'' to OB''. (5) These facts reveal that on a purely technical level the ultimate problem posed by real wage contracts may not be so much one of inflation as of unemployment. If the excessive real wage is enforced, then free enterprise employment must drop, and monetary policy can neither increase nor reduce that impact. The levels of employment and of real income are wholly determined by the basic functions of figure VIII together with the real wage: B' is directly determined, hence real income of \$2,000, and hence employment of OB''; the SI–LM curve can in no way alter that, but can merely affect prices. It should be added, however, that as shown in paragraph 3 of the following section, a sufficiently sharp increase in money wages may make inflation inevitable despite any action of the central bank.

It should be emphasized that this analysis assumes that labor is unable to increase its real wages by reducing other income shares in the economy or by increasing productivity. The possibility of these should be fully examined before any policy implications of a specific action are drawn.

The geometric analysis given above may be interpreted algebraically by simply replacing equation (7) on page 253 with equation (7''). As the graphical analysis indicated, this shows that the last three equations may now be solved for employment and real income without any reference to the supply of money or the saving-investment functions. The supply of money will, however, affect the price level.

Fixed Money Wages and Fixed Real Wages

If we consider this analysis in conjunction with the study of the constant money-wage model, we may draw certain policy implications, subject, of course, to the simplifications of the models themselves.

1. *If labor demands a money wage that is higher than the one consistent with full employment at going prices, then monetary policy is forced to choose between inflation and unemployment.* It cannot avoid both, however adroit it may be. Let us suppose, for example, that we began with M equal to \$1,740, so that the SI–LM curve passes through H_3, providing full employment there with money wages equal to w_3 and prices equal to

½ p_0. Now labor demands slightly higher money wages (e.g., w_2), moving $WwPp$ to the right and shifting the equilibrium to u. The banking system may restore full employment by increasing the money supply until SI–LM shifts up to intersect H_3H at H_2. The result of maintaining full employment, however, is a higher price level. Alternatively, the banking authorities may reduce the supply of money until SI–LM shifts down to intersect $WwPp_2$ at K_2, indicating the same price levels as formerly (i.e., ½ p_0) but reducing employment to OB″. If the monetary authorities keep M constant, then the location of u shows that the result of the higher money wage will be felt partly in higher prices and partly in lower employment.

2. *If labor demands higher money wages and also has an escalator clause which is wholly effective in enforcing the desired real wage, then monetary policy may or may not be able to prevent inflation, but it cannot prevent unemployment.* By the same token it cannot worsen employment even if it is so framed as to prevent inflation, as it may indeed be able to do. But such anti-inflationary action would *appear* to cause unemployment, and the political realities suggest, therefore, that the monetary authorities would find it extremely difficult to follow such a policy. This fact is doubly emphasized by the observation that in both types of wage increase the only monetary policy that would prevent inflation is one that would actually reduce (not merely hold constant) the quantity of money in the face of increasing demand. This is asking a great deal of the monetary authorities.

In the case of constant real wages it may be added that even fiscal policy cannot increase employment except by governmental hiring of labor at wages greater than their productivity warrants. Thus a true federal subsidy is the only way to maintain full employment at an excessive real wage.

3. Figure VIII reveals another fact about the limited power of the monetary authorities. Suppose that in the first example cited above, where labor demanded an increase in money wages without escalator clauses, it had demanded w_1 instead of only a slight increase from w_3 to w_2. Then no shift of SI–LM would be capable of reducing prices to their former level at ½ p_0. Geometrically this is because $WwPp$ does not have sufficient elasticity below real incomes of about \$2,000; i.e., at all levels of income, it lies to the right of ½ p_0. Economically speaking, this is because however low the level of employment may be pushed, the marginal productivity of labor, and hence the real wage, cannot thereby be caused to rise enough to satisfy the money wage demanded while prices remain as they are; only rising prices can make the required money wage consistent with a feasible real wage. The monetary authorities are unable to prevent inflation by any action.

4. Combining points 1 to 3, this conclusion may be stated. If union ac-

tion raises money wages faster than the rate at which productivity is rising, then the best hope is that the monetary authorities may be able to choose between inflation and an increase in unemployment. However, if on the one hand the money-wage increase is sharp, then *inflation* may be inevitable regardless of monetary action, and the central-bank option is whether to prevent unemployment despite the fact that this may cause an even greater rise in prices. If, on the other hand, there are escalator clauses, then *unemployment* is inevitable whenever the increase in real wages sought goes beyond the full-employment level, and the only option open to the central bank is to decide whether to permit inflation as well.

5. Although these models are drawn with the conventional focus upon employment and wages, it is essential to emphasize that they could have been related to the examination of monopolistic prices for goods rather than for labor services. The moral concerning the implications of any monopolistic price increase is similar. Evidence suggests that not only trade unions struggle to retain or increase real income. When monopolistic business and politically powerful agriculture also have similar goals, the difficulties of maintaining stability are, of course, greatly magnified. Furthermore, in the face of other monopolistic efforts to increase shares of income there are times when labor's attempts to obtain a determined level of real wages are not efforts to secure excessive real wages, and labor may be blamed for inflation when other price increases should bear the responsibility.

Inflation Caused by Excessive Demand

A number of conclusions concerning cost-push inflation have been indicated in the preceding analysis of the establishment of rigid real wages or rigid money wages by union contracts. The more traditional explanation of inflation, excessive demand in relation to productive capacity, may be analyzed equally well with the model developed in this chapter.

Before variable prices were introduced into my analysis, I stated that equilibrium would lie at the intersection of *SI* and *LM*, and that the level of real income implied by this intersection would not necessarily lie along the full-employment wall; only the introduction of variable prices provided a mechanism for so shifting *LM* and *SI* as to force the intersection toward that position. In this entire discussion it was implicitly assumed that the intersection would lie somewhere within the box, implying underemployment if not full employment. Obviously there is no reason *a priori* for presuming that the normal forces of supply and demand would cause this intersection to lie below rather than above the full-employment level. If demand for output is very great, for instance, L″ in IVc may lie below I, so that *SI* intersects *LM* only in the imaginary extension of these curves beyond the full-employment wall.

In elementary economics this situation might be illustrated by a vertical wall indicating 1 per cent interest in figure IV*c*, a wall that is extended beyond the box on the right and on which the investment and saving surfaces will trace a near-horizontal investment curve crossed from the left and below by a steeper saving curve, with the intersection lying to the right of the full-employment level of income. The indication is that income will be pushed up toward this equilibrium, but that the growing income can be expressed only in rising prices, since real output cannot be expanded. Because of the simplifying assumptions of this model the situation appears to be explosive, but the more complete analysis developed in this chapter permits a more adequate resolution of the problem. This resolution depends upon the variability of both prices and interest rates, neither of which is depicted in the elementary view described above.

When prices begin to rise under the impact of excessive demand, the liquidity surface begins to rotate clockwise, reflecting the concomitant increase in requirements for cash balances. This shift of the *L* surface pushes the *LM* curve upward. Meanwhile the rising price level is also reducing the real value of balances in the economy, increasing saving and reducing investment, and thereby lowering the *SI* curve. Each of these movements brings the intersection of *SI* and *LM* toward the full-employment wall, and the movement continues so long as prices continue to rise. But prices will continue to rise so long as the excess demand persists. Thus the intersection of *SI* and *LM* is forced back into the box. The inflation is choked off by the forces it has itself generated.

We noticed earlier that deflation might not be effectively ended by its own natural forces, basically because *LM* might not be capable of falling to the low levels at which *SI* might intersect the full-employment wall. The result, we found, was the possibility of a persistent contradiction within the system, with continued unemployment. It is interesting to note that such a dilemma is hardly possible in the case of inflation. However horizontal the *L* surface may become at its intersection with *M* as *M* moves to the right, it cannot remain horizontal indefinitely as *M* moves to the left. While inflation persists, the transactions demand alone must create a strong demand for funds even at high rates. Sooner or later *LM* must rise as prices increase, and the equilibrium level of income is forced down to the level of full employment without further inflation.

The conclusion suggested is that an inflationary pressure has its own built-in cure in a way that underemployment may not have. This conclusion, however, may easily prove misleading if not carefully understood. In the first place it assumes that the money supply is not permitted to increase, and in the second place it does not suggest that prices will return to their previous levels. Typically the problems which inflation itself raises for government are such that the temptation to add fuel to the flames in the form of increased government spending and increased money supply is too powerful to be easily overcome, and the inflation is indeed cumulative if not also explosive.

Before leaving these brief comments on inflation it may be useful to consider the relation between cost-push inflation and excess-demand inflation. The previous discussion makes the two sound entirely unrelated. In fact, as is well known, they are closely interdependent, and some of the reasons can be illustrated with the model we are using here. In the first place, resistances to cost-push inflation may be powerful if demand is weak. There are several possible reasons. Consider the consequences of an increase in money wages from w_1 to w_0 in figure VIII; equilibrium shifts from K_1 to N_0, with employment dropping from OB″ to OA″. If the unions think even partly in terms of this kind of analysis they will be less anxious to press their demands.[24] Even if they do not so think, business may. It will recognize that if it tries to pass on the wage increase in terms of higher prices, sales may drop, which is its version of what our model states. The resistance to the wage increases will, therefore, be much stronger in times of weak demand.

In contrast to the situation when demand is weak, consider boom times, with equilibrium corresponding to H_3. Both labor and business know that demand is growing actively, and that consequently the SI–LM curve is steadily shifting outward. By the time wages rise from w_3 to w_2, SI–LM will have moved out to intersection with the full-employment line at H_2. Workers get their money-wage increase and business has passed the charge on to consumers without loss of sales.

It may be that in boom times the rising SI–LM is forcing employment above OF″ (because of money illusion or lags in response). Real wages are below even the full-employment level because of rapidly rising prices without concomitant wage increases. Equilibrium is moving to the right along $WwPp_3$. Rising money wages would bring marked increases in real wages, and would cut only the overemployment. Resistance to the wage boost might be quite small, and public opinion would accept the justice of such a rise in the face of earlier price rises.

---

[24] The typical position of labor may be one that would deny the assumptions of this analysis for any of several reasons. In the first place our analysis abstracts from the effects of distribution on aggregate demand. Labor will argue that wage increases reduce unemployment by raising consumption, hence SI–LM. It may also assume that no administration will dare permit extensive unemployment, and that government spending or monetary policy would raise SI–LM similarly. To the extent that labor so argues it will push for higher wages even without the presence of excess demand. To the extent that it can force its will on business, higher wages will be achieved. And to the extent that the central bank or the treasury does as labor assumes it will, cost-push inflation will take place without excessive demand. There is enough likelihood of this that an inflationary trend seems probable. But there still seems little doubt that this kind of pressure will be greatest when demand is strong rather than when it is weak.

Land-poor and Capital-poor Countries

One who is nurtured on Keynesian economics often gains the impression that the universal way to deal with the problem of unemployment is to increase effective demand. *The General Theory* was written in the 30's from the perspective of the mature economy, and its focus surely gives this impression. The model we have developed, however, makes it possible to analyze with equal ease a situation in which underemployment may result from very different causes, and in which an increase of effective demand will serve only to produce inflation.

Countries that are poor in capital or in land will suffer a rapidly declining marginal productivity of labor as employment expands, even while large numbers of workers are still unemployed. This situation may be pictured in figure VIII by merely redrawing the supply curve of labor. Assume the number of men wishing work at the subsistence wage of 10 is OS''. The supply curve therefore becomes SS', and equilibrium is at C'. The price-income equilibrium corresponding to this is at T in VIII*d*. Suppose we now try to increase employment by raising effective demand — i.e., by moving *SI–LM* upward. The effect is a shift of T horizontally to the right, indicating a price rise without any change in the real variables. The only way to obtain real improvement is to increase productivity. By greater capital or better techniques the marginal product of labor is increased, the demand curve of VIII*b* rises to the right, and more workers find employment.

This is a somewhat rigid picture because of the simplified model on which it is built, but it represents elements of reality. Millions of man-hours of available labor are lost in underdeveloped areas because there is neither the capital nor the land to permit adequately productive work. A less rigid example that shows a similar but not identical result would be to assume that money wages are sticky at w_2, causing equilibrium at u. A shift of *SI–LM* upward caused by monetary or fiscal policy will be felt partly by higher income and employment, but largely and increasingly by rising prices, as seen by the movement of u up and to the right along $WwPp_2$. The fundamental differences between this solution and the mature-economy parallel is that here marginal productivity declines because of the shortage in factors with which labor can work, whereas in the mature economy it declined chiefly because the efficient labor supply was being exhausted.

It is not pretended that this analysis includes enough variables to permit direct and unqualified application to the real world. But I believe it does include important parts of a total analysis.

CONCLUSIONS REGARDING
MONETARY AND NONMONETARY
THEORIES OF INTEREST

With this general equilibrium system before us we can now compare and partly appraise the monetary theories of interest described in Part Two and the nonmonetary theories described in Part One. The latter, in showing the rate of interest as determined by equilibrium in saving-investment relations, essentially said no more than that the rate of interest would lie somewhere along the *SI* curve. For this reason these theories provided full determination of the rate of interest only when income was assumed to be given, thereby locating the point on the *SI* curve where equilibrium would rest. These nonmonetary theories were embedded, however, in a classical general-equilibrium theory according to which equilibrium would be at a level of full employment, and it is this assumption which really made the nonmonetary theories fully determinate, with the solution at I in figure IV*c*. Clearly, nonmonetary theories are theories of long-run-equilibrium interest-rate determination, with all the associated strengths and limitations.

The monetary theories of interest focus attention on the fact that the rate of interest is determined somewhere along the *LM* curve. This conclusion holds whether the loanable-funds or the liquidity-preference theory is used. Once again the theory remains indeterminate unless some income level is assumed whereby it may be determined at what point along *LM* equilibrium will lie. As commonly used, the monetary theories are partial-equilibrium theories, and hence the level of income is simply assumed as given rather than being determined, as in the nonmonetary theories, in a general-equilibrium solution. Thus the monetary theories are typically used as short-run theories of interest-rate determination.

The preceding paragraph indicates that if income is assumed to be given, as in the short-run analysis, then monetary theory is sufficient without direct application of the nonmonetary theories. The solution lies where *LM* intersects the assumed level of income. But our study shows that even in this case the elements of nonmonetary theory necessarily enter into the analysis. This fact is shown in figure VI, where the two familiar monetary theories are depicted: saving and investment curves are directly included in the loanable-funds formulation, and they are implicitly included in the transactions demand of the liquidity-preference presentation. To the extent that nonmonetary theories give insights into the determination of saving and investment, therefore, they shed light on even the short-run monetary analysis, despite the fact that the saving-investment equality postulated by nonmonetary theory may not be realized.

If an equilibrium level of income is presumed to have been realized at some determined point, such as that of full employment in the classical model, or at some other level as in the case of fixed real wages (see p. 273), and if we provisionally abstract from real balance and real bond effects, then nonmonetary theory is sufficient without application of the monetary theories. The solution lies where SI intersects the determined level of income. It may be added, however, that monetary theory would, in this case, serve equally well; for SI and LM would intersect the equilibrium-income wall at the same point. This is simply a consequence of the fact that in long-run equilibrium, changes in hoards and in the supply of money are assumed to be zero, so that the difference between the two types of theory vanishes (see, for instance, figures VIe and VIf). If real balance and real bond effects are admitted, then this solution will have to be modified by recognition of shifts in the surfaces which they bring about. Both monetary and nonmonetary elements are now required, but once the location of the surfaces is determined it is still true that either SI or LM in conjunction with the level of income shows the equilibrium solution for r and Y.

For some purposes we do not wish to take income as given either by "short-run assumption" or by "long-run determination"; for example, in the problem of determining a kind of "middle-run" equilibrium under the assumption of constant money wages. For this solution the nonmonetary and the monetary theories must both be used. This conclusion follows from recognition of the fact that in this frame of reference the level of income is essentially determined by the intersection of SI and LM. In other words, the equilibrium level of income here is that level which satisfies simultaneously the conditions of both the monetary and the nonmonetary theories, with all surfaces located according to the price level necessitated by the given money wage. This is probably the most familiar Keynesian model.

It may now be useful to describe the process of adjustment to a disturbance of equilibrium in the model I have drawn. This description will be in terms of three types of adjustment that start simultaneously but require different amounts of time for completion. Reference to Vd may aid in following this review. Let us assume that M equals \$1,740, so that the relevant LM curve is $L'M'$. Suppose, for instance, that the initial disturbance causes a disequilibrium relation between interest and income represented by a point somewhere between SI and LM, beyond and to the right of their intersection (for example, take a point very near Q but slightly toward B). Disequilibrium exists in every respect: there is inequality between supply and demand for cash, between saving and investment, and between supply and demand for labor. The first and quickest adjustment will be in interest rates, which will fall until supply and demand for money is equated at the going level of income; this reaction can be very rapid indeed because of the rapidity with which securities markets adjust. In other words the shortest-run equilibrium will be quickly achieved on the *LM* curve corresponding to the initial level of income. This shows the rate of interest determined by monetary theories. This temporary solution does not lie on the *SI* curve, but will be somewhere to the right of and above it, indicating an excess of saving over investment. Income will now begin to adjust by the process described in the earlier discussion of figure VI. The decline in income will take some time, and it may be represented by the movement of equilibrium down to the left along *L'M'*, approaching the intersection of this curve with *SI*, at which point saving would equal investment. Now the equilibrium conditions of both the monetary and the nonmonetary theories are fulfilled. This picture is oversimplified, however, for it fails to recognize the possibility of downward wage and price movements. If the persistent unemployment implied by all relations described above tends to reduce wages and prices, then the *L* surface will be rotating counterclockwise, so that *LM* is shifting toward the front and to the right in figure V*d*; meanwhile, *SI* will be moving backward and to the right because of the real-balance effect of the falling prices. Hence the equilibrium intersection of *SI* and *LM* will be gradually moving to the right. The ultimate equilibrium of the classical school is finally achieved if and when this intersection reaches the full-employment wall.

QUALIFYING COMMENTS ON THE MODELS USED IN PART TWO

The theory of interest developed in Parts One and Two of this study is not alleged to offer any major advance in refinement over the conventional theory of interest as generally taught in intermediate economic analysis today. If the study has made a contribution it is in integrating, unifying, and tidying up the corpus of accepted interest theory. Even here I have not yet incorporated all that is essentially involved in the presentation of an adequate, elementary theory of interest. Some of the major oversimplifications implied by my models must now be described explicitly.

One of the most serious inadequacies of these models is the fact that investment has been drawn as a function of the rate of interest and the level of income only. There is every reason to believe that investment is largely a function of variables not included here. The acceleration principle describes the way in which investment is greatly influenced by *changes* in the level of output; furthermore the response to these changes in output is in turn greatly influenced by the relation between level of output at a given time and potential output at full capacity. Although analysis shows that under some circumstances the ultimate equilibrium is not influenced by the operation of the acceleration principle, the path to equilibrium is greatly influenced thereby, and part of my analysis purported to show possible paths to equilibrium. Many other variables have been tested, especially profits. Lagged variables and rates of change also enter dynamic equations that attempt to explain levels of investment.

The investment function is not alone among the relations that can best be described only with the aid of dynamic variables. Klein suggests models in which equation (7) on page 253 might define changes in money wages as a function of the difference between full employment and the actual level of employment.[25] The search for an adequate consumption function still goes on in ways too numerous to describe in this summary reference. Furthermore, a major determinant of all functions in the economy is the expectation concerning future events, and an adequate theory must discuss explicitly the ways in which changing expectations are likely to cause shifts of functions.

The nature of an interest theory depends crucially upon the shapes of the functions involved. I have presented these functions in fairly conventional form without attempting to examine thoroughly the realism of these assumed shapes. An adequate theory of interest must go beyond this to find what empirical or subjective considerations suggest about realistic shapes of functions in our society today.

Finally, no theory of interest is complete without full recognition of the fact that there is no such thing as "the interest rate." There is an entire structure of rates, with at least two major dimensions: one measured by the term of securities to maturity, and the other by the risk of nonpayment. In short, an adequate theory of interest must tell us the meaning of the "interest rate" found by it, for each security will have its own yield, and that yield will differ according to the two criteria just mentioned. Part Three will examine term structure of rates and attempt to relate the theory of the structure of rates to the general theory of interest discussed in Parts One and Two.

---

[25] "Theories of Effective Demand and Employment," *Journal of Political Economy* (April, 1947), reprinted in Richard V. Clemence, *Readings in Economic Analysis*, Vol. I (Cambridge, Mass.: Addison-Wesley Press, 1950), p. 268.

PART THREE

THE TERM STRUCTURE OF INTEREST RATES

INTRODUCTION TO RATE STRUCTURE

ON METHOD

I should like to begin with an analogy. For a very long time, value theory was almost wholly restricted to a study of competitive markets, together with some analysis of monopoly but very little indeed of oligopoly. The reason was not wholly a failure on the part of economists to recognize the practical importance of oligopolistic markets: the analysis of these markets was laid aside largely because the problems raised were said to be "indeterminate." And as William Fellner has pointed out, it was really quite inappropriate to say this — after all, price does get determined, even in oligopolistic markets.[1] What is meant by calling such problems indeterminate is simply that they cannot be solved without introducing more variables, and more principles of behavior, than those which constitute the time-honored axioms of economic doctrine. The new problems introduced into economic analysis by oligopoly are especially difficult to handle, partly because their essential variables defy quantification and seemingly make prediction impossible. Fortunately for the usefulness of economic analysis the difficulties posed by these problems did not permanently preclude them from economic attack. However unsatisfactory our answers may be, we must at least do what we can to build methods of study that can guide us in the real world.

It seems to me that there is much similarity between the treatment of oligopoly in value theory and the treatment of rate structure in interest theory. Every elementary course in economics deals with the "theory of interest" in at least some measure, yet many graduate students know little indeed about the structure of rates. We lay the latter subject aside as an addendum for the curious to explore if they wish. Yet the knowledge is commonplace that there is no such thing as the "rate of interest." This is not only an abstraction, but one that most of us have not taken time to relate to the great complex of rates which we meet in the market for money and credit. In short, it is my view that no discussion of the theory

---

[1] William Fellner, *Competition Among the Few* (New York: A. A. Knopf, 1949), chapter i.

of interest should close without examining the relation between "the rate" which it describes and the more specific rates that are found in the market. The analysis of rate structure is thus seen to be important because it is an essential part of any theory of interest.

There are other and more directly practical reasons as well for insisting that interest theory include this aspect of study. We develop a theory of interest, after all, in order to help find answers to real-world problems. It is difficult to name one of these problems which can be adequately faced with a theory that is content to determine only "the rate" of interest. Monetary policy, for example, draws heavily upon general interest theory in order to define both its function in the economy and its specific implementation. But monetary policy is concerned with the purchase and sale of specific government securities, and the question is immediately raised, which securities? Should transactions be limited almost entirely to the short end, as present policy directs? If so, why? If not, then what policy should define the types of securities to be bought and sold? Or again, monetary policy involves direct control over one specific rate — the discount rate. What effect does this have on the structure of other rates? What rates most influence business activity, and how can these be reached by monetary action? Still again, monetary policy determines reserve requirements. But banks deal primarily in short to intermediate Governments. How do changes in reserve requirements influence rates on other securities than these?

We study interest theory for other reasons than the implications for monetary policy. Government debt management is equally dependent upon an understanding of the factors that influence interest rates. Here especially the problem can never be confined to an understanding of the abstraction called "the interest rate." The different influences resulting from debt structures of different length are the heart of the problem that debt management must solve.

Many of the institutions that engage in the investment of funds must constantly make judgments about the probable shifts in rate structure before they can most wisely fill their responsibilities. Security dealers and investment-banking houses must do the same. Business corporations investing temporarily available funds face similar problems. And all large enterprises on the other side of the market — those seeking funds for economic expansion — must decide when and how to borrow whenever they need to obtain new funds or to refund outstanding debt.

Unfortunately the analysis of the structure of interest rates, like the analysis of oligopoly, is not only important but also difficult. Here too we must use new methods of study and admit less-tractable variables than those with which we have been working up to now. To be sure, it would be possible, as in the more general theory of Parts One and Two, to develop a neatly determinate static theory. Indeed, I do precisely that in what I shall call the "neoclassical" theory with which this Part will begin. But such an analysis leaves us so far from a practically applicable theory of the structure of rates that we simply cannot discontinue the study at that point. In other words, the implications of uncertainty and of changing expectations are so central to any realistic understanding of the structure of rates that these considerations must be introduced promptly in any theory dealing with this issue. The obvious consequence of this methodological conclusion is that our resulting theory will be far less precise in appearance than one in which we could point to a geometric intersection and suppose that this provided the answer to our problem. More important, the testing of our theory will be far more difficult than if all elements entering it were objective and readily quantifiable: since expectations are crucial determinants, any testing of the theory obviously requires a judgment concerning what expectations actually were during the period of the test. These judgments are very hard to make, and differ greatly even among informed and able observers.

It should not be inferred from these comments that the general "theory of interest" described in the previous Parts of this study is satisfactory or complete while it retains its static assumptions. This volume can be regarded as no more than an introduction to the theory of interest until it has admitted dynamic considerations. But my preliminary attempt to develop a dynamic theory of interest suggests that the introduction of dynamics can proceed only after examination of at least an elementary theory of the structure of rates. For this reason I shall first introduce dynamic analysis in conjunction with this Part, reserving its application to more general interest theory for a later work.

A theory of rate structure must answer a number of questions about the behavior of rates and the relations among rates over time. I shall direct major attention to a few selected questions concerning rate behavior. My method of analysis will involve first a review of the "first approximation" of the structure of interest rates given by neoclassical doctrine. I shall then consider the ways in which it would appear that this approximation must be modified in order to include major aspects of reality from which it abstracts. Next I shall examine the questions referred to above in order to see how the answers of experience compare with the answers that might be expected from my theoretical discussion. The historical period taken for the empirical work was primarily that from the Treasury–Federal Reserve accord of March, 1951, through the end of 1954. I recognize the near anachronism of now publishing a study of rate structure that omits the four most recent years, during which changes in the structure of rates have been dramatic, but this study was originally completed in the summer of 1955 and a reworking of data cannot be carried through in available time.

SIMPLIFYING ASSUMPTIONS OF THE CONVENTIONAL THEORY OF RATE STRUCTURE

Definitions

Friedrich Lutz has given an excellent synthesis of "received doctrine" concerning the determination of the structure of interest rates,[2] beginning with a highly simplified model that is characterized by the following assumptions: (1) abstraction is made from disturbing institutional factors such as tax laws, and from other characteristics of securities besides term and risk, such as call features and rights; (2) all securities are assumed to be riskless so far as payment of interest and principal are concerned; (3) a set of expectations regarding short rates is held with complete confidence running far into the future; (4) arbitrage between maturities of different term is unimpeded, and the profit-maximizing motive is sufficient that such arbitrage is perfectly complete.

In addition to giving this first approximation Lutz goes on to indicate the modifications imposed by a number of more realistic assumptions. I shall first present an essentially similar exposition of this first approximation, and shall refer to this simplified theory as the "neoclassical theory." In order to test the theories with which we are working, however, I shall also utilize another model which represents a special case of the neoclassical theory, and which adds still another element of unrealism to those already inherent in the neoclassical analysis. In this model, which will be referred to as the "perfect-foresight model," I assume not only that expectations concerning future rates are held with confidence by all investors, but also that these expectations are realized. Only by adding this last assumption is it possible to build a theory whose predictions can be meaningfully tested empirically. It is important to remember, however, that when we test the theory with this addendum included, we are testing the combined effects of the neoclassical theory and the assumption that investor's predictions are accurate. To give a specific example, if a yield curve does not behave over time the way the perfect-foresight model implies that it should, then this fact does not prove that today's rates are not determined by expectations, precisely according to neoclassical theory. We know only that either the neoclassical theory was wrong, or the expectations were wrong — or, of course, some combination of the two. This

---

[2] F. A. Lutz, "The Structure of Interest Rates," *Quarterly Journal of Economics* (1940–41); reprinted in American Economic Association, *Readings in the Theory of Income Distribution* (Philadelphia: Blakiston, 1946), chapter 26, pp. 499–532.

qualification concerning the adequacy of our findings must be borne in mind. (A "yield curve" is one which, like those of charts 1, 2, and 7, shows the yield to redemption on various securities as a function of the time from the date of the curve to the redemption of the security.)

The rest of this chapter will consist of comments on the significance of the simplifying assumptions made by the perfect-foresight model of neoclassical theory. This discussion will show that correction for a number of these simplifications, though important for detailed investment decisions, may be safely neglected in a general analysis. Two of the simplifications, however, must be dropped if we wish our theory of rate structure to be at all applicable to the real world. Modification of the theory to remove these inadequacies will be developed in the following chapters, and the resulting theory will be referred to as the "modified theory."

Abstraction from Selected Institutional Factors

For reasons to be described later on page 293, this study will be chiefly devoted to the behavior of United States government securities. The analysis, however, will not include the study of a number of important differences among government obligations that arise from particular institutional characteristics that are not inherent in the study of interest theory. A brief comment on these considerations will, therefore, be made at this point. The most important features of this kind operating between 1951 and 1954 were probably (a) tax status, (b) call features, (c) bank eligibility, and (d) coupon rate.

Tax Status. — Obviously, tax-exempt securities tend to show a lower before-tax yield than others, but the amount of this spread will depend upon the volume of such securities, the progressiveness of the income-tax schedules, and the investment decisions of those investors to whom the tax-exemption feature is important. Thus it may be presumed that if the volume of tax-exempt securities is small, the marginal buyer will be one in high brackets who gains much by purchasing a tax-exempt investment, and the before-tax spread between these and other yields will be great. On the other hand, if the volume of tax-free securities grows, marginal buyers will be those in relatively lower brackets, the before-tax spread will be reduced, and the after-tax yield to those with high incomes will rise accordingly.

A second feature of tax status which "distorts" the yield pattern is the differential between tax rates on income and those on capital gains. Because of this differential the after-tax gain from price appreciation of securities is greater than that from an equivalent amount of interest income. For this reason before-tax yields might be expected to be slightly less on securities selling at a discount than on those of equivalent maturity selling at par or at a premium. Another factor tending toward the same result is the fact that interest income is taxed sooner than capital gains because it is realized sooner.

Call Features. — Securities subject to call are less attractive than others to the extent that the market is uncertain as to when the security will be redeemed. For this reason, callable bonds will often tend to yield more than others having a maturity in the same range. In this study, if securities are selling above par, I will follow the convention of calculating the yield on the assumption that the security will be redeemed on the first call date; if below par, redemption will be assumed to be at maturity. This procedure is probably the best available, although it permits sudden aberrations in the yield curve from one month to the next if the prices of callable securities are fluctuating above and below par.

Bank Eligibility. — As might be expected, securities not eligible for bank ownership generally yield somewhat more than eligible securities. It may be noted in passing that this provides empirical evidence of an incompleteness in arbitrage activities which is in contradiction to the neoclassical theory. This distinction was important in the early years covered by this study, but now all government issues are bank-eligible, and hence this cause of a yield differential among government securities has disappeared.

Coupon Size. — Finally, though simplified theories of rate structure usually assume that coupon size should not have any effect upon yield to redemption, some evidence suggests that high-coupon bonds do sell at such a price that they yield more than those with lower coupons. Studies by Durand and Winn[3] covering a number of 25-year state and municipal issues in 1944, 1945, and 1946 showed surprisingly large differences in yield according to coupon, the yield range being from about 1.1 to 1.6 per cent on a number of issues which appeared to be identical in every respect but coupon. Reasons for these differences apparently all relate to the fact that high-coupon bonds must sell at a higher price than those with a lower coupon in order to give equal yield. Consequences include these: (1) high-coupon bonds, if callable, are more likely to be called than others; (2) high-coupon bonds are less attractive tax-wise in the light of considerations described above; (3) it is sometimes argued that lower-priced bonds appear more like bargains to the unsophisticated. The limited number of Treasury issues with essentially equal maturities has made it impossible to reach a convincing conclusion from empirical observation about the effects of coupon size upon yield of government se-

---

[3] See David Durand and W. J. Winn, *Basic Yields of Bonds 1926–47: Their Measurement and Pattern,* Technical Paper No. 6 (New York: National Bureau of Economic Research, 1948), pp. 31–40. Also W. B. Hickman, *The Term Structure of Interest Rates: An Exploratory Analysis* (New York: National Bureau of Economic Research, 1942; mimeographed), p. III–21.

curities during the period of this study (1951–1954). Superficial examination showed no consistent relationship.

All in all, the institutional distortions described in this section are not great enough to obstruct achievement of the purposes of this study and we shall not examine them further. Empirical observation gives general support to the comments made above, though the evidence is not always uniform or unambiguous.

Default Risk

By concentrating our study on United States Treasury securities we eliminate the problem of the risk of default, and hence permit our study to conform to the theoretical assumption in this respect.

Perfect Arbitrage and Uncertainty: General Comments

The two types of simplifying assumption of the theory of rate structure already examined do not cast doubt upon the basic conclusions suggested by the neoclassical theory, though they might call for important adjustments in applying it to investment decisions. The two remaining assumptions are of major importance, and the theory of rate structure must allow for substantial modification in order to describe the consequence of relaxing these assumptions. These two simplifications are, it will be remembered, (1) the assumption of firm, uniform, and correct expectations of future rates, and (2) the assumption of perfect arbitrage between maturities.

In examining the theory from this point on I shall proceed as follows. First, I shall explore the meaning and some of the implications of the neoclassical theory with and without the assumption of expectation fulfilment. I shall then examine a number of questions about rate structure. Each question will be studied first from the standpoint of the perfect-foresight model; second, from the standpoint of modifications imposed upon that theory by admitting risk and market segmentation; and, finally, from the standpoint of empirical observations.

XV

THEORETICAL ANALYSIS

THE NEOCLASSICAL THEORY

The Meaning of Yield

It should be understood that throughout Part Three, "yield" of securities means "yield to redemption." Precisely, this means that the yield is the rate at which it would be necessary to discount all subsequent payments (interest and principal) in order to make the present value of these payments equal to the present price of the security. Less precisely, it means that yields include both interest and capital gain or loss, always assuming the compounding of interest receipts.

Outline of the Neoclassical Theory

The neoclassical theory of rate structure, derived from the simplifying assumptions described in chapter xiv, but without the assumption of perfect foresight, states that the yield to maturity on any long-term security will be approximately equal to an average of the short-term rates expected to rule over the remaining life of the security. Roughly speaking, in other words, the yield to maturity on January 1 of a security maturing at the end of the year would be equal to the average of the present yield on three-month bills, the expected yield on three-month bills to be issued April 1, the expected yield on bills to be issued July 1, and that on bills to be issued October 1.[1] This conclusion is based on the assumption that investors calculate the most profitable term of securities to hold for whatever time their funds are to be invested. If the holding of a successive sequence of shorts would yield more than the continuous holding of a long, then arbitrage would cause price changes large enough to eliminate the yield differential. An illustration will clarify this argument and also show one of its major implications.

If the present rate on one-year money is 1 per cent, and if the market could confidently expect a 3 per cent rate on one-year money a year from today, then the rate for two-year money now must be approximately 2 per cent. Assuming that shifting can take place freely, instantaneously,

---

[1] It would, of course, be equally possible to relate the one-year rate to averages of rates on one-week bills, or even on federal funds, if one assumed accessibility of these markets to a sufficient number of investors.

and without charge, no one would buy a two-year security yielding appreciably less than 2 per cent if he could buy one-year maturities now at 1 per cent and reinvest at 3 per cent one year hence. Similarly no one would pay more than 2 per cent for two-year money if he could secure one-year funds now for 1 per cent and could refinance at the end of the year at 3 per cent. In other words, price adjustments on securities must be such that the return for two years is equal (about 2 per cent) by the two investment procedures.

As stated at the outset, the generalization derived from the above observation is that, under the assumptions of the neoclassical theory, arbitrage should bring rates into such a relation that any long rate would approximately equal the average of intervening expected short rates. We must say "approximately" because of the problem introduced by compounding of interest. In the example given above, for instance, the two-year security would yield slightly less than 2 per cent, for the following reason. The present value of a two-year 2 per cent security with a face value of 1 would be $.02/1.01 + 1.02/(1.01 \cdot 1.03) = 1.00029$. The present value of returns on funds invested for one year at 1 per cent and then for 1 year at 3 per cent would be $.01/1.01 + 1.03/(1.01 \cdot 1.03) = 1.00000$. Since the present value of the 2 per cent security is greater than that of the alternative investment opportunity, its price would be bid up until it would yield less than 2 per cent.

An equation for long rates which employs appropriate discounting procedures follows:

$$R_n = \frac{(1+r_1)(1+r_2)\ldots(1+r_n)-1}{(1+r_2)(1+r_3)\ldots(1+r_n)+(1+r_3)(1+r_4)\ldots(1+r_n)+\ldots+(1+r_n)+1}$$

where r stands for short rates expected to hold in the year of the subscript, and R_n stands for the long rate in year 1 on securities maturing in year n.[2] Table 6 has been derived by this formula from an assumed sequence of future short rates, and it illustrates many implications of the theory thus far outlined.

Column 13 is introduced to show the amount of error involved when calculations of long rates are made by a simple average of short rates instead of by use of the more exact equation shown above. A comparison of this column with column 3 illustrates the fact that if the range of short rates is not great, the long rate secured by simple averages will generally serve quite well for fairly short-term securities, but may give increasing distortion as the term increases.

This discrepancy between rates on long-term securities when calculated correctly and the corresponding rates when derived by a simple average

---

[2] The derivation of this equation, together with a discussion of a different one developed by J. R. Hicks, will be found in appendix A to this chapter.

suggests one point of importance. The use of simple averages would make it impossible for changes in current short rates to have any noticeable effect on long-term yields, because the latter would be entirely dominated by the long sequence of future (expected) short rates. Use of the correct formula shows that long-term rates should be expected to be appreciably more responsive to current rate changes than a theory of simple averages would imply.[3] The correct formula for long rates gives added weight to the most recent years because current rates determine present values of all of a series of future payments, but future rates determine only the value of payments made after those future rates apply. The important influence of changing current short rates on the yields even of perpetuals is demonstrated by the changing yields shown in table 6, A, bottom row.

With the aid of the table we can now present an example which emphasizes the equalities that are brought about, and those that are not brought about, by arbitrage as assumed under the neoclassical theory. Suppose that I wish to invest a sum of approximately $100 for one year. Two of the alternative procedures I might follow would be: (1) I could buy a one-year 2 per cent certificate for $100, receiving par and $2 at the end of the year, or (2) I could buy a 5-year 4 per cent bond and sell it at the end of the year, with results as follows:

I pay	$104.63	(part B, col. 3, row 5)
I receive at year end	102.72	(part B, col. 5, row 5)
Capital loss	1.91	
Interest earned	4.00	
Net receipts	$ 2.09	= 2.0% of $104.63

Thus it is seen that I earn 2 per cent on my funds whichever way I decide to invest them.[4] Arbitrage has equated the return over one year on one-year certificates with that on five-year bonds. This example illustrates a highly important implication of the neoclassical theory of rate structure:

---

[3] Indeed, the use of simple averages would make the entire theory basically inconsistent internally under all assumptions except that of identical rates for all securities at all times. This follows from these considerations: if long rates were determined by simple averages of short rates, then changes in current short rates could not affect the yields on perpetuals, which would be wholly dominated by the infinite series of future short rates. But the implication of these constant yields would be that the prices of perpetuals could not change (still assuming a fixed pattern of expected rates). These constant prices would imply that the net return on perpetuals during any time interval must equal the constant yield to perpetuity. Since arbitrage would equate all short rates to this given long rate, the implication of the entire analysis would be that the only internally consistent set of short rates would be equal ones for all periods. The theory would reduce to an inevitably horizontal yield curve at all times. Incidentally, it may be noted that the Hicks formula for long rates is subject to the same limitation as the simple average so far as this problem is concerned.

[4] The generality of this illustration is demonstrated in appendix B to this chapter.

TABLE 6

STRUCTURE OF YIELDS AND PRICES ASSUMING PERFECT ARBITRAGE TAKES PLACE
(Short rates are arbitrarily assumed; other derivations are explained in appendix C, p. 308)

A. YIELDS OF BONDS MATURING AT END OF YEAR SHOWN BY COLUMN I

(1)	(2)	(3)	(4)	(5)	(6)	(7)	(8)	(9)	(10)	(11)	(12)	(13)
		At start of year I		At start of year 2		At start of year 3		At start of year 4		At start of year 5		Column 3 by simple average
Year	Short rates (Per cent)	Yield	Term	Yield	Term	Yield	Term	Yield	Term	Yield	Term	
1	2	2.00	1	...	...	...	...	...	...	...	...	2.00
2	5	3.46	2	5.00	1	...	...	...	...	...	...	3.50
3	3	3.31	3	4.01	2	3.00	1	...	...	...	...	3.33
4	1	2.75	4	3.03	3	2.00	2	1.00	1	...	...	2.75
5	4	2.99	5	3.26	4	2.65	3	2.47	2	4.00	1	3.00
6	4	3.15	6	3.40	5	2.97	4	2.96	3	4.00	2	3.17
10	4	3.45	10	3.65	9	3.45	8	3.52	7	4.00	6	3.50
15	4	3.60	15	3.75	14	3.63	13	3.69	12	4.00	11	3.67
20	4	3.67	20	3.80	19	3.71	18	3.76	17	4.00	16	3.75
Perpetual	4	3.82	∞	3.89	∞	3.85	∞	3.88	∞	4.00	∞	4.00

B. PRICES OF 4 PER CENT BONDS MATURING AT END OF YEAR SHOWN BY COLUMN I

(1)	(2)	(3)	(4)	(5)	(6)	(7)	(8)	(9)	(10)	(11)	(12)	(13)
		At start of year I		At start of year 2		At start of year 3		At start of year 4		At start of year 5		
Year	Short rates (Per cent)	Price	Term	Price	Term	Price	Term	Price	Term	Price	Term	[Does not apply to part B]
1	2	101.96	1	(100.00)	0	...	...	...	...	...	...	
2	5	101.03	2	99.05	1	(100.00)	0	...	...	...	...	
3	3	101.93	3	99.97	2	100.97	1	(100.00)	0	...	...	
4	1	104.63	4	102.72	3	103.85	2	102.97	1	(100.00)	0	
5	4	104.63	5	102.72	4	103.85	3	102.97	2	100.00	1	
6	4	104.63	6	102.72	5	103.85	4	102.97	3	100.00	2	
10	4	104.63	10	102.72	9	103.85	8	102.97	7	100.00	6	
15	4	104.63	15	102.72	14	103.85	13	102.97	12	100.00	11	
20	4	104.63	20	102.72	19	103.85	18	102.97	17	100.00	16	
Perpetual	4	104.63	∞	102.72	∞	103.85	∞	102.97	∞	100.00	∞	

NOTE: "Term" refers to the number of years remaining before retirement regardless of initial issue date. The columns marked "term" in part A therefore show terms for the yield curve drawn for the year at the head of the column in which the corresponding yields appear.

for any defined period of time, however long or short, the expected net
effective yield (including capital gains and losses) will be identical on all
riskless securities regardless of their term.

This important conclusion does not mean that either the coupon rate
or the yield to maturity on securities of different term are equal at any
one time. Indeed, in the example given the certificate paid 2 per cent and
yielded 2 per cent to maturity; but the bond paid 4 per cent and yielded
2.99 per cent to maturity. The return for one year on the latter was
reduced to 2 per cent by capital loss.

It is important to observe that the neoclassical theory in no way implies
that the 2 per cent rate on the certificate in some sense "caused" the 2
per cent yield on funds invested for that year. Indeed, when we say that
the short rate was 2 per cent, we refer to the one-year return for holding
five-year bonds just as much as we refer to the return for holding one-year
certificates during that period. These comments leave unanswered the
question of what did "cause" the 2 per cent short rate. The theory of
the structure of rates as presented above takes these short rates as given,
but the full meaning of the theory cannot be grasped, unless the determinants of these given rates are explained. For this reason it is now necessary
to digress from the main stream of the argument and describe the relation
between the theory of rate structure and the general theory of interest.

The Structure of Rates and the General
Theory of Interest

Parts One and Two above concern the theory of "the interest rate." We
now find ourselves describing a whole structure of rates. Our first problem, therefore, is to determine which of these rates is the one described by
"the theory of interest." Often it is implied that the theory of interest gives
the long-term rate; at other times it seems to be assumed to give a sort of
average, the middle of a wide belt within which the specific rates tend
to hover.[5] The preceding review of the neoclassical theory of rate structure opens the way for a clear answer to the question raised here. I have
just shown that under this theory, even though coupon rates and yields
to redemption on outstanding securities may differ appreciably, the effective rate of return for any given period of time will be the same on securities of all maturities so long as capital gains and losses as well as in-

---

[5] Keynes frequently refers to the "complex of rates" in his *General Theory,* and his
discussion shows he was thoroughly familiar with what we have called the neoclassical
theory of the structure of rates. Yet he is quite vague about how these rates fit into his
analysis, which seems to determine a single r, since the supply and demand for money
can give only one value. A typical comment is that found in his footnote 2 on p. 167,
where he states that "it is convenient to mean by the rate of interest the complex of
the various rates of interest current for different periods of time, i.e., for debts of different maturities." Does he refer to an average of the complex? One cannot tell.

terest income are included in this return. It is this rate which is given by the "theory of interest," whether that theory be liquidity-preference or loanable-funds.

The liquidity-preference theory, built upon the stock concept of supply and demand for cash at a moment of time, would determine the rate on funds for each instant during whatever time interval elapses before these functions shift. The loanable-funds theory, built on flow concepts, would similarly give the rate for the period during which the functions it describes continue to rule. The supply and demand functions, whether for cash (liquidity-preference theory) or loanable funds (loanable-funds theory) would represent all funds demanded or supplied for the time described regardless of the term of the securities involved. The rate determined by these functions is the effective return on any and all riskless securities during the interval described by those functions.

It will be convenient to imagine a time interval sufficiently short that the interest rate determined by the theory in question is essentially constant throughout it. Yields for time periods of this length may be called "short rates." These yields will, of course, be equal to the nominal rates on securities whose terms are identical with this short time period. But, as shown above, this yield will also equal the effective return on holding for this period securities of any maturity. Thus there is consistency between the fact that a unique rate is determined by the general theories of interest over a given short period of time and the fact that according to the neoclassical theory of rate structure a unique rate of return will be found to apply to securities of all terms over any given time span. Likewise the single, unified market for loanable funds implied by the general theories of interest is consistent with the implication of the neoclassical theory of rate structure that, since returns for given time periods are equal on all securities, there is no reason for preferences between securities according to term.

The theory thus far presented is seriously incomplete and to this extent unrealistic. Only by adding the complexities introduced by uncertainty and market segmentation can we begin to develop a theory which rings true to experience. But so long as we work with a theory of "the" rate of interest we can probably do little better than describe the kind of relations referred to here. Once we recognize the realities of a world in which uncertainty and market segmentation exist, we are forced to admit fundamental changes in both the general theory of interest and the theory of the structure of rates.

Prices of Securities

Returning to the discussion of relations implicit in the neoclassical theory of the structure of rates we may now derive the prices of securities on the basis of assumed short rates. This may be done simply by finding the present discounted value of the sum of payments represented by the security, including annual interest and ultimate repayment of principal. The equation is the familiar one:

$$V = \frac{A}{1 + r_1} + \frac{A}{(1 + r_1)(1 + r_2)} + \cdots \frac{A + P}{(1 + r_1)(1 + r_2) \ldots (1 + r_n)},$$

where V represents the current value (market price), A represents the amount of the coupon, P represents the principal value, r_1, r_2, r_3, etc., represent the assumed short rates during the life of the security, and n refers to the year of maturity. Further comments on these derivations will be found in appendix C to this chapter under discussion of the construction of part B of table 6.

Derivation of Rate Structure from Yield Curves

It is shown above that all present and future yields on all maturities are determinate if the expectations regarding all future short rates are given. It may similarly be noted now that if we know the present yield curve for all securities up to the year n, then we can derive the implied expected short rates to the year n, and hence all subsequent yield curves within these time limits. The determination of the future expected short rates may be illustrated as follows: The yield curve shows the yield on present two-year securities. But this (known) yield is the "average" of present (known) and next year's (unknown) short rates. From this, next year's short rate may be readily calculated. Similarly the present three-year rate (read from the yield curve) equals the "average" of the present one-year rate (read from the yield curve), next year's short rate (derived above) and the third year's short rate (to be hereby derived). Obviously this process can be continued to the short rate of the year n.

Recapitulation and Conclusions: The Determination of Rates in the Neoclassical Theory

I may now summarize the theory developed thus far concerning the determination of interest rates on riskless securities under the assumption of perfect arbitrage, firm and uniform expectations of future rates, stable prices of goods, and the absence of institutional distortions caused by such matters as tax laws or special features of the securities involved: (1) General theories of interest provide a means of determining going rates of interest for any time by analysis of the supply and demand for funds. These rates represent the cost of securing funds for the time period involved, regardless of the securities sold to obtain those funds. Since rates are constantly changing, it is convenient to develop the analysis in terms of short periods during which the change is negligible, and the rates for these periods may be called "short rates." (2) These short rates will, of course, equal the nominal rate on securities with terms of equal length. But they also equal the net return (including capital gain and loss) on any security held for that period of time. (3) The conclusion that net returns for any given time are equal on securities of different term results from the assumption that investors maximize their returns, together with the assumption that they know what future short rates will be. (4) A consequence of this equality in effective returns over any given time period is that at any time, long rates (i.e., yields to maturity) will be approximately the average of short rates over the intervening time. (5) Given the short rates it is easy to calculate the present price of any security of which the coupon and maturity are known. This may be done by simply finding the present value of regular payments equal to that coupon, plus the present value of the final payment of principal, using the known short rates for the discounting formula.

In order to avoid misinterpretation of this theory a number of its characteristics should be highlighted. (1) Short rates are not uniquely related to the return on short-term securities, but represent the short-period return on any security. (2) These short rates do not in any sense "cause" long rates. Rather, all rates are caused by present and expected future supply and demand for funds. The long-term rates depend upon the supply and demand conditions expected to rule throughout the life of the securities involved. To say that today's long rate will equal the average of future shorts implies that today's long rate will be determined, as will today's and tomorrow's short rates, by today's and tomorrow's supplies and demands for funds. (3) The fundamental behavioral assumption of the neoclassical theory is not that investors calculate long rates by averaging expected short rates, but rather that investors will seek to invest in such a way as to maximize their returns on the basis of their expectations about the future levels of interest rates and security prices.

This theory and its implications will be drastically modified below. Expectations are, in fact, quite vague as investors look beyond the fairly near future. Action to maximize returns will be modified by the desire to avoid risk and by institutional impediments to free and rapid action. But the neoclassical theory of rate structure proceeds on the assumption that the best way to secure a realistic picture is to examine first the implications of the simplified assumptions we have made above and then to modify the conclusions to the extent required by the most crucial considerations from which the simplified model abstracts.

RATE CHANGES OVER TIME

The neoclassical theory provides two ways by which the structure of rates might change over time. In the first place, since this theory does not describe how expectations are formed, there is room for any influence that may change them to alter the value of any or all future short rates, and hence to produce a wholly new rate structure. Thus it is possible to make any pattern of change in the structure of rates compatible with the neoclassical theory by merely assuming the appropriate changes in the sets of expected short rates.

There is a second kind of change in rates over time, however, which does not depend upon any changes of expectations whatever, but which would follow inevitably and predictably whenever the series of expected short rates is not uniform. This kind of change, because it is predictable on the basis of originally given data, provides a useful bench mark from which to begin the analysis of many problems. The rate behavior involved here is that indicated by our perfect-foresight model, since perfect foresight implies, of course, that expectations regarding future short rates never change.

In this model rates will change over time because the calculation of any long rate will include different short rates as time passes. As each "day" or "year" goes by, the current short r disappears and a new one, representing what was formerly that of the year $n + 1$, is added.

At this point it may be useful to note the distinction between changing yields or prices "on n-year securities" and the change in yield or price of "an" n-year security. Examination of yield structures over time compare yields on n-year securities at one date with those on n-year securities at another date. This means that the specific securities involved will be continually changing, since the term to maturity of any one would be constantly declining. A number of problems, however, concern what happens to the price or yield of a specific security. Such a question, of course, involves the comparison of an n-year security today with an $(n - 1)$-year security a year hence. Whenever this is the purpose of the study the change in yield according to the perfect foresight model would depend only upon the elimination of today's r, since the r for the year $n + 1$ would not be involved.

MODIFICATION OF THE
PERFECT-FORESIGHT MODEL TO
PERMIT UNCERTAIN EXPECTATIONS

Recognition of uncertainty leads to a drastically different behavior in the rate structure from that implied by the model that assumes perfect foresight, and it appreciably modifies even the simple neoclassical theory in which no assumption is made concerning the fulfillment of expectations.

Of course it does not logically follow that uncertainty must necessarily be associated with imperfect foresight, but we shall assume that the two do go together and examine the joint consequences of these two closely related changes in the underlying assumptions of the model just described. The main way in which these considerations affect the conclusions drawn from the perfect-foresight model is that the changes in rates over time are no longer limited to the sloughing off of one r and its replacement by another, but they occur also — and in long terms primarily — because of changed values for many or all of the intervening short r's. We shall observe the consequences of this later when we examine the characteristics of yield curves.

Aside from imperfection of foresight and the consequent changes in expectations over time, uncertainty also has direct bearing on the behavior of those who buy and sell securities. The fact of changing expectations causes security prices to vary in such a way that yields over any given time period do not turn out to be equal on securities of different term. For this reason shorts are not perfect substitutes for longs, and choices will differ among people according to their varied expectations and according to their varied attitudes toward the assumption of risk. At this point, it will be noted, modification is imposed not only on the perfect-foresight model, but also on the central characteristics of the neoclassical theory. The specific implications of these facts for the shapes of yield curves will be given in the following analysis, but for the moment it is sufficient to note the general nature of the ways in which uncertainty and imperfect foresight alter the conclusions of a more simplified analysis.

MODIFICATION OF THEORY
BECAUSE OF MARKET IMPERFECTIONS
AND IMPERFECT SUBSTITUTABILITY
OF SECURITIES

For a variety of institutional reasons, the perfect arbitrage[6] assumed to be possible by the neoclassical theory is most nearly realized only in the long run; that is, the effects of changes in one sector will be reflected throughout the entire structure only after a lag — perhaps never fully — and chiefly among securities other than those of very short term. The cost and inconvenience of investment and disinvestment in securities of very short term may at times be quite important in preventing "arbitrage." This cost not only includes the actual outlay in the form of commission or dealer's spread, but also the cost of maintaining a staff to watch the market closely for opportunities of gain. One consequence of these costs

---

[6] The existence of either uncertainty or market segmentation makes the term "arbitrage" somewhat inappropriate when we leave the simplifications of neoclassical theory, since the "commodities" being exchanged are no longer identical under these assumptions. I shall use the term, as it is both convenient and conventional, but I shall place it in quotes in order that the observation made here may be kept in mind.

is that many persons whose funds can be committed for only a brief period will hold idle cash. A second is that the active trading in shorts will be chiefly limited to large institutions like the money-market banks, whose funds are so large that they are in a position to gain enough from small margins to employ a staff capable of managing such operations. This provides one of the reasons for specialization of institutions in securities of particular term.

In still other ways the varied character of the institutions dealing in the market for funds and securities results in an element of market separation between securities of different term. Partly because of uncertainty and the desire to minimize risk, many of the large investing institutions place their funds in investments whose maturities are similar to the life of their own liabilities, so that the likelihood of a forced prematurity sale on the one hand, or frequent reinvestment on the other, is small. Life insurance companies, for instance, typically invest in long-term securities, commercial banks in short and intermediate bonds (mostly governments), and so forth. I shall refer to the effects of institutional preferences like these as "market segmentation."

Furthermore, rigid patterns of investment develop within these institutions even with respect to the varieties of securities they do hold. Thus the investment officer will frequently have to operate within limits which define the approximate proportion of securities in each maturity range which he may hold. Changes in such allocations will require action at the highest administrative level, and such changes will not usually be considered in quick response to a changed market situation.

Another type of market imperfection arises from the institutional impossibility of making very large security "swaps" rapidly without causing market dislocations. Not only do the participants in the market take care to avoid creating such disturbances, but dealers also act to maintain order in the securities markets. If a large firm wished to unload a particular security even at rapidly deteriorating prices, it would soon find the dealers simply backing away from transactions and would find itself unable to complete the sale.

I have described above some of the broad implications of modifications which realistic considerations impose upon the neoclassical theory. Many more specific consequences of these modifications will be spelled out in the analysis of questions described in the following chapter.

APPENDIX A: DERIVATION OF EQUATION FOR LONG RATE OF INTEREST

The equation on page 295 that expresses the equilibrium relation between the long rate of interest and a series of short rates is presented but not derived or fully explained by Lutz.[7] Alvin Marty has suggested to me the following simplification of my derivation. Its rationale rests on the fact that the appropriate long rate will be the one that makes the present value of receipts from investment of a given principal exactly equal to the amount of the principal invested. These receipts are the annual coupons plus the return of the principal itself at maturity. Each must be discounted according to the short rates assumed. This condition may be stated algebraically as follows, assuming that P represents principal, r_1, r_2, r_3, etc. represent the series of assumed short rates, and R represents the long rate which is equivalent for the investor to a sequence of short investments. With these assumptions PR will of course represent the annual coupon of the long-term security.

$$P = \frac{PR}{1 + r_1} + \frac{PR}{(1 + r_1)(1 + r_2)} + \ldots + \frac{PR + P}{(1 + r_1)(1 + r_2) \ldots (1 + r_n)}. \quad (1)$$

Dividing through by P and multiplying by the least common denominator we obtain:

$$(1 + r_1)(1 + r_2)(1 + r_3) \ldots (1 + r_n) = R(1 + r_2)(1 + r_3) \ldots (1 + r_n)$$
$$+ R(1 + r_3)(1 + r_4) \ldots (1 + r_n)$$
$$+ \ldots + R(1 + r_n) + R + 1. \quad (2)$$

Transposing 1 to the other side and solving for R we have:

$$R = \frac{(1 + r_1)(1 + r_2)(1 + r_3) \ldots (1 + r_n) - 1}{(1 + r_2)(1 + r_3) \ldots (1 + r_n) + (1 + r_3) \ldots (1 + r_n) + \ldots + (1 + r_n) + 1}, \quad (3)$$

which is the equation used in the text.

In case the logic of this demonstration is not convincing one may well use a rationale which is closer to that of the problem stated in the text. Specifically, our task is to find a long rate (R) which will make the present value (P_a) of a security bearing that uniform rate precisely equal to the present value (P_b) of the opportunity to invest in successive one-year securities bearing rates of r_1, r_2, r_3, etc. in sequence. We may state the values of these two options as follows:

$$P_a = \frac{P_a R}{(1 + r_1)} + \frac{P_a R}{(1 + r_1)(1 + r_2)} + \ldots + \frac{P_a R + P_a}{(1 + r_1)(1 + r_2) \ldots (1 + r_n)}; \quad (4)$$

$$P_b = \frac{P_b r_1}{(1 + r_1)} + \frac{P_b r_2}{(1 + r_1)(1 + r_2)} + \ldots + \frac{p_b r_n + P_b}{(1 + r_1)(1 + r_2) \ldots (1 + r_n)}. \quad (5)$$

Since the required condition is that $P_a = P_b$, we may set these two expressions equal to one another and substitute P_a for P_b in the second. This gives:

[7] F. A. Lutz, "The Structure of Interest Rates," *Quarterly Journal of Economics* (1940–41); reprinted by American Economic Association, *Readings in the Theory of Income Distribution* (Philadelphia: Blakiston, 1946), chapter 26, p. 500, footnote 2.

$$\frac{P_a R}{(1 + r_1)} + \frac{P_a R}{(1 + r_1)(1 + r_2)} + \cdots + \frac{P_a R + P_a}{(1 + r_1)(1 + r_1) \ldots (1 + r_n)} = \frac{P_a r_1}{(1 + r_1)}$$

$$+ \frac{P_a r_2}{(1 + r_1)(1 + r_2)} + \cdots + \frac{P_a r_n + P_a}{(1 + r_1)(1 + r_2) \ldots (1 + r_n)}. \quad (6)$$

It can readily be proved by mathematical induction that the expression on the right is equal to P_a, and we thus obtain the equation with which Marty's proof begins.

It may be useful to compare our (Lutz') value of R with that derived by Hicks in his *Value and Capital*.[8] His procedure is to equate the receipts that might be obtained by two investment procedures — one in a single long and the other in a sequence of shorts as above — assuming that all funds are retained in the investment until ultimate maturity of the long term security. Thus the maturity value of option 1 for him is $P_1 (1 + R)^n$, and the maturity value of option 2 is P_2 (which equals P_1 by hypothesis) multiplied by $(1 + r_1) (1 + r_2) (1 + r_n)$. Setting these two values equal to one another and cancelling out the P_1 we obtain Hicks' equation:

$$(1 + R)^n = (1 + r_1)(1 + r_2) \ldots (1 + r_n).$$

Solving this for R we obtain:

$$R = [(1 + r_1)(1 + r_2) \ldots (1 + r_n)]^{1/n} - 1.$$

The reason that Hicks finds an expression for R so different from that of Lutz is twofold. In the first place, Hicks assumes that under each option interest and principal are left invested until the long term security matures, at which time all proceeds are collected. Lutz, on the other hand, presumes that under each option only the principal is left invested, coupons being clipped and their present value determined through discounting. Thus Hicks works with the ultimate value of the total accumulation at maturity, whereas Lutz finds the present value of each payment (interest and principal), discounted from the date it becomes due. For this discounting, the assumed short rates are, of course, used.

There are a number of difficulties with Hicks' derivation, the most elementary of which may be described as follows: If a bond is initially sold at its face value (X), then the discounted value of the subsequent payments that it represents should exactly equal X. Assuming we know the short rates that will obtain during the life of the bond, we can readily calculate the discounted value of the receipts from the bond once we are given the coupon rate. However, when we presume that this coupon rate is the long rate as calculated by Hicks' method, then the present value of

---

[8] J. R. Hicks, *Value and Capital*, 2d ed. (Oxford: Clarendon Press, 1946), p. 145.

the payments it represents will not in general equal the assumed face value. Therefore Hicks' method fails to meet this elementary requirement. Lutz' method clearly does satisfy this test, for his derivation of R consists of finding precisely the R that does meet it, as shown by Marty's simple proof above.

APPENDIX B: EQUALITY OF EFFECTIVE YIELDS ON SECURITIES OF DIVERSE MATURITY DATES

The purpose of this appendix is to show that under relations assumed in the neoclassical theory, the gain of one who buys a long-term security, holds it for a year, collects the coupon and sells again, will be equal to that of one who invests the same amount in one-year securities. This equality was illustrated but not proved in the text (p. 296).

The gain of the investor in a long-term security will be his capital gain (positive or negative) plus the coupon rate, R. Our first problem is to express this gain in terms of the funds invested and the assumed short rates. P will be used to represent the face value of the long, and the amount of the coupon is, therefore, PR. V_1 will stand for the value of the bond when bought, V_2 the value when sold. We may, therefore, state as equation (1):

$$\textit{Gain for holder of long-term security for one year} = V_2 - V_1 + PR. \quad (1)$$

If we assume the security has already run $i - 1$ years when bought, and matures in the year n, we may state the values when bought and when sold as follows:

$$V_1 = \frac{PR}{(1 + r_i)} + \frac{PR}{(1 + r_i)(1 + r_{i+1})}$$
$$+ \ldots + \frac{PR + P}{(1 + r_i)(1 + r_{i+1})(1 + r_{i+2}) \ldots (1 + r_n)} \quad (2)$$

$$V_2 = \frac{PR}{1 + r_{i+1}} + \frac{PR}{(1 + r_{i+1})(1 + r_{i+2})}$$
$$+ \ldots + \frac{PR + P}{(1 + r_{i+1})(1 + r_{i+2}) \ldots (1 + r_n)}. \quad (3)$$

Multiplying both sides of equation (2) by $(1 + r_i)$, we obtain:

$$V_1(1 + r_i) = PR + \frac{PR}{(1 + r_{i+1})}$$
$$+ \ldots + \frac{PR + P}{(1 + r_{i+1})(1 + r_{i+2}) \ldots (1 + r_n)} = PR + V_2 \quad (4)$$

by substitution from equation (3).

$$\therefore V_2 = V_1(1 + r_i) - PR \tag{5}$$

and

$$V_2 - V_1 = V_1 r_i - PR. \tag{6}$$

Substituting from (6) in (1):

$$Gain = (V_1 r_i - PR) + PR = V_1 r_i. \tag{7}$$

But this is precisely the gain that would be obtained by investing the same sum (V_1) for one year at the going short rate, r_i. Our conclusion is that if market prices equal the discounted values of promised receipts, as implied in Lutz' derivation of R, then investment for any given time period will offer the same effective return regardless of the term of the security employed. The example given in the text on page 296, therefore, illustrates an entirely general relationship.

APPENDIX C: DERIVATION OF TABLE 6

Part A

Columns 1 and 2: Assumed.

Column 3:

$$R_n = \frac{(1+r_1)(1+r_2)+\dots(1+r_n)-1}{(1+r_2)(1+r_3)\dots(1+r_n)+(1+r_3)(1+r_4)\dots(1+r_n)+\dots+(1+r_n)+1}$$

or, by successive procedure:

$$\text{If } R_s = \frac{a}{b} \text{ by above, then } R_{s+1} = \frac{(a+1)(1+r_{s+1})-1}{b(1+r_{s+1})+1}.$$

Columns 5, 7, 9, and 11: Same principle as column 3, but beginning with expected short rates for year 2, then for year 3, then year 4, and finally year 5.

Column 13: Simple averages of expected short rates:

$$\frac{r_1 + r_2 + \dots r_n}{n}$$

Row for perpetual yields: In year 1, by the basic equation on page 295 of the text,

$$R_n = \frac{(1.02)(1.05)(1.03)(1.01)(1.04)^{n-4} - 1}{[(1.05)(1.03)(1.01)(1.04)^{n-4} + (1.03)(1.01)(1.04)^{n-4}}$$
$$+ (1.01)(1.04)^{n-4} + (1.04)^{n-4} + (1.04)^{n-5} + \dots + 1].*$$

As $n \to \infty$, $\frac{-1}{[*]} \to 0$, and therefore we have:

---

* This denominator is represented in the following line by an asterisk in brackets.

Equation 1:

$$\frac{1}{R_n} \to \frac{1}{1.02} + \frac{1}{(1.02)(1.05)} + \frac{1}{(1.02)(1.05)(1.03)}$$

$$+ \frac{1}{[(1.02)(1.05)(1.03)(1.01)]**} + \frac{1}{[**](1.04)}$$

$$+ \frac{1}{[**](1.04)^2} + \cdots \frac{1}{[**](1.04)^{n-4}}.$$

Similarly multiplying by 1.04, we may write equation 2: As $n \to \infty$,

$$\frac{1.04}{R_n} \to \frac{1.04}{1.02} + \frac{1.04}{(1.02)(1.05)} + \frac{1.04}{(1.02)(1.05)(1.03)} + \frac{1.04}{[**]}$$

$$+ \frac{1}{[**]} + \frac{1}{[**](1.04)} + \frac{1}{[**](1.04)^2} + \cdots + \frac{1}{[**](1.04)^{n-5}}.$$

Subtracting equation 1 from equation 2 we have:

$$\frac{.04}{R_n} \to \frac{.04}{1.02} + \frac{.04}{(1.02)(1.05)} + \frac{.04}{(1.02)(1.05)(1.03)} + \frac{1.04}{[**]} - \frac{1}{[**](1.04)^{n-4}}$$

hence

$$R_\infty = \frac{.04}{(.04)\left[\dfrac{1}{1.02} + \dfrac{1}{(1.02)(1.05)} + \dfrac{1}{(1.02)(1.05)(1.03)}\right] + \left[\dfrac{1.04}{[**]}\right]}.$$

Similar equations determine r_∞ for other years.

Part B

Columns 1 and 2: Assumed.

Column 3: Derived by aid of conventional discounting formula as given on page 300 of the text above, where $A = 4$, $P = 100$, the short rates are those indicated in column 2, and the year of maturity in column 1.

Columns 5, 7, 9, and 11: Similar to column 3.

A useful equation may be developed for derivation of prices in years following the time when the short rates are assumed to level out at a constant figure. We shall assume symbols as before, but two additional ones are required: ρ represents the rate at which short rates remain constant after some year i (the rate in the year i is the last that does not equal ρ). The following comments may clarify the derivation. Equation (1) simply states the present value by showing the discounted value of all subsequent payments. To obtain equation (2) we multiply both sides of equation (1) by $(1 + \rho)$. Equation (3) is obtained by subtracting equation

** This expression is represented in the following calculations by two asterisks in brackets.

(1) from equation (2). Equation (4) is secured by dividing both sides of (3) by ρ.

$$V = \frac{A}{1 + r_1} + \frac{A}{(1 + r_1)(1 + r_2)} + \cdots \frac{A}{[(1 + r_1)(1 + r_2)\ldots(1 + r_i)]***}$$
$$+ \frac{A}{[***](1 + \rho)} + \frac{A}{[***](1 + \rho)^2} + \cdots \frac{A + P}{[***](1 + \rho)^{n-i}} \quad (1)$$

$$V(1 + \rho) = \frac{A + A\rho}{1 + r_1} + \frac{A + A\rho}{(1 + r_1)(1 + r_2)} + \cdots \frac{A + A\rho}{[***]}$$
$$+ \frac{A}{[***]} + \frac{A}{[***](1 + \rho)} + \cdots \frac{A + P}{[***](1 + \rho)^{n-i-1}} \quad (2)$$

$$V\rho = \frac{A\rho}{1 + r_1} + \frac{A\rho}{(1 + r_1)(1 + r_2)} + \cdots \frac{A\rho}{[***]} + \frac{A}{[***]}$$
$$+ \frac{P}{[***](1 + \rho)^{n-i-1}} - \frac{A + P}{[***](1 + \rho)^{n-i}} \quad (3)$$

$$V = \frac{A}{1 + r_1} + \frac{A}{(1 + r_1)(1 + r_2)} + \cdots \frac{A + (A/\rho)}{[***]}$$
$$+ \frac{P}{\rho[***](1 + \rho)^{n-i-1}} - \frac{A + P}{\rho[***](1 + \rho)^{n-i}}. \quad (4)$$

The last two terms may be consolidated by multiplying numerator and denominator of the first by $(1 + \rho)$, as follows:

$$\frac{P(1 + \rho)}{\rho[***](1 + \rho)^{n-i}} - \frac{A + P}{\rho[***](1 + \rho)^{n-i}} = \frac{P\rho - A}{\rho[***](1 + \rho)^{n-i}} \quad (5)$$

$$\therefore V = \frac{A}{1 + r_1} + \frac{A}{(1 + r_1)(1 + r_2)} + \cdots \frac{A + (A/\rho)}{(1 + r_1)(1 + r_2)\ldots(1 + r_i)}$$
$$+ \frac{P\rho - A}{\rho[***](1 + \rho)^{n-i}} \quad (6)$$

In any case where the coupon on the security is presumed to represent the same percentage of the principal as the rate of interest which rules in the market after the period i we may state that $A/P = \rho$, or $A = P\rho$. Making this substitution in the final term causes it to vanish. But this is the only term that includes any reference to years beyond the year i. This means that under the assumptions just stated securities that are identical except for term will have equal present value so long as their term reaches beyond the year i. Indeed this yield will be the same as that of an i-year security, as may be seen by substituting P for A/ρ in the next to last term of equation 6.

*** This expression is represented throughout the rest of this derivation by three asterisks in brackets.

If we had assumed that rates after the year i settled at some rate other than the coupon rate, the conclusions of the preceding paragraph would not follow, for then $A \neq P/\rho$, and the final term would not vanish. In this event, however, the denominator of that term rises without limit as n approaches infinity, so that this term does vanish in the case of a perpetuity, the value of which may, therefore, be calculated readily from the other terms of equation (6).

EMPIRICAL TESTS
OF THE THEORY OF RATE STRUCTURE

We turn now to the series of questions concerning the behavior of rates on securities of different term referred to on p. 293.

1. To what extent should one expect rates on securities of different term to move in the same direction when changes in rates occur?

Perfect-foresight Model. — According to common sense one might expect all segments of the rate structure to rise or fall simultaneously even if not equally when there are rate changes anywhere. It should be noted, however, that the neoclassical theory implies no need for such similarity in direction of movement to occur, even if expectations remain unchanged and are wholly fulfilled. Consider, for example, table 7.[1]

TABLE 7

Year	Assumed one-year rate (Per cent)	Derived two-year rate (Per cent)
1	4	$\dfrac{4+2}{2} = 3$
2	2	$\dfrac{2+6}{2} = 4$
3	6	. . .

Here the long rate rose from 3 to 4 while the short rate fell from 4 to 2 per cent. In general, the long rate for securities maturing in the year n will rise between year 1 and year 2 even though the short rate falls if the expected short rate in the year $n + 1$ (that being newly included in the calculation to replace year 1) is higher than the short rate in year 1.[2]

---

[1] In simple illustrations like this I derive long rates by the use of simple averages.

[2] The explanation given here contradicts that of F. A. Lutz, "The Structure of Interest Rates," *Quarterly Journal of Economics* (1940–41); reprinted in American Economic Association, *Readings in the Theory of Income Distribution* (Philadelphia: Blakiston, 1946), chapter 26, p. 502. Lutz appears to be in error.

This model would suggest that rate movements might be in the same direction more often than not because one of the elements which is changed in the "average" (the elimination of r_1) is common to all of them. But movements in different directions could surely be common.

Modifications. — When uncertainty is admitted, the chief factors influencing rate movements are almost entirely changed from those described in the perfect-foresight model but conflicting forces will still be at work. Two major considerations would lead to the expectation that rates should move together much more often than not, whereas two others might tend to cause diverse rate movements.

Using the terminology of the theory, it may be noted in the first place that expectations regarding rates in the far future, or even the intermediate future, will be held so vaguely that the influence of the new r_{n+1} will be negligible. Second, a change in rates will typically be dominated by a change in actual or expected supply and demand in the markets for money and credit, not by a mere passage of time in the context of unchanged expectations. Still using the terminology of the neoclassical theory, this means that a whole host of successive expected short rates will change together, so that the effect on any individual security arising from a new r_{n+1} will be swamped by the changes in the other expected short rates making up its average. Thus the impact which is common to most securities — the changed expectations regarding short rates — will be dominant, causing rates to move together. The terminology of the market short-cuts these complex logical relations and states simply that investors, having changed their expectations concerning future supply and demand in the market for money and credit, assume at once that long rates will be correspondingly changed and they offer or bid for securities accordingly.

The considerations just described would lead to the expectation that rates on securities of different term would usually move in the same direction. This would apply especially among intermediate and long-term securities, since it is unlikely that a changed situation would lead to the expectation of a rising short rate in one distant period (i.e., increased tightness in one distant period) and a falling short rate (easier money) in another distant period. Expectations of diverse movements like this are not unlikely in relation to the more immediate future, however, so that diverse rate movements may be expected more frequently among very short-term issues, or between these and longs rather than among longs. But the general effect of uncertainty from the standpoint of these considerations all taken together is clearly to increase the probability that rate movements will be in the same direction.

In contrast to this, two considerations serve to increase the possibility of diverse rate movements. First, the frictions which are common in real-world markets may cause lags in adjustment which would permit a reversal in the direction of a general rate movement to appear in some maturities before it appears in others. Second, for reasons which I shall discuss later (pp. 318 ff.), the prices of longs generally fluctuate much more than do those of shorts. One consequence is that a marked change in expectations may lead persons to wish to shift between longs and shorts. Thus, for instance, expectations of declining yields will suggest rising security prices, and investors would wish to benefit from the relatively larger change in long prices.[3] This changed relative attractiveness of different maturities could readily cause rates to move in opposite directions.

The implications of theory regarding the similarity in direction of rate movements may now be summarized. Rate movements on securities of different term should generally be expected to be in the same direction. This similarity should be most consistent among longs, different issues of which will typically respond in a similar way to changed expectations. Diverse movements among shorts, or between shorts and longs, may not be uncommon, however. This is partly because expectations are held more specifically over the near future, making the neoclassical theory more applicable to this group of securities. But diversity of movement between longs and shorts results also from the fact that changed expectations may sometimes cause a desire to shift between longs and shorts in order to avoid capital loss or to acquire capital gain.

This analysis of the relation between rate changes on securities of different term should be compared with a commonly presented explanation of the way a change in the yield of one security is transmitted to that of others. This explanation would run as follows. Suppose that the Federal Reserve raised the yields on bills by open-market sales. Then marginal holders of certificates would find rates on bills relatively more attractive than before, and would shift to bills. The sale of certificates would force up yields on these, and then holders of slightly longer term securities would shift to certificates. This process of "arbitrage" works its way throughout the entire structure, raising longer rates to levels appropriate to the new level of bill rates. A new equilibrium is established with all rates higher than before, but with bill rates lower than they would have been without the "arbitrage" here described. Thus any rise in rates at one point in the rate structure will result in a rise throughout the other maturities in the market.

In a large measure this description is realistic, and analysis shows it to be nearly a direct translation into simple terminology of the argument that long rates change when there are changes in the expected short rates that make them up. But this explanation of what happens to the structure

---

[3] See pp. 318–321 for discussion of relative price changes.

of rates when a disturbance is brought to bear on one sector is oversimplified in ways which may sometimes be misleading. Two major qualifications should be mentioned. One is that the process here described is not
the only kind of rate behavior that may take place, since this process requires rate movements in the same direction, whereas both theoretical
analysis and empirical observation show that changes in expectations may
at times cause diverse rate movements. A second qualification in the simplified explanation just presented is somewhat more complex. According
to that presentation bill rates would first rise sharply and would then fall
to a new equilibrium as former holders of longer terms switched to the
bills. In part and at times this may well be what takes place, partly because the institutional structure of the market is one in which newly supplied bills will first be absorbed by dealers and banks, to be subsequently
distributed more widely. But in part the picture given here implies a
larger volume of shifting than need actually take place. Buyers and sellers
of all securities will normally discount the changes in all rates that might
be expected to occur as a result of a disturbance at one part of the rate
structure, and consequently all security prices may often adjust quite rapidly to the new equilibrium levels without the necessity of a great volume
of shifting.

Empirical Studies. — In chart 3 yields on six different series of United
States government securities are plotted for 1951 through 1954.[4] The fre-
quency with which rates moved in the same direction is obvious, and a
test of statistical significance overwhelmingly confirms the hypothesis of
a strong tendency for covariation. The calculated likelihood that the
movement of the series together is the result only of chance is so small
as to be entirely negligible.[5]

The extent of correlation between rates on securities of different term
which these movements suggest is further clarified by the aid of scatter
diagrams, four of which are presented in chart 4. These cover the same
period as that shown in chart 3, namely, January, 1951, through December, 1954. Whereas the calculation of the chi-square value for these series
showed the similarity in *direction* of monthly movements of different
rates, the scatter diagram permits visualization of the degree to which the
levels of rates are correlated with one another. As is to be expected, and
as the theory of rates suggests, the correlation is not only clear and positive, but is also much higher when the securities compared are of long
term than when shorts are involved in the comparison. Although various

---

[4] All charts referred to in this chapter are found on pages 361–367.

[5] The chi-square value of the series is 178, whereas a value of only 16.3 would be
significant at the .001 level. Our 288 observations are insufficient to provide high re-
liance upon the value of chi-square, but the figure found is so high that its implication
would be unchanged even if it erred very greatly indeed.

considerations might explain this finding, the interpretation described in general terms by the modified theory probably provides the major explanation. Supply and demand for immediate funds and expectations for the very near future move much more sharply than do corresponding expectations concerning supply and demand in the more distant future. A practical illustration of this generalization is the fact that short-term securities are the instruments of the money market, where trading is most active and where the shocks of changing monetary conditions are first felt. Sharp fluctuations may thus be expected to appear here when longer-run changes are not anticipated, and when, therefore, the prices of long-term securities would not be expected to change appreciably.

The exceptions to the high positive correlation during these years offer important suggestions for the theory of rate structure, but these can be best interpreted in relation to another issue, that of the shape of yield curves, and this analysis will therefore be postponed until that question has been examined. Meanwhile we shall review the evidence of the closely related questions, the amplitude of fluctuations in yields and in prices of securities with different term.

2. *When yields change, what is the relation between the size of change on shorts and on longs?*

Perfect-foresight Model. — It has been shown above that so long as we assume perfect foresight, the only reason that the yields on long-term securities would change over time is because of the gradual sloughing off of successive short rates from the "averages" that make up the long yields, together with the addition of the $n + 1$ rates of the years coming into view. But the longer the term of the security the larger will be the number of unchanging short rates in the "average" to off-set the effects of the change caused by the one rate that disappears and the one that enters. Thus long rates will remain quite stable. On the other hand, if short rates vary sharply, then these changes will be markedly reflected in the yields of moderately short term securities.

Modifications. — In a world of imperfect foresight the yield changes of longs from period to period will be appreciably greater relative to those of shorts than is implied by a model that assumes the realization of expectations. This is because imperfect foresight permits changes of rates to arise from new situations or new expectations, which have the effect of altering a whole series of expected short rates. Consequently the long rate will move more than is implied under unchanging expectations, though typically less than short rates. Again translating to familiar language, although expectations concerning rate levels of the intermediate or more distant future are typically vague and not subject to sudden changes, they are, nevertheless, somewhat volatile. They do not remain wholly unchanged, as implied by a perfect-foresight model.

Although the relations just described are common, there is nothing in the theory to preclude the possibility that future expectations may sometimes change while current supply and demand remain unaltered. In such cases, long rates would change while shorts were unaffected. Indeed, the previous section demonstrated that shorts and longs could even move in opposite directions. The analysis, therefore, provides a basis for both (1) the generalization that rates will normally move together, with longs moving least, and (2) the recognition of circumstances in which this generalization will not be fulfilled.

Empirical Evidence. — Chart 5 shows yields on prime commercial paper and high-grade corporate securities from 1900 to 1942.[6] It is clear from inspection of this chart that the amplitude of fluctuation in yields quite consistently diminishes as the term lengthens. Chart 8, which shows basic yield curves for the period 1900 to 1942, illustrates the same fact. My own empirical study relates only to the years 1951 to 1954. Three months have been chosen to illustrate times when rates were, respectively, at low, high, and low points. The average monthly yields on three different term classes of government securities for these months are shown in table 8. It will be noted from the last two columns that with one exception yields always moved more widely for securities of shorter term. Chart 3 shows that this tendency is fairly generally characteristic of yield changes during the post-accord period, though it is most clearly marked during

TABLE 8

Monthly Averages of Yields on Selected
United States Government Obligations

Term classification	April 1952	April 1953	July 1954	Change in yield	
				Period 1 to 2	Period 2 to 3
Three-month treasury bills	1.57	2.19	.72	+.62	−1.47
Three- to five-year government issues	1.93	2.61	1.69	+.68	−.92
Long-term bonds	2.64	2.97	2.47	+.33	−.50

sustained rather than brief periods of yield movements, and especially when rate changes have been substantial. Chart 4 depicts this same tendency much more clearly than chart 3 in some respects, and may be interpreted as follows: Since in each scatter diagram the longer of the two securities is plotted vertically, the more nearly each implied regression

---

[6] The idea for this chart was derived from a similar one in David Durand and W. J. Winn, *Basic Yields of Bonds 1926–47: Their Measurement and Pattern*, Technical Paper No. 6 (New York: National Bureau of Economic Research, 1948). Data used in my chart are taken from the Board of Governors of the Federal Reserve System, *Banking and Monetary Statistics* (Washington, D. C.: National Capital Press, 1943), pp. 448 and 477.

line approaches the horizontal the greater is the indicated excess of the amplitude of yield fluctuation of the short-term security over the long-term. In all four of these diagrams the slope of the regression line (not drawn in) is less than 45 degrees. The steepest is that of part D, where two long terms are compared; the nearest to horizontal is part B, where bills are contrasted with long-term bonds. The other slopes fall appropriately between these two.[7]

It will thus be observed that the relative amplitude of yield movements on longs and shorts is generally consistent with the expectation suggested by the modified theory of the structure of rates.

3. What is the relation between the size of price changes on longs and on shorts?

Perfect-foresight Model. — Since empirical testing of price changes will have to relate to specific securities, we shall now consider the price changes of individual issues instead of comparing some abstract price of *n*-year bonds today with that of *n*-year bonds next year. The essential nature of the conclusions is not different, though numerical values would diverge significantly on short-term issues.

In contrast to what might be supposed, the perfect-foresight model of classical theory implies that changes in prices of securities over time will be nearly equal regardless of term. An illustration may be drawn from the example described in table 6 (p. 297). Consider, for instance, a comparison between the start of year 1 and the start of year 2 (table 9). Dur-

TABLE 9

Year	Short rate	Price of 4 per cent bonds at start of year shown in first column	
		Security maturing at end of year 2	Perpetual security
1	2	$ 101.03	$ 104.63
2	5	99.05	102.72
Decline in price		$ 1.98	$ 1.91

ing this period compare price changes on two-year bonds with those on perpetuals. It may be seen from this calculation that the difference in price changes recorded was only 7 cents despite the fact that short rates changed from 2 per cent to 5 per cent, and the terms of the securities were

---

[7] J. M. Culbertson gives similar evidence for selected years between 1920 and 1957. His data lead him to the same conclusion I have reached and described regarding the consistently wider amplitude of movement in short than in long rates. See "The Term Structure of Interest Rates," *Quarterly Journal of Economics*, 71 (1957): 504–506.

two years on the one hand and perpetual on the other. Furthermore, what difference there was between amounts of price change might appear to suggest greater price movements in shorts than in longs!

Generalization from this illustration would explain the nearly equal price change implied by the neoclassical model as follows. I have shown that the net yield on funds invested for any given year must be the same regardless of the issue held. Since this illustration compares securities of equal coupon, the price change must therefore be approximately equal in order that the total effective yield for the interval may be equal. The small difference in price change which does appear results from the fact that the initial prices differ, and hence equal percentage yields will be found only if the absolute receipts are higher on the higher priced securities. It follows that this small price change can run in either direction between longs and shorts.[8]

Modifications. — The contrary but generally accepted view that prices of longs will move much more widely than the prices of shorts when the general level of interest rates changes, is typically explained by an illustration like the one in table 10.

TABLE 10

Year	Rate of interest	Price of 4 per cent bond assuming rates shown in second column	
		2-Year security	Perpetuity
1	2	$\dfrac{\$4}{1.02} + \dfrac{\$104}{(1.02)^2} = \$103.88$	$\dfrac{\$4}{.02} = \$200.00$
2	5	$\dfrac{\$4}{1.05} + \dfrac{\$104}{(1.05)^2} = 98.14$	$\dfrac{\$4}{.05} = 80.00$
Price decline from year 1 to year 2		$ 5.74	$120.00

[8] Compare the above illustration, when the price change was greatest on the short-term security, with the following illustration, also taken from table 8, but beginning in the second year of that table:

Year	Short rate	Price of 4 per cent bonds at start of year in column 1	
		2-Year security	Perpetuity
1	5	$ 99.97	$102.72
2	3	100.97	103.85
Rise in price		$ 1.00	$ 1.13

The difference in implicit assumptions which produces this great contrast in result is chiefly this: in the example illustrating the neoclassical theory we examined price changes over time as we moved from a period of low to one of high short rates, assuming that all expectations were fulfilled or unchanged. In the second and more familiar illustration we implicitly assumed horizontal yield curves at each time (i.e., rates on all maturities are implicitly assumed to be equal at any one time) and hence the change in rates which caused the change in security prices represents an equal change in all expected future rates.

The illustration just presented shows the direction in which modification of the perfect-foresight model must be made. In the language of the neoclassical analysis one consequence of uncertainty is that many expected short rates will usually change together if expectations change. I have already shown that the result of this is a greater change in yields on longs than the assumption of perfect certainty would suggest. But long *prices* changed equally with short prices when yields changed as indicated by the perfect-foresight model. Therefore long prices must change more than short prices in the modified theory, since their yields change more in this than in the perfect-certainty model.

The modified theory of the structure of rates thus suggests that price changes should clearly be greater on longs than on shorts, though not nearly so great as would be implied by the classroom model described above.

Empirical Evidence. — It is generally assumed by those working in securities markets that prices of longs fluctuate more widely than those of shorts. I do not know of any thorough empirical research on the problem, but the following check of 1951–1954 data gives support to this assumption. Table 11 shows prices of a number of government securities which were outstanding during the entire period under review. As in the study of yields I here compare three dates representing extremes in yield fluctuations.

TABLE 11

PRICES OF SELECTED UNITED STATES TREASURY SECURITIES, 1952–1954

Date of call and maturity	Years to call and maturity from April, 1952	Prices[a] (end of month)			Price change[a]	
		4/52	4/53	7/54	52–53	53–54
3/55	3	99.3	98.4	100.18	−0.31	+2.14
3/56–58	4–6	101.27	98.3	102.12	−3.24	+4.9
9/56–59	4½–7½	100.25	96.30	101.26	−3.27	+4.28
6/62–67	10–15	100.8	94.28	101.21	−5.12	+6.25
3/65–70	13–18	98.19	92.23	100.23	−5.28	+8.0
9/67–72	15½–20½	99.8	92.6	100.17	−7.2	+8.11

[a] Figures after decimal indicate number of 32nds of a point.

It is clear from the last two columns that during both the period of price decline and that of price rise, the prices of longer-term securities always varied more than the prices of securities with shorter term. At the extremes, notes maturing in 1955 fell $3\frac{1}{32}$ and rose $2\frac{14}{32}$ points in these two periods while the bonds of 1967–1972 fell $7\frac{2}{32}$ and rose $8\frac{11}{32}$ in the same periods. Thus the perfect-certainty model is not borne out, but the modified theory is wholly supported by the experience of the post-accord price fluctuations recorded here.

4. Should one expect the yield curve to be monotonic?

Perfect-foresight Model. — Nothing in the neoclassical theory, either with or without the assumption of accurate forecasting, would suggest that the yield curve need be monotonic (i.e., have the same direction of slope throughout its length at any one time). Sharp alternating differences in expected short rates for successive future periods will cause the slope of the yield curve to alternate between positive and negative values as is illustrated in chart 1 for the data presented in table 6. It may be noted, however, that mild fluctuation in short rates may not prevent the yield curve from being monotonic. For example, note the curve derived from the expected short rates shown in table 12.

TABLE 12

Term to which rate applies	Rate in per cent			
	Year 1	Year 2	Year 3	Year 4
One-year rate (assumed)	2	5	4	5
Two-year rate (derived)	3.46	. . .ª	. . .	. . .
Three-year rate (derived)	3.63	. . .	. . .	. . .
Four-year rate (derived)	3.95	. . .	. . .	. . .

ª Figures for these spaces are not required for this analysis

In this case, the curve is monotonic from the start, successive yields being 2, 3.46, 3.63, and 3.95, despite the fluctuation in expected short rates.

Furthermore, it should be recognized that forces preventing a monotonic yield curve will be much greater among relatively short terms than among others. Suppose, for instance, the shorts should be expected to oscillate perpetually between 5 and 1 per cent. In this event the yields on securities of successive term beginning with the shortest would be as follows: 5.00, 3.01, 3.65, 3.01, 3.38, 3.01, 3.27, 3.01, 3.20, 3.01. . . . If we suppose any influences causing a generally rising or generally falling curve, fluctuations would soon be buried under the larger influence of the trend. A crude example would be that given in table 13. In this example, the yield curve is monotonic beyond the third time period.

TABLE 13

Year or term	Expected short rates	Yields in year 1 on securities of term in first column
1	3	3.000
2	1	2.005
3	4	2.651
4	2	2.491
5	5	2.959
6	3	2.965
7	6	3.349
8	4	3.419
9	7	3.749
10	5	3.844

The conclusion to be reached is that under the assumption of neoclassical theory yield curves can be other than monotonic despite fixed expectations of future rates, but that the fluctuations tend to be damped as maturities lengthen, and that consequently yield curves with a clear trend are likely to be monotonic beyond the shortest end of the curve.

Modifications. — The existence of uncertainty will increase the probability that the curve will be monotonic compared with the perfect-foresight model. Since expectations may be fairly firm for the immediate future, the neoclassical theory, with its possibility of a jagged yield curve in that area, is not altered. However, the greater uncertainty over later times would cause general and vague long-term rate expectation to be much more influential in that range than estimates of precise short-duration rate changes. Hence the smoothing of the yield curve would presumably begin much "earlier" (nearer the short end) in a world of uncertainty than in a world of perfect certainty. If a noticeable hump or U should appear in a region of the curve representing terms greater than one or two years it might be best attributed to market segmentation, though a peculiar sequence of expectations should also be considered.

Empirical Evidence. — Yield curves as drawn were nearly always monotonic up to and through the period of this study.[9] This is partly because the scatter of points is sufficiently ambiguous that economists with preconceived notions of the appropriate shape can readily take enough liberties to draw them in this way. Empirical study indicates that the arbitrary act of drawing monotonic curves is largely, but not wholly, justified.

It can be seen in chart 3 that except for sections of the structure representing terms of one year or less there were only two places in which the

---

[9] Since this draft was written a hump-backed curve has emerged.

curve would not have been monotonic.[10] (These are places where curves on the chart intersect.) On the yield curve for securities maturing or callable within a year, however, there are several places where the slope of the implied yield curve would differ from what it would be farther to the right. It is, however, precisely within this region — at the short end of the yield curve — that one has the greatest difficulty interpreting what appear to be aberrations in the curve, especially because maturing securities typically have rights values large enough to result in their sale at very low or even negative yields. Furthermore, since the Federal Reserve System conducts its open-market operations largely in bills, and since corporations and banks adjust their cash positions to a large extent by transactions in bills, there may be times when bill rates are pushed out of line with others before the market can fully react to these changes at other points. A study of the post-accord period through 1955 has not revealed any instances where negative slope at the short end of the curve for securities whose yields are plotted in chart 3[11] can be clearly explained by the factors envisaged in the perfect-foresight theory, though these may have played a part sometimes.[12] Market frictions appear to be a more important explanation of the aberrations noted. (See pp. 332 ff. for further discussion.)

In order to examine the rate structure within a range of even shorter terms, but without the confusion caused by rights values, I have studied the yields on bills of different term during 1954. Bid and asked values on the thirteen outstanding issues were recorded for each Wednesday during the year. In this study yield curves were regarded as monotonic (upward) if no bill yielded less than the one preceding it, so that series of equal successive yields did not eliminate a curve from the monotonic classification. On this basis twenty-five weeks showed monotonic rising yield curves by study of both the bid and asked rates; the curves for ten more weeks were virtually monotonic. Where irregularities appeared they were generally represented by a short stretch of negative slope at the short end, but often this U-shape appeared only in bid values or only in asked values, but not in both. It seldom extended beyond the three shortest terms of bills. In only three cases did the declining section extend beyond the third week on both bid and asked sides, though it went beyond that point on one side (bid or asked) fifteen times. Neoclassical theory would lead

---

[10] On May 31 and June 30, 1953, the 2¼'s of 1962–1967 yielded very slightly more than the 2½'s of 1967–1972; and at the end of August, 1953, an 11½ month security yielded more than one due in 2 years 3½ months.

[11] I.e., including only securities of 90 days or more. It will be noted that this theory may well explain observations concerning relations among rates on shorter securities.

[12] It is quite plausible, however, to attribute the post-1956 hump in part to a pattern of expectations which would cause just such a hump according to the neoclassical theory.

us to expect that these U-shaped curves would appear when the money market was temporarily tight but expected shortly to ease. This is true of every major U-shaped yield curve for bills, as may be seen by high rates on federal funds at a time when policy was known to call for continued ease.

Under conditions in 1954 expectations regarding future rates did not appear sufficiently precise and varied to result in many wavelike yield curves for bills with a term longer than one month (though some may be noted), and thus the curves are, if anything, more monotonic than neoclassical theory might lead us to suppose. On the other hand, the theory itself would lead us to expect normally monotonic curves beyond a fairly short term, and this expectation has been generally realized. Frictional lags in response to money-market pressures, together with special features of many securities, appear to explain most of the waves in yield curves beyond the terms of 3-month bills.

5. *What factors control the direction of slope of the yield curve?*

Perfect-foresight Model. — If one assumes a generally monotonic curve beyond the immediate future, then the question is whether any particular direction of slope can be expected on the basis of the theory of rate structure. As table 8 and chart 1 indicate, there is nothing in the perfect-foresight model of neoclassical theory to prevent the yield curve from sloping either positively or negatively. Indeed, since long rates are modified averages of shorts, it would appear that the curve would slope one way about as often as the other if and when it was monotonic enough to slope consistently in any direction.

Modifications. — Since it has been shown that in the absence of perfect foresight price changes are usually greater on long terms than on short terms, purchase of longs offers the possibility of greater gain and the risk of greater loss than does purchase of shorts. It is not unreasonable to presume that investors in bonds are generally seeking to avoid risk, and that they will usually prefer a return that is sure over one with equal actuarial value but greater uncertainty. If this behavioral hypothesis is valid, then it is reasonable to presume that longs would have to yield more than shorts when prospects of gain are about equal to prospects of loss, in order to compensate for the greater risk involved in holding the longs. This presumption would lead to the conclusion that long rates should exceed short rates more often than not. Put somewhat differently, the desire of investors in bonds to avoid risks should give the yield curve bias in the direction of positive slope.

The implication of this would be that yield curves might have negative slope when rates are quite high, but not otherwise. Rolph suggests another factor which may give a similar result. In prosperous times people are generally optimistic, and thus show a far less asymmetrical attitude toward risk than that just described, so that the positive bias of the curve may lessen when the economy is strong. But good times also generally bring high interest rates. Thus there may be a negative correlation between the level of rates and the slope of the yield curve although neither causes the other, because each results from a third cause — prosperity.

Uncertainty presents two other causal elements that influence the shape of the yield curve. Because the slope of these curves was positive for over twenty years (before 1955) it has been expected that this direction of slope would persist, and this expectation has been to a large extent self-fulfilling. For example, whenever the curve approached the horizontal, the view that this was abnormal caused many persons to believe short prices too low, or long prices too high, or both. The consequent purchase of shorts, or sale of longs, or both, tended to restore the positive slope of the curve. This may go far to explain the secular stability of the slope of yield curves during most of the time since the 1920's. It is interesting to note, however, that there is one respect in which the expectation of persistent positively sloped curves tends to work against the fulfillment of the expectation. To the degree that one can assume that the present levels and structure of rates will continue, one can presume that long-term bonds must sell at a premium before maturity, since their coupon will be appreciably above short-term rates. This means that the yield to some date preceding maturity would exceed the yield to maturity, and that in consequence persons considering this will buy securities of longer term than they would otherwise buy.[13] Clearly the "lengthening of demand" which would thus result from the expectation of an unchanging yield curve will reduce the long rates relative to shorts, and thus reduce the positive slope of the yield curve. Sophisticated investors definitely take account of this, but the self-fulfilling tendency of expectations seems to have been more powerful up to the time of the empirical studies used in this book (1954).

In the present institutional framework, the asymmetry of attitude toward risk is of very great importance. All large institutional investors have it. Banks' and corporations' holdings of government securities are almost entirely at the short and intermediate end partly because these institutions do not regard speculation in securities with more volatile prices as one of their functions. Life insurance companies can afford to buy longs only because their liabilities are sufficiently long term that they will not normally be forced to liquidate before maturity. These institutional preferences become a central cause of the market segmentation frequently referred to in this analysis.

---

[13] See appendix B to this chapter for an illustration of this process on the basis of a 1954 curve.

The influence of this market segmentation on the slope of the yield curve could conceivably be great. Lutz argues that it will tend to result in yield curves sloped positively more often than in those sloped negatively, because "there will be relatively few funds whose owners can part with them irrevocably for a very long time, whereas the demand for long-term funds will be relatively large owing to the importance of fixed capital." [14] This tendency to a positive slope would, of course, be reduced or overcome if the government functioned as a balance wheel by increasing its short borrowing and reducing its long borrowing to compensate for the small supply of shorts that private borrowers wish to issue.

In this connection it seems appropriate to comment on some questions raised by Keynesian analysis of liquidity preference. It is sometimes stated that the Keynesian theory of interest implies that the yield curve must always be positively sloped. The argument runs that this theory describes the interest rate as the price for sacrificing liquidity, and that therefore the longest-term securities, where more liquidity is sacrificed, should always yield the greatest return.

It will be shown later that empirical yield curves appear often to have been downward sloping before the 1930's, and it therefore becomes important to find whether the liquidity-preference theory can be reconciled with this observation. Such a reconciliation may be sought in either of two ways. One is suggested by Lutz: It is generally agreed that the concept of liquidity preference must include not only the time before repayment, but also the certainty of payment in full. If this be true, then it might be argued that the prospect of payment in excess of the initial obligation represents liquidity above 100 per cent; thus when long-term securities offer prospect of price rise, their liquidity is greater than that of shorts, and hence their yield may be less. The implied definition of liquidity is bizarre though not illogical. In any event, whatever words are used to describe the proposition, it is surely reasonable to presume that longs are going to be more attractive than shorts with equal yield if the expectation of rising security prices is sufficiently general and confident.

The second way to reconcile liquidity-preference theory with the downward slope of the yield curve is that described by the neoclassical theory. This shows clearly that liquidity need not be the only element affecting rate differentials. So long as we retain the assumption of perfect arbitrage and firm expectations of future rates, all maturities have equal liquidity, since all can be sold at predictable prices, and the effective yields over given time periods are equal. The shape of the yield curve in this case cannot reflect the degree of liquidity of different term securities, but only the expected future short rates. If these are generally falling, the yield

---

[14] F. A. Lutz, "The Structure of Interest Rates," p. 506.

curve would have to be negatively sloped. This suggests that a pure liquidity explanation of rate structure is at least incomplete.

An argument which may seem similar to that of Keynes is one concerning the continuity between money and other forms of debt. Despite the latitude offered by our theoretical discussion, yield curves usually appear to be monotonic. If we regard government securities as "near-moneys," with the nearness to money growing closer to identity as the maturity approaches zero, then the question is raised, would not the yield curve be expected to rise continuously from zero — the yield on money — to whatever long rate rules? Looking at the curve in the other direction (i.e., beginning at the long end) how could the yield on securities be expected to rise monotonically as the term shortens and then suddenly to drop to zero when the limit, zero-term securities (money), is reached?

Three comments suggest themselves in answer to this question. In the first place, the yield on money is not zero so long as service charges of banks vary inversely with the size of balances. In the second place, if the yield curve did rise monotonically all the way from the longest to the shortest rates, and if future rate expectations were held with confidence, it is very doubtful that persons would hold any idle balances except where habits, convenience, or costs of investment and disinvestment impeded the purchase of securities. In the third place, the typical monotonic appearance of yield curves does not always hold all the way to the very short-term obligations (e.g., especially three weeks or so) and the shortest rates of all — those on Federal funds — fluctuate readily above and below bill rates. There is, therefore, nothing surprising about sharp discontinuities in rates as one moves from zero-term (money) to one-day loans, and so forth. The reason for these sharp differences follows simply from the fact that there is a substantial difference between money today and a promise of money tomorrow. A consequence of the discontinuities is that a yield curve of generally negative slope need not conflict with the zero return on money.

Empirical Evidence. — Yield curves have been positively sloped so consistently since 1931 that many persons have come to assume this shape almost without explanation, but a longer look at history raises a question about the cause of this characteristic. David Durand's analysis of high-grade corporate securities over the first 42 years of this century showed that yield curves clearly declined in 17 years, were fairly close to horizontal in 12, and rose appreciably in 13.[15]

---

[15] Since this study was completed history has again demonstrated the danger of assuming the inevitability of positively sloped yield curves. The interpretation of Durand's charts is mine; the charts appear in David Durand, *Basic Yields of Corporate Bonds,* Technical Paper No. 3 (New York: National Bureau of Economic Research, 1942), pp. 25 ff.

According to the modified theory of rate structure developed above, the curve should be negatively sloped only when interest rates are generally high relative to long-run concepts of normal rates. Durand's data show roughly horizontal curves from 1900 to 1906, when most rates were rising from lower levels than they had reached for several decades. By 1907 short rates rose above longs, and, except for a sharp war-time interruption beginning in 1916, both rose persistently until they reached a peak in 1921, after which a decline began that continued until early 1928. Just as the neoclassical theory would suggest, yield curves sloped downward consistently during most of this period, when rates were generally high. The 1916–1917 decline in yields was associated with horizontal and positively sloped curves. From 1925 through 1928, when rates had fallen substantially from levels of the early 20's, yield curves were horizontal to slightly rising, but after a fairly sharp increase in rates in 1928 and 1929 the yield curve returned to a negative slope. In 1930, with rates already falling from their 1929 peak, shorts moved downward rapidly. The yield curve that year was almost horizontal, and it was positively sloped consistently from that time through the period of this study (1955).

These data would appear to be almost completely consistent with the theory of the structure of rates as modified by admitting uncertainty. It seems reasonable to believe that this theory does offer much of the explanation for the general shape of yield curves over the first half of the twentieth century. On the other hand, other factors than levels of rates were often important. The great demand for call money during the stock market boom might provide the full explanation of the negatively sloped curve in 1929 and the subsequent return to positive slope. This kind of explanation would fall within the category of "market segmentation" in the theory as expounded here.

Further qualification of the view that the slope of the yield curve has been determined by the deviation of rates from levels viewed as normal is suggested by noting that the close fit of theory with fact during the half-century reviewed is partly the result of the very broad strokes of our description. An examination in more detail would raise a number of questions requiring much more thorough analysis. Two issues will be explored here: (1) Does the theory seem consistent with the shapes of post-accord yield curves? (2) To what extent may the facts reported here be explained by other elements than the general level of rates (as, for instance, in 1929)?

Since yield curves were always positively sloped during the post-accord period of my research, the problem to be studied is that of the steepness of the curve rather than of the direction of slope. Chart 2 depicts two of the flattest and two of the steepest yield curves between the end of 1950 and the end of 1954. According to the theory, we should expect these to represent the periods of highest and lowest rates, respectively. It turns out that one of the steepest curves is that of June, 1954, which is seen by chart 3 to be the low point of yields for the four-year period; and one of the curves nearest to horizontal is that of April, 1953, clearly during the period of highest rates. Furthermore, chart 3 shows that during this latter period yields were almost identical for all securities of five-year term or more; and at the end of June and July the 2½'s of 1967 (the next to the longest term shown) yielded even more than those of 1972 (the longest shown). If the movement taking place during the first half of 1953 had continued much longer we might have seen a clear negatively sloped curve. Thus far the post-accord experience would add support to the theory modified to admit uncertainty.

Turning to the two other yield curves selected for this period we find the explanation must be of a different order entirely. These are the curves for October, 1953, and for July, 1952. The former is quite steep, yet its long rates are appreciably higher than those of the much more horizontal curve for 1952. In each case the explanation appears to lie in what might be dubbed "psychological friction." By October, 1953, the Federal Reserve System had been rapidly buying bills, at intervals from early May, in a vigorous effort to remove the tightness in the market which had become serious around the first of June. Between the end of July and the end of October the volume of United States government securities in the hands of the public maturing within one year declined four and a half billion dollars while longer-term outstandings increased nearly three billion. These supply changes by themselves would be expected to cause declining short rates and rising longs, but the over-all policy of ease transformed the change into one of rapidly falling short-term yields together with slowly falling long rates. A degree of skepticism regarding the turn toward ease apparently added to the delay in the rise of long-term prices.

The nearly horizontal yield curve of July, 1952, resulted from a persistent four-month rise in short rates which was only gradually reflected in longer rates. The Federal Reserve System had been keeping steady restrictive pressure on the money market in order to prevent unduly inflationary consequences of the Korean War, and although this resulted in virtually no change in the volume of shorts held by the public, it forced down free reserves from a weekly average of $992,000,000 at the end of March to a deficiency of $650,000,000 at the end of July. Meanwhile commercial banks sold approximately $105,000,000 worth of bills and $290,-000,000 worth of certificates. Furthermore about four and a quarter billion dollars worth of new government six-year bonds were issued on July 1, which pushed up rates in the intermediate ranges. All these pressures were ultimately reflected in long rates, but the rise at that end was very slight through July. One cause for this sluggishness in response may well be the fact that 1952 long-term yields were already higher than they had been for fourteen years and the expectation of further price declines did not come quickly.

The post-accord evidence regarding the slope of yield curves may be summarized by the conclusion that extremes of high and low yields were accompanied by slopes of just the kind that the modified theory would lead us to expect. At times the relation between the level of rates and market concepts of "normal" seemed to dominate. At other times the slope of yield curves can best be understood only by assuming a lagged response of long to short rates. The second type of situation is clearly inconsistent with either model of the neoclassical theory.

One other possible explanation of the shape of yield curves deserves examination. This explanation grows out of the segmented nature of the market. The question raised is whether supplies of shorts in recent years, for instance, have been small relative to the specialized demand for shorts. Evidence concerning this question will be examined in the following section.

6. How does the term mixture of outstanding securities influence the structure of rates?

Perfect-foresight Model. — The answer to the question of the influence of term mixture on the structure of rates is implicit in much of the previous discussion, but it deserves the emphasis of explicit comment. A major feature of the neoclassical theory is the conclusion that the expected net yield on funds invested during any given period will be identical for securities of different maturities.[16] On the basis of this, the entire structure of rates was derived. No reference was made to the term mixture of outstandings because by the nature of the theory this question was irrelevant. To the extent that expectations could be relied upon with certainty, all securities became perfect substitutes for one another, and only the aggregate supply and demand at different times had influence on the structure of rates. In this setting arbitrage is complete, and no one need be concerned with the maturities of securities offered by the Treasury or with the terms of Governments traded by the Open-Market Account.

Modifications. — The unrealistic implications of the perfect-foresight model at this point are clear. After introducing uncertainty, together with its implication of segmented markets, it is no longer true that the effective yield for holding securities during a particular period of time will be the same regardless of the term bought. This makes it impossible to speak of "the interest rate" even for riskless securities held during a given time interval. Actual yields will be modified upward or downward according

---

[16] Note that this does not mean that yield curves are horizontal. See p. 298 above.

to the specific supply and demand for securities of given term. An important consequence for monetary policy is the fact that central-bank purchase or sale of a particular maturity will not necessarily alter other yields to the degree assumed by perfect arbitrage. If institutional rigidities cause only a lag in adjustment, then the distortion here concerns only the period immediately following the open-market operations. But it would appear entirely possible that the market segmentation may be great enough to cause a persistent distortion, so that a desired change in long rates would require more extensive action in the short end than would be required in perfect markets. If this be true, then a policy which confined operations to the short end could increase the inconsistencies within the yield curve, and might in some cases move us farther from "competitive" rates than would operations throughout the entire structure.

From the standpoint of debt management, the degree of market segmentation will affect the consequences of a policy that shapes government debt structure without reference to the needs of major investing groups. To the degree that market segmentation permanently limits the extent of "arbitrage," supply mixture can readily distort the yield curve from the shape it would take if there were no market segmentation. The question of how far the specialized desires of investors will lead them to sacrifice interest in order to hold their preferred maturities is one requiring empirical investigation.

Empirical Evidence. — It is conceptually possible that changes in the supply of longs or of shorts might be perfectly arbitraged at once, implying that term mixture has no importance; or the arbitrage might take place fully but only gradually; or it might never be wholly effective, so that the term structure is permanently altered by a change in the relative supplies of different maturities, or by changes in the demand of buyers in specialized segments.

The question — which of these conditions holds? — is highly important, but despite a number of empirical approaches made in this study, much further research would be required before firm conclusions could be reached. Although no single aspect of the analysis in this section yielded wholly convincing results, the conclusions suggested in each approach seemed to dovetail into a unified whole, and this consistency may justify more confidence in the over-all conclusions than any one part alone would permit.

The investigation began with an examination of the maturity pattern of the holdings of major lending institutions in order to observe the degree to which "arbitrage" may be limited by the fixed requirements of each type of institution. Next, a study was made of four periods since 1920 in which yield curves took fundamentally contrasting shapes, and each period was examined superficially to see whether these differences might be explained in part by differences in supply and demand relations among securities of different term. This method should be pursued much more thoroughly, for the hasty test conducted here gave suggestive results. Then a study was made of the term structure of total debt and its various components at year-end dates from 1950 through 1954, in order to see whether these data would help explain the shape of yield curves on these dates. After this I studied the impacts of monthly changes in the maturity composition of debt upon the monthly movements of different rates. Finally, I examined the implications of a study by W. B. Hickman, wherein he compared actual yield curves at various times with those which would be inferred from application of the perfect-foresight model to earlier yield curves.[17]

The conclusions suggested by this group of studies are as follows: (1) A study of the behavior of yield curves gives important suggestive evidence, but is far short of proof, that changing relations between supply at the long end and supply at the short end, as well as changing specialized demand for securities of different term, can have both temporary and lasting influence on the structure of rates. (2) Under existing institutional conditions there is a demand for short-term debt instruments that is sufficiently strong to cause these yields to be clearly lower relative to long rates than would seem explainable on the basis of wholly rational maximizing assumptions, even making allowance for the direct effects of uncertainty. (3) This view is given very modest support by post-accord rate behavior, and somewhat clearer support by longer-run movements. It also appears reasonable when one examines the supply of shorts in relation to apparent institutional needs for these. (4) Aberrations in the shapes of yield curves or in the movements of rates with respect to one another appear in monthly data, revealing lags in the response of some rates to changes in others. These lags do not always appear following sudden changes in supply, and no understanding of them can be gained without study of all details in relation to each period examined. When lags do occur they usually take the form of long rates lagging shorts, and they frequently last as much as one or even two months. Many such delayed responses would be observed if daily and weekly changes were studied.

We now turn to a more detailed résumé of the findings revealed by each of the approaches described above.

a) Institutional pattern of holdings of government securities by term: Chart 6 records the holdings of government securities by various institutions on selected dates which represent sharply different circumstances in the postwar period. The right-hand section of the chart reveals the great importance of commercial banks among institutions holding gov-

---

[17] W. B. Hickman, *The Term Structure of Interest Rates: An Exploratory Analysis* (New York: National Bureau of Economic Research, 1942; mimeographed).

ernments in 1954, and the left side shows the large proportion of these holdings which are in short-term or intermediate securities. The chart also shows the very wide fluctuations in commercial bank holdings of five to ten year bonds (six and a half billion in 1948, two and a half billion in 1951, and thirteen billion in June, 1954). Bank "arbitrage" beyond ten-year terms would appear to be sharply limited under present practices, but such activity up to that length is apparently substantial. Mutual savings banks and "all others" appear to be capable of fairly important shifts between five to ten year bonds and those of longer term. Life insurance companies have held a nearly constant and very small volume of short terms, but since World War II they have steadily liquidated their long-term government securities, exchanging them for private investments. In the "all other" category, nonfinancial corporations are largely limited to short terms, and state and local governments appear to hold mostly longs, so that "individuals," with sixteen billions in marketable bonds and fifty billion in nonmarketable, are the major group which may perform wide ranges of "arbitrage."

Two implications of significance are suggested by chart 6. One is that the present (1955) supply of shorts may be none too large in relation to the desire for them by institutions wishing to meet liquidity requirements. If it is assumed that minimum desires of banks and insurance companies are close to the smallest amounts actually held during this period, and if it is recognized that corporations' desires are largely for shorts, then most of the 1954 supply may have been absorbed by institutions with special needs for them. If this is true, then it could help explain a tendency for short rates to be lower than they would be if such specialized demands were absent.

The second implication of chart 6 is that although many institutions concentrate their holdings in one segment of the term spectrum, their demands overlap enough to permit effective though not perfect arbitrage across the whole range, thus eliminating discontinuities in the yield curve though not preventing distortions in its general shape.

b) Secular changes in maturity pattern of outstanding government securities: It might be that the negatively sloped yield curves of the 1920's could have resulted from relations between specialized demand and outstanding supplies wholly different from that of the present. An adequate study of this question would be difficult, partly because of inadequacy of data. I have examined commercial-bank statistics only, but these institutions provide so important a part of the total demand for short-term securities that the changing relative importance of banks as holders of government securities may suggest the changes in that part of demand which is specific for short and intermediate instruments. The result indicates that these supply and demand relations may indeed have bearing on the shape of the yield curves.[18] Table 14 gives relevant data for June 30 of three interwar years.

TABLE 14

Date (June 30)	Commercial bank holdings of governments as per cent of total outstanding governments	Bills and certificates as per cent of total outstanding governments	Bills, certificates, and notes as per cent of total outstanding governments
1921	14.3	11.4	29.2
1929	29.7	9.9	23.4
1941	35.7	2.9	13.3

It may be noted that figures suggestive of demand for short terms[19] vary consistently from lowest to highest over time, while the supply figures move successively from highest to lowest. These findings are entirely consistent with the movement of the yield curves from a steep negative slope to a steep positive slope between 1921 and 1941.

Postwar data might be interpreted as contradicting the neat picture implied by these earlier observations. On June 30, 1954, bank holdings had dropped (relatively) to represent only 21.6 per cent of all public marketable government securities, while bills, certificates and notes had risen to 26.0 per cent of outstanding marketable governments. These supply data and demand data would suggest a 1954 yield curve with slope between that of 1921 and 1929, whereas in fact the slope was similar to that of 1941.

The 1954 data are less damaging to the hypothesis under study than might appear, because important new sources of demand for shorts, especially by corporations, had arisen, thus tending to drive these yields down as compared with those on longer-term issues. It must be recognized that more years and many more elements would have to be examined before these conclusions are accepted as more than a suggestion. But the evidence is at least consistent with the idea that the current positive slope of the yield curve may at least in part reflect a substantial institutional demand for shorts relative to their supply.

[18] Culbertson has studied this period extensively. In an article published since my analysis was completed he gives a much more adequate review of the empirical evidence than is included here. His conclusions firmly support the thesis that the term-mixture did influence the rate structure during the twenties and thirties. See "The Term Structure of Interest Rates," pp. 509–516.

[19] "Demand," of course, refers to a schedule. The implication of this section is, however, that specialized needs for shorts make demand so inelastic that it may be crudely represented by a single figure for "quantity desired." Commercial-bank holdings of government securities may suggest something of the relative magnitude of this figure. I have tried to emphasize the fact that such crude yardsticks as these are at best suggestive rather than conclusive.

c) Post-accord changes in debt outstanding: I have made two studies of post-accord changes in outstanding debt in order to compare term mixture with changes in the yield curve. One study was based on annual, the other on monthly changes.

The difficulties of securing and interpreting data are so great that findings are far from conclusive, and I shall summarize them only briefly here. In each study supply changes were examined both for government securities in the hands of the public and for total public and private debt so far as data were available. The only possible term classification was that of "long-term" versus "short-term," the dividing line between the two being a term of one year. A more complete report of these studies is given in appendix A to this chapter.

The study of annual data included consideration of demand changes to the extent that these may be suggested by changes in the total assets of commercial banks (a major source of demand for shorts)[20] and those of life insurance companies, mutual savings banks, and savings and loan associations (a major source of demand for long terms).

The study of supply changes alone would suggest that if demand were unaltered the yield curve should have flattened out during 1951, and should have grown successively steeper at each following year-end. Since the annual lengthening of total debt in the United States was much more marked in 1954 than in any of the earlier years studied, the steepening of the yield curve in that year should have been most marked. In the meanwhile, however, the demand data described above would also suggest a lengthening of demand during the same period. The combined impact of supply and demand changes on the yield curve is therefore difficult to determine, though the much greater lengthening of supply in 1954 might suggest fairly definite expectations of a steepening of the curve in that year. In fact the curve shifted somewhat ambiguously until the end of 1952 and then grew successively steeper, the difference being substantial in 1954. The general lowering of rates was not sufficient to explain the shifts noted in the last of these years, and it seems reasonable to suppose that the term mixture of outstandings in relation to specialized demand may have contributed to the changing structure of rates.

The study of monthly data on changes in term mixture revealed a notable inconsistency in the apparent impact of supply changes upon rate structure. It was completely impossible to find a simple correlation between even sharp changes in outstandings and changes in the structure

---

[20] Nonfinancial corporations provide another major source of "specialized demand" for shorts, but total holdings of government securities by these corporations varied so little since 1951 that this source of possible disturbance was neglected. Such holdings at the end of the years 1951–1954 respectively were, in billions of dollars: 20.7, 19.9, 21.0, 19.3.

of rates. Yet a detailed study of individual changes in the structure of rates during the four-year period showed that the rate behavior was often explainable only by consideration of supply changes. This finding may appear quite meaningless, and surely a clear correlation between supply changes and rate behavior would be more satisfying. It would appear, however, that some fairly clear conclusions are suggested by even the inconsistent relations observed: (a) The many other variables determining rate structure are important enough to make useless any simple correlation analysis of rate movements with supply changes. The most practicable method of studying these relations involves a detailed investigation of each specific instance in which changes occur. (b) Supply changes frequently did cause distortions in the yield curve which persisted at least one or two months. (c) At least as often as not supply changes at one point in the term structure were sufficiently discounted in advance by investors in securities of different maturity that no distortion in the yield curve at the time of actual supply change was noticeable in monthly data. (d) The temporary distortions which did occur appear to result far more often from sudden changes in conditions at the short end than from changes in the supply of longs. Thus the increasing long rates associated with new issues of long terms appear almost without exception to have been promptly reflected elsewhere, but tightness or ease in the money market frequently caused only a lagged response at the long end. It should be remembered, of course, that these comments refer to monthly data and may not be true of shorter period changes.

d) Chronological review of "inconsistent" rate movements from the accord to the end of 1954: Explanation of some cases in which rates on securities of different term moved in opposite directions will illustrate the wide variety of factors that can cause negative correlation in rate movements.[21] (1) In April, 1951, long rates continued to rise, while intermediate and short rates fell. Here the dominating influence at the long end was probably the continued response to the unpegging of long-term securities agreed to in the Treasury–Federal Reserve accord. (2) In October, 1951, long rates again rose while intermediate and short rates declined. No clear explanation of the long-term price weakness is apparent.[22] (3) In April, 1952, bill rates rose appreciably while yields of longer-term securities all fell fairly sharply. These contradictions can be explained only in part by changed supplies. The Treasury borrowed $600,000,000 through new bill issues, and the Federal Reserve sold $165,-000,000 net, virtually all these sales being certificates. Thus the pressure toward upward rates at the short end is readily understood. Meanwhile banks continued to buy long terms in an effort to lengthen their portfolio

---

[21] It will be useful to examine chart 3 in conjunction with this review.
[22] *Monthly Review*, Federal Reserve Bank of New York, November, 1951, p. 154.

maturities, and generally pessimistic views regarding business prospects (partly related to rumors of Korean peace) led to the expectation, and hence the realization, of lower long-term yields. Toward the middle of May, long-term bond prices turned downward gradually as business expectations improved slightly and as the market began to anticipate fairly substantial Treasury financing throughout the year. The money market continued tight, and all yields moved upward together until June, 1953, with the exception of the period from August through October, 1952, which I shall now examine. (4) During the latter part of August, 1952, yields on bills turned down, followed a month later by those on one-year securities and two months later by all longer maturities. During October bill rates turned upward again, to be followed in November by all other terms. The September inconsistency of rate movements was partly the result of fairly substantial open-market purchases toward the middle of the month, which were largely extended to facilitate the refunding of ten billion dollars' worth of certificates maturing October 1, combined with intermediate and long-term yield increases representing lagged responses to earlier rises in shorter rates. A further reason for the opposing rate movements in August and September is the fact that the expectation of higher long yields made shorts an attractive haven for funds, with the result that long rates were forced up and short rates down. Over-all October data suggest contradictory movements again, though in the opposite direction from those of September: they suggest a much greater period of divergent movement than actually occurred, however, since both bill rates and long-term yields fell during most of the month. Near the end of October bill rates rose sharply enough to result in an increase for the month as a whole, and longs followed promptly in November. (5) From this time until March, 1954, there were no significant divergences in rate movements. On the latter date the long, sharp decline in rates that began in June, 1953, was briefly interrupted on the short end when corporations liquidated bills in preparation for March tax payments, and seasonal elements tightened the money market generally. From April through June short rates fell again before reversing direction and continuing upward throughout the rest of the year. In the meantime long and intermediate rates followed the same course except for a sharp temporary rise during May, caused, apparently, by fears that Indochinese developments might necessitate Treasury borrowings, together with general optimism concerning business prospects and the consequent view that Federal Reserve policies might tighten somewhat.

This review of instances where short and long rates moved in opposite directions reveals that supply changes frequently but not always played an important role. It should be remembered in this connection that open-market operations are included among supply changes. However, an examination of supply changes, whether in relation to government securities alone or to all securities, demonstrated the complete impossibility of predicting divergent rate movements from observation of these supply movements alone. Frequently the sharpest divergences between changes in the outstanding volume of longs and of shorts would show no corresponding reflection in diverse yield movements. The cause is, of course, the one mentioned above: many other powerful variables are at work, and one of the most important of these is the ever-elusive category of expectations.

e) Forecasting the shapes of yield curves: In the theoretical discussion it was pointed out that to the degree that expectations are held with confidence and fulfilled in fact, the yield curve at any time should provide the data necessary for drawing future yield curves. By examining these curves for successive periods it is therefore possible to test the adequacy of the perfect-foresight model.

W. B. Hickman systematically compared the actual yield curves for the period 1936 to 1942 with those that theory would imply to have been "expected" on the basis of previous years.[23] He then contrasted these projections with those which would have been achieved if the theory had been disregarded and it had been simply assumed in each case that the previous year's curve would continue unchanged.

This comparison implies disaster for any investor who staked his funds on the assumption that the curve would shift as indicated by the perfect-foresight model of the neoclassical theory. Only twice did the theorist do better than those who assumed a continued status quo — 1938 and 1942. These successes are not a coincidence: they represent the only times that the yield curve moved upward. Chart 7 shows three yield curves from the post-accord period together with implied predictions, and the results are entirely similar to those of the Hickman study. In short, the monotonic upward slope of all yield curves during the two decades before 1954 should, on the basis of the perfect-foresight model of the neoclassical theory, imply an expectation at all times that rates will rise in both the near and more distant future.

These observations provide the sharpest kind of evidence that the perfect-foresight model is strongly at odds with empirical evidence. How far this goes to show inadequacy of the neoclassical theory itself is a matter of conjecture, because the answer depends upon how much one blames imperfect foresight for the conflict between projection and reality. I, for one, would accept the view that it is unreasonable to presume the market is so consistently and grossly wrong in its expectations that poor foresight could wholly explain these observations. And this means that the neoclas-

---

[23] Hickman, *The Term Structure of Interest Rates,* p. III–13.

sical theory is itself seriously inadequate as a theory of the structure of rates. On the other hand, this conclusion does not lead me to the view that this theory should be rejected as irrelevant. The modified theory which I have outlined, in which the implications of the neoclassical theory are adjusted for the consequences of uncertainty and market segmentation, is in no way contradicted by the behavior of these projections. For me the meaning of Hickman's data and my own is that 1955 yield curves are sharply biased toward positive slopes. Just such a bias as this is what I would expect to occur in the light of various considerations growing out of my previous analysis. Possible explanations of this bias, some of which have already been suggested above, would include the following elements.

1) It may be generally characteristic of bond buyers that they are willing to sacrifice yield in order to avoid the gamble of holding longs even if that gamble offers equal chance of gain or of loss. (2) There seems to be a variety of evidence that at present the supply of shorts is less adequate than that of longs relative to the specialized demands for these two kinds of securities. This specialized demand comes largely from institutions like banks and nonfinancial corporations which are subject to obligations that are short term or which wish to remain highly liquid in order to shift funds rapidly into other uses. (3) Two long-term historical reasons may tend to give the slope of present yield curves a positive bias. One of these is the fact that a history of positively sloped curves since the early 1930's leads to continued expectation of this shape, and such expectations tend to be partly self-fulfilling. The other is that rates may have still seemed low by long-term historical standards, so that the expectation of ultimately declining prices still lingered.

The statement that there is insufficient supply on the short end is not easy to establish firmly, but many observations give consistent even if mild support to it. Besides the evidence from secular change since 1921 (see page 333) and a slight suggestion of similar changes since the accord, there are two other supporting data. One is Hickman's evidence of the irrational upward bias of yield curves, which does not seem adequately explained by reasons 1 and 3 just given. Another is the observation that in June, 1953, when rates were at their highest levels since the 1930's and expectations turned gradually toward declining yields, shorter rates came nowhere near crossing the longer ones although the intermediate and long end of the yield curve moved very close to the logically appropriate negative slopes.

A summary of the findings of this chapter together with their implications for the theory of the structure of rates and the general theory of interest will be included in the next chapter as a part of the general summary and conclusions to Part Three.

APPENDIX A: ANNUAL POST-ACCORD
CHANGES IN TOTAL DEBT OUTSTANDING

The following pages present more details of the studies leading to the conclusions reported on pp. 332 and 335.

The problems of interpreting supply-demand data are many and great. One difficulty arises from the fact that debt classified as short-term may increase sharply simply because passage of a month's time moves the term of a single large issue from $12\frac{1}{2}$ months to $11\frac{1}{2}$ months. Adjustments which eliminate these changes can be made in the government sector (where figures are available) but the adjusted figures which result from the elimination of such sharp discontinuities are themselves partly inappropriate, for it is clearly wrong to erase the full effect of the passage of time on terms of outstanding securities. I believe that a reasonable interpretation of term changes in the period covered would lie between "actual change" and the "adjusted change," as recorded in table A, which gives both kinds of data.

A second problem of interpretation concerns the treatment of private debt. My examination of the yield curves in the post-accord period covers the return on government securities only, but there is so much opportunity for funds to flow between the government and the private sector that these yields on government securities can be understood only after study of total debt figures. Both private and governmental debt are shown in the tables in this appendix.

A third major difficulty of interpretation results from the fact that it is impossible to know the effects of supply-demand changes without first knowing what would have happened without them, and this cannot be known without measuring the effects of all elements which alter expectations. Obviously that task would be momentous and to a great extent subjective.

A fourth difficulty concerns the heterogeneity of basic data available. For example, corporate debt is classified according to term at time of issue, whereas the term of government debt shows the number of years securities still have to run. Consequently no total of government and private securities according to term is logically permissible. It appears, however, that during the period studied major changes in the number of private longs and shorts as recorded would give a fairly good reflection of changes in the term mixture according to the criteria applied to governments. A total of private and government securities according to term is therefore presented with this warning regarding its nature.

At best only uncertain and subjectively based conclusions can be derived from examination of post-accord changes in supply and demand.

Yet even these may be better than nothing, and it seems useful in any event to see how much the data do reveal.

Available statistics do not permit a compilation of total debt by term, but a number of major elements can be so classified if rough estimates are made at some points. Table B shows a crude classification of this kind. Yearly changes derived from that table are shown in table C.

TABLE A

Changes in Year-end Yields of Short-term
and Long-term Government Securities

Term	1950–1951	Apr. 30 to Dec. 31, 1951	1951–1952	1952–1953	1953–1954
Short-term	+.42	+.37	+.15	−.52	−.38
Long-term	+.42	+.11	+.07	−.19	−.15

NOTE: Long-term includes averages of selected securities with term greater than one year, since supply data is defined on that basis. Short-term yields are averages on 3-month bills and one other issue with terms of roughly 9 to 12 months. Issues used are those shown in chart 3.

The interpretation of these data requires comparison with information on actual rate movements. These data are given in table A. Since there was a sharp rise in long rates during March, 1951, which was apparently the result of the accord and related events, the second column of table A is used rather than the first.

Findings from comparison of these two tables include the following: (1) Rate changes appear to be much more meaningfully related to adjusted than to unadjusted data. (2) Rate changes appear to be more meaningfully related to changes in total debt than to changes in government debt alone. (3) Most conclusions would be qualitatively similar whichever data are used. (4) The results of this test are generally consistent with the assumption that rate structure is influenced by the term mixture of securities outstanding. The evidence is as follows: If the percentage changes in the amount of short-term and long-term debt outstanding are compared, then it would appear from table C that supply changes, *ceteris paribus,* would have raised short rates relative to longs in 1951, raised longs relative to shorts in 1952 and 1953, and raised long rates even more, relative to shorts, in 1954. In fact table A shows that short rates did rise more than longs from April to December, 1951, and about equally for the full year, and short rates did fall much more than long rates in

TABLE B

YEAR-END DATA ON DEBT IN HANDS OF PUBLIC
(In millions of dollars)

	1950	1951	1952	1953	1954
SHORT TERM					
Private					
Nonfarm commercial, financial, and consumer loans	37,594	39,392	45,486	49,666	53,236
Farm production loans	6,149	6,977	7,985	9,122	9,424
Net corporation short-term (1 year or less)	81,912	95,927	97,696	99,127	92,864
Total private	125,655	142,296	151,167	157,915	155,524
U. S. government and agencies[a]	51,518	66,014	65,062	68,531	52,190
Total private and U. S. government	177,173	208,310	216,229	226,446	207,714
LONG TERM					
Private					
Nonfarm mortgage	59,337	67,382	75,079	83,626	94,459
Farm mortgage	6,071	6,588	7,154	7,656	8,200
Net corporation long-term	60,146	66,589	73,334	78,812	83,724
Total private	124,554	140,559	155,567	170,094	186,383
U. S. government and agencies	144,570	126,926	131,744	134,583	154,112
Total private and U. S. government	270,124	267,485	287,311	304,677	340,495
State and local government net debt as of June 30	20,723	23,347	25,771	28,559	33,381

NOTE: All U. S. Government debt is exclusive of that held by Treasury agencies and Federal Reserve Banks. Private debt figures are taken from pp. 6–12, *Survey of Current Business*, U. S. Department of Commerce, May 1955. Public debt figures from *Treasury Bulletins*. Federal debt classified according to maturity or first call. These data include Federal agency debts and all nonmarketable Government securities; all of the latter but savings notes are regarded as long-term.

State and local government debt is not included in the totals because there is no available data on classification by term. New debt in this category is quite consistently two thirds long-term.

[a] Includes savings notes.

TABLE C

Changes in Selected Categories of Debt in the Hands of the Public According to Term

(in billions of dollars)

Type of debt	1951 Actual change		Adjusted change[a]		1952 Actual change		Adjusted change[a]		1953 Actual change		Adjusted change[a]		1954 Actual change		Adjusted change[a]	
	Amount	%	Amount	%	Amount	%	Amount	%	Amount	%	Amount	%	Amount	%	Amount	%
U. S. government																
One year or less	+14,496	+28.1	−1,864	−3.6	−952	−1.4	−4,712	−7.1	+3,469	+5.3	−1,642	−2.5	−16,341	−23.8	−27,895	−40.6
Over one year	−17,644	−12.2	−1,284	−.9	+4,818	+3.8	+8,578	+6.8	+2,839	+2.2	+7,950	+6.0	+19,559	+14.5	+31,023	+23.1
Private debt																
One year or less	+16,641	+13.2			+8,871	+6.2			+6,748	+4.5			−2,391	−1.5		
Over one year	+15,005	+12.0			+15,008	+10.7			+14,527	+9.3			+16,289	+9.6		
Total private and U. S. government[b]																
One year or less	+31,137	17.6	+14,777	+8.3	+7,919	+3.8	+4,159	+2.0	+10,217	+4.7	+5,106	+2.4	−18,732	−8.3	−30,226	−13.3
Over one year	−2,639	−1.0	+13,721	+5.1	+19,826	+7.4	+23,586	+8.8	+17,366	+6.0	+22,477	+7.8	+35,818	+11.8	+47,312	+15.5

Source: Derived from data in table B. Excludes debt held by Federal Reserve Banks and Treasury agencies (see text above).

[a] Eliminates spurious appearance of abrupt changes resulting from gradual shift of term on large government issues which passage of time brought into short-term category. Retains effects of retirements, new issues, and operations of Treasury and Federal Reserve Banks. See text at start of section for comment.

[b] An important lack of comparability between private and public debt arises because the former classification of term is based on the term at time of issue, whereas U. S. government debt is classified according to the period securities still have to run. See text for comment.

both 1953 and 1954. In 1952 rate changes were in slight contradiction to the theoretical expectation.

It should be noted, however, that the movements described here might also be explained by the general tendency of short rates to move more widely than long rates, and the significance of the above observations therefore depends upon whether the slope of the yield curves has been changed more than would be expected in the light of changes in the general level of rates. Study of these curves reveals only one clear case of this kind: in 1954 the curve is appreciably steeper than previously, even though not lower at the long end, thus proving consistent with the hypothesis that its shape may be influenced by the marked lengthening of both private and government debt during the year. Comparison of the curves for April, 1951, December, 1952, and December, 1953, also suggest the possible influence of supply elements on the rate structure described above, but the suggestion is very modest and some might debate it.

I have been unable to devise any method of measuring changes in the relation between the demand of institutions for one-year securities and the corresponding demand for longer instruments. It is clear, however, that a large part of the growing assets of investing groups has gone into long-term securities, and it seems reasonably certain that the steepening slope of yield curves, which data on supply indicate for the period since 1951, would have been quite marked if this growing source of demand for longs had not existed. Changes in the assets of some of these institutions at year-end dates are shown by table D.

TABLE D

TOTAL ASSETS OF SELECTED LENDING INSTITUTIONS

Institution	Amounts, December 31					Annual changes in per cent[a]			
	1950	1951	1952	1953	1954	1951	1952	1953	1954
Commercial banks	168.9	179.5	188.6	193.0	202.4	6.3	5.1	2.3	4.9
Mutual savings banks	22.4	23.4	25.2	27.1	29.3	...	...	...	...
Life insurance companies	64.0	68.3	73.4	78.5	84.1	...	...	...	...
Savings and loan associations	16.8	19.1	22.6	26.6	31.7	...	...	...	...
Total of last three	103.2	110.8	121.2	132.2	145.1	7.4	9.4	9.1	9.8

SOURCE: *Federal Reserve Bulletins.*
[a] Figures not relevant to the analysis are not given.

Throughout the period studied the proportionate growth of assets of holders of longs was substantially greater than that of the holders of shorts. Thus the growing demand for longs might have largely canceled the effects of the growing supplies of longs. The major exception is 1954, when the supply changes showed a much sharper lengthening of debt than previously, and the demand changes did not. It is precisely in this year that the yield curve was most clearly steeper than it might be expected to be from the changing levels of rates alone.

In summary: Data covering the post-accord period are consistent with the hypothesis that the term mixture of outstanding debt, and the clearly defined demand for securities of particular term, do have a persistent effect on the shape of the yield curve. "Arbitrage" does not wholly eliminate the effects of marked changes in the term mixture of supply and demand for debt instruments. The evidence for this conclusion is by no means conclusive, and too many variables are involved to permit meaningful, simple correlations.

APPENDIX B: ONE-YEAR YIELDS ON SECURITIES ASSUMING YIELD CONSTANT AS OF JULY 30, 1954

The accompanying table shows the effective yield which investors could obtain on securities of different term if they invested funds for one year beginning on July 30, 1954, and if the yield curve remained unchanged at the same date in 1955.

YIELDS TO BE REALIZED FROM HOLDING VARIOUS SECURITIES FOR ONE YEAR FROM JULY 30, 1954, ASSUMING CURVE UNCHANGED AT END OF YEAR, AND COUPON OF 2 PER CENT

Term	Yield	Price$_1$	Price$_2$	$P_2 - P_1$	Interest received	Net yield (per cent)
1	.80	101.19	100.00	−1.19	+2	.81 ÷ 101.19 = .80
2	1.20	101.57	101.19	−.38	+2	1.62 ÷ 101.57 = 1.59
3	1.53	101.37	101.57	+.20	+2	2.20 ÷ 100.37 = 2.17
4	1.80	100.77	101.37	+.60	+2	2.60 ÷ 100.77 = 2.58
5	2.00	100.00	100.77	+.77	+2	2.77 ÷ 100.01 = 2.77
6	2.16	99.10	100.00	+.90	+2	2.90 ÷ 99.10 = 2.93
7	2.25	98.39	99.10	+.71	+2	2.71 ÷ 98.39 = 2.75
10	2.43	96.21	96.93	+.72	+2	2.72 ÷ 96.21 = 2.83
15	2.50	93.78	94.23	+.45	+2	2.45 ÷ 93.78 = 2.61

It is obvious from the last column that a person with funds to invest for one year would never buy one-year securities (thereby earning only .8 per cent) if he assumed that the July yield curve would still hold a year hence. He could secure an effective yield of 2.93 per cent by buying a six-year security, holding it for one year, and selling again. It is of interest to note that this yield is appreciably greater than the yield to maturity on even the longest-term securities. In this case the sophisticated buyer who wishes to invest funds for one year might buy securities somewhere short of six years on the assumption that rates will probably rise, but he would surely not act upon the assumption that yields for one year's investment will be the same regardless of the term he buys.

A common observation about the changes in security prices as securities approach maturity should now be recognized as another implication of what has just been observed. As shown by the table, a fifteen-year 2 per cent bond would be selling at 93.78 if the yield curve looked as it did on June 30, 1954. The yield to maturity would be 2.50 per cent. But this security would be destined to rise in price to a premium of 1.57 three years before maturity if the yield curve were to remain unchanged. The yield of the security to that time would be 2.75 per cent.

XVII

RATE STRUCTURE:
SUMMARY AND CONCLUSIONS

This chapter reviews the major findings of the analysis of the term structure of rates and also presents conclusions not developed in the somewhat piecemeal analysis presented thus far.

Like most generalizations in economics, the theory presented here is constructed by adding successive modifications to an unrealistically simplified basic theoretical structure. The fundamental assumptions of the basic theory are that investors act as if uncertainty were wholly absent, that securities are free of the risk of nonpayment, and that investors are able to, and do, maximize their expected returns by unimpeded arbitrage among securities of different term. This is the neoclassical theory of the structure of rates. In order to facilitate empirical testing I have also presented a model which includes still another simplification: the assumption that expectations are not only held confidently, but are also fully realized in subsequent developments. This I have called the perfect-foresight model of the neoclassical theory.

The rationale of the neoclassical theory (with or without the perfect-foresight assumption) is that the endeavor of investors to maximize their returns forces security prices so to adjust that effectiv returns for any defined period are equal on all securities, regardless of term. This does not mean either that the coupon rates, or the yields to maturity, will be identical on securities of different term. It means only that the net return for investment over a given period, including capital gains and losses, will be equal. On the logic of the assumptions underlying neoclassical theory, this argument is scarcely debatable. If the return on one maturity were greater than that on another, demand and supply would raise the price of the first and lower that of the second until the differential was eliminated.

This theory of the structure of rates fits neatly into the theory of interest as presented in Parts One and Two, for each implies a unique rate of interest on riskless securities for a defined period of time. That rate, according to the neoclassical theory of term structure, is the uniform effective yield, including interest payments and capital gain or loss, while the security is held. Over periods brief enough that functions do not shift, that unique rate may be found from the theories elaborated in Parts One and Two. Similarly, for all other short periods the rate will be determined by the elements described in the theory of interest. Given these short rates for a long sequence of future periods, the entire structure of rates for today is determined. Thus a complete integration may be attained between the theory of interest (Parts One and Two) and the theory of the structure of rates (Part Three). One qualification should be mentioned, however, even at this level of abstraction. The motives for holding speculative balances include implications of uncertainty which would clash with the assumption of perfect substitution between securities. To this extent a satisfactory synthesis of the theory of interest and the theory of the structure of rates would require modification of the demand curve for money presented in Part One.

The chief inadequacy of this integrated theory is inherent in the simplified, static nature of the model, which abstracts from dynamic and institutional considerations such as uncertainty and market imperfections. Even within the limitations imposed by this frame of reference, however, one refinement should be made. The integration just suggested would imply that saving, investment, and hoarding functions are drawn in terms of simultaneous short rates. It would be more realistic to recognize the ways in which each of these independent variables may be influenced by predicted future short rates, or what is equivalent in this theory, by current long rates. It is easy to state a set of equilibrium equations that relates the general equilibrium functions of Part Two to the theory of term structure in Part Three and at the same time recognizes this interdependence. First, of course, a set of behavioral assumptions must be made.

One highly simplified set of such assumptions which emphasizes what might be the crucial variables would be that investment and saving decisions are primarily dependent upon long rates of interest (since investment and saving decisions are often long term), but that the decision to hold funds idle depends upon short rates. Assume also for simplicity that "long rates" are three-year rates; and that expected short rates are equal after the third year. The following symbols will be used:

I = investment	T = long (three-year) rate
S = saving	M_1 = funds available for active balances.
Y = income	
r = short (one-year) rate	M_2 = funds available for idle balances.
R = two-year rate	

Subscripts a, b, and c indicate the year of reference: e.g., R_c = the two-year rate in year three. Barred symbols are given data. L, f, and ϕ are functional notations for the demands for money, for desired saving, and for desired investment, respectively. Subscripts 1 and 2 related to L indicate active and idle money.

The preceding assumptions define the following set of equilibrium equations:

$$\overline{M_a} = M_{1a} + M_{2a}; \; \overline{M_b} = M_{1b} + M_{2b}; \; \overline{M_c} = M_{1c} + M_{2c}. \tag{1}$$

$$M_{1a} = L_{1a}(Y_a); \; M_{1b} = L_{1b}(Y_b); \; M_{1c} = L_{1c}(Y_c). \tag{2}$$

$$M_{2a} = L_{2a}(r_a); \; M_{2b} = L_{2b}(r_b); \; M_{2c} = L_{2c}(r_c). \tag{3}$$

$$S_a = f_a(T_a, Y_a); \; S_b = f_b(T_b, Y_b); \; S_c = f_c(T_c, Y_c). \tag{4}$$

$$I_a = \phi_a(T_a, Y_a); \; I_b = \phi_b(T_b, Y_b); \; I_c = \phi_c(T_c, Y_c). \tag{5}$$

$$S_a = I_a; \; S_b = I_b; \; S_c = I_c. \tag{6}$$

$$R_a = \frac{(1 + r_a)(1 + r_b) - 1}{(1 + r_b) + 1}; \; R_b = \frac{(1 + r_b)(1 + r_c) - 1}{(1 + r_c) + 1}; \; R_c = r_c. \tag{7}$$

$$T_a = \frac{(1 + r_a)(1 + r_b)(1 + r_c) - 1}{(1 + r_b)(1 + r_c) + (1 + r_c) + 1}; \; T_b = \frac{(1 + r_b)(1 + r_c)^2 - 1}{(1 + r_c)^2 + (1 + r_c) + 1};$$

$$T_c = r. \tag{8}$$

This system provides twenty-four equations for the solution of these twenty-four unknowns — M_1, M_2, I, S, Y, r, R and T for each of the three years — and could be easily modified to recognize the influence of both long and short rates on investment and saving decisions if that seemed appropriate. These equations present a simplified general-equilibrium framework, with the solution corresponding to the intersection of SI and LM in the models of Part Two. A particular equilibrium model corresponding to the conventional liquidity-preference theory (i.e., to the intersection of LM with a given level of income) would be represented by equations (1) to (3) and (7) to (8), with Y assumed as given. It is essential to note that at any given time the functions for future times must be expected ones. Thus today's interest rates are determined in part by current expectations regarding future functions such as saving, investment, and the demand for idle balances. Recognition of this dependence suggests that interest-rate forecasts are much more difficult even than they appeared to be when they depended only on today's functions.

This model provides an explicit integration of the theory of interest and the theory of the structure of rates. It also includes elements of realism which the simpler integration lacks. Unfortunately, however, even this model exemplifies all the shortcomings of the unmodified neoclassical theory, which is explicitly included through the seventh and eighth equations. The major weaknesses of that theory arise from its implied assumption of perfect confidence in expectations, together with its disregard of market segmentation and market imperfections. As a result of these limitations the entire neoclassical theory of rate structure has been sharply challenged not only by practical men engaged in security operations, but also by academic economists.[1] My own empirical work supports the view that this simplified theory by itself is wholly unsatisfactory as a device for explaining rate behavior in the real world. The same study indicates, however, that a modified theory which begins with this basic core and adds the recognition of uncertainty can yield "predictions" that are highly consistent with observed facts and offers credible explanations of actual developments in rate structure.

A number of questions are raised by these observations. (1) What is the nature of the modified theory toward which we are led? (2) What do the modified theory and empirical evidence suggest about the nature and the behavior over time of the structure of interest rates? (3) Can we fit the modified theory into the framework of the general interest theory described in Parts One and Two, and if so, how? (4) Does the modified theory give too large a role to the neoclassical theory in the determination of the structure of rates? These four questions will be reviewed in turn. Answers to the first and second consist of no more than a brief review of the findings discussed above. Answers to the third and fourth require facing directly issues that have been touched upon only lightly before.

OUTLINE OF MODIFICATIONS TO
THE NEOCLASSICAL THEORY

The most fundamental fact which forces modification of the neoclassical theory is that of uncertainty. Some of the important consequences are these: (1) Expectations about conditions in the market for money and credit for the intermediate and long-term future are typically very vague or almost entirely unformed. Thus, long rates may be largely influenced by changes in short-term expectations and by considerations not described in the neoclassical theory. (2) One of these other considerations is the fact that long-term securities offer more prospect of capital gain or loss than do shorts. The essential reason is that a simultaneous change in all expected short rates will cause a much larger change in long prices than in short prices, and a general change in expectations tends often to color the far as well as the immediate future, thus causing a similar if not an equal alteration in a substantial sequence of expected short rates. (3) A conse-

---

[1] See, for instance, F. R. Macaulay, *The Movements of Interest Rates, Bond Yields, and Stock Prices in the United States Since 1856* (New York: National Bureau of Economic Research, 1938), p. 3; W. B. Hickman, *The Term Structure of Interest Rates: An Exploratory Analysis* (New York: National Bureau of Economic Research, 1942; mimeographed), pp. III-21; Joan Robinson, *The Rate of Interest* (London: Macmillan, 1952); J. M. Culbertson, "The Term Structure of Interest Rates," *Quarterly Journal of Economics,* 71 (1957): 485–517.

quence of the more speculative character of longs is the tendency of institutions requiring a high degree of liquidity (e.g., banks and nonfinancial corporations) to hold very few longs. (4) Another consequence is that longs often yield more than shorts, partly as compensation for risktaking. Hence institutions not requiring much liquidity may hold longs partly in order to benefit from the high yield. Furthermore, even when yields are not higher on longs than on shorts, institutions with long-term liabilities may find it both convenient and safe to buy securities with terms comparable to those of their obligations, thereby assuring themselves of a known income during the intervening years. (5) A result of 3 and 4 is that the markets for securities of different term become partly segmented. An important consequence for the theory of interest is that there is no longer a single rate of interest even over defined short periods of time as there was in the unmodified theory. Thus securities of different term are no longer perfect substitutes for one another, and a rate determined by the theory of interest is no longer unambiguous.

THE BEHAVIOR OF THE STRUCTURE OF INTEREST RATES

A number of empirical studies were made, chiefly covering the years 1951–1954, but in some cases referring to a substantially longer period, in order to discover what answers are suggested by the data to a number of questions regarding the nature of the rate structure and the way that structure changes over time. These findings were used to check the plausibility of the theoretical models just reviewed. As stated in the opening page of this chapter three models have been examined — the general neoclassical model, a perfect-foresight model of the neoclassical theory, and a modified theory which recognizes a number of changes imposed on the neoclassical theory by the existence of uncertainty and market segmentation. The following review summarizes briefly both the theoretical presumption and the empirical evidence regarding answers to each of the questions raised about rate structure.

Direction of Rate Movements (Review of pp. 312–316)

Nothing in the neoclassical theory would contradict the possibility that rates of different terms might move quite differently from one another, some up and some down, in the same period. This theory would lead to the expectation, however, that any two rates would move together more often than not, even under the assumption of perfect foresight. Introduction of uncertainty and imperfect foresight would imply still greater uniformity in direction of rate movements. The theory thus modified suggests that long rates, and even intermediates, would quite consistently move together, though short rates would occasionally move in different directions from one another or in different directions from longs. Short and long rates might often move in opposite directions when there are sudden changes in expectations regarding future rates or sharp changes in supply. Empirical data support all of the expectations suggested by the modified theory, in which imperfect foresight is assumed. The general implications of the neoclassical theory are not here contradicted, but detailed studies indicate leads and lags which require the recognition of imperfections not recognized in that theory.

Size of Changes in Yields (Review of pp. 316–318)

The neoclassical theory would lead one to expect that changes in yields would generally be much greater on shorts than on longs. The modified theory would suggest much more change in long yields than would neoclassical analysis, but it would still lead one to expect greater changes in short yields than in long yields. Empirical evidence is entirely consistent with the modified theory, and does not necessarily conflict with the implications of the neoclassical analysis, so long as imperfect foresight is admitted.

Size of Price Changes (Review of pp. 318–321)

Surprisingly enough, the neoclassical theory suggests that unless foresight proved erroneous price changes should be almost exactly equal among different securities of equal coupon regardless of term to maturity. The modified theory, primarily because it admits imperfect foresight would lead one to expect price changes to be greater for longer-term than for shorter-term securities. Data examined in this study were entirely consistent with the modified theory but sharply inconsistent with the perfect-foresight model of the neoclassical theory.

Monotonic Character and Direction of Slope of Yield Curve (Review of pp. 321–330)

The neoclassical theory permits any slope if and when the yield curve is generally monotonic, but the over-all direction of slope might be expected to be downward when current rates are high in historical terms, and rising when rates are low by these standards. The modified theory retains this general conclusion, though commonly restating it in terms of hopes and fears of change in capital values. It also adds, however, two considerations that would provide the basis for expecting a bias in the direction of positive slope during the past two decades or more. The first of these reasons would, indeed, suggest such a bias at all times, for it rests on the assumption that bond-buyers will in general be willing to pay an actuarially excessive premium through sacrifice of interest, for the opportunity of avoiding risk of capital loss. The other reason for expecting a bias toward positively sloped curves is specific to these times and rests on the assumption that markets are segmented enough to permit interest differentials arising from supplies of shorts that are, relative to demand, small compared to the supplies of longs.

Empirical data for this century would seem to be almost entirely consistent with the modified theory, though yield curves have been generally more monotonic than this theory might seem to indicate. The bias toward positive slope suggested by both the data and the modified theory are in contradiction to both models of the unmodified neoclassical theory, however. Furthermore, the relation between shape and shifts of yield curves over time wholly refute the perfect-foresight model, and seem to argue strongly against the adequacy of even the general neoclassical theory.

Term Mixture of Outstanding Securities (Review of
    pp. 330–339)

A number of attempts were made in this study (1) to discover how far changes in the term mixture of outstanding securities might be followed by significant lags in the response of rates other than those directly affected by the disturbance, and (2) to see whether lasting changes in term mixture might cause a permanent distortion in the yield curve. No single approach gave convincing results, but all together seemed to suggest fairly credible answers to these questions. The answer to the first question is a mixed one: on a number of occasions there were clear lags in permeation of yield changes throughout the rate structure following changes in the term mixture of securities outstanding; but at other times fairly massive supply changes were sufficiently discounted in advance that no distortion in the rate structure appeared at all. Concerning the second question: the empirical findings were always somewhat ambiguous, but there was fairly convincing evidence that the general slope of the yield curve may be influenced even secularly by the term-mixture of outstanding securities. These observations clearly contradict the neoclassical theory with or without the assumption of perfect foresight. They are entirely consistent, however, with the modified theory.

Looking back over the tests to which I have subjected the theory of the structure of rates presented here, I conclude that the neoclassical theory, when modified to recognize the implications of uncertainty and market segmentation, provides a workable analytical framework for the interpretation of real-world relations between securities of different term in the United States today. This does not prove the theory valid, and comments will be made below on alternative approaches. The plausibility of this framework is strongest if we presume that expectations of future rates are generally held in fairly vague terms beyond a reasonably short period.

The evidence seems equally clear that the perfect-foresight model of the neoclassical theory is not consistent with experience. A somewhat weaker case, though one that is entirely convincing to me, suggests the inadequacy of the unmodified neoclassical theory even without the assumption of perfect foresight. The problem of verification here arises from the impossibility of dogmatizing about what expectations are or have been at any time: without knowing these, disproof of the neoclassical theory is not possible. In relation to the first three of the questions about yield curves reviewed above — similarity in direction of rate movements, size of yield changes, and size of price changes — there is little clear evidence against the neoclassical theory. The study of question 4, however, which concerns the monotonic character and the slope of yield curves, reveals shifts of these curves over time that would be inconsistent with the neoclassical theory unless one assumes the market to be unbelievably bad at forecasting future movements of rates. In this connection the evidence of an upward bias in the slope of the yield curve is entirely inconsistent with neoclassical theory even without the perfect-foresight assumption. Furthermore, study of question 5 tends also to contradict neoclassical theory by evincing definite effects of term-mixture on the shape of the yield curve extending well beyond the period of briefly felt frictions.

INTEGRATION OF MODIFIED
STRUCTURE THEORY WITH THE
GENERAL THEORY OF INTEREST

Although the perfect-foresight model has been demonstrated to be entirely unsatisfactory, the failures of the more general neoclassical theory appear to be less numerous. Indeed, if we abstract from frictions, which qualify the validity of most economic models, there are only two modifications clearly suggested by the evidence reviewed above. One is the correction for a positive bias in the slope of the yield curve, and the other is a correction required because of the segmentation of the market. The statement that there are "only two modifications" required is not intended to imply that these are of minor importance, but it suggests the nature of changes which these considerations require in the structure of the neoclassical model. Only extensive empirical work would show the best way to express these changes in the neoclassical functions, and the model I propose below is intended to be only suggestive of the way in which the modified theory might be integrated with the general theory of interest.

The equations here are generally similar to those used for the unmodified theory (p. 349 above), but the presentation has been simplified by confining it to the first year. Symbols are the same except for six new ones that have been added. Small r still stands for the short rate that would rule if no modifications in the neoclassical theory were required, but this fact requires the introduction of a new symbol Q to represent the current short rate that exists because of the distortions recognized by the modified theory. The symbols m and n are multiplicative coefficients required to give the yield curve its positive bias. The symbols α, β, and γ represent additive adjustments made necessary by market segmentation. They may be defined as the premium which the marginal buyer (or seller) of a security is willing to pay because of the buyer's particularized demand for a given term (or because of the seller's wish to borrow by use of a particular term). They could, of course, be functions instead of being parameters.

Any appearance of precision and completeness which the mathematical form of presentation may lend to this model is admittedly spurious. This set of equations simply provides a convenient means of suggesting the way that a modified theory of rate structure like that presented here may be related to general interest theory. I have here begged all the really difficult questions, which have to do with the values of the parameters and the determinants of expectations. As a schematic representation the system still seems useful. After all, economists have found saving and investment curves analytically helpful for a long time even though they are still groping for light concerning the crucial question of their elasticities.

The proposed set of equations follows:

$$\overline{M} = M_1 + M_2. \tag{9}$$

$$M_1 = L_1(Y). \tag{10}$$

$$M_2 = L_2(Q, R, T). \tag{11}$$

$$S = f(T, Y). \tag{12}$$

$$I = \phi(T, Y). \tag{13}$$

$$S = I. \tag{14}$$

$$Q = mr_a + \alpha. \qquad 1 > m > 0; \; \alpha \lessgtr 0. \tag{15}$$

$$R = \frac{(1 + r_a)(1 + r_b) - 1}{(1 + r_b) + 1} + \beta. \qquad \beta \lessgtr 0. \tag{16}$$

$$T = \left[\frac{(1 + r_a)(1 + r_b)(1 + r_c) - 1}{(1 + r_b)(1 + r_c) + (1 + r_c) + 1}\right] n + \gamma. \qquad n > 1; \; \gamma \lessgtr 0. \tag{17}$$

Since equations for years b and c are not given, we must assume r_b and r_c to be known. This leaves as unknowns: M_1, M_2, Y, S, I, Q, R, T, and r_a. No multiplicative coefficient is given in the equation for R since we assume two-year terms to be the fulcrum about which the yield curve rotates in obtaining its positive bias.

EVALUATION: THE MODIFIED
THEORY AND ALTERNATIVES

Even if I am correct in arguing that the theory of rate structure described here is consistent with the facts of recent experience, the validity of the theory is by no means proved. An entirely different theoretical framework might provide conflicting but better explanations of the same events. Since the most widely criticized element in this analysis would probably be the neoclassical core on which it is built, the objections to that framework must be examined and appraised.

One of the most recent studies of the structure of rates is an article by John Culbertson which was published since the text of this book first went to the printer. In one observation after another Culbertson and I have independently reached similar conclusions. Yet concerning the usefulness of the neoclassical theory he appears to take an entirely opposite position: he rejects completely what I seem to have made the cornerstone of my edifice! "We find the expectational theory [i.e. the neoclassical theory] unsatisfactory on theoretical grounds and inconsistent with the behavior of the rate structure in the postwar period." [2] Again, "the explanation of broad movements in the term structure of rates must be sought principally in factors other than in behavior governed by interest rate expectations." [3]

It is by no means wholly clear to me how far Culbertson's position and mine really differ, despite this apparent conflict. I, too, have rejected the unmodified neoclassical theory, and I have emphasized the major importance of modifications to it. In making it the starting point of my theory I do not wish to imply that the final product closely resembles it. The modifications I have imposed include an upward bias in the yield curve caused partly by investors' desire to avoid risk, and an emphasis on the segmentation of markets, both of which are major planks in Culbertson's theory of rate structure. Another modification indicated in my text is the recognition of the likelihood that expectations will be held with definiteness only in relation to the fairly near future, with longer-run ideas being vague. This assumption seems reasonable, and it is necessary in order to explain the normal lack of undulation in the yield curve beyond the very short run. Culbertson takes a similar if not identical position.

There are places where Culbertson seems to do what others have clearly done, namely, to condemn the neoclassical analysis on the basis of evidence that really contradicts only the perfect-foresight model of that

---

[2] Culbertson, "The Term Structure of Interest Rates," p. 488.
[3] *Ibid.*, p. 502.

theory — a model which is surely not implied by the theory itself, and one which I have also rejected. This identification of the two theories by implication is indicated in statements implying that the tendency of long and short rates to move together, and the response of long rates to credit conditions, are inconsistent with the neoclassical theory.[4] It is clear that the perfect-foresight model would prevent substantial effects on long rates following any change in a single short rate, although it has been shown above (page 296) that these changes would be greater than implied by simple averages. However, there is every reason to believe that changed credit conditions or other events affecting the nearest short rate will also influence expectations for a number of short rates appreciably beyond the immediate present, thereby causing a still more marked effect on long rates.

In sum, then, it does not seem at all clear that Culbertson's rejection of the neoclassical position is based on considerations that would force a similar rejection of its use as one building block in a larger structure. At the same time it is probable that he and many others would object to the emphasis which my model still leaves upon the thought processes implied by the neoclassical theory. While I am not prepared to dogmatize in favor of the procedure followed here, I still believe there are good reasons for adopting it, and these reasons should be reviewed.

In the first place, it seems to me that the neoclassical theory describes behavior that is far more plausible than its critics would usually admit. The thought process implied is not one of investors estimating future bill rates and then calculating the yield to be expected on other securities. Rather, it is one of estimating whether it will be more profitable to invest funds over a given period by purchasing shorts and reinvesting as they mature, or by buying a security whose term matches the time funds are to be invested, or by buying a still longer-term issue and considering the capital gain or loss as well as the yield for the period involved. To the extent that investors think in terms like these they are thinking in terms consistent with the presumptions of neoclassical theory. It seems to me beyond question that managers of large accounts often do think in just these terms.

The fact that the neoclassical theory does imply this kind of behavior does not seem to be recognized by many of its critics. Culbertson says, for example,

The influence of the expectational theory [i.e., neo-classical theory] seems to have been confined mainly to academic economists. The view most common among those close to debt markets seems to be the older one, that interest rates generally move up and down together because of overlapping among debt markets. Some also have emphasized the role of 'arbitrage' of specialists in debt markets in bringing about such behavior.[5]

In my outline of the neoclassical theory at the start of chapter xv I have shown why I believe that behavior of the kind presumed in this statement is precisely the mechanism by which the relations described in the neo-classical theory are brought about.

A closely related misconception of neoclassical theory is the view that since this theory describes equilibrium long rates as an "average" of short rates, it presumes that causation runs from rates on shorts to rates on longs. This is not the case. The yield earned by holding a long for any short period is just as much a short rate as is the yield for holding a short, and the supply of longs on the market today is just as significant an influence in determining rates as is the supply of shorts. The solution for each rate is part of an interdependent set of relations involving all other rates, as seen in the equations of page 355 above.

These arguments admittedly relate to periods for which some reasonable guess may be made regarding the movement of rates. What of the longer run? It is certainly true that we have no very clear notion about the level of rates ten years from today. Why is it that long rates have so persistently remained higher than shorts for two and a half decades? It is possible, of course, that market segmentation, together with supplies of shorts that have been inadequate to fill the demand for them, and an oversupply of longs, would explain this phenomenon. I have argued that this probably helps to explain observed facts, but I have not seen evidence that it provides an adequate explanation. It is clearly true that the differential between short and long rates decreased when all rates rose and was even reversed in parts of the curve when rates became quite high, but I have seen no evidence that these periods were also periods in which the relative supply and demand for longs and shorts were abnormal. On the other hand, if people think at all in terms of some long-run normal rate above the levels of those that commonly ruled throughout the thirties and forties, or if for safety they act on the presumption that higher rates may return, then the neoclassical theory would explain the reluctance of long rates to fall. A more natural way to think of this would be in terms of the floor under long rates established by what Keynes described as the speculative motive. But the operation of this motive can surely be translated into a process that combines the neoclassical theory (without perfect foresight!) and the view that bondholders are willing to pay a premium to avoid risk. The essential difference is that Keynes' simplified picture included only money and long-term securities, whereas the motive he described is used here to explain shifts between securities of different term.

---

[5] *Ibid.*, p. 487.

In any event the fear that expected rates may rise in the future would be shown by the neoclassical equations to imply the fear of much greater capital loss on longs than on shorts and would justify bearishness on the former when rates are low in comparison with historical standards or standards that caution sets above the levels of actuarial expectation.

Finally, I believe that it would be generally accepted that any events that may affect the supply and demand for money and credit, now and in the foreseeable future, would influence expectations about future rates. These would include business conditions, saving patterns, international events, and monetary policy. And these are just the elements that are assumed to determine supply and demand for funds in the theory of interest developed in this book.

A formulation of structure theory that appears to be quite different from the one sketched here begins by regarding each security (or each term-group) as an individual "good," whose price is determined by supply and demand. If the "arbitrage" across the maturity range is believed to be small, then this procedure would be preferable to mine, for it faces much more squarely the problems that I pass over in my use of α, β, and γ on page 355. If there is significant "arbitrage," however — as I believe all the evidence indicates — then this method of approach would face as great or greater problems because of the need to determine cross-elasticities throughout the entire chain of maturities. And it would still have to find some means of dealing with the problem of bias in yield curve, just as I have had to do. In the end, there is no reason that these approaches need give different results.

I would willingly grant that economists close to the market may be expected to resist the formulations of the neoclassical theory, just as practical businessmen have often resisted the marginal analysis in price theory. For their purposes these academic formulations are remote from conscious decision-making and seem far more complex than necessary. Yet I believe that the theorist who is trying to see underlying relationships can often benefit substantially by such formulations. And I see nothing illicit about defining the elements that enter decision-making in terms that may not be those used by the decision-maker himself. The issue is the one made famous by Machlup's parable of automobiles.[6] My sympathies have always been with his view that it is meaningful to describe the driver's decisions to pass a car in terms of rates of acceleration, velocity of approaching car, and so on, even though some drivers never heard of acceleration and few could estimate the figure even crudely in relation to the potential of their own car.

---

[6] Fritz Matchlup, "Marginal Analysis and Empirical Research," *American Economic Review*, 36 (1946): 534; reprinted in Richard Clemence, *Readings in Economic Analysis*, Vol. II (Cambridge, Mass.; Addison-Wesley Press, 1940), p. 139.

These comments indicate my reasons for believing that the neoclassical theory contributes necessary elements to an adequate theory of interest. I hardly need restate the conviction that needed modifications may be substantial, and I recognize they may include important ones I have not enumerated. But there do seem to be reasons of convenience in starting here. Perhaps the most important is that it provides, at least conceptually, a basis for determining the level of various rates, in contrast to a theory which simply makes statements about the way rates should be expected to behave. The theory of the structure of rates presented here is tied in clearly with the general theory of interest, and *the* rate of that theory is replaced by a structure of rates.

This completes my introduction to the theory of interest and of rate structure. The major steps which need to be taken next are the introduction of uncertainty and dynamic elements into the basic theory of interest as presented in Parts One and Two, a more thorough examination of institutional relations including the channels through which monetary policy is implemented, and empirical work directed to finding the elasticities of the major functions such as saving, investment, and the demand for idle balances. Economic journals reveal much exploratory work along all these lines but the review and evaluation of findings must await another volume.

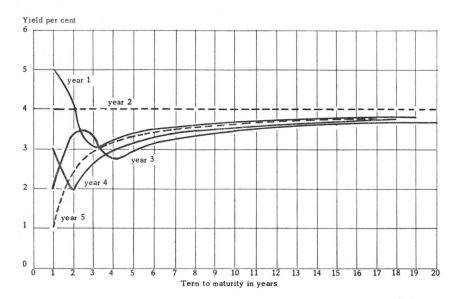

Chart 1. Hypothetical yield curves. Based on short rates as assumed in table 6, p. 297.

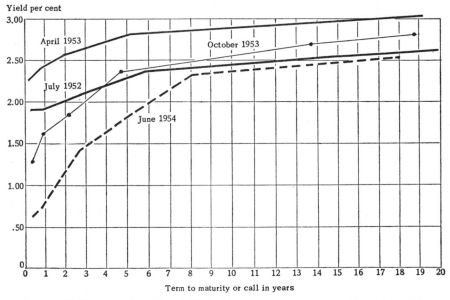

Chart 2. Yield curves for selected United States government securities, selected dates 1952–1954. SOURCE: *Treasury Bulletins*. Securities used are those shown in chart 3.

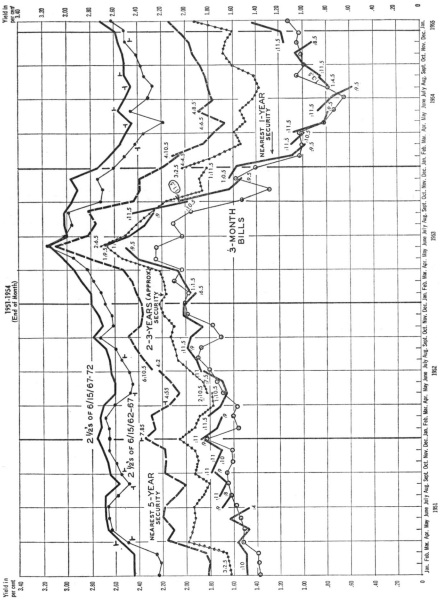

Chart 3. Yields on selected United States government securities, 1951–1954, end of month. Numbers indicate years to maturity at time and for security indicated. Number before colon is years; number after colon is months. Whenever yield calculation shifts from call to maturity basis the first point of change is shown by ⊢ ; opposite changes are shown by ⊣ . SOURCE: *Treasury Bulletins.*

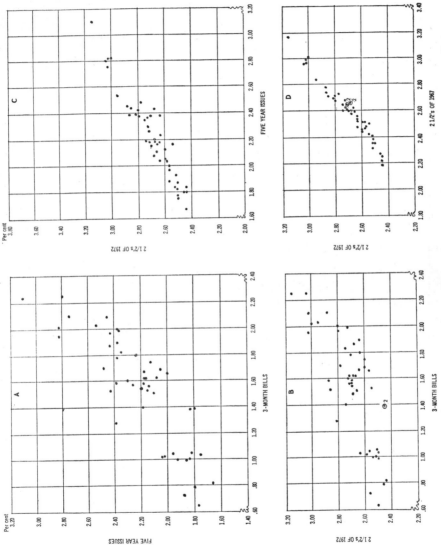

Chart 4. Scatter diagram: rates of securities of different term, 1951–1954. SOURCE: *Treasury Bulletins.*

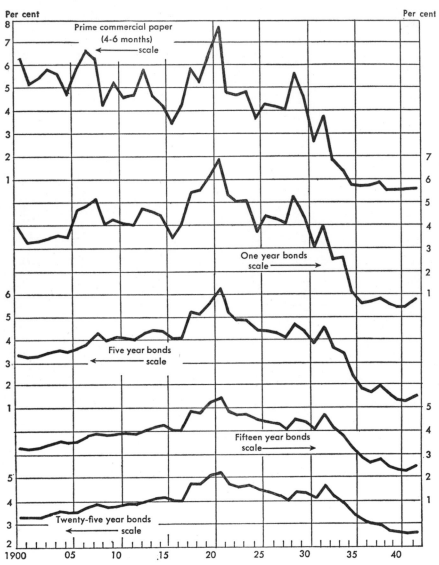

Chart 5. Yields on nongovernmental securities of different term, 1900–1942. Source: For commercial paper rate, calculated average of rates during first three months of each year on basis of data from Federal Reserve System, Board of Governors, *Banking and Monetary Statistics* (Washington, D. C., 1943), pp. 449 ff.; for bond yields, *ibid.*, p. 477.

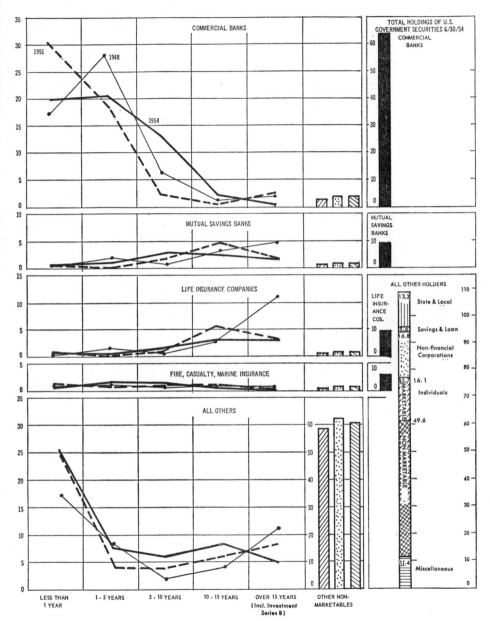

Chart 6. Selected data on United States government security holdings of major investors, June 30, 1954, and December 31, 1948 and 1951. In billions of dollars. SOURCE: *Treasury Bulletins.*

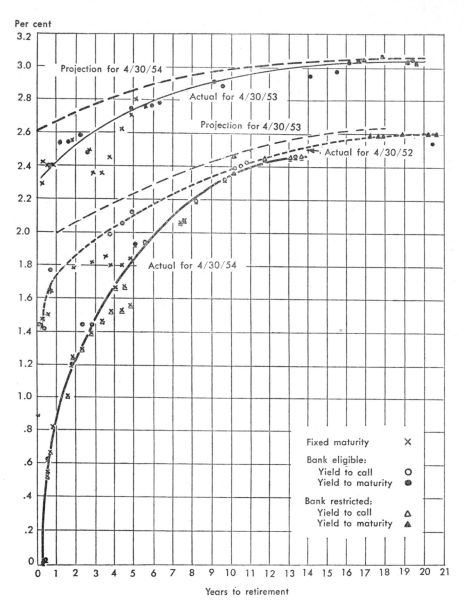

Chart 7. Actual and projected yield curves, selected dates. The years for retirement are years to call date for securities selling above par, years to maturity for others. Source: Actual data, *Treasury Bulletins;* the projected curves were calculated from the data.

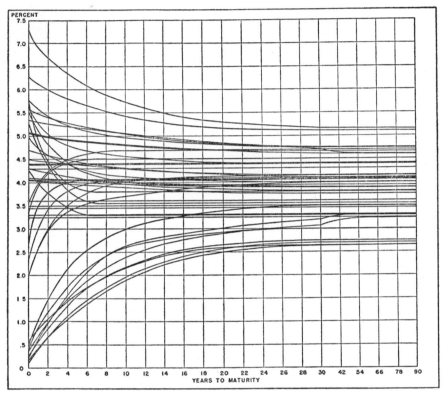

Chart 8. Superimposed basic yield curves, 1900–1942. Yields used in preparing this chart were based on a study of 3,000 high-grade domestic corporate bonds, though only a small fraction of these were finally used in the calculations. The selection of securities is described on pp. 4 ff. of the source from which this chart was reproduced. Only bonds with ratings of A or higher were included. Price quotations used were the averages of the high and the low for each of the first three months of the year shown. It should be noted that the horizontal scale changes at 30 years from two-year intervals to twelve-year intervals. SOURCE: David Durand, *Basic Yields of Corporate Bonds, 1900–1942,* Technical paper 3 (New York: National Bureau of Economic Research, 1942), p. 17.

INDEX